Psychology
An Evolutionary Approach

Steven J. C. Gaulin

and

Donald H. McBurney

Prentice Hall

Upper Saddle River, New Jersey 07458

Library of Congress Cataloging-in-Publication Data

Gaulin, Steven J. C.
   Psychology : an evolutionary approach / Steven J. C. Gaulin, Donald H. McBurney.—
1st ed.
     p.   cm.
   Includes bibliographical references and index.
   ISBN 0–13–759994–3
   1. Genetic psychology.   2. Human evolution.   I. McBurney, Donald   II. Title.
BF701 .G297   2001
155.7—dc21

                                    00–020213

VP, Editorial director: Laura Pearson
Executive editor: Bill Webber
Editorial assistant: Deborah Fenster
Managing editor: Mary Rottino
Production liaison: Fran Russello
Editorial/production supervision: Bruce Hobart
   (Pine Tree Composition)
Prepress and manufacturing buyer: Tricia Kenny
Marketing manager: Sharon Cosgrove
Cover designer: Kiwi Design
Cover image: © Bettman/Corbis

This book was set in 10/12 New Baskerville by Pine Tree Composition, Inc., and was printed and bound by R. R. Donnelley & Sons Company. The cover was printed by Phoenix Color Corp.

For permission to use copyright material please refer to p. xiv which is hereby made part of this copyright page.

© 2001 by Prentice-Hall, Inc.
A Division of Pearson Education
Upper Saddle River, New Jersey 07458

Printed in the United States of America

10 9 8 7 6 5 4 3 2 1

ISBN 0-13-759994-3

Prentice-Hall International (UK) Limited, *London*
Prentice-Hall of Australia Pty. Limited, *Sydney*
Prentice-Hall Canada Inc., *Toronto*
Prentice-Hall Hispanoamericana, S.A., *Mexico*
Prentice-Hall of India Private Limited, *New Delhi*
Prentice-Hall of Japan, Inc., *Tokyo*
Pearson Education Asia Pte. Ltd., *Singapore*
Editora Prentice-Hall do Brasil, Ltda., *Rio de Janeiro*

This book is dedicated to our grandchildren

Sylvia
René
Jeremy
Anna
Paris
Christopher
Joel
Erica
Nicolaas
Adam
and
James

That an appreciation for the process and the products of evolution
might enrich the lives of their generation.

Contents

Chapter 6: Consciousness   110

Chapter 7: Learning: How Experience Modifies Behavior   129

Chapter 8: Cognition   155

Chapter 11: Families and Development   231

Chapter 12: Motivation and Emotion   257

Chapter 13: Health   278

Chapter 14: Abnormal Psychology   297

Chapter 15: Social Behavior   314

Chapter 16: Culture   342

Preface

"Is it not reasonable to anticipate that our understanding of the human mind would be aided greatly by knowing the purpose for which it was designed?" (Williams 1966, p. 16).

In one important way this book is very different from other introductory psychology texts. Traditional psychology largely ignores the question of what the mind is for. This oversight puts traditional psychology seriously out of step with the rest of the life sciences, where design-for-a-function is recognized as the normal result of evolution by natural selection. The reader may hesitate but there's little room for doubt: Psychology is a life science. It studies the behavior of living things, not rocks or stars or electrons. The theory of evolution has inspired countless thousands of discoveries throughout the life sciences—in physiology, ecology, medicine, and the like. It's time to consider what this theory can offer to psychology.

In a sentence, natural selection shapes organisms by preserving those chance genetic variants that aid survival and reproduction. Contemporary biologists are convinced that every single species, including our own, owes its present form to a long history of natural selection. And their conclusion applies with equal force to every organ system; the mind and the behaviors it fosters are in no way exempt from this process. Thus our working assumption is that human psychology was designed by evolution, over millions of years, to solve the various challenges that faced our ancestors in their struggles to survive and reproduce.

We have chosen to write an introductory textbook for one simple reason. Evolutionary psychology is *not* a specialized subfield of psychology, such as personality psychology or abnormal psychology. Instead, it is a different way of thinking about the entire field. Its insights and methods should be the groundwork for the study of psychology, not an afterthought. Our goal is that, after reading this text, students will be able to think like evolutionists, not only about human behavior but also about a wide range of related matters.

But what of traditional psychology? Let us be clear. Traditional psychology it is a rich and vital field. But we have two general criticisms of it. First, because traditional psychology has no overarching theory of what we call "mind design," it can only take a trial-and-error approach to discovering the mind's operating principles. Unfortunately, trial and error is slow and inefficient, and it has led to some spectacular blind alleys, such as Freudian theory. Second, most of traditional psychology's reliable findings, about perception, thought, learning, motivation, social behavior and the like are more sensible and more informative when they are interpreted in an evolutionary framework. For example, long-standing debates such as the one over nature versus nurture, are illuminated and usefully resolved by evolutionary thinking.

Thus we begin in Chapter 1 by mapping the differences between evolutionary psychology and the more traditional non-evolutionary approach. Evolutionary psychologists and traditional psychologists often differ in how they develop their theories, in the kinds of questions they pose, and in the sorts of statements they accept as valid answers. There is an old saying that you can't understand what a person is saying unless you know who he's arguing against. Let's be explicit then; in a real sense we are arguing against many of the assumptions and interpretations (but few of the findings) of traditional psychology.

Studying psychology from an evolutionary viewpoint requires a clear understanding of the theory of evolution. Thus, one of our key missions is to explain what evolution is (and isn't), and what it can (and can not) do. These matters are the focus of Chapters 2, 3 and 4. There may be a temptation on the part of both students and professors to skip or deal briefly with these chapters in order to get on to the "meat" of the course—psychology. We beg you not to yield to the temptation! Every high-school graduate "knows what evolution is." But most harbor serious misconceptions: Evolution always fosters what is good for the species; because of their basis in genes, evolved traits are fixed and unresponsive to experience; species can usefully be arranged on a ladder from lower to higher. Wrong; wrong; and wrong again! According to a large majority of modern evolutionists all three of these ideas are dangerously off the mark. And there are many other pitfalls and misconceptions that must be discussed before evolutionary theory can be productively applied, to the study of psychology or to any other set of questions. Thus, a thorough grasp of the basics of modern evolutionary theory, especially as it relates to behavior, is essential to a full appreciation of the argument and evidence in this book.

The remaining chapters, 5 through 16, each treat one of the central topics of modern psychology. The topics include sensation and perception, development, learning, cognition, social psychology, abnormal psychology, motivation, individual differences and several others. In each of these chapters, our focus is not on reviewing the entire literature, either from a traditional or an evolutionary perspective. Instead, by discussing eight or ten examples in each chapter, we try to show what evolutionary psychology is, how it reorients the study of mind and behavior and how genuinely novel its conclusions can be. Our goal in exemplifying the evolutionary approach over such a wide range of topics is two-fold. Of course we intend that each reader will take away a richer understanding of human behavior and the psychological mechanisms that underlie it. But we also hope to demonstrate the considerable power of Darwin's theory. For any question about living things—from the sensory abilities of moths to the complexities of human cognition—an approach that neglects evolution is unlikely to produce full and satisfying answers. Charles Darwin explained the fundamental logic at the core of all living things. If we wish to understand our own, our friends', our mates' or our children's behavior, we'd be foolish to ignore the insights afforded by an evolutionary perspective.

As will be obvious from our citations and bibliography, we are not the first to imagine the outlines of an evolutionary psychology. Many students of human behavior, not only from the field of psychology, but also from biology, anthropology, economics and the other social sciences have contributed to the emergence of this field. Our primary debt, then, is to these colleagues, who had both the vision to foresee a synthesis between the evolutionary and behavioral sciences, and the interdisciplinary knowledge to build it. We hope that we have portrayed your pioneering efforts as clearly as you would have, and that many others will be encouraged to follow you down the Darwinian path.

In particular we thank our colleagues, Liz Cashdan, Martin Daly, Denys deCatanzaro, Jack Demarest, Jennifer Higa-King, L. Scott Johnson, Bruce MacDonald, Janet Mann, B. Kent Parker, Kathleen Ross, Kenneth Wildman, David Sloan Wilson, Matthew Winslow, and Thomas Zentall who offered frank, thorough and genuinely useful criticisms of parts, or in some cases all, of the book manuscript. You were (nearly) always right, and we have done our best to implement the various improvements you suggested while keeping in mind the kind of book we wanted to produce.

Indispensable editorial and organizational advice and support was generously provided by Cynthia and Claire Gaulin, Deborah Fenster, Frances Russello, Sharon Cosgrove, and especially our editor, Bill Webber. Bruce Hobart, our production supervisor, was the model of organization and good humor. We thank you all; it was a pleasure working with you.

Steven J. C. Gaulin
Donald H. McBurney

Photo Credits: p. 32, PURSE, RENEE/Photo Researchers, Inc.; p. 98, Geostock/PhotoDisc, Inc.; p. 105, Dr. Merlin Tuttle/Photo Researchers, Inc.; p. 121, Dr. Daniel Povinelli/New Iberia Research Center, University of Southwestern Louisiana; p. 126, Hisham F. Ibrahim/PhotoDisc, Inc.; p. 186, Anthro-Photo File; p. 200, Konner/Anthro-Photo File; p. 210, Karl Grammer/Institute for the Urban Ethology at the Institute for Human Biology, Vienna, Austria; p. 246, Ken Karp/Pearson Education/PH College; p. 248, Birnbach/Monkmeyer/Monkmeyer Press; p. 261, Harlow Primate Laboratory, University of Wisconsin; p. 263, Novastock/PhotoEdit; p. 264, Paul Ekman, Ph.D., Professor of Psychology; p. 271, Corbis; p. 293a, Tim Hauf/Visuals Unlimited; p. 293b, Scala/Art Resource, N.Y.; p. 294, Hulton Getty/Liaison Agency, Inc., p. 300, Courtesy Alan Pollock, National Transportation Safety Board; p. 304a, Photo Researchers, Inc.; p. 304b, Cindy Lewis Photography; p. 309, Gianni Dagli Orti/Corbis; p. 350, Gregory Pace/Corbis Sygma

1

Introduction: What Is Psychology Like Without Evolution?

What causes us to think, react to others and behave in the ways we do? Why do people behave differently from each other? How do our experiences shape us? These questions fascinate all of us. And these are the questions on which the science of psychology is founded. Like any comprehensive introduction to psychology, this book attempts to address these and other questions about the human mind and human behavior. This book is unusual, however, because it explores these questions from an evolutionary perspective.

EVOLUTIONARY PSYCHOLOGY IS AN APPROACH TO ALL OF PSYCHOLOGY

Psychology includes many specialized areas, such as learning, perception, and personality. Each one focuses on a particular aspect of behavior. Evolutionary psychology is different from these specialties because it uses evolutionary thinking to answer questions in all areas of psychology: learning, perception, personality, and the rest. For this reason, you will find a chapter in this book on each of the topics typically discussed in an introductory psychology book. We want to explore the results of applying Darwin's insights to the broad range of psychology.

A Note on Organization

One pedagogical problem is how to deal with those issues that naturally arise in some readers' minds as they first begin to think about the implications of evolution. We cannot deal with all the matters that follow from an evolutionary perspective in this first chapter simply because they require an understanding of material that comes later. One approach we have used is to note key ideas and frequently misunderstood concepts with "Trail Markers" highlighted in the text. You will encounter some in this chapter. Think of these as signposts that will guide you through the material. You may turn to the appendix for a list of trail markers.

Is the Evolutionary Perspective New to Psychology?

Evolutionary psychology (EP) is an approach to psychology that takes seriously the fact that the human species is a product of evolution. It is both old and new: It started with Charles Darwin himself, who applied evolutionary thinking to human behavior in his 1872 book, *The Expression of the Emotions in Man and Animals*. At the same time it is new, because until the last decade or so, the theory of evolution has had relatively little impact on the field of psychology. It is true that prominent, early psychologists such as William James and James McDougall consciously included evolutionary concepts in their work. And some psychologists have continued in that tradition. But it is demonstrably true that evolution has had much less impact on psychology than on biology. A cursory look at the index of any introductory psychology text published before 1990 shows scant evidence that Darwin ever lived.

PSYCHOLOGY WITHOUT EVOLUTION

There are many reasons why evolution has had so little impact on psychology. We will discuss them as we progress through the book. For now, we will mention one. This is the idea that humans are somehow "higher" than the (other) animals and that, to some degree, our evolved biological nature is no longer relevant. In this respect, many psychologists still seem to be influenced by the ancient notion of the Great Chain of Being (or *scala naturae*, the "scale of nature"), according to which humans stand between animals and angels on a ladder that rises from inanimate objects to God (Great Chain of Being, 1994).

That doctrine holds that beings share certain similarities with their nearest neighbors—in our case, angels above us and animals below. Beings higher on the scale are considered to have "higher" natures. Because they view as higher than animals, people who think in terms of the Great Chain of Being believe that we have somehow transcended our biological nature, although they concede that we bear some similarities to the animals. For example, whenever someone argues that human capacity for culture frees us from the bonds of our animal nature, they are implicitly appealing to the Great Chain of Being, even if they have never heard of it by that name (see Figure 1–1).

Let's be clear about this: The idea of a Great Chain of Being is mistaken, and for two main reasons. First, it implies that evolution proceeds in a linear fashion, with "higher" creatures directly related to "lower" animals. In fact, evolution is not

The Great Chain of Being

God
:
Angels
:
Humans
:
Apes
:
Cats
:
Clams
:
Plants
:
Rocks

Figure 1–1. *The Great Chain of Being.* The mistaken notion that evolution implies that organisms can be ranked from highest to lowest is actually an ancient notion that includes all of nature in a scale of increasing perfection.

linear, like a ladder; it is branching, like a tree or bush (see Figure 1–2). Picture a bush that has been trimmed into a flat hedge for many years. All the leaves and shoots on the inside have died, and green, growing leaves are only found on top. The dead twigs represent creatures that have died out over the course of evolution. And the green leaves represent all the kinds of organisms alive today—including bacteria, oysters, mushrooms, sycamores, trout, snakes and people. They are all on top because they have all been evolving for an equally long period of time. No one is an ancestor to any of the others. Instead, all share a common ancestor that lived as much as several billion years ago. To give another illustration, humans did not evolve from chimpanzees; humans and chimpanzees are "cousins" who share a common ancestor that is now extinct.

Second, the idea of a Great Chain of Being implies progress—that evolution has the goal of producing more and more sophisticated creatures. Only if evolution meant progress would it make sense to rank animals on an evolutionary

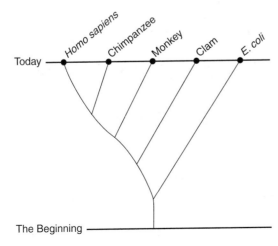

Figure 1–2. *The evolutionary tree.* The evolutionary tree is actually more of a bush. All organisms are the result of the same amount of evolutionary fine tuning.

ladder from lowest to highest. Naturally, people who think that evolution means progress place humans near the top of the ladder, "a little lower than the angels." This idea is also mistaken, because evolution does not imply progress, only change.

Trail Marker: Evolution does not mean progress, only change.

People who believe that evolution is progressive often argue that, over time, evolution builds increasingly complex creatures. This is a certain kind of half truth that, if we take it for the whole truth, will give us a distorted picture of the world. In fact, evolution builds complexity sometimes, but it also sometimes does the opposite. True, humans are more complex than bacteria. But *every* kind of living thing represents the latest model produced in a never-ending process that chooses the best possible creature to fit a particular environment. Some of these models, like humans, are complex, and we did evolve from simpler organisms. But some models get along quite well in their simplicity. That is, being simple is a good way to survive and reproduce in certain environments.

Sometimes evolution takes a complex design and simplifies it. Consider tapeworms, parasites that live in the intestines of vertebrates. They evolved from nonparasitic, free-living worms that had to find food and fend for themselves. Modern tapeworms, on the other hand, depend heavily on their hosts; in fact, they have handed over responsibility for almost every life process except reproduction (see Figure 1–3). Because their hosts provide so many "services" tapeworms have evolved towards simplicity, not complexity. In summary, evolution provides organisms with the traits they need to survive and reproduce. Sometimes this demands complexity; other times simplicity.

We will get a clearer idea of what evolution is and how it works as we proceed through the next few chapters. For now it is sufficient to realize that evolution and the Great Chain of Being are two very different ideas. We believe that confusing the two has led some scientists to imagine that humans are above biological influences.

THE STANDARD SOCIAL SCIENCE MODEL

Psychology is a vast and varied field: Psychologists study everything from learning in single-celled organisms to hostage-taking by terrorists. And their methods and theories are as varied as the phenomena they study. Thus it is impossible to say what all psychologists believe about their science. But we agree with John Tooby and Leda Cosmides (1992) that many psychologists hold to a general set of beliefs called the Standard Social Science Model (SSSM), that has a pervasive influence on their research and theories. As you will see, the SSSM emphasizes the dominant influence of experience and culture in shaping human behavior.

(a)

(b)

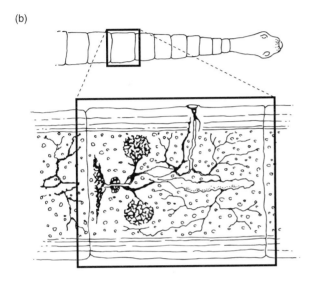

Figure 1–3. *Trematode worm and tapeworm.* The tapeworm (b) lacks digestive tract of its close relative, the trematode, *Opisthorchis sinensis.* Detail shows tapeworm is filled with reproductive structures. (From *Evolutionary Analysis* by Scott Freeman and Jon C. Herron. Copyright © 1998 by Scott Freeman and Jon C. Herron. Reprinted by permission of Prentice Hall, a division of Pearson Education.)

The SSSM notes that human infants have the same behavioral characteristics the world over. On the other hand, adults are much less uniform. For example they speak and act somewhat differently in different parts of the world. The SSSM assumes a particular relationship between these two facts: As babies grow up, the differences between them increase because they are shaped by different experiences and cultures. A belief in the profound influence of culture and experience on behavior lies at the heart of the SSSM. The SSSM rests on the following propositions:

1. *There is a psychic unity of human nature.* Humans the world over have essentially the same basic mental characteristics; there is a "human nature" that all people share. That's why infants are fundamentally alike. (Evolutionary psychologists agree with this first proposition, but they disagree about what that human nature is, as we will see later on.)

2. *Differences between people arise from differences in their experiences and cultures.*

3. *Biological constraints on human behavior are unimportant.* Humans have few, if any, "instincts" and only a few basic, biological drives, such as hunger, thirst, and sex.

4. *Learning operates by one or a very small number of general-purpose mechanisms.*

5. *The job of psychology is to discover how culture and experience, operating by means of the general purpose learning mechanisms, produce variation in human behavior.*

To repeat, the propositions of the SSSM are not shared by all psychologists. And a few mainstream psychologists have challenged some of these propositions in recent years, as we will see shortly. But these propositions reflect the thinking of many psychologists, particularly those who see psychology as a social science. The SSSM encapsulates the view that dominates most introductory psychology texts.

CRITIQUE OF THE STANDARD SOCIAL SCIENCE MODEL

Evolutionary psychology (EP) finds the Standard Social Science Model deeply flawed. Tooby and Cosmides (1992) list three major problems with the model.

1. *The SSSM misunderstands the nature of development.* Just because a trait is absent at birth does not prove that it results from learning or experience. Babies lack teeth, beards, and breasts, but these structures are not the product of experience; they appear through the process of maturation.

> **Trail Marker:** Absence of a behavior at birth is not proof that it results from experience.

Likewise newborns do not walk or talk, but these behaviors develop more or less spontaneously over time. Although we commonly say that baby has learned to walk, or has learned to talk, we all appreciate that this is quite different, say, from learning to play the violin. We don't seriously believe that experience is all that is responsible for the emergence of walking and talking. For example, it would be very difficult to *prevent* babies from talking and walking as they grow up. But under no circumstances would they master a musical instrument without explicit instruction and huge amounts of practice!

In part babies aren't born walking and talking because the nervous system must mature further before the baby is capable of these activities. In some cultures, babies are tightly bound to a cradling board for the first several months of life. Researchers found long ago that cradled babies walked as early as those who were free to move their limbs (Dennis & Dennis, 1940), so "practice" seems relatively unimportant. Likewise, deaf children born to parents who are not fluent in sign language spontaneously improve upon their parents' version (Pinker, 1994). Of course, culture determines which language a child will learn to speak. But, as you will learn in Chapter 7, babies the world over go through the same stages of language development at the same ages in spite of wide variations in experience. Clearly "learning" to walk or talk is different from learning geometry or European history. EP recognizes that biological influences on behavior do not have to appear full blown at birth. As you will learn, they typically begin to assert themselves at the time the particular behavior is likely to be needed.

2. *The SSSM draws a false dichotomy between nature and nurture.* The nature-nurture controversy is older than psychology itself. For centuries, people have wondered how heredity and environment work in causing behavior. We will deal with this extraordinarily important issue at length in Chapter 4. For now we will anticipate that discussion by saying simply that the idea that behavior is *X* percent caused by heredity and *Y* percent caused by environment is fundamentally misguided.

> **Trail Marker:** It is a mistake to divide the causes of behavior between nature and nurture.

That makes as much sense as saying that walking depends 50 percent on your left leg and 50 percent on your right leg. Walking depends 100 percent on each one, because without two legs you can't walk at all. Just as your legs work *together* when you walk, nature and nurture work *together* in shaping a person's behavior. Instead of trying to divide the causes of behavior between nature and nurture, we need to understand how nature and nurture interact to produce behavior (see Chapter 4).

3. *General purpose mechanisms cannot explain behavior.* For many decades, psychology took as one of its main tasks the search for general laws of learning. Every introductory psychology text has a chapter on learning that discusses the theories of Pavlov, Watson, and Skinner. These theories are the most prominent, and the best remembered, from the period of the "big theories." During the 1930s through approximately the 1960s, psychologists worked mightily to develop theories that would explain all types of learning in all sorts of animals. Hundreds of psychologists labored in dozens of laboratories, conducting thousands of learning experiments, mostly on two species, white rats, *Rattus norvegicus*, and people, *Homo sapiens*. It was not, as the old joke goes, that psychologists believed that humankind evolved directly from the white rat. Rather they believed two separate, but related ideas: 1) The same laws of learning operated in all species, and 2) learning involved making connections between arbitrarily chosen stimuli and responses. In other words, the process by which a rat learned to press a bar in a Skinner box was believed to be not much different from that used by a college student to learn Shakespeare.

B. F. Skinner once published a graph that showed the learning performance of several different species. He said:

> Pigeon, rat, monkey, which is which? It doesn't matter. Of course these three species have behavioral repertoires which are as different as their anatomies. But once you have allowed for [anatomical] differences in the ways in which they make contact with the environment, and in the ways in which they act on the environment, what remains of their behavior shows astonishingly similar properties. Mice, cats, dogs, and human children could have added other curves to this figure. (Skinner, 1956, pp. 230–231)

One of the first cracks in the "big-theory" program came from the work of Keller and Marian Breland (1961). The Brelands were students of Skinner who wanted to use his principles to train animals to perform tricks for zoos and commercial displays. For example, they tried to train a pig to pick up an oversized coin and drop in into a piggy bank. Unfortunately, the pig preferred to push the coin around the floor with its snout, throw it in the air, and push it around some more. They also tried to train a raccoon to do the same task. The animal picked the coin up all right, but instead of dropping it in the slot, the raccoon repeatedly put it in and took it out again, rubbed it, but wouldn't let go. They wrote up their findings in an influential article called, "The Misbehavior of Organisms."

It may have occurred to you, as it did to the Brelands, that pigs root for food by pushing things around with their snouts. Repeatedly putting the coin into the slot and taking it out again parallels the behavior raccoons show in washing their food before eating. Eventually, the Breland's concluded that training animals required them to take account of the behaviors typical of each species. Thus they changed their tactics and did things such as "teaching" chickens to dance by placing them on a slippery surface, making use of chickens' habit of scratching the ground in their search for food.

Although Skinner claimed that he taught animals to perform arbitrary tasks to obtain food, we can see that it was no accident that he trained rats to press a bar on the wall, but pigeons to peck a key. Rats explore their environment by raising themselves by their forepaws, and pigeons peck for food. Partly in response to these findings, Martin Seligman (1971) introduced the concept of "preparedness" to account for the differences in ease of training certain behaviors. Animals are "overprepared" to perform certain behaviors, and "underprepared" for others. Humans are underprepared to do calculus or juggle. But we are overprepared to talk or walk. Every normal child learns to do these things without systematic instruction. In Chapter 7, we will give several detailed examples to show that evolution has prepared different species to learn quite different tasks.

Eventually the period of big theories ended—for the simple reason that the effort failed. Learning to press a bar for food is fundamentally different from learning to find one's way through a city, or learning to recognize emotions on people's faces. There is no general learning mechanism because it wouldn't serve any useful purpose. Evolution would not have designed the brain to be a general purpose problem solver because there is no general purpose problem to be solved! Instead, the real world poses many quite specific problems.

Consider a computer analogy. Hard as it might be to imagine, when personal computers first came on the market in the 1970s they weren't very popular. Here's why: They were "general purpose" computers. They had some computational power but, right out of the box, they couldn't do much; they were not designed for any specific real-world problems. If you wanted to write term papers, you had to buy a word-processing program. If you wanted to manage your finances, you needed to install a spreadsheet program, and so on. Because these general purpose computers weren't very useful, the manufacturers began to pre-load more and more kinds of software into their computers at the factory. This made them much more attractive and computer sales skyrocketed. The point is, a general purpose mind is just as useless as a general purpose computer. As a consequence, evolution has "pre-loaded" lots of "software" that allows our brains to perform a wide range of specific tasks. For example, as we have mentioned above (and will discuss in detail in Chapter 7), human infants are born with "programs" or "modules" that allow them to master the sounds, meanings and grammar of any language they hear. This is just one module out of many: Clearly a language-decoding module would not be very good at mastering routes and spatial relationships in the local landscape. Indeed, we should expect the brain to contain specialized modules that evolved to solve each of the problems faced by our ancestors: Is this edible? Which way is home? Is that person a suitable mate? Is my neighbor trustworthy? And many others.

John Tooby and Leda Cosmides offered the analogy of a Swiss Army knife to make the same point. A Swiss Army knife wraps many specialized tools (screw drivers, can opener, saw, corkscrew) into a single compact package. That's why these pocket tool collections are so popular. And they nicely exemplify our two part-lesson: Useful objects are useful precisely because they are tailored to the tasks of the real world; and because the real world poses many different problems we need many different tools.

> **Trail Marker:** The brain can't be a general purpose computer; computers need task-specific software.

Although not detailed by Tooby and Cosmides (1992) there are two additional problems with the SSSM.

4. *The Standard Social Science Model drives a wedge between the natural and social sciences.* By claiming that the job of psychology is to study how culture produces behavioral differences, the SSSM divorces psychology from the natural sciences in general, and biology in particular. This denial of the role of biology in human behavior is widespread, both inside and outside the scientific arena. What this stance overlooks is that our biology makes possible *everything* we do. We think the way we do because of our evolved cognitive mechanisms just as we see colors the way we do because of the particular pigments in our eyes.

The wedge between the natural and social sciences can be illustrated by the fact that psychologists and biologists for the most part study behavior in isolation from each other, as indicated by the way they approach differences between men and women. Both psychologists and biologists agree that, on average, men desire to mate more often and with a greater variety of partners than women do. But they disagree about the causes of the sex difference. Psychologists who follow the SSSM tend to attribute these differences to cultural influences, whereas the biologists have an evolutionary explanation (which we will discuss in detail in Chapter 10). For now we'll merely point out a weakness in the cultural explanation. Is it plausible that the male-female differences found in humans are simply the result of culture when the identical pattern appears in hundreds of other mammal species?

Unless humans share the same culture with all these other mammals (an idea no social scientist could accept), the cultural explanation makes no sense.

There is an even more general point to be grasped here. Not only are the natural and social sciences linked, *all* of science is a single coherent enterprise. This is true even though there are many disciplines within science. First, note that all of science is based on common assumptions and methods. But equally important, the web of scientific laws, theories, and explanations must form a coherent fabric across disciplines. This is clear from the way disciplines blend into each other. Biophysics links biology with physics, and biochemistry links biology with chemistry. But linkage is always required, even if there is no named discipline to fill the gaps.

Here's an example of how science is really a single enterprise. A few years ago, a team of chemists announced that hydrogen atoms could be made to fuse together (as they do in the sun) but without producing large amounts of heat. They called the process "cold fusion." Unfortunately, given what modern physics has uncovered about the nature and structure of atoms, cold fusion is theoretically impossible! This was a crisis. The behavior of atoms *must* be compatible with the principles of physics; they can't follow different laws in the chemistry lab than they do in the physics lab. Either the chemists were wrong about cold fusion, or the physicists needed to revise their principles. Contradictions are not allowed in science, and teams of chemists and physicists got working on the problem. In case you're wondering, physics is okay. There is no cold fusion; it was a false alarm. It didn't have to turn out that way, however. The chemists could have been right, in which case we would have had to make some very important revisions to our picture of the physical world. Either way, by the rules of science, the findings of the two fields would have to be brought into alignment; no exemption is possible.

This book isn't about chemistry or physics but the general point holds: Science is a single endeavor linked by a coherent set of laws, principles and theories. Now, notice the fundamental contradiction that occurs when psychology (or any of the social sciences) tries to divorce itself from biology. No such exemption is possible! Psychologists study the behavior of living things. Living things are biological objects and thus conform to the principles discovered by biologists. The single most powerful principle in biology is the principle of evolution by natural selection (Chapter 2). The conclusion is obvious: The behavior of living things must be explicable in terms of evolution. Trying to exempt the behavior of organisms from the principles of biology is like trying to exempt the behavior of atoms from the principles of physics. Such maneuvers are not permissible within the framework of science.

Is this conclusion too strong? Let's review the pieces separately. Could biologists be wrong about evolution by natural selection? Of course any scientist or group of scientists can be wrong. In fact, it's the willingness to be shown wrong, and to offer testable predictions, that makes one a scientist. And over the centuries, a great many scientists have been shown to be wrong by this very process.

But when a theory stands for a long time—when it offers many and varied predictions, and these predictions are consistently verified by experiment and observation—scientists begin to talk about the theory as if it were a fact. In terms of how well established they are, the theory of evolution by natural selection is just as much a fact as the theory that the earth goes around the sun. In short, if it's not right, it's so close to right that it's hardly worth worrying about. The relevant evidence is presented in Chapter 2.

What about the claim that science is one endeavor? Curiously, some say it's two. Those who believe this say that the natural sciences are united with each other and the social sciences are united with each other but that the two major divisions are separate. This is a common claim among those social scientists who want to wall off their efforts from biology. Here's one way of seeing that the wall is imaginary.

Social scientists study social behavior. Humans are by no means the only social species; there are thousands of others. And there is a great deal of work in biology showing how evolution has adapted the social behavior of various species to their environments (Chapter 15). In other words, biology, and its central principle of evolution, seems highly relevant to understanding the behavior of many nonhuman species. By what logic would it be irrelevant to understanding human behavior? The wall crumbles. First, it's social behavior that is off limits to evolutionary analysis. When that's shown to be impossible, then it's human social behavior. But evolutionary theory applies with equal force to humans. In short, there is no scientifically defensible division between the natural and social sciences. Science is demonstrably one enterprise, not two. And living things are products of evolution. Anyone studying living things will be at a disadvantage if they pretend otherwise.

5. The final and perhaps most important criticism of the SSSM is that *the Standard Social Science Model lacks an overarching theory of design.* Psychology is a vigorous branch of science with a large body of findings, theories, and applications. It stands as one of the significant intellectual achievements of our day, and contributes enormously to human welfare. We do not in any way intend to minimize the accomplishments of psychology. Rather EP should be seen as providing an added perspective that enriches psychology. What is missing in the SSSM, and what EP adds to psychology, is an overarching theory that unifies these findings and allows one to predict them in advance. *Why* are men more inclined to promiscuity than women (Chapter 10)? *Why* should watching violence on TV cause people to become more violent instead of less violent (Chapter 4)? *Why* are some logical problems difficult and others easy (Chapter 8)? *Why* are family ties so important to us (Chapters 4 and 15)? *Why* do we care about our reputations (Chapters 4 and 15)? *Why* does inequality lead to violence (Chapter 16)? *Why* can't we be happy all the time (Chapter 12)? *Why* do we crave foods that are unhealthy (Chapter 14)? The SSSM model attributes these effects to culture and experience, with no further comment! Evolutionary psychology makes sense of them.

"HOW" QUESTIONS AND "WHY" QUESTIONS

One way to see that EP adds a theory of design to psychology is to note that standard psychology asks "how" questions, whereas EP asks "why" questions. "How" questions are questions about how the human mind works: What are the conditions under which learning takes place? What parts of the brain are involved? What chemicals transmit the messages? Standard psychology books are chock full of answers to these kinds of questions. Biologists call these questions *proximate* questions. Proximate questions ask for information about the plumbing and wiring of the system, about how it works.

EP, however, asks "why" questions: Why do men and women evaluate partners by somewhat different criteria? Biologists refer to "why" questions as *ultimate* questions, because they explore why the system exists in terms of the function it was designed to serve. The value of the evolutionary approach is that it adds the ultimate "why" explanation. It explains why humans are the way they are.

> **Trail Marker:** Proximate answers explain how a mechanism works; ultimate answers explain why the mechanism exists, in terms of the function it serves.

Both questions contribute to understanding behavior. Birds fly north in the spring to nest and raise their young where there is a seasonal abundance of food. In the fall, they return to escape the cold and the reduced food supply of winter. This is the "why." The "how" includes their response to changes in day length (triggering the hormones that drive migration), their use of celestial navigation cues, and the like.

You may wonder how stating the function of a thing can explain why it exists. And you are right to wonder: In many arenas, it can't. But in the realm of living things, traits exist only because of the function they serve. In fact, that was one of Darwin's most brilliant insights. In the following chapter, we explain how evolution builds functional design as a matter of course, and thus how the function of a trait explains its existence. Human-designed objects such as thermostats can also be said to have a function; thermostats were designed to maintain a constant temperature. It was human needs and engineering that built them in the goal of maintaining temperature. Evolved mechanisms have the goals that were built into them by the process of evolution.

In summary, psychology has done an excellent job of discovering many of the proximate mechanisms that shape our behavior. But psychology has largely failed to address the fact that these mechanisms must somehow have been designed. EP looks at psychology from a design perspective, asking "Why did evolution build that kind of mechanism?"

THERE IS A HUMAN NATURE

As we mentioned earlier, EP agrees with the SSSM that there is a human nature: People around the world have basically the same psychology. But make no mistake. The two disagree quite profoundly on what that human nature is. The SSSM says that human nature is a blank slate; almost anything could be written on it by experience. Thus, according to the SSSM, human behavior is almost infinitely flexible. The form it takes is largely the result of arbitrary environmental influences such as learning and culture. In sharp contrast, EP says that human nature is not blank at all; it consists of a large number of evolved psychological mechanisms. According to EP, these psychological mechanisms shape human behavior by fostering specific patterns of response to the environment.

The SSSM View of Human Nature

Scientists who hold to the SSSM point to the many differences among peoples around the world to argue for the importance of learning in shaping human behavior. They believe that human behavior is almost infinitely malleable: For example, people would be kind and gentle if society did not encourage them to be mean and aggressive.

Introductory psychology textbooks are full of what Steven Pinker (1994) calls "our society" statements. They say, "In our society boys are encouraged to be tough, and girls are encouraged to be gentle," or "women tend to be the caretakers of children," or "men are more aggressive than women," and so forth. The implication is that these things are true only in "our society," not everywhere. What these books seldom present, however, is any evidence that our society is in any way unusual in regard to the behavioral trait under consideration. This technique is known as begging the question—assuming what you want to prove.

When pressed to give evidence that our society is different from others, proponents of the SSSM generally point to the work of anthropologist Margaret Mead. Mead is world famous for her writings on the culture of Samoa, a chain of islands in the Southwest Pacific. In her classic book, *Coming of Age in Samoa*, Mead (1928/1973) drew a picture of a carefree society in which there was no selfishness or jealousy, and people avoided competition. Mead claimed that children were reared communally without attachment to their parents, and so roamed freely in a sort of paradise where everyone shared in their upbringing. Adolescents were pictured as engaging in sexual relations without emotional entanglements until marriage; even then adultery was not considered particularly serious, and rape was unknown. Mead's book was enormously popular, and she became the most famous anthropologist of her time. Contemporary reviewers hailed her work as leading the way to a new style of life that would be characterized by "free love," absence of jealousy, and communal child rearing.

The only problem with this picture is that it is totally at odds with the facts of Samoan life. Derek Freeman is an anthropologist who studied Samoan culture during many field trips, stretching over several decades. To make a long story short, he found that Samoans are far from the carefree people of Mead's writings (Freeman, 1983, 1996). They are strict in raising their children in nuclear families; the virginity of girls is carefully guarded until marriage; adultery is taken very seriously; and Samoan men are at least as prone to rape as men in America and other Western cultures. Freeman's thorough documentation of Samoan culture leaves no doubt that Mead's picture was wide of the mark.

How could Margaret Mead have been so wrong? This is a story in itself, but in a nutshell, Mead went to Samoa as a twenty-three-year-old graduate student with two year's study of anthropology, little preparation in field research, and no knowledge of the Samoan language. She stayed in Samoa for only nine months, the first six weeks of which she spent picking up the rudiments of the language. Mead lived with an American family in the U.S. Navy, which had a large presence there. She preferred Western-style accommodations over living with an indigenous family because she didn't think she would like the native food or being in close quarters with the people. Mead obtained her information about Samoan culture by interviewing a group of girls who attended a school operated by the U.S. Navy.

Probably her biggest mistake was that she went to Samoa precisely to find the evidence she believed she found. Her adviser in graduate school at Columbia, the famous Franz Boas, sent her to find evidence that would support his extreme environmentalist position, which was very popular in the 1920s.

Margaret Mead, and many others like her, tried to show that human behavior is almost infinitely malleable—that human behavior is, for all interesting purposes, learned. This effort did not succeed, although the fact is often lost to students of psychology and anthropology. One reason that extreme environmentalist ideas flourished was because people went out to prove them. In fact, it is not too extreme to say that anthropologists have generally gone looking for differences between cultures at the same time that they ignored the similarities between them. We can see why. You may have gone to visit your relatives in another state and been intrigued by differences in family customs, such as holiday traditions and eating patterns. The novelty kept you from noticing the striking similarities between your family and your cousins' family.

Margaret Mead's work has long since been superceded by better studies. Nevertheless we have described it in some detail because it has passed into popular thought as *the* classic demonstration of cultural relativity. Orans (1996) reviewed the controversy over Mead's work in Samoa. He sums up his evaluation by saying that Mead failed to follow standard scientific rules of evidence. Therefore,

> Her work may properly be damned with the harshest scientific criticism of all, that it is 'not even wrong'. . . . In short, if Mead is taken as having done science, she did a bad job of it, and the procedures she followed would have produced unreliable results whatever her hunches. (p. 155)

In summary, Mead's work cannot be taken as evidence for an arbitrary cultural variation in sexual mores and other cultural practices.

The Universal People

Donald Brown (1991) argues that anthropologists have vastly underestimated the similarities among cultures simply because they are as invisible to us as the air we breathe. He has described what he calls the *universal people*—whose behavior is typical of every single human culture. This is the human nature that would be seen by the hypothetical Martian who landed randomly anywhere in the world, whether suburban North America, or hunter-gatherer Amazonia.

According to Brown the universal people are social. They live in groups; they observe rank and status; they are polite and enforce rules of etiquette. They communicate both via language and nonverbally. They have a wide range of facial expressions for anger, sadness, and the like, that everyone recognizes immediately. They cry, flirt, mimic, joke, tease, and show affection.

The universal people exchange gifts, keep track of favors, and retaliate for injustices. They show hospitality and throw feasts. They dance and make music. They have rules that define rights and obligations, and have mechanisms to deal with theft, rape, and murder.

The universal people live in families centered on mother and children and a man. They recognize marriage, which defines socially recognized sexual access to a fertile woman. They pay attention to kinship, marking father and mother, son and daughter, aunt and uncle. There is division of labor by age and sex. Women do more child care. Men are more aggressive than women and dominate political affairs.

They show modesty about sexual behavior and bodily functions even if they go about naked.

They have supernatural beliefs and develop theories of misfortune, disease, and death. They plan for the future, have rituals to observe life passages, and mourn their dead.

This is a very partial sampling of Brown's description of the universal people. But it should be obvious that people everywhere act in ways that are obviously and distinctly human. What we all have in common is far more than something we share with other animals, even our nearest relatives, the apes. Brown's description of the universal people should make us think twice about claiming that human behavior is infinitely variable and that this variability is the result of experience.

Before we go any further, we need to make it clear that human behavior does vary from culture to culture. Obviously human cultures differ in many interesting ways. There are thousands of languages around the world. Marriage systems vary considerably—including monogamy, where one woman and one man live together; polygyny, where one man has several wives; and (rarely) polyandry, where two or more men share a single wife. But this variation is no embarrassment to EP because EP does not predict fixity of behavior. According to EP, the role of our evolved psychological mechanisms is to adjust our behavior to prevailing conditions. We will illustrate this extraordinarily important point over and over in this book. Human behavior is variable, but the variability is not random and arbitrary. Instead human behavior is patterned. And those patterns make sense only in the light of evolution.

A SOURCE OF CONFUSION: THE NATURALISTIC FALLACY

Evolutionary psychology is controversial in some circles. Some psychologists oppose it strongly, others are skeptical, and still others are just becoming aware of its existence. There are a number of reasons for this state of affairs, including the indisputable fact that some people have misused evolutionary ideas to excuse such evils as racism, sexism, and social injustice in general. Make no mistake: We reject repression in all its many forms. We believe that any use of evolutionary theory in this way is a distortion of the theory, not a proper application of it. In the chapters that follow, you will learn how to recognize such distortions. We will also show that EP has a wide range of progressive implications. Remember, any scientific theory can be used for good or evil. An understanding of radioactivity can be used to build nuclear weapons or to cure cancer. Science is merely a tool for satisfying our needs and wants; as Richard Dawkins (n.d.) has said, "the trick is to want the right things."

Some readers will be bothered right from the outset by one important issue, so we will address it now. It is the mistaken idea that EP excuses many of the evils in society on the basis that they are "natural," being the product of evolution. For example, some people react negatively when they learn that abuse of stepchildren or marital infidelity may have their roots in certain evolved psychological mechanisms. We evaluate these ideas in Chapter 13 and 10, respectively. For now we simply need to note that many behaviors that we find undesirable, to put in mildly, can be seen as the products of evolution. But is that a reason to reject EP, or to study it more intently?

> **Trail Marker:** The naturalistic fallacy confuses "is" with "ought." Something is not morally acceptable simply because it is "natural."

Evolutionary psychology explains behavior; it does not justify it. Imagining that it offers a justification is known as the *naturalistic fallacy* (e.g., Buss, 1990). In a nutshell, the naturalistic fallacy confuses "is" with "ought." It confuses the situation that exists in the world with our moral judgment about that situation. Earthquakes, volcanic eruptions, floods, pestilence, AIDS, cancer, and heart attacks are all natural phenomena. Yet we study their causes, not to justify them, but to be better able to eradicate them or alleviate their effects. By the same token, we hold that studying the possible evolutionary origins of child abuse or infidelity is a good way to understand and therefore address the problems.

Suppose you woke up to find yourself as a character in a horror movie, with a strange creature outside your house, acting in a frightening manner. You immediately would ask, "What is this thing? What does it want? What makes it tick?" Only when you understand "the nature of the beast" are you in a position to deal with it. Ignorance of the causes of behavior definitely is not bliss. It can lead to actions that are useless at best, and deadly at worst. In short, we study all sorts of behaviors in order to understand them. With the understanding we gain, we are in a better position to encourage the desirable behaviors and discourage the undesirable ones.

A particularly well-known example of the naturalistic fallacy goes by the name of *social Darwinism.* Herbert Spencer (1820–1903) was a contemporary of Darwin who believed that social inequality is justified by evolutionary theory.

> The poverty of the incapable, the distresses that come upon the imprudent, the starvation of the idle, and those shoulderings aside of the weak by the strong . . .

are the decrees of a large, farseeing benevolence. (Herbert Spencer, quoted by Bartlett, 1992, p. 492.)

Although Spencer was an enthusiastic supporter of Darwin, he doesn't appear to have understood the theory. For one thing, he believed that evolution meant progress, a misunderstanding we have already discussed. Second, Spencer committed the naturalistic fallacy when he urged that we should not meddle with social forces. Social Darwinism would better be called social Spencerism, because it represents neither Darwin's own thinking nor that of present-day Darwinians (Hergenhahn, 1996). Whatever we call it, however, it became enormously popular.

> **Trail Marker:** Social Darwinism is a prominent example of the naturalistic fallacy. It also mistakenly holds that evolution means progress.

As you can imagine, American capitalists of the turn of the century found Social Darwinism much to their liking. Andrew Carnegie, the Scottish immigrant to Pittsburgh who became fabulously wealthy in the steel industry, enthusiastically supported social Darwinism, which he even elevated to a religious principle. Be that as it may, social Darwinism represents a serious misconstrual of evolutionary thinking and a prominent example of the naturalistic fallacy.

It is important to remember that no evolutionary explanation, whether it deals with humans or not, constitutes a moral claim. Evolution explains why things are as they are. It does not suggest that they are "right" or "good." Nor does it suggest that we ought to blindly accept them as "natural" if our moral principles tell us otherwise.

SUMMARY

1. Evolutionary psychology (EP) is an approach to all of psychology, not simply another specialty within psychology such as learning or perception.
2. Darwin and some early psychologists such as William James and James McDougall incorporated evolutionary thinking into the study of behavior, but most contemporary psychologists ignore the implications of evolutionary theory.
3. There is no "evolutionary ladder." All contemporary organisms are equally suited to their environments, and all have equally long evolutionary histories.
4. Evolution means change, not progress.
5. The Standard Social Science Model (SSSM), which dominates contemporary psychology, downplays the influence of biology and evolution; instead it emphasizes the importance of learning and culture.
6. The SSSM has a series of flaws. It:
   a. misunderstands the nature of development,
   b. misunderstands the nature/nurture issue,

    c. fails to recognize the limitations of general-purpose behavioral mechanisms,

    d. ignores the unity of science, and

    e. lacks an overarching theory of design.

7. EP asks ultimate, or "why" questions, whereas SSSM psychology asks proximate, or "how" questions.

8. According to the SSSM, human nature is a blank slate; thus human behavior is almost infinitely flexible.

9. According to EP, human nature consists of a large number of evolved psychological mechanisms. The mechanisms shape human behavior by fostering specific patterns of response to the environment.

10. Donald Brown's Universal People demonstrate a large set of complex behavior patterns common to all known societies. These commonalities suggest that human behavior is far from infinitely flexible.

11. The naturalistic fallacy confuses "is" with "ought." It is an error to conclude that a situation is morally acceptable simply because it is natural.

12. Social Darwinism is an example of the naturalistic fallacy and a misapplication of evolutionary thinking.

13. Evolution provides no moral seal of approval. Evolved traits should not be automatically accepted as "good" if they conflict with our moral code.

2　Evolutionary Theory

In the last days of December 1831, a twenty-two-year-old British naturalist named Charles Darwin embarked on a study of biological diversity that would take him around the world. He returned to England five years later with a large collection of animal and plant specimens. Intrigued with their variety, he set out to solve the question of why there are so many kinds of creatures. In doing so, he developed what may be the single most important and far-reaching scientific theory that has ever been formulated. After amassing his arguments and evidence, Darwin published *On the Origin of Species* in November of 1859. In it he detailed the theory of evolution by natural selection. The 1,250 copies of the first edition sold out in a single day, and the echoes of that fateful day have been reverberating through scientific, religious, and popular thought ever since.

Darwin's ideas are important to psychology because the theory of evolution by natural selection is not just a theory about where species come from. Rather, the theory details a process that continually designs species. Picture a machine on the shop floor of a manufacturing plant. If someone explains to you how the machine works, you will have some idea of what kind of product it makes. So it is with natural selection. Anyone who understands the workings of natural selection will have profound insight into the kinds of creatures it can create. Darwin's theory implies that all living things are designed, not by a conscious designer like a human engineer, but by the inanimate force of natural selection. And the theory of evolution by natural selection is quite explicit about what these living things are designed to do, which is a matter of great importance to psychologists and anyone else who hopes to understand behavior. Let's take a look at how natural selection works.

THE MECHANISM OF NATURAL SELECTION

Darwin's great insight about how evolution happens, and how organisms are designed along the way, can best be understood as a series of logical statements and conclusions.

1. *Natural populations (of giraffes, daisies or people) could grow exponentially.* Let's take a simple example: a single asexual organism that reproduces once per day. If we begin with one of these organisms we will have two tomorrow, four the next day, eight the next, and so on. After a month we will have 2^{29} (about 540 million) and after two and half months we would have more of these creatures than there are atoms in the universe! This conclusion may seem to be a consequence of the fact that we have chosen a creature that reproduces daily, but it is not. To illustrate this very point, Darwin discussed the most leisurely reproducer he could think of, elephants. Based on reproductive rates in zoos he assumed that a female elephant would begin reproducing by the time she was 30 years old and that she would then produce one offspring every 10 years, up to a total of six offspring, when she would die of old age. Given these assumptions, he calculated that after a mere 500 years such a female would have 15 million living descendants. Darwin ran out of computational power at that point, but modern computers can show that after a few thousand years she would have so many descendants—each of whom would be in the process of producing yet more descendants—that the earth would be a ball of elephants expanding outward at the speed of light! This is exponential growth.

2. *Despite this potential for exponential growth, natural populations normally are relatively stable.* The last time you looked, this sector of the universe was not a ball of elephants expanding outward at the speed of light. There are no mistakes in the calculations, so what's wrong? It must be that some elephants do not produce six offspring over their lifetimes. The calculations tell us what would happen if they did. Since the conclusion is false, the assumptions are wrong. In other words:

3. *Many individuals do not leave as many offspring as they might.* This failure is often due to limited resources. What would a ball of elephants expanding outward at the speed of light eat? What would they breathe? The resources needed to make more elephants are finite. And every time elephant *A* reproduces, her offspring use food, water, and other resources that would have otherwise been available for the offspring of elephant *B*. When a population colonizes a new, unexploited area it may grow exponentially for a while. But its very success means that it will soon grow to the point where, again, there are not enough resources to support the reproduction of all.

> **Trail Marker:** Natural selection refers to the fact that those who are better suited to the current environment tend to produce more offspring.

4. *Those best suited to the prevailing environment leave the most offspring.* By virtue of their unique endowments, some individuals are better at finding food, avoiding

predators, fending off parasites, or coping with the vagaries of the local climate than other members of their population. Those better-suited individuals tend to leave more offspring. This is the kernel of the idea of natural selection. In each generation *nature selects* from the population those individuals best able to cope with the prevailing environmental barriers to reproduction. It selects them in the sense that they pass the various tests of the environment and thereby succeed in reproducing. Those that fail the tests of the environment leave fewer or no offspring. It's often useful to think of the environment as a filter that lets some types pass through to the next generation but prevents other types from passing (see Figure 2–1).

    5. *Because of heredity, offspring are like their parents.* The advantages that allowed certain individuals to reproduce, in spite of the local environmental challenges, will be passed on to the next generation. And the disadvantages that caused some individuals to fail the tests of the environment will not be passed on. This means that the results of the natural selection in one generation form the starting point for another round of selection in the next. Thus:

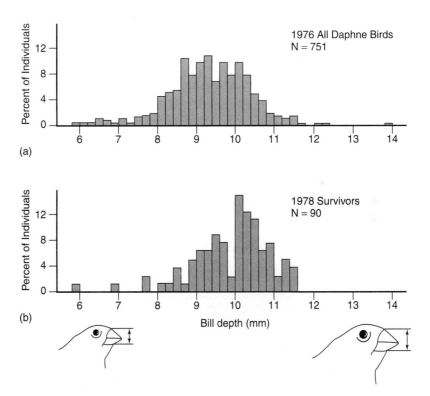

Figure 2–1. *Natural selection of bill depth in a seed-eating bird.* During a drought between 1976 and 1978 the supply of softer seeds dwindled. Birds with deeper bills were better at processing the harder seeds that remained. Few of the small-beaked birds survived to breed, but many of the large-beaked birds did. As a result the average beak size changed over the course of the drought. (From *Ecology and Evolution of Darwin's Finches* by P. Grant. Copyright © 1986 by Princeton University Press. Reprinted by permission of University Press.)

6. *Over many generations, natural selection builds individuals that are progressively better adapted to their environment.* Because those individuals best suited to prevailing conditions leave more offspring, the traits that make them well suited become more common in the population over time.

These six points capture Darwin's central argument. Many people summarize his theory of evolution by natural selection with the popular phrase "survival of the fittest." This phrase was not coined by Darwin but by his contemporary, Herbert Spencer, who as we saw in Chapter 1, had many mistaken ideas about evolution. And Spencer didn't get it quite right here either. "Survival of the fittest" is *not* an accurate summary of natural selection; it requires two important modifications. First, reproduction is what makes a difference to the process of natural selection, not mere survival. If an individual survived for hundreds or even thousands of years but never reproduced, that individual's traits would be lost when he or she eventually died. According to the theory of evolution by natural selection, advantageous traits become common because they are passed on to more offspring than are disadvantageous traits. Mere survival can never make a trait more common. Thus we ought to say "reproduction of the fittest."

The second qualification to Spencer's phrase concerns the meaning of "fittest." It must not merely mean "those that reproduce." If it does we end up with the circular idea, "reproduction of those that reproduce." To capture the logic of Darwin's theory, fittest must refer to the fit between the organism and the environment; the fittest are the ones best able to cope with local environmental challenges. The phrase then becomes a bit bulkier but much more precise: "reproduction of those best suited to the prevailing environment." This phrase is now a good summary of the theory of evolution by natural selection. It emphasizes that unless a trait is reproduced it will eventually be lost. And it also stresses that what is fit depends on the environment, because each environment poses a unique set of challenges.

NATURAL SELECTION CRAFTS ADAPTATIONS

The process of natural selection, the reproduction of those best suited to the prevailing environment, is constantly designing organisms. It shapes them for one ultimate purpose—reproduction. This is true simply because only those that reproduce pass on their traits to the next generation. Designs for reproduction are transmitted to offspring; other kinds of designs are not transmitted and therefore disappear. Designs for reproduction are called *adaptations*. They are preserved by natural selection because they aid reproduction in some way. This idea is central to modern evolutionary theory and deserves further examination.

> **Trail Marker:** Natural selection produces designs for reproduction called adaptations.

It is important to realize that the phrase "designs for reproduction" does not merely refer to the reproductive organs themselves. Living things have many complicated, integrated, functional traits that any engineer would marvel at. Bats evolved echolocation millions of years before humans invented its technological equivalent, sonar. The human eye is sensitive over at least thirteen orders of magnitude of light intensity—equivalent to the range from 1 to 10,000,000,000,000 (that's ten trillion or ten million million), far more than the most expensive video cameras (see Chapter 5). Cheetahs can run faster than cars can travel across the African savanna. Bat sonar, the human eye, and the cheetah's agility were designed by natural selection because they solved some immediate environmental problem such as obtaining food or avoiding danger. But there is no contradiction here. Natural selection can design traits like sonar, eyes, and agility to the extent that they contribute to reproduction. For example, if better nourished individuals produce more offspring then natural selection will be able to shape a wide array of traits that help organisms locate, capture, and digest food, because individuals who lacked these traits would leave fewer offspring.

Variations among individuals are constantly being tested against the environment. Any variation that aids reproduction, whether it happens to be in the liver, the lung, or the brain, will be passed to the next generation. An improvement in the brain that aids reproduction is just as much a design for reproduction as is an improvement in the ovaries. Both are properly thought of as adaptations. Adaptations exist because they enhance the fit between the organism and the environment and thereby increase the chances of reproduction.

Of course, some of the features of organisms should not be regarded as adaptations. Such nonadaptive features could arise simply by chance; or they could be incidental side effects of other traits that are adaptations. For example, your nose should not be regarded as an adaptation for holding up your sunglasses because it was not designed by natural selection for that purpose. How, then, do we recognize adaptations? Adaptations are structurally complex, typically made up of several integrated parts. And they show evidence of design for a particular function in that the parts work together to efficiently accomplish that function. Let's return to the example of the human nose. Most of its features are much more consistent with the idea that it was designed to filter, humidify, warm, and conduct air to and from the lungs, than with the idea that it was designed to support glasses. A few cases may be controversial, but with adequate information about the trait in question it is usually not too difficult to decide whether or not it is an adaptation.

> **Trail Maker:** Adaptations are complex, integrated and show design for a clear function that contributes to reproduction.

For example, all the features of the vertebrate eye work together in a way that convinces us it is an adaptation for seeing (see Figure 2–2). Any other idea, such as the suggestion that its parts might have fallen into their present arrangement by chance, or that it is really designed for something other than seeing, are inconsistent with what we know about its structure and workings.

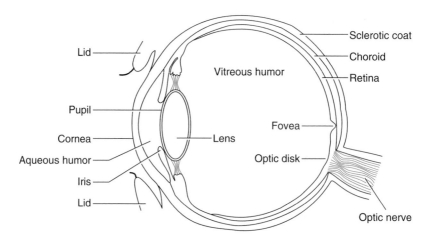

Figure 2–2.   *Diagram of the vertebrate eye showing the functional integration of its parts.* Note how each element fits together with the others to form a single organ that is very good at seeing (detecting certain wavelengths of light), but not very good at anything else.

Adaptations Are Specialized

For the most part, each adaptation is narrowly suited to solving a particular kind of problem. For example, the heart pumps blood through the body, the lungs aerate it, the kidneys purify it, and the like. Each organ is specialized for a narrow function. To understand why, think about a carpenter's tool box. It contains drills, saws, planes, hammers, files, clamps: a wide array of specialized implements each finely tuned for particular tasks. You could cut a board in half by drilling a series of closely spaced holes across the middle. But we'd bet that, given the choice, you'd use the saw; that would be much more efficient and produce a much better result. Remember that selection is constantly refining adaptations to achieve better and more efficient results. So this general principle, that tools are specialized for specific functions, applies to adaptations as well. Each adaptation tends to be specialized for solving a narrow class of problems simply because less specialized designs didn't work so well and selection tended to weed them out. For example, the vertebrate eye discussed above, shows a marvelous degree of specialization for resolving images from reflected light. It's stunningly good at that task and downright miserable at most others.

SELECTION BUILDS PSYCHOLOGICAL ADAPTATIONS

When we look at a flock of sparrows or sea gulls we see just that, a flock. We might with some effort be able to distinguish two types within the group, perhaps females and males. And we may notice that some are young individuals and some are full-grown adults, but our ability to distinguish among them ends there. We cannot separate individual adult females; they all look the same to us. On the other hand we recognize hundreds and even thousands of individual humans, principally by their faces, but also by their voices, postures, and gestures. This is a very special ability. Remember, we can't do it with sparrows. And just imagine trying to program a computer to recognize individual humans (or sparrows). Where did such an amazing ability come from?

One way to start answering this kind of question is to ask what life would be like without the ability. We all know people we regard as kind and generous and others we think of as mean and selfish. Some people we can count on for support. And there may be people we regard as enemies: people who have treated us badly, or taken advantage of us. Imagine that we could not tell these people apart. On any given occasion we would not know whether we were dealing with friend or foe! Our actions would often be precisely wrong. Clearly this could get us into trouble, trouble that would sooner or later reduce our chances of reproducing.

Being unable to tell people apart is so far from our normal experience that it is difficult to imagine. But there are certain kinds of brain injury that can disrupt the abilities we use to recognize individuals. For example, people who suffer from *prosopagnosia* cannot recognize faces (Benton 1980, Johnson and Morton, 1991). Patients with prosopagnosia say things like, "Are you my mother? I think you might be because my mother has a dress like that." They can recognize objects and patterns, even voices, but not faces. One patient with prosopagnosia wondered why a stranger kept staring at him as he sat in his club. When he complained to the waiter, he discovered he had been looking at his own face in a mirror (Goldstein, 1996). Notice that, as predicted, the mechanism responsible for face recognition is highly specialized, since prosopagnosics can still recognize people by their voices but not by their faces. By studying such patients it is possible to learn a great deal about the small part of the brain that does the job of face recognition (e.g., Sergent et al., 1992). And it is also apparent how difficult these patients find even the simplest transactions of social life.

Evolutionary psychologists think of brain elements like the one that recognizes faces as mental organs designed for a particular job. The face-recognition organ was presumably designed by natural selection to enhance our fitness in a complex social world where appropriate or inappropriate interactions with others can greatly effect our reproductive prospects. Thus, the face-recognition organ is almost certainly an adaptation, a psychological adaptation, preserved by natural selection because of its contributions to reproduction.

Evolutionary psychologists believe that selection has designed *many* specialized mental organs, each fulfilling a particular function. Remember the analogy of the carpenter's tool box. Specialization is an expected consequence of evolution because specialized adaptations do a better and more efficient job. Evolutionary psychologists use a variety of terms when talking about this mental specialization. For example, they point out that the mind is modular, not a single organ but a collection of many organs or modules, each designed for a different task. Similarly each module or organ is said to be domain specific. This phrase means that each module is designed to accept a particular kind of input and produce a particular kind of output, and to be more or less unresponsive to other sorts of stimuli. Modules are not necessarily made up of identifiable chunks of brain tissue. Some may involve a wide network of connections in the brain. What makes it useful to talk about them as modules is their narrow range of responsiveness, their specialization for a specific task.

Psychological Adaptations and Adaptive Behavior

Psychological adaptations have been designed by natural selection to produce adaptive behavior. Behaving appropriately is an important part of being fit. An animal with the anatomy of a wolf and the behavior of a sheep would leave few progeny. In fact, when we look around us in the world we see that the behavior of each type of animal is marvelously adjusted to its particular environment.

But how does selection work on behavior? Adaptive behavior is the norm not because selection has designed behavior directly. Instead selection designs the organs that underlie and produce behavior. Selection can, for example, choose among alternative neurological plans or alternative hormonal regimes. The fitter alternative would be the one which produced more adaptive behavior. This indirect action of selection is not limited to psychological traits. It's equally true for any aspect of performance. For example, selection can improve the efficiency of blood circulation only by improving the design of the circulatory organs such as the heart, arteries, and veins. Sometimes when they see adaptive behavior evolutionary psychologists can point to the underlying adaptation. For example, we know quite a bit about the brain mechanisms responsible for language (Pinker, 1994). In other cases the behavior is clearly adaptive, but we haven't yet identified the underlying mental organ. But in all cases it is important to remember that natural selection designs the psychological organs that produce behavior, not behavior itself.

> **Trail Marker:** Natural selection cannot design behavior directly. It designs psychological organs that produce adaptive behavior.

This is not meant to minimize the importance of adaptive behavior. On the contrary, behavior is critical to fitness, and selection has designed a huge array of psychological adaptations precisely for the purpose of guiding that behavior. In fact, there is an important corollary to the idea that selection operates on psychological mechanisms and not directly on behavior. Selection can design psychological mechanisms only to the extent that they influence behavior.

For example, imagine an emotion, let's call it *jyn*, that has no impact whatever on the people who experience it. Feeling jyn does not make you more or less likely to do anything. Others cannot tell when you feel jyn, so it does not influence their behavior towards you in any way. An emotion like jyn would be completely invisible to natural selection because it would have no effect on fitness. For this reason, emotions like jyn are not expected to evolve. Emotions and other psychological traits have been shaped by selection to produce adaptive behavioral output.

ADAPTATIONS ARE FORMED SLOWLY

Natural selection is powerful, but it takes time to craft adaptations. There are two principal reasons for this. First, the natural pace of evolution is measured in generations. In each generation, individuals are tested against the prevailing environment and the fitter ones pass on their traits. Traits cannot spread any faster than the members of the population can reproduce. Thus the pace of evolution is governed by the pace of reproduction, or what is called generation time. The generation time of humans, the time from birth to reproduction is roughly twenty years. The generation time of bacteria can be twenty minutes, so bacteria can evolve much more quickly than humans can.

The second reason evolution takes time is that natural selection can only choose among naturally occurring variants or alternatives; it cannot create entirely new variants. This is reflected in the very name of the evolutionary process: natural selection. To select means to choose from among existing possibilities. For example, selection can't favor an organism with three eyes instead of two unless a three-eyed individual actually exists.

Figure 2–3 illustrates evolution in a hypothetical population of grazing animals. Two types of individuals occur naturally in the population: They differ in how much time each spends scanning for predators. The diagram shows what might happen if the number of predators increased. This sort of environmental

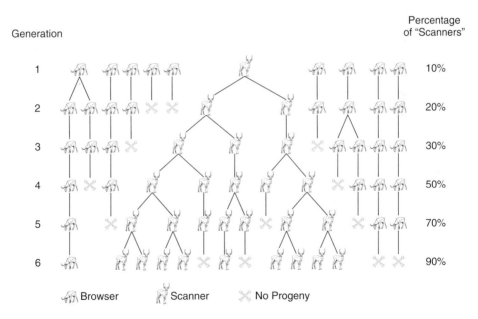

Figure 2–3. *A hypothetical case of natural selection.* This example assumes there has been a recent increase in the number of predators. Thus, individuals who spend more time scanning their environment ("scanners") have a better chance of surviving and reproducing. Initially scanners are rare but, due to their reproductive advantage, they become the predominant type.

change would probably give an advantage to the "scanners." Although initially rare, scanners would increase in frequency under these conditions.

Of course evolution can happen quickly when selection is strong, that is, when successful individuals leave many more offspring than unsuccessful ones. In Figure 2–3 the "browsers" have an average of 0.75 offspring while the "scanners" have an average of 1.44, nearly twice as many. This large difference in reproductive success allows a lot of evolution in a few generations. Often, differences in reproductive success are smaller and thus evolution typically happens more slowly.

> **Trail Marker:** Selection works by choosing among existing alternatives, not by inventing entirely new ones.

Suppose the environment changes in a way that poses a new challenge. There are two possible evolutionary outcomes. One possibility is that, by chance, a few members of the population have a trait that helps them cope with this new challenge. These few individuals will be more likely to reproduce than those who lack their advantage. An initially rare trait can spread through the population as those that fit the environment reproduce more than those that don't. Eventually all, or nearly all, members of the population will possess the advantageous trait, though this may take many generations. (Again you can refer to Figure 2–3 to help visualize the spread of an advantageous trait.)

The second possible outcome is that no member of the population has a trait that helps it cope with the new challenge. In this case, there is no advantageous alternative for natural selection to spread. If one does not soon arise by chance, the population may go extinct. In fact, the majority of species that have ever existed are now extinct, probably for this very reason. In other words, sometimes natural selection cannot build a good adaptation because the variation it needs is not present. We will talk more about the causes of variation in the next chapter, but for now it is sufficient to understand that selection builds adaptations by choosing among existing variants, not by inventing entirely new ones.

It might seem that the slow cycle of generations and the fact that natural selection can only draw on existing variability make natural selection a weak force. But this is a mistaken conclusion because it fails to recognize three important facts. First, selection has literally all the time in the world to do its work. Since the earth's crust cooled about four thousand million (i.e., four billion) years ago, there has been plenty of opportunity for selection to operate. Second, most natural populations consist of many millions of individuals. As a consequence, there is a great deal of natural variability, and thus there is often an advantageous variant available to selection. Third and finally, to be favored by natural selection a trait does not have to fully solve some environmental problem; it merely has to help. Any variant that confers a reproductive advantage relative to its alternatives will spread. Later, even better alternatives may arise and be substituted or added to the initial solution by selection. Thus the process of evolution by natural selection is cumulative, with solution being layered on solution over many generations.

Selection Is Cumulative

The vertebrate eye, discussed by Richard Dawkins in his excellent books *The Blind Watchmaker* (1986) and *Climbing Mount Improbable* (1996), is a classic example of how selection can add refinements over time to build complex adaptations. How did the eye evolve? Was a freak animal with eyes born into a population of blind, eyeless ones? Almost certainly not. The eye must have been built through the accumulation of small improvements, each one an adaptation in its own right. For example imagine an eyeless creature living in a world where exposure to sun or shade had reproductive consequences, perhaps because sunlight allowed more rapid metabolism or because a predator typically cast a shadow in the moment before attack. Any individual who happened to be born with a patch of light-sensitive cells would have a reproductive advantage because it could seek sunlight or avoid shadow. The light-sensitive patch would therefore have spread by natural selection. Some starfish, jellyfish, leeches, and other worms have very simple "eyes" of this type.

> **Trail Marker:** Evolution is cumulative with new adaptations being layered on older ones.

Perhaps much later, when all the members of the population had light-sensitive patches, one was born with its patch formed into a slight depression. This arrangement would add the refinement that light direction could be sensed, and would similarly spread through the population. ("Cup eyes" of this general design are common among invertebrates such as clams and limpets.) Subsequently a lens could have been added, providing focus, by the same cumulative process. The first crude lens would not have to equal our precise modern ones. If it gave some advantage over the alternative of not having any lens at all, it would spread. Further selection could improve the lens, making it more fully transparent, refining the curvature to sharpen the focus, and the like. Natural selection will retain any chance variation that provides a reproductive edge. In this way, it can build very complex adaptations bit-by-bit from simple elements. The functional integration of the vertebrate eye shown in Figure 2–2 emerged gradually as new adaptations were layered on top of older ones.

ADAPTATIONS MAY BE OUT-OF-DATE

Real world environments are often changing. This means that adaptive solutions are moving targets. If we combine the slow pace of evolution with the fact of changing environments, we see that organisms are often better adapted to the past than to the present. The adaptations we see around us today are here because they have survived the tests of the past. Natural selection is this very minute evaluating whether they solve present environmental problems!

Some kinds of creatures may experience relatively slow environmental change. In that case, past and present environments are similar and so past adaptations tend to still be effective. This points up the fact that change is not the only result of evolution by natural selection. In stable environments, selection tends to prevent change in order to maintain previously constructed adaptations. On the other hand, rapidly changing environments make past adaptations out of date. This idea is important in thinking about human evolution because our technology is a recent source of rapid environmental change. For example, it's not surprising that we can't breathe automobile exhaust. Our respiratory systems were designed many millions of years before the first automobiles. The same line of thinking illuminates some of our psychological traits. Over much of human evolution, our ancestors probably lived in small social groups where everyone knew everyone else. Some of the social stresses of living in large, anonymous urban populations must be as evolutionarily novel as automobile exhaust. These issues will be discussed in more detail in Chapter 13.

> **Trail Marker:** Adaptations were designed to solve past environmental problems and may not perfectly match present challenges.

In summary, the great age of the earth means that selection has had large amounts of time to work. The individual variation present in large populations allows selection to evaluate many alternative designs. And the fact that selection incorporates any small improvement allows it to build up complex adaptations from simple elements. All these facts tend to make natural selection powerful. But two factors slow the pace of evolution by natural selection. Selection cannot create new variants but instead can only draw on existing variability. And the rate of evolution is limited by generation time. This means that when environments change too rapidly selection can not keep up, and adaptation will be imperfect.

SEXUAL SELECTION IS A SPECIAL KIND OF NATURAL SELECTION

Most of us have seen peacocks in zoos or aviaries and no doubt have been impressed. The male is an outrageous animal, with his fabulously long, flamboyant tail and glistening colors. But now that you are learning how selection designs organisms, it's time to reconsider the peacock from an evolutionary perspective. How did the peacock's tail evolve? It's hard to imagine how such a tail might help the peacock find food, or escape predators, or fend off parasites. In fact just the opposite is more likely the case: His tail must surely be a handicap in most respects, making it more difficult for him to survive. And yet the peacock is not a rare freak; many other birds have equally extravagant plumage. New Guinea's birds of paradise or the resplendent quetzal of Central America are more adorned. Even the tiny coquette hummingbirds outshine the peacock in many respects. And such extravagance is not limited to birds. Why do males of every known deer species have bones growing out of their heads? That's what antlers are after all. What a strange thing for evolution to do! And most puzzling, why in all these species is it the males—the peacock and not the peahen, the male birds of paradise, the male quetzals, the male coquettes, and the male deer—that have evolved all this ecologically useless decoration?

Darwin and his contemporaries knew about traits like the peacock's tail and wondered if the theory of evolution by natural selection could explain them. Darwin himself believed that it could but only if it were extended. And so in 1871, some dozen years after the publication of *The Origin*, he offered his theory of *sexual selection*. The essence of the idea is simple and does not fundamentally contradict any aspect of the theory of evolution by natural selection. Let's remind ourselves how natural selection works before we attempt to see what Darwin was suggesting with his theory of sexual selection. Under the influence of ordinary natural selection, certain traits spread if they lead to higher reproductive success than their alternatives. Of course, no trait is free: Each has developmental and maintenance costs and often risk costs as well. Traits don't spread because they are cheap. They spread because they yield a net profit in eventual reproductive success: In the bottom-line currency of offspring, they pay back more than they cost.

When natural selection is viewed this way, it's clear that it includes what Darwin and others call sexual selection. Here is why. The peacock's tail does impose all kinds of costs, making the bird more conspicuous to predators, slower in its escape when it is attacked, and leaving fewer energetic resources to spend on important activities such as foraging and fighting off disease. The trait is "ecologically harmful" in that it doesn't help the organism solve any environmental problems; it is actually a hindrance. But it can also provide an important benefit by making the bird more attractive to members of the opposite sex. In other words, it does solve one very special "environmental" problem after all: It helps in acquiring mates. So a long-tailed male is more likely to die than a short-tailed one, but more likely to mate while he is alive. Under these conditions, would long tails become more common in the population? The answer is the standard one we have learned in the realm of natural selection. The trait will spread if the benefits outweigh the costs. Thus, if the mating advantage provided by a long tail is large enough to compensate for the fact that many long-tailed males are taken by predators and disease, the trait will spread through the population.

We have described sexual selection as a kind of natural selection; but exactly what kind is it? It's a kind of selection favoring genes that provide advantages *only in the mating context.*

> **Trail Marker:** Sexual selection favors traits that provide benefits only in the mating context.

The main reason to recognize sexual selection as a distinct type of natural selection is that sexual selection often acts unevenly on the two sexes. Only peacocks have evolved long tails, while their mates, the peahens, remain relatively unadorned. Natural selection can, but seldom does, lead to the evolution of marked sex differences. In contrast, conspicuous sex differences are a normal result of sexual selection (see Figure 2–4).

> **Trail Marker:** Unlike natural selection, sexual selection typically leads to the evolution of sex differences.

Thus, the first puzzle—why evolution has produced costly traits like peacock tails—is easy to solve. These traits increase fitness by paying back in mating opportunities more than they cost in decreased survival. But the second puzzle, of why these mating opportunities are not equally valuable to females and males, is a bit more challenging. Consider the following. In most species the two sexes eat the same foods and are vulnerable to the same predators and diseases. In short, they are subject to the same natural selection pressures and thus evolve very similar traits. For these reasons male pigeons are more like female pigeons than they are like male eagles or male robins. So why are males and females not also subject to the same *sexual* selection pressures? The question can be framed in several different ways. Why does a costly trait that provides a mating advantage not yield similar reproductive benefits to both sexes? Aren't females and males equally dependent on matings to achieve reproductive success? To understand why sexual selection often acts more strongly on one sex we need to know what causes sexual selection.

Figure 2–4. *Male and female peafowl.* A male, the peacock, displays to a much less ornamented female, the peahen. In some species sexual selection has favored striking sex differences. This comes about when males and females can reproduce at very different rates.

What Causes Sexual Selection?

The answer is not immediately obvious. In fact Darwin did not get it quite right, and neither did modern evolutionists until very recently. To understand the modern theory of sexual selection you need to realize that males are usually, but not always, the bearers of ecologically harmful adornments. In some species neither sex is adorned, and in still others it is the female who has been beautified by sexual selection while her partner remains drab. A good theory would identify a key variable that predicts which sex, if either, would have been modified by sexual selection. Building on earlier work by George Williams (1966) and Robert Trivers (1972), Tim Clutton-Brock and Amanda Vincent (1991) suggested that the key variable is reproductive rate. Reproductive rate refers to how many offspring an individual can produce per unit time. In some species the sexes have nearly identical reproductive rates, but in other species members of one sex have the potential to reproduce much more rapidly than their partners. An example will be helpful.

Consider a male and female deer that have just mated. The female will gestate her offspring for six months and lactate for another six. Thus, if she is to succeed in this new reproductive venture she will not be free to start another one until she weans the first offspring in about a year. In other words, her maximum reproductive rate is one offspring per year (or perhaps two if she produces twins). The male's situation is rather different. How soon could he begin another reproductive venture without compromising the one he has just initiated? Five minutes, perhaps ten! Of course this is because, unlike the female, he invests nothing in the offspring beyond his initial contribution of sperm (Williams 1966, Trivers 1972). Thus the uncommitted male can potentially inseminate a series of females and produce many offspring per year, while each of his partners produces only one or two. Let's see how differences in reproductive rate like these cause sexual selection.

Many things in nature are balanced and symmetrical by sex. For example, as you will see in the next chapter, females and males make essentially equal genetic contributions to each of their offspring. Similarly, many factors relevant to the quest for mates are also balanced and equal. Sex ratios in nature are about 50:50. In other words, in most species there are roughly equal numbers of males and females, so on this basis neither sex should find partners scarce. Also, every (reproductive) copulation involves one male and one female, and that copulation temporarily removes each of the participants from the mating pool, that is from the pool of fertile potential mates. But from this point on, differences in reproductive rate begin to distort the balance because they produce differences in the length of time males and females are removed from the mating pool.

Using our deer example, a copulating female won't be fertile again for twelve months. Thus she will be effectively unavailable as a reproductive partner for a year. A copulating male will be fertile again almost immediately. If each copulation removes one female from the mating pool for a year and one male from the pool for a few minutes, the pool of fertile males will always be much larger than the pool of fertile females. The result of this imbalance is that when a female is available to mate she finds a large pool of willing and able partners and few other fertile females to distract their attention. In contrast, when a male is available to mate he finds a small pool of potential partners and many other fertile males competing for these scarce mating opportunities.

> **Trail Marker:** Sex differences in reproductive rates affect the availability of mates for males and females.

Remember that sexually selected traits are costly but provide a net benefit because they confer advantages in the competition for mates. The key point is simply that the competition for mates will always be less intense in the sex with the slower reproductive rate. Female deer have little need to compete for mates: They confront a long line of suitors and few competitors. Selection would be unlikely to favor some costly trait that allows a female deer to get more of something she already has in abundance, potential mates.

> **Trail Marker:** Sex differences in reproductive rate cause sexual selection by making mates scarce for just one sex.

Male deer on the other hand find matings genuinely scarce and must outmaneuver many competitors to get them. For a male, considerable costs could be outweighed if they allowed him to capture a larger share of the available mating opportunities. Thus, costly traits that help in acquiring mates are more likely to be favored in the sex with the faster reproductive rate because this sex is more likely to experience a shortage of mates.

Which Sex Is Fast?

Males are usually but not always the fast sex. What we have said about deer is true of mammals in general: Females alone gestate and females alone lactate and this tends to make them reproduce more slowly than their mates, who typically shoulder little of the burden of offspring production. In general, with some interesting exceptions among frogs and fishes [see Clutton-Brock and Vincent (1991)] that won't concern us here, doing the work of rearing the young slows down reproduction (Williams, 1966; Trivers, 1972). What that work is varies from species to species, but it's not difficult to recognize. For example, birds do not gestate their young but they do build nests, incubate their eggs, and feed their nestlings. In some species, females do this work alone; in others males do; and in yet many others the sexes perform these chores together. What would our theory of sexual selection predict for these various kinds of cases? It's very simple. When females are the primary care givers, they are slow to return to the mating pool and males end up competing for scarce mating opportunities. When males alone care for the young, this slows down their rate of reproduction and females must compete for scarce mating opportunities. When both sexes care for the young, they tend to return to the mating pool at about the same time and thus the sexes have about equal difficulty finding mates.

Traits Favored by Sexual Selection

When the females and males have similar reproductive rates sexual selection tends to act on them in similar ways with the result that the sexes evolve similar traits. But when males and females have different reproductive rates, sexual selection acts differently on the two sexes. In the fast sex, sexual selection favors traits that help increase the *number* of matings; in the slow sex, it favors traits that increase the *quality* of matings. This is so because members of the fast sex can never find enough matings to realize their full reproductive potential. But members of the slow sex will need very few matings to realize their reproductive potential and so should hold out for the best possible matings.

There are two broad ways of getting more matings. One way is to exclude your same-sex competitors from mating by force or threat of force. The other is to so dazzle members of the opposite sex that they essentially ignore all your would-be competitors. The first mode of competition for mates leads to the evolution of aggressive traits such as large size, strength, weapons, and a quick temper. In the other mode, sexual selection favors elaborate ornamentation and display. These two kinds of traits frequently evolve in the fast sex. In the slow sex, sexual selection favors choosiness and traits that force members of the fast sex to reveal their true qualities.

Hopefully you are already beginning to think about how the theory of sexual selection might apply to humans. Can one sex reproduce more rapidly than the other? Can our patterns of mate choice, courtship, and competition for mates be understood in terms of sexual selection? To what extent will sexual selection have shaped different psychological adaptations in women and men? Chapter 10 explores these issues in depth.

MANY KINDS OF EVIDENCE SUPPORT DARWIN'S THEORY

Many separate lines of evidence indicate that evolution is a fact. These have been admirably summarized by Mark Ridley (1993).

1. *The pattern of the fossil record.* As we discussed in Chapter 1, evolution does not imply progress. Nevertheless, selection proceeds by sorting among existing alternatives and by layering new adaptations on old ones. Thus an evolutionary view suggests that multicellular organisms probably evolved from earlier single-celled creatures. For this reason we would be very surprised to find that multicellular creatures came first in the fossil record. They do not; and there are many other test cases (e.g., reptiles follow rather than precede amphibians). The overall pattern of the record is entirely consistent with the idea that it was produced by natural selection.

2. *Homology.* Homology refers to the fact that the same structural elements are found in very different kinds of creatures. Often the function of these elements

is the same in different organisms. But sometimes their function is different. The forelimb of vertebrates is a good example (see Figure 2–5). The part closest to the body is based on a single bone, the humerus. Below what we call the elbow there are two bones, side by side. Next is the wrist made up of a large number of bones, and lastly there are five digits (fingers). A wide array of mammals, from people to dogs to bats to whales, show this same arrangement of elements. This is striking because these animals use their forelimbs very differently. Indeed it is clear that while the same elements are present, they have been greatly modified in a way that matches their different functions. Selection can only draw on existing variation as it adapts organisms to their environment. Thus, both the preservation of elements and their modification for specific uses is consistent with selection.

3. *The universality of genetic code.* The specifics of the genetic code will be discussed in Chapter 3. For now the important point is that the genetic code of all living things is structurally the same. This does not mean that all creatures have the same genes. It means that their genes are made out of the same elements, arranged according to the same rules. The genetic code is thus the greatest homology of all.

4. *The analogy with artificial selection.* Darwin noted how many different breeds of dogs, sheep, and other domesticated species had been created simply by selective breeding. Suppose a sheep breeder wanted sheep with denser wool. The breeder would choose as breeding animals the sheep with the densest available wool and repeat this process over several generations. Another breeder might like sheep's milk cheese and thus choose to breed for the richest milk. Still another breeder might sell lambs to the butcher and thus decide to breed for tender flesh, or for twinning. As different breeders carried out their separate breeding programs different breeds of sheep emerged. Different kinds of animals were created from one initial kind. Darwin called this process artificial selection and he saw a parallel between it and natural selection. In the case of artificial selection, humans breed for whatever characteristic they desire and the frequency and intensity of the desired trait slowly increases in their herds. In the case of natural selection, the challenges of the local environment determine who gets to breed. But in both processes differential breeding causes certain traits to be passed on and certain traits to be eliminated. As a result, the makeup of the population changes over time. Darwin argued that if short-lived human breeders could produce such changes, the unrelenting force of natural selection could be a potent designer of organisms.

5. *Direct observation.* The theory of evolution by natural selection predicts that, because of environmental pressures, some individuals will leave more offspring than others. And it predicts that the traits of these advantaged individuals will become more common over time. Both of these predictions are testable by direct observation of natural populations. There are many studies of this type (Endler 1986). The work of Peter and Rosemary Grant (e.g., Grant, 1986) and their students on Darwin's finches is an excellent example (Figure 2–1). They have studied these birds for more than twenty-five years in the Galapagos islands. Each

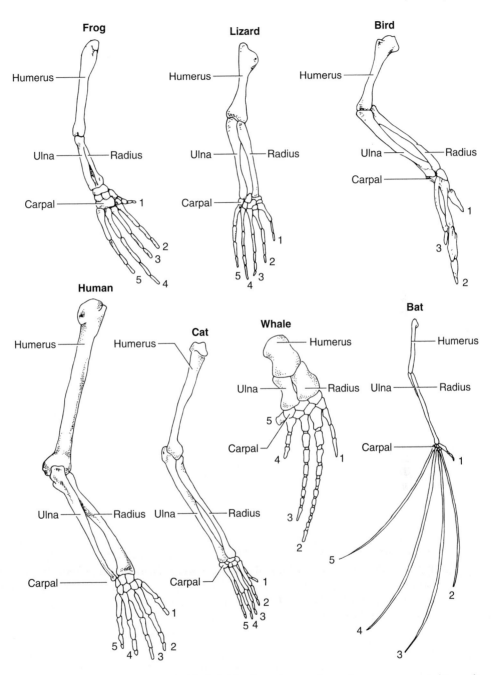

Figure 2–5. *Homologies of the tetrapod forelimb.* Note how the same bony elements are repeated in modified form in each of the different species. The repeated pattern suggests that all these species share a common ancestor.

climatic fluctuation has favored a particular class of birds (e.g., those with deeper beaks), and the favored type has consistently increased in the population. Studies like the Grants' show that evolution is not a dusty idea about something that happened long ago. Evolution by natural selection is going on all around us, all the time.

In summary, there are many different kinds of evidence which all point to the conclusion that evolution by natural selection is real. Of course, good scientists know that no theory can ever be proven once and for all. (This is because there may be other theories that can explain the same observations.) But our confidence in any scientific theory is greatest when it is supported by a wide array of evidence. By this standard, the theory of evolution by natural selection should be regarded as very well-established.

ALL CREATURES ARE SUBJECT TO NATURAL SELECTION

We have argued that natural selection is a powerful evolutionary force and the key architect of adaptation. But how general is it; is it happening everywhere? There are two ways to answer this question. One is to study many different populations and assess whether natural selection is at work. As mentioned above, where this has been done the answer is "yes." But no matter how many populations are evolving, a skeptic could argue that there are still many unstudied ones that are not. Fortunately there is another way of deciding how widespread natural selection is. To do this we determine what the preconditions or prerequisites are for natural selection. Where the prerequisites are met, natural selection will be operating; where they are not, it won't. It turns out that there are just three prerequisites.

1. *Variation.* There must be variation in the population; the individuals must not all be the same. Variation is necessary because, without it, there would be no alternatives for natural selection to choose among. In all the species that interest psychologists, sexual reproduction insures that no two individuals are the same (except for the rare case of identical twins). So clearly there is a great deal of variability, and this prerequisite is satisfied.

2. *Differential reproduction.* For natural selection to operate, some individuals must leave more offspring than others. If there were no differential reproduction all types would be equally successful and there would be no change in the makeup of the population. Each type would replace itself to precisely the same degree. But differential reproduction is so much a part of life that it's hard to imagine a world without it. How could we stop differential reproduction? The Chinese tried with their "one-baby program," but many couples ignored government directives and had two or more. There are even bigger problems to overcome to really eliminate differential reproduction. For example, what about infants born with terminal defects, or fetuses that spontaneously abort due to genetic anomalies? How could it be arranged so that these individuals also grow up and have their quota of offspring? Individuals are not equally equipped to meet the challenges of the environment and therefore leave different numbers of offspring. Thus the second prerequisite is also satisfied.

3. *A reliable system of heredity.* Natural selection causes adaptive evolution because fit individuals pass on their traits more often than unfit individuals. But this assumes that when an individual reproduces he or she passes on his or her traits. If there were no system of heredity, offspring would not resemble their parents. In such a world, the advantages of fitter individuals would not be transmitted to the next generation and favorable traits would not spread. Of course this is an imaginary world. On this planet, at least, there is a very reliable system of heredity called genetics (the subject of the next chapter). The reliability of the hereditary system is relevant. In a system where the resemblance between parent and offspring is tight and reliable, natural selection will spread favorable traits relatively quickly. When the resemblance is weak and uncertain natural selection will be relatively ineffective in promoting adaptive evolution. Because all life, as we know it, has a hereditary system based on genes, the third prerequisite is fully satisfied.

To show that some population is not subject to evolution by natural selection we would have to show that at least one of these prerequisites is not satisfied. But that is not at all likely. The conclusion to be drawn from this analysis is that all three prerequisites—variation, differential reproduction, and reliable heredity—are facts of life. Therefore evolution by natural selection is also an inescapable fact of life.

ARE PEOPLE STILL EVOLVING?

Sometimes we hear that, because of all the changes humans have brought about—antibiotics, artificial insulin, eyeglasses, the elimination of predators, central heating, and the like—we are no longer subject to natural selection. The idea is that we have insulated ourselves from the environment to such a degree that the harsh judgement of natural selection is no longer separating the fit from the unfit.

This idea is wrong for two reasons. First, it fails to recognize that environments have been changing since the origin of life. Evolution explains why many kinds of organisms can keep up with environmental change—because any new variant that fits better with the new environment tends to spread. True, technology is driving environmental change at an unusually fast pace. But that simply means that we are rapidly creating new selection pressures. Second, as we noted above, selection occurs any time there is variation, differential reproduction, and a reliable system of heredity. Because of genetics, which you will learn about in the following chapter, humans are variable and reliably transmit their differences to offspring. The fact that some people leave more offspring than others is also indisputable. Because the three prerequisites are satisfied, human populations are evolving. The causes of differential reproduction may not be the same as they were in the past; that is because environments and hence selection pressures are changing. But in human populations, as in all other species, natural selection continues to sort among available variants and to preserve those variants that fit best with the prevailing environment.

SUMMARY

1. Charles Darwin proposed the theory of evolution by natural selection to account for species diversity and to explain why organisms seem to fit so well with their environments.
2. Natural selection occurs because individuals who are better suited to their local environments leave more offspring and because, when they do so, their advantageous traits become more common in the population.
3. Natural selection can spread even small advantages. By doing so over many generations it crafts designs for reproduction called adaptations.
4. Natural selection builds psychological adaptations not by designing behavior directly, but by shaping the psychological traits that produce behavior.
5. Natural selection is powerful but often slow. It can build complex and efficient adaptations but it takes time to do so.
6. If the environment changes rapidly adaptations may be out of date.
7. Sexual selection is a kind of natural selection; it favors traits that help in acquiring mates.
8. Sexual selection happens because the faster reproducing sex experiences a shortage of mates.
9. When the sexes differ in reproductive rate, sexual selection favors different traits in females and males.
10. Many lines of evidence suggest that evolution by natural selection has been and continues to be an important force.
11. When three prerequisites (variation, differential reproduction, and reliable heredity) are met, natural selection will be operating. Because these conditions are virtually universal among living things, natural selection is expected to be similarly universal.
12. Human populations currently satisfy the three prerequisites and thus are still subject to evolution by natural selection.

3 The Genetic Basis of Evolution

Every theory of evolution rests, at least implicitly, on an assumption about the nature of heredity. For example, later you will learn how Lamarck's erroneous ideas about evolution were derived from his equally mistaken assumptions about the inheritance of acquired characteristics. And, as we saw in Chapter 2, natural selection itself cannot operate without a reliable system of heredity.

Darwin's difficulties in winning acceptance for his theory help demonstrate the connection between evolution and heredity. In Darwin's day, the power of natural selection was widely underestimated. This was not because his presentation was unclear. Instead, it arose because of a widespread misconception about the nature of heredity. In the nineteenth century, people mistakenly believed that the stuff of heredity was a fluid, perhaps because semen is a liquid. When mixed, fluids blend and dilute each other. If heredity really worked this way, any favorable new trait would be diluted to 50 percent intensity by the contributions of the mate. And this dilution would continue each generation, so that grandchildren would have only a 25 percent advantage, great-grandchildren a 12.5 percent advantage, and so on. One of Darwin's contemporaries, a Scottish engineer by the name of Jenkin, recognized that the advantage of a favorable new trait would be diluted down to nothing long before the force of natural selection could spread it through the population. His criticism was valid, given the assumption that the stuff of heredity behaves like a fluid. But the hereditary material is not a fluid, as we will soon see.

MENDEL DISCOVERED THE BASIS OF HEREDITY

To make our theory of evolution by natural selection thoroughly modern, and to fully understand what we expect natural selection to do, we must detail the hereditary system on which it rests. On earth (at least) that hereditary system is genetics. Again we will introduce the topic historically by reviewing the work of its discoverer, a brilliant Austrian monk by the name of Gregor Mendel.

Using garden peas as his model organism, Mendel quite consciously set out to discover how heredity works. He began first by breeding pure strains of different recognizable types: tall plants, short ones, plants with green pea pods, plants with yellow pods. Over many generations, he purified each strain by eliminating any individuals that did not breed true to type. Thus, if a tall plant produced any short progeny, it and all its progeny went out of the garden and into the soup pot. In this way, he produced a number of clearly identifiable types that could be counted on to produce offspring like themselves and that had nothing but ancestors like themselves. These so-called "pure" types were his experimental subjects. Using carefully planned matings among these pure types, he was able to formulate and test a theory of heredity. Although Mendel performed many experiments, one series will capture his methods and main conclusions.

In a well-known pair of experiments, Mendel first performed a hybrid cross between two pure strains. For example, he took pollen from pure-bred tall plants and used it to fertilize the flowers of pure-bred short plants (or vice versa; it made no difference which parent gave the pollen). These hybrid crosses typically yielded offspring of only one type. For example the tall × short cross produced only tall offspring. This result contradicted the fluid model of inheritance. The hybrid offspring were just as tall as their tall parents, not intermediate in height. The contributions of their short parents didn't dilute their tallness one bit.

In the second experiment, Mendel bred these hybrid offspring among themselves. Remember, the hybrids were all tall but, unlike the pure strains from which they came, they each had one tall and one short parent. How do you think the offspring of these hybrids looked? The dramatic result is that matings among apparently uniform tall parents produced two distinctly different sizes of offspring, and in stable proportions. About 75 percent were tall but 25 percent were short, just as short as their short grandparents had been. The fluid model also fails to account for this second result. Mendel repeated this set of experiments many times using different trait pairs, and he found a regular pattern. Just like shortness did, one condition would reliably disappear in the hybrid offspring, but consistently reappear in 25 percent of the progeny when the hybrids were mated among themselves. What an astounding regularity!

Elegant as these experiments are, Mendel's great contribution was a simple model of heredity that explained the pattern of results. His model posited the following:

1. *The stuff of heredity consists of particles, not fluids.* The particles retain their integrity and are not diluted or reduced when combined with the particles of the

mate. This is why short pea plants could reappear in the second experiment. We call these particles *genes*.

2. *Each normal adult carries a pair of genes for each trait.* This pair might consist of two identical genes and be what we call *homozygous*. Or it might be made up of two different genes and thus be *heterozygous*. In essence, when Mendel initially purified his strains he was making sure that each pea plant was homozygous. Thus his pure-bred tall plants had two genes for tallness, while the pure-bred short plants had two genes for shortness.

3. *When breeding, each parent gives one, and only one, of its pair of genes for each trait.* As a result of each parent giving one gene, the offspring will end up with a pair. In this way, the alternation between reproduction and growth involves an alternation between states. Normal reproducing adults have pairs of genes (the *diploid* state). And they produce sex cells which have only one member of each pair (the *haploid* state). When two sex cells combine, the diploid state is restored and development begins.

4. *Although pairs of genes do not dilute or change each other permanently, they can influence each other's expression.* For example, some genes can overshadow the effects of others. In peas, the tall gene completely overshadows the short gene. For this reason, peas that carry the heterozygous pair [TALL, SHORT] are just as tall as peas that have the homozygous pair [TALL, TALL]. Thus we say that TALL is *dominant* to SHORT, or that SHORT is *recessive*. Recessive genes are only expressed in the homozygous condition, because they are overshadowed in the heterozygous condition.

Let's see if these four ideas can explain Mendel's experimental results. By convention, we'll use an uppercase initial to represent the dominant gene, and the corresponding lowercase initial to represent the recessive gene. Thus,

T = a gene for tallness.

t = a gene for shortness.

These are just genes. The individual pea plants in Mendel's experiments were normal adults and hence were diploid. With respect to genes for height, three kinds of individuals are possible, two homozygotes and one heterozygote:

T,T = a homozygous tall individual.

t,t = a homozygous short individual.

T,t = a heterozygous individual, tall due to dominance.

Note that T,t and t,T are equivalent since the notion of order is meaningless in genetics. One gene came from the mother and one came from the father; neither came "first."

Because Mendel did not begin his experiments until he had bred pure strains, he assumed that his first hybrid cross (tall × short) was between two homozygous individuals, one tall (T,T), and one short (t,t).

	PURE TALL PARENT
PURE SHORT PARENT	T, T
t,	
t	

Each parent would have given one gene for height, combining with the gene of the other parent to produce a new diploid individual. The T,T parent could only have given T and the t,t parent could only have given t. Thus all the offspring would have to be heterozygotes, T,t.

	PURE TALL PARENT	
PURE SHORT PARENT	T,	T
t,	T,t	T,t
t	T,t	T,t

Because of the dominance of T over t, all these heterozygotes would be tall. So far, so good. The model explains why a hybrid cross between purified tall and short strains would produce only tall offspring.

What about the second experiment? What does the model predict will happen when the hybrid offspring are bred among each other? Here the parents will be the heterozygous offspring of the first experiment.

	HETEROZYGOUS PARENT	
HETEROZYGOUS PARENT	T,	t
T,	T,T	t,T
t	T,t	t,t

Genetically speaking, this second experiment produces three distinct kinds of offspring: some homozygote dominants (T,T), some heterozygotes (T,t and t,T), and some homozygote recessives (t,t). And in any reasonably large sample of such experiments it should produce them in relatively constant proportions of 1:2:1, that is, roughly equal numbers of the two kinds of homozygous plants and about twice as many heterozygous plants. Moreover, because of dominance the heterozygous individuals (T,t and t,T) will look just like the homozygous tall plants (T,T). Thus the 1:2:1 ratio will appear as 3:1, that is, 75 percent tall and 25 percent short. Mendel's model not only predicts some tall and some short offspring from uniformly tall parents, it accurately predicts how many of each type!

Of course Mendel tested his model in a wide variety of ways and found that its predictions tightly matched his experimental results. Here's another experiment that Mendel performed: mate short individuals with the offspring of a pure-tall × pure-short hybrid cross. As we saw in the first experiment, the offspring of a pure-tall × pure-short hybrid cross are all tall. In this new experiment it looks as if we are again mating tall with short. However, Mendel's model told him that these tall individuals were not pure tall, but heterozygote. What did his model predict would happen when heterozygotes were mated with short individuals? Because short is recessive the short individual must be t,t, so the mating looks like this.

| | HETEROZYGOUS PARENT | |
SHORT PARENT	T,	t
t,	T,t	t,t
t	T,t	t,t

The expected result is 50 percent tall heterozygotes (because of dominance) and 50 percent short. And that is the result that Mendel obtained when he performed this experiment. Note that this tall × short cross produces a very different result than the tall × short cross of the first experiment. It was the ability of his model to predict these unexpected patterns that gave Mendel—and indeed gives us—confidence that his model is essentially correct.

To summarize, Mendel's model posits that the hereditary system is based on particulate genes, not fluids, It assumes that normal adults are diploid, carrying their genes in pairs, but that they give only one member of each pair to each offspring. According to the model these genes do not change each other as a consequence of pairing, but they can influence each other's expression through interactions such as dominance.

THE NATURE OF GENES

One of the peculiar twists in the history of science is that Gregor Mendel both published (in 1865, only six years after Darwin) and perished! Not one person understood Mendel's brilliant insights for thirty-five years. His work went entirely unnoticed, no doubt partly because his ideas dramatically contradicted the prevailing folk belief in a hereditary system based on fluids. But in the year 1900, three teams of researchers working independently rediscovered Mendel's principles. In doing so, they ushered in the era of modern genetic research, which continues at an ever-accelerating pace.

Genes Are Organized into Chains Called Chromosomes

While the modern era has essentially verified all of Mendel's findings, it has added vast amounts of important detail to our understanding of how heredity works. For example, we now know that genes do not float around loose inside us. An organized set of your genes can be found in the nucleus of each cell in your body. The organization consists of the genes being linked together into long strands called *chromosomes*. Each chromosome has a definite structure; genes for a particular trait are reliably found at a particular place or *locus* (plural, *loci*) on the chromosome. Thus peas have a height locus, a particular spot on a particular chromosome where the genes T or t can occur. Genes for pod color or pea shape cannot occur at the height locus. That would violate the organization of the chromosome and such errors are usually lethal. Pod-color genes and pea-shape genes each have their own locus. A normal set of human chromosomes is presently estimated to contain somewhere between 50,000 and 100,000 loci.

Genes that can occur at the same locus (like T and t in peas) are said to be *alleles* of each other. Alleles are different "versions" of the same gene, in the case of T and t, different versions of the height gene. While many genes do come in different versions, many others do not. For example, roughly two-thirds of human loci are genetically invariant. That means that currently all humans are homozygous for the same allele at those invariant loci. The remaining one-third of loci are genetically variable; there are two or more alternative alleles that could occupy these loci. These variable loci are the source of any and all genetic differences between us.

But how do these alternative alleles arise in the first place? The answer is simple: by mistake. In order for genes to be passed to the next generation, they must be copied. You can't give your actual genes to your offspring because you need them to run your own body. So in the process of producing sex cells, you copy your genes. Very rarely errors occur during this copying process. Such errors in gene copying are called *mutations*. Whenever a gene mutates the result is a new allele, a new version of the old gene. We will have more to say about mutations in Chapter 4.

People and peas and most other creatures are diploid. Thus we have two copies of each chromosome, one that came from our mother and one that came from our father. The maternal and paternal chromosomes have the same organization. If they were to lie side by side—which they sometimes do—their loci would line up. For example, in peas the paternal locus for pod color would be right next to the maternal locus for this same trait. This matching facilitates the accurate transmission of genes from parents to offspring. Remember, parents are diploid and produce haploid sex cells which combine to form new diploid individuals. When a diploid individual forms sex cells, locus by locus she gives either the gene that came from her mother or the gene that came from her father, but not both. The side-by-side matching of loci insures that this sorting process happens accurately so that the sex cell contains one and only one gene for each locus. Without this sort of locus matching, sex cells would invariably have two genes for some traits and none for others, and such errors would often be lethal. The chromosomal organization of the genetic system minimizes these kinds of errors. For this and other reasons, the genetic system provides a very accurate and reliable system of heredity, just the sort of system that natural selection requires.

Genes Shape the Traits of the Phenotype

Mendel and his modern counterparts rely on a distinction between traits and the genes that shape those traits. Traits are things like height or pod color or seed shape. Traits have one or more states. In peas, height can take the states tall or short. Pod color has the alternative states green or yellow. And seed shape can be smooth or wrinkled. When we talk about traits and their states, we are talking about the observable (measurable) features of the organism, its *phenotype*. The states manifested in the phenotype are at least partly caused by the genes it carries, its *genotype*. We saw how genes affect the height of pea plants. The genotypes T,T and T,t both produce tall phenotypes, whereas the genotype t,t produces a short phenotype. Thus, in Mendel's second experiment (above) 1:2:1 was the genotype ratio, while 3:1 was the phenotype ratio.

GENES ARE A CHEMICAL CODE

Because of the close ties between genetic and evolutionary processes we cannot form a detailed picture of how selection works until we understand more about how genes shape phenotypes. Genes are composed of a long, two-stranded spiraling molecule known as *deoxyribonucleic acid,* or *DNA*. For our purposes it is not essential to detail the molecular structure of DNA. But it is important to understand that DNA has some variable elements that constitute a sort of alphabet of genetics. The genetic alphabet consists of just four chemical compounds—adenine, thymine, cytosine, and guanine which geneticists abbreviate to their initial letters (a, t, c, and g). Just as the English alphabet can be used to form words that carry information, the chemical elements of the genetic alphabet can be used to form meaningful instructions.

The Chemical Code Has Its Own Grammar

The language of genetics contains some rules about how messages can be written. You know that English has rules about what letters can go together. For example, the letter q must be followed by u. A word could begin with fr or fl, but not with fg or fh. The rules of genetics are even more strict. The elements of the genetic alphabet always form complementary pairs across the two strands of the DNA spiral. If there is a "c" on one side, there will always be a "g" on the other side. Similarly, "a" and "t" always form complementary pairs. Because of this complementarity, if you had just half of a DNA molecule, and a stockpile of spare elements, you could replace the missing half without error (Figure 3–1).

DNA's internal complementarity lies behind its two unique and most important abilities. The first ability is that DNA can make perfect copies of itself. To do this the two halves of the spiral separate, and *each* half specifies its missing counterpart. The result is two identical copies of the original DNA molecule. Because of this process, parents can pass perfect copies of their genes to their offspring (with rare exceptions where mutation occurs).

The Chemical Code Contains Recipes for Proteins

Of course DNA's second important ability is that it can shape the phenotype. Let's begin with an analogy. Suppose you had a set of irreplaceable master plans for a large building project. It would be unwise to leave the plans strewn around the construction site where they could be blown away by the wind, obscured by spilled coffee, or run over by bulldozers. You'd want to keep them in a safe place where you could

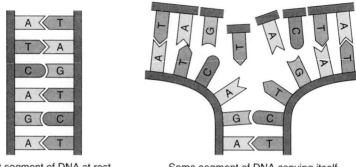

Short segment of DNA at rest   Same segment of DNA copying itself

Figure 3–1. *The structure of DNA allows faithful copying.* The "alphabet" of the genetic code consists of four chemical bases, here represented as A, T, C and G. Each base can pair only with one other. As a result one half of the DNA strand contains all the information necessary to construct the other strand. To copy itself, the strand simply "unzips" and each half recruits the A, T, C and G units needed to assemble its missing half.

make clean photocopies for your subcontractors, as needed. Of course DNA is a master set of plans for a monumental construction job, building an organism. The safe place where the master plans are kept is the cell nucleus. From there copies are sent out in the form of *RNA, ribonucleic acid.* RNA is similar to DNA in structure and is formed, using DNA as a template, by the same sort of complementarity rules that allow DNA to copy itself. Actually, photocopies are not a perfect analogy; photographic film and prints would be more precise. DNA is the white-on-black negative, whereas RNA is the black-on-white print. Thus, the variable elements in the RNA exactly mirror the message carried by the a's, t's, c's, and g's of the DNA (Figure 3–2).

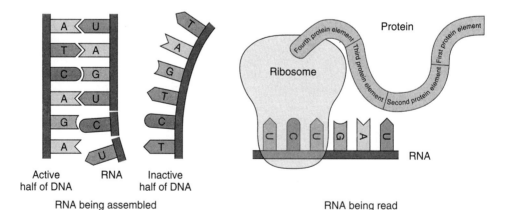

Active   RNA   Inactive
half of DNA   half of DNA

RNA being assembled   RNA being read

Figure 3–2. *Using RNA, DNA specifies the formulas for proteins.* Using base-pairing rules like those that apply for DNA (except that uracil replaces thymine), DNA directs the assembly of RNA. The RNA message is "read" by the ribosome, which interprets each set of three elements (for example UAG) as specifying a particular kind of protein building block. As it reads along the RNA molecule, the ribosome assembles a whole protein by stringing building blocks togther in the specified sequence.

Discrete traits, such as height in the pea plants studied by Mendel, are typically affected by genes at a single locus. In such cases there are usually a small number of possible genotypes and thus a small number of possible phenotypes. In peas the three genotypes TT, Tt, and tt are reduced to just two phenotypes—tall and short—by dominance. Thus the results of Mendel's second experiment (Tt × Tt) could be graphed as shown to the left. The graph shows what Mendel found: roughly three times as many tall plants as short plants, with no plants of intermediate size.

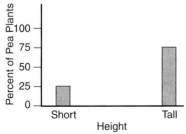

Height in pea plants is a discrete trait

To model the polygenic case, now suppose that height is affected by genes at many loci. This seems to be true for humans. Let's assume that ten loci are involved, *a, b, c, . . . j*. And to keep the model simple, let's assume that at each locus there are just two possible alleles, one of which tends to increase height (like T in peas) and one of which tends to decease height (like t). At each locus, *a, b, c,* etc, let's denote the allele for tallness as 1 and the allele for shortness as 0. Thus the partial genotype *a1,a1, b0,b0, c1,c0* is homozygous tall at the *a* locus, homozygous short at the *b* locus and heterozygous at the *c* locus.

The main point can be grasped in terms of simple probability. The most likely genotypes are the ones that carry a roughly equal proportion of 1's and 0's. Genotypes comprised of mainly 1's or genotypes composed of mainly 0's will be uncommon for the very same reason that you are unlikely to flip a long series of tails or a long series of heads in a coin toss. Extreme genotypes such as all 1's are possible but very rare. This simple model predicts a normal bell curve for polygenic traits, with average values being the most common and more extreme values being progressively rare.

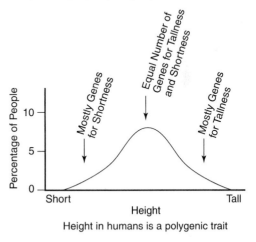

Height in humans is a polygenic trait

Box 3–1.   On the Distributions of Discrete and Polygenic Traits.

The RNA message is then read by the subcontractors of the cell, *ribosomes*, whose job it is to make proteins. Through the sequencing of their variable elements, as transcribed in the RNA, genes specify the formulas for proteins. Each gene specifies the formula for a different protein.

Proteins Build the Phenotype

It should be clear now that genes don't directly make bones, muscles, or brains. Instead they orchestrate the assembly of specific proteins. These proteins are the almost infinitely varied building material of all living things. Because we have tens of thousands of genes, our cells produce tens of thousands of proteins. It is the many different interactions among these proteins that form our phenotypes.

Some gene products, some proteins, have relatively simple phenotypic effects. For example, a gene that makes pea pods yellow instead of green might simply code for a kind of protein that is a yellow pigment. A gene that makes pea plants taller would probably work in a more complicated way. Most likely it would operate by specifying a protein that affects the activity of genes at one or more other loci that influence growth. For example, such a protein might increase the activity of genes that govern the rate of cell division. Or it could delay the action of genes that tell the plant to stop growing and start reproducing. Genes for tallness might operate through very different pathways in different creatures.

Sometimes a trait state depends on the summed effects of genes at several loci. Such traits are said to be *polygenic*. Height in humans is polygenic; genes at perhaps a dozen loci produce different proteins that have an additive effect on adult height. Traits that are shaped by genes at one locus typically exhibit a discrete or discontinuous distribution of trait states. In contrast, polygenic traits usually exhibit a more continuous and normal distribution of trait states (see Box 3–1). But no gene acts in a vacuum; the environment in which every gene acts is a protein environment specified by many other genes. Thus our phenotypes are the consequence of many thousands of interactions among these gene products.

GENES SHAPE THE PHENOTYPE—NEVER THE REVERSE

The flow of instructions from genotype to phenotype is a one-way street. Genes transcribe their messages to RNA, and ribosomes translate these messages into particular proteins. Then these proteins interact to build the phenotype. A change in the gene would change the protein and hence change the phenotype. But there is never any reverse transcription. By that we mean that no altered phenotype or protein ever has its structure read back into the genes. This idea, that instructions flow outward from the genes, never inward, is central to both modern genetics and to our picture of evolution.

The eighteenth-century biologist Jean-Baptiste Lamarck is remembered for his mistaken view that acquired traits could be inherited. For example, Lamarck's theory predicts that the children of body builders would be more muscular than average even at birth. We know today that this is false. The reason it is false is that there is no reverse transcription. Our genes, and the copies of those genes we pass to our offspring, are unaffected by changes in our phenotype.

But how can exercise change the phenotype if it does not change the genes? In fact, there is no contradiction here. Experience can and does change the phenotype. But such phenotypic changes are not read back into the genes. The genes are insulated against revision by the one-way nature of RNA flow. There is no way for phenotypic changes to revise the genetic code. This means that, while experience can and often does alter our phenotypes, the effects of this experience are not passed on to offspring.

Do not imagine that we underestimate the importance of the environment. In a very real sense, environmental effects are the most interesting forces in both traditional and evolutionary psychology. A central objective of this chapter has been to detail the structure and workings of the genetic system itself, so we have dwelt on what genes are and what they do. Now it is time to extend the focus to the important relationships between genes and the environment. In the remaining sections of this chapter, you will learn that, for very good evolutionary reasons, the environment often plays an absolutely critical role in shaping phenotypes.

MANY GENES ARE VERY RESPONSIVE TO THE ENVIRONMENT

As we have just discussed, our experiences will not change our genotypes, so our experience cannot be genetically transmitted to our progeny. But, experience can still be profoundly important in shaping our own phenotypes.

Many people think that traits with a genetic basis are automatically fixed and inflexible. But this way of thinking is simplistic and often just plain wrong. Geneticists recognize that genes differ in how responsive or how resistant they are to the environment. They find it useful to characterize two types of gene-environment relationships, called obligate and facultative. Genes with *obligate* effects resist environmental interference. They tend to produce much the same phenotypic result regardless of the environment. The traits Mendel studied in peas—height, pod color, pea shape—were relatively obligate. (If they had not been, he would have never succeeded in discovering the rules of heredity.) Genes that govern overall body plan provide another example of obligate effects. You would have developed with two arms, legs, and eyes regardless of whether you had grown up in the snows of the Himalayas or sands of the Sahara, regardless of whether your parents were loving or self-absorbed, and regardless of whether you had been fed meat and potatoes or manioc and beetle grubs.

Before we paint too extreme a picture however, let us note that even obligate traits do depend importantly on experience. Imagine, for example, that pregnant women accidentally exposed to high levels of pesticides give birth to deformed infants. Tragic as such a thing would be, it does not change our conclusion that the genes governing bilateral symmetry are obligate. We use the term obligate when the genes are relatively insensitive to experience over a wide range of *normal* environments.

In contrast, genes with *facultative* effects are highly responsive to normal environmental variation. These genes code for systems that respond constructively to environmental change. It sounds like magic but facultative effects are obvious in every organ system in our bodies. Suntanning provides a useful example. When we suntan, the color of our skin adjusts to the amount of solar radiation we receive in the uv_b part of the spectrum. Suntanning is caused by increased production of a particular protein, a dark pigment called melanin. As we are exposed to progressively more uv_b the gene that codes for this pigment becomes increasingly active. The result is that more melanin is deposited in the skin and the skin therefore darkens. Suntanning is not like toasting bread. If you put a piece of bread in the toaster it will also darken, but the darkening of the toast is caused by burning, to the destruction of organic material (that's what happens in sunburning). In contrast, suntanning is an active response on the part of the organism that actually reduces the harmful effects of solar radiation.

In terms of fitness, sunburning by itself is a not a major risk. Of much greater significance, however, is the fact that overexposure to uv_b radiation can cause fatal skin cancers. The protein melanin specifically blocks uv_b radiation from penetrating to the levels of the skin where it can cause these cancers. So the design of the melanin molecule and the linking of its production to uv_b exposure constitute sophisticated adaptations. But why didn't selection design us to play it safe? If uv_b exposure is risky, why not produce lots of melanin all the time and thus screen out all the uv_b? The answer is that uv_b is also beneficial. In fact, it is absolutely necessary for the synthesis of vitamin D, an essential substance that is absent from almost all naturally occurring foods. People who produced too much melanin would screen out too much uv_b and thus die of vitamin D deficiency.

This is bad news. The environment poses two contradictory challenges (Harm 1980). How can we screen out enough uv_b to avoid skin cancer while getting enough uv_b to produce adequate vitamin D? The problem is especially complicated because the amount of uv_b varies with the seasons (as well as with latitude). The solution is to build a screen when there is too much uv_b and take it down when there is too little. That's exactly what the facultative suntanning adaptation does, producing more melanin when we experience high levels of uv_b and disassembling the melanin molecules when uv_b levels drop. (To understand why human populations differ in baseline levels of melanin synthesis see Box 3–2.) Suntanning is clearly a useful adaptation. Organisms as different from us as sharks exhibit a melanin-based suntanning response when they inhabit shallow tropical waters where levels of uv_b are high (Lowe and Goodman-Lowe, 1996).

Each facultative trait produces its own unique pattern of phenotypic responsiveness. For any facultative trait, the relationship between environmental change and phenotypic change can be graphed. Such graphs summarize what we call the *norm of reaction* of the trait. Figure 3–3 shows the norm of reaction for suntanning.

Rest assured that facultative traits like suntanning do not involve any reverse transcription. True, the melanin gene is expressed more when there is more uv_b radiation. But the gene itself is not changed in any way. A person who carries the melanin gene will transmit precisely the same gene to his offspring, regardless of whether he experienced high or low levels of uv_b during his lifetime.

Every normal (non-albino) human suntans. The more uv_b radiation we receive the more melanin we produce. So why do people differ so much in skin color? Part of the answer is that their recent exposure to uv_b differs. But another part of the answer is that their ancestors' exposure to uv_b differed.

The dangers posed by uv_b vary from one part of the planet to another. For example, in Scotland the risk of skin cancer has been very low because Scotland lies at high latitude and is very cloudy. The main problem there has been to produce enough vitamin D. So the average skin color of Scots is very pale, although they can produce more melanin if their exposure to uv_b is gradually increased. In contrast, uv_b exposure has been much more dangerous in equatorial regions. There, average uv_b levels are high and the risk of skin cancer would be great unless people produced much more melanin. Thus, all human populations have the ability to suntan, that is, to increase their baseline levels of melanin synthesis when uv_b levels increase. But there are also significant differences in baseline levels of melanin synthesis between human populations living in regions of high or low *average* uv_b radiation.

All of this makes profound evolutionary sense, and many separate observations support this explanation. For example, early in this century the discovery of widespread vitamin D deficiency among African-Americans living in Northern cities such as Boston led to an understanding of the role of melanin in blocking uv_b, and to the public-health decision to add vitamin D to all milk. The opposite sort of effects are now visible in Australia. Australia was colonized in the last century by people of European, primarily British, ancestry. But Australia is largely a tropical country. Thus, you should not be surprised to learn that Australians of British ancestry have skin cancer rates twenty times higher than their countrymen who did not emigrate. With this additional insight, try to expand on Figure 3–3 to show two suntanning norms of reaction, one for an average Scot and one for an average Kenyan.

Box 3–2.   About Skin Color Differences

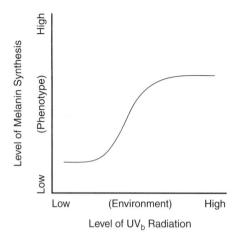

Figure 3–3. *The norm of reaction for suntanning.* A norm of reaction shows how the phenotype changes in response to changes in the environment. In suntanning, melanin synthesis responds to changes in uv_b radiation. The curve has the shape it does because each of us has some baseline level of melanin synthesis which we never drop below and some maximum level of melanin synthesis we can never exceed. Between those minimum and maximum levels, the more uv_b radiation we experience, the more melanin we produce.

NATURAL SELECTION SHAPES THE LEVEL OF RESPONSIVENESS

Now that the usefulness of facultative traits is clear, you may wonder why all traits are not facultative. As with any evolutionary question the answer lies ultimately with the environment. Selection will often design a facultative adaptation when:

1. the environment is variable within the lifetimes of individuals (e.g., the amount of uv_b varies from summer to winter, or from one part of the habitat to another), and

2. the fittest alternative varies from one environment to the next (e.g., the ideal level of melanin production depends on the season).

Under these conditions, genes that monitor the environment and adjust the phenotype appropriately will win out in competition with less responsive alleles.

On the other hand, sometimes a single solution is best over a wide range of environments (e.g., our overall body plan works well almost everywhere). In these cases, obligate adaptations would be superior because they would resist environmental interference. That is not to say that their development is independent of experience. Selection designed them to produce their more-or-less constant results in the environments that normally prevailed. In that sense then, obligate traits "expect" a certain range of environments. When that normal range is exceeded, the results are unpredictable. This points up the important fact that, over the development of each individual, the environment is important in shaping both obligate and facultative traits.

In summary, selection will prefer facultative or obligate traits depending on whether phenotypic responsiveness would increase or decrease fitness, respectively. In contrast with certain anatomical adaptations like body plan, behavioral traits are useful precisely because of their potential for rapid flexibility. It would be difficult to respond to a new environment by suddenly reorganizing your body plan (although some organisms such as butterflies do). But it would be relatively easy to do so by modifying your behavior. Thus as you might expect, selection has designed most behavioral adaptations to be facultative. For this reason, the facultative model is especially important to psychology.

NEO-DARWINISM: THE UNION OF SELECTION AND GENETICS

Darwin wrote in *The Origin* that selection would cause favorable traits to become more common. He said this because he knew that individuals with favorable traits would leave more offspring. And he knew what was obvious to anyone, that parents pass on their characteristics to their offspring. The argument is logical, but a critical detail is missing: Darwin could not say exactly how traits were transmitted to offspring. That was the weak link that Jenkin attacked (see the introduction to this chapter). The genotype/phenotype distinction helps resolve the problem.

To begin, note that selection cannot evaluate genes directly; it only "sees" the phenotypes they produce. On the other hand, successful (that is, fit) phenotypes are not directly passed on to the next generation; only the genes that built the phenotypes are. One analogy would be to say that, each generation, genes audition for the future by building phenotypes. The phenotypes that perform well get to pass on some of (remember, sex cells are haploid) the genes that directed their performance. In this way, the genes that build the best performers become more common. Put another way, favorable traits become more common because individuals who have genes that assemble favorable traits leave more offspring. In so doing they leave more copies of the genes that assembled the favorable traits. In this way, the differential reproductive success of phenotypes changes the frequency of the underlying genes (see Figure 3–4).

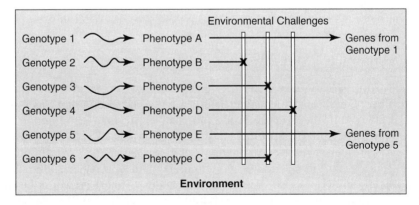

Figure 3–4. *Successful phenotypes contribute more genes to the next generation.* Environments influence how genotypes are translated into phenotypes. Environments also pose a series of challenges. The phenotypes that best meet those challenges pass on more of the genes that built them. (Note that due to dominance effects or environmental influences different genotypes could produce the same phenotype.)

Another implication of these facts is that natural selection can only act on genetically based traits. If a trait confers a reproductive advantage it will *not* automatically be more common in the next generation. It will only spread if those who have the advantageous trait somehow pass it on when they reproduce. But they can only pass on genes, not traits. So only those traits that have a basis in the genes can be passed on. And hence only traits that have some basis in the genes are subject to evolution by natural selection.

Because this condition of having a genetic basis is central to the process of evolution, we should be very precise about what it means. Simply stated, a trait has a genetic basis if a change in the genotype—for example, substituting one allele for another—would change the phenotype. This is logical. Selection evaluates the phenotypic effects of alternative alleles. If an allele substitution changed the phenotype in some way that caused an increase or a decrease in fitness, selection would begin to work, spreading the favorable allele, and eliminating the inferior one.

EVOLUTION CAN BE THOUGHT OF AS A CONTEST AMONG GENES

As Richard Dawkins (1989) has pointed out, one very powerful way to understand evolution is to take the gene's perspective. Think of evolution as a game where the players are genes. The objective of this game is simply to stay in it. A gene wins when it is passed on to the next generation; it lives to play again. It loses when the body it sits in dies without reproducing. What kinds of genes would be winners in this game? Simply put, the answer is genes that are good at getting passed on. With certain important exceptions to be discussed in Chapter 4, genes get passed on when the body that carries them reproduces. Hence, one good way of getting passed on is to increase the fitness of the surrounding body. The genes that we carry today are the survivors of many, many rounds of this game. They are here today because they have been very good at getting into the next generation.

Explaining Genetic Variation

In this evolutionary game the alleles that can occur at a locus are competitors. Every height locus occupied by T is a piece of genetic real estate that is not available to t. If selection favors the phenotypes produced by T, then T will be copied more often than t is. If this goes on long enough, T will eventually occupy all the height loci in the population. In other words, when T wins enough evolutionary rounds and t loses enough, t is completely out of the game. Because evolution has been going on for so long it might seem that the game would be over by now. At each locus the superior allele should have already won. Remember that two-thirds of human loci do have only a single allele, so our intuition is correct for those cases. But what about the remaining one-third? Why has evolution not gotten rid of all but the best allele at these loci? There are several reasons.

The first reason is that some alleles may be *selectively neutral;* the alternative alleles at a particular locus may produce equally fit phenotypes. In cases like this, there will be no differential reproduction and therefore no natural selection; no adaptations will be constructed. The frequency of neutral alleles will just fluctuate randomly. While this idea is easy to understand, it is very controversial in practice. If someone claims, for example, that the ABO blood types represent neutral alleles, within a few years there will certainly be several publications about the particular advantages conferred by each blood type, say in relation to disease resistance. Thus, the existence of genuinely neutral alleles remains a topic of debate.

Environmental variation is a second factor that can prevent one allele from completely replacing its alternatives. Phenotypes produced by T might be favored for a few hundred years and then, perhaps due to some climatic change, phenotypes produced by t would have an advantage. In such cases T would increase in frequency for several centuries; then it would begin to lose ground to t as a consequence of the new selective regime. Peter and Rosemary Grant's (1986) study of finches in the Galapagos (mentioned in Chapter 2) indicates that these kinds of selective reversals are commonly associated with multiyear cycles of high and low rainfall that affect the supply of different kinds of food.

There is probably a tendency to think of environmental change as taking place through time. But environments can also change in space, say from one part of a species' range to another. These spatial changes may similarly preserve genetic variation because one allele may be favored in one part of the range while a different allele is favored elsewhere.

A third reason why some loci continue to have multiple alleles is *heterozygote superiority*. We saw earlier that some alleles are dominant to others, but that is not the only way that alleles can interact. In some cases, two different alleles work together in the heterozygote to produce a different phenotype than either allele would in homozygotes. If the phenotype produced by the heterozygote is fitter, then heterozygotes—individuals who carry both alleles—will pass most genes to the next generation. The reproductive success of heterozygotes will inevitably maintain both alleles in the population.

The disease known as sickle-cell anemia provides a famous example of heterozygote superiority. This fatal disease occurs when an individual is homozygous for the recessive s allele at the hemoglobin locus. Considering its lethality, this disease is surprisingly common in certain African populations. The reason is that heterozygous (*Ss*) individuals are more resisant to malaria (a potentially deadly tropical disease transmitted by mosquitoes) than are homozygote *SS* individuals. So in areas where malaria is common, *ss* individuals die of sickle cell and *SS* individuals die of malaria. Thus *Ss* individuals have the highest fitness and their reproduction maintains both alleles in the population.

Frequency-dependent selection is another mechanism that maintains more than one type of individual in a population. In such cases, the fitness of a phenotype depends on how common it is in the population. To see how this can happen consider the following example. In some predatory insects, males offer prey items to females with whom they are attempting to mate. (This "nuptial feeding," as it is called, probably evolved because it reduces the chance that the female will eat the courting male, but that's not the point of this example.) Of course, finding and capturing the nuptial gifts is costly to males in terms of time, energy, and risk. Randy Thornhill (1979) has studied one species of predatory insect (a kind of scorpion fly) where selection has come up with a way for males to avoid these costs. Instead of hunting for nuptial gifts, some males adopt the posture of a female who is ready to mate and then steal the nuptial gift of any other male who approaches them!

This is a pretty good trick, and you can imagine that the first mutant male using this deception would have had high reproductive success, because of all the time and energy he saved and all the hunting risks he avoided. But think about what happens next. Obviously, as this deceptive strategy spreads though the population, hunting males become rarer and rarer. That matters because hunters are the only ones supplying nuptial gifts; deceivers just pass around the gifts that were originally procured by hunters. So as hunters become rare, deceivers waste more and more time waiting for hunters to provide nuptial gifts. The point is that deceiving is a good strategy when it's rare. But as it becomes more common its advantage decreases, eventually to the point that it provides no advantage at all. At that point, hunters and deceivers have precisely the same fitness. If two types are of equal fitness, selection will not eliminate either of them: Both types will remain in the population.

A final factor that can explain why selection has not eliminated all but the best allele is *mutation*. Remember, mutations are just gene copying errors; they are the ultimate source of all genetic variation. Genes ordinarily make very precise copies of themselves, but mistakes do sometimes occur. When a gene mutates by copying itself incorrectly, a new allele is created—a new alternative that will be evaluated by selection. Ordinarily copying errors interfere with gene function. So ordinarily the phenotype produced by a new mutant allele is less fit than the phenotype produced by the ancestral allele from which it derived. Selection quickly eliminates these harmful new alleles. But every once in a while, by chance, a new mutant allele produces a phenotype that is actually fitter than the one produced by the ancestral allele. This is the stuff of evolution, the stuff of new adaptations. Such beneficial new alleles spread because of the higher reproductive success of the phenotypes they produce. Of course it can take many generations for the new allele to replace the ancestral one. Thus, sometimes when we see a locus with two alleles, we are just witnessing evolution in progress. A favorable new mutant is in the process of spreading, but it has not yet completely replaced its alternative allele.

In Chapter 2 we noted that selection could not create entirely new variants, but only choose among existing alternatives. It should now be clear that these alternatives are the phenotypes produced by alternative alleles. And we know that alternative alleles arise by mutation. In other words, the raw material for natural selection originally comes from random errors in the genetic process. This is why selection cannot create variation. Variation comes into existence through genetic, not selective processes. Selection evaluates these alternatives once they exist, eliminating the harmful ones and spreading the beneficial ones.

SELECTION ON POLYGENIC TRAITS

Up to this point, we have concentrated on how selection works on genes at a single locus. Our message has been that, ordinarily, selection will eliminate all but the best allele, but that five factors or situations (neutrality, environmental variation, frequency-dependent selection, heterozygote superiority, and mutation) may sometimes prevent that outcome. Now we need to consider how selection works on polygenic traits, that is, traits where the phenotype depends on genes at several different loci.

Polygenic traits are very common: It may even be the exception for a trait to be shaped principally by genes at a single locus. As you saw in Box 3–1, polygenic traits tend to show a continuous, and often bell-shaped or normal distribution; and we've mentioned the example of height in humans to illustrate this. What would happen if selection favored an increase in human height?

Each individual carries genes at several loci that, in interaction with environmental factors, affect his or her height. On average, tall individuals have more genes for tallness than short individuals. More precisely, this means that, at the loci affecting height, they have more alleles promoting tallness than do shorter individuals. It follows, then, that if taller individuals are experiencing higher reproductive success that alleles for tallness will be passed on at a higher rate than alleles for shortness are. Alleles for tallness will thus increase in frequency, with two results. First, the average height of the population increases, because the average individual will have more alleles for tallness than was the case before selection. Second, the whole distribution will shift to the right: The shortest types will completely disappear from the population and the tallest individual will be taller than any seen before. This, too, is a result of the changing mix of genes for tallness and shortness in the population. As genes for shortness decrease in frequency, the combinations of many "short" alleles that produce the shortest individuals become very unlikely. And in parallel, as genes for tallness increase in frequency, the combinations that would produce very tall individuals become more likely. In this way, selection on polygenic traits tends to move the entire bell-shaped curve until it becomes centered on the current optimum value.

Effects of Sexual Reproduction on Polygenic Traits

All of the five factors (discussed earlier) that prevent selection from reducing each locus to a single allele may also operate in the case of polygenic traits. This is obviously so because selection of polygenic traits is just the sum of selection on each of the contributing loci. But there is an additional force that needs to be considered when we think about polygenic traits: sexual reproduction.

Sexual reproduction shuffles genes. It produces new combinations of genes each generation, because each parent takes a selection of genes from its two parents and, by mating, mixes them with a selection of his or her mate's parent's genes (see *Genes Are Organized into Chains Called Chromosomes,* above). What are the consequences of this shuffling? The most important for psychology is a bit unnerving: Many individuals will not exhibit the optimum value for polygenic traits! Let's take a hypothetical example just to make the theoretical point clear. Let's posit that the tendency to be anxious is a polygenic trait (affected by genes at several loci), and that there is an optimal level of anxiety. The idea of an optimal level simply means that, over human evolution, individuals who were too anxious and individuals who weren't anxious enough did poorly. Individuals who were too anxious spent so much time monitoring their surroundings that they didn't have enough time for foraging, courting, tending their young, and other fitness-enhancing activities. Individuals who were insufficiently anxious tended to be eaten by predators, taken advantage of by their competitors and the like. Some individuals, because they have the right polygenic combination of anxiety genes, exhibit the ideal or optimum level of anxiety. It's these optimally anxious individuals who would have had the highest reproductive success.

Now here's the key point: Because of the genetic shuffling of sexual reproduction, even these optimally anxious individuals will produce offspring with diverse combinations of anxiety genes, and who thus exhibit a range of non-optimal anxiety levels! Here's a hypothetical example to help you understand why sexual reproduction automatically produces non-optimal phenotypes. Let's imagine that there are 5 loci that carry genes affecting anxiety. Since we are diploid this means that we each carry 10 (= 2 × 5) genes that have some influence on our anxiety level. Each of those 10 could either be a gene that fosters high anxiety levels or a gene that fosters low anxiety levels. Finally, suppose that medium anxiety levels are optimal, and that they result when 5 of an individual's 10 genes are high-anxiety genes and the other 5 are low-anxiety genes.

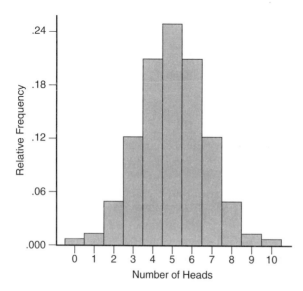

Figure 3–5. *Probability of various numbers of heads, given ten flips of a fair coin.*

Now imagine a mating between two optimally anxious individuals, each of whom carries the ideal mix of 5 high- and 5 low-anxiety genes. What will their offspring be like? The outcome is like flipping a coin 10 times in a row. It is possible to get 10 heads, or 10 tails, but either of these outcomes is very unlikely (see Figure 3–5). It's true that the most likely outcome is 5 heads, but notice that even the most likely outcome is not all that likely: less than one in four. So even though both our hypothetical parents had the optimal value on this trait, more than 3/4 of their offspring would be either more or less anxious than is optimal. This is an important demonstration. The very nature of sexual reproduction means that, for polygenic traits, the population will always include considerable scatter around the optimum value. This realization will be especially important when we consider behavioral disorders in Chapter 14.

> **Trail Marker:** For polygenic traits, the population will always include considerable scatter around the optimum value.

THE GENETIC FALLACY

The *genetic fallacy* is the mistaken idea that genes are destiny, that genetic traits cannot be changed. When we talk about evolved features of human psychology we are inevitably talking about behavioral adaptations that are rooted in our genes. This idea makes some people nervous because they mistakenly believe the genetic fallacy and thus see genes as ruling the phenotype in a rigid and inflexible way. They believe that if a trait has a genetic basis it cannot be changed. Perhaps they have overgeneralized from what they know of Mendel's experiments with peas and erroneously think that all genes have obligate effects on the phenotype.

As you have already learned, their discomfort is unnecessary. Especially in the realm of behavior, facultative adaptations are expected to be the norm, and unlike obligate traits, facultative traits respond to the environment. Thus a failure to understand the full implications of the facultative model lies at the heart of many social scientists' misgivings about evolution.

> **Trail Marker:** The genetic fallacy is the mistaken idea that genetic traits cannot be changed.

Let's consider our model facultative trait, suntanning, one last time. We know that suntanning has a genetic basis. Here are several important conclusions that you should now be able to deduce on your own:

1. The fact that suntanning has a genetic basis does *not* imply that skin color is fixed and invariant. Within a moderate range, skin color could be darkened or lightened simply by adjusting uv_b dosages up or down, that is, by manipulating the environment in the

appropriate way. For any facultative trait, an evolutionary approach can be helpful in discovering what kind of environmental manipulation will produce the desired effect.

2. The fact that suntanning has a genetic basis does *not* imply that individuals with different skin colors necessarily have different genes governing their melanin production. They could have the very same genes but differ in skin color because of their different experience with uv_b.

3. Family members, such as parents and offspring or brothers and sisters, will resemble each other in skin color partly because they share many genes and partly because they share much of their environment.

These three ideas will be critical to your understanding of the theories and examples you will encounter in this book. They make it clear that, just like SSSM psychology, evolutionary psychology is fundamentally environmentalist in outlook. For example, in the next chapter we will develop an evolutionary argument about why viewing violence on television makes people more inclined to be violent. Such an argument does *not* imply that we can't change our violent tendencies because they were shaped by natural selection. In fact, it implies the reverse! Understanding the evolutionary basis of violence suggests particular environmental manipulations that could reduce the level of violence in society.

As we saw in Chapter 1, the naturalistic fallacy is the idea that what is natural, for example because it evolved, is good. And in this chapter, we explained the genetic fallacy: the idea that genetically based traits cannot be changed. Of course these are fallacies, but their logical flaws often go unexamined. Hence many people draw important conclusions without realizing that they are based on one or both of these erroneous ideas. Consider this doubly fallacious argument: Trait *X* can be shown to have evolved by natural selection, so it is both good (the naturalistic fallacy) and unchangeable (the genetic fallacy). The implication is that we should not try to change it because it is already the way it ought to be and because we couldn't change it even if we tried. Together these two mistaken ideas have formed a powerful philosophical barrier to the acceptance of evolutionary thinking. With these fallacies swept aside, the way is clear for a more accurate application of neo-Darwinian ideas.

Evolutionary psychologists do not fatalistically resign themselves to our imperfect human nature. We know that evolution can and does design adaptations—such as a propensity for violence—that while "natural" may not be "good." And we also know that any facultative trait can be changed by the appropriate environmental adjustment. Once we reject both the naturalistic fallacy and the genetic fallacy, we see that evolutionary thinking is not the cause of our ills but one of the best routes to curing them.

We may feel that some human behaviors are admirable but far less frequent than we would like. And we may agree that other behaviors are despicable and all too common. In either case our practical task is to discover what environmental adjustments will produce the desired behavioral change. The difference between SSSM psychology and evolutionary psychology is that the SSSM offers no theoretical guidance to help us discover the relevant environmental parameters. Because it lacks an overarching *theory about what humans are designed to do*, SSSM science can only discover underlying norms of reaction by trial-and-error methods. But as we showed in the case of suntanning (and will soon argue with respect to violence), thinking in evolutionary terms can yield clear and testable predictions about the underlying gene–environment interactions. Only when we understand these interactions are we in a position to plan effective environmental intervention. In this way, evolutionary models of behavior provide a useful set of tools for those who seek constructive social change.

SUMMARY

1. Using garden peas as a model Gregor Mendel first discovered the rules of genetics.
2. Genes are particles, not fluids.
3. Diploid adults produce haploid sex cells.
4. These haploid cells combine to form new diploid individuals.
5. Recessive genes are only expressed in homozygotes.
6. Genes are organized into chromosomes, and genes for a particular trait are always found at the same locus on the chromosome.
7. Most loci have only a single allele, but about one-third of human loci currently have more than one.
8. Mutation is the ultimate source of all new alleles and, hence, of all genetic variation.
9. Genes are made out of DNA and, through the intermediary of RNA, they code for the structure of proteins.
10. These proteins interact with each other and with the environment to produce phenotypes.
11. Genetic changes such as mutations can change the phenotype, but phenotypic changes have no effect on the genotype.
12. Genes with obligate effects resist environmental interference.
13. Genes with facultative effects allow the phenotype to respond productively to environmental change.
14. When a single phenotype has the highest fitness over a wide range of environments, selection favors genes with obligate effects.
15. When environments are variable in time or space and the optimal phenotype varies among environments, selection favors genes with facultative effects.
16. Behavioral adaptations are expected to be significantly facultative.
17. Genes are not directly evaluated by selection, but phenotypes are.
18. Phenotypes vary in fitness.
19. The genes that shape the fittest phenotypes are most likely to get passed to the next generation.
20. For these reasons, only traits that have a genetic basis are subject to natural selection.
21. The genetic fallacy is the idea that genetically based traits cannot be modified; the facultative model shows that this idea is false.
22. Evolutionary thinking offers a systematic approach for discovering norms of reaction and thus for developing effective environmental intervention.

4

Implications of Neo-Darwinism for Psychology

As we have seen, neo-Darwinian theory is a bit more subtle than Darwin's original theory. For example, traits don't spread automatically. They spread if the underlying genes are passed on at a higher rate than their alternative alleles. There are several other implications of neo-Darwinism that are not immediately obvious but are nevertheless essential to a modern evolutionary treatment of psychology. This chapter will address these remaining issues. We'll explore questions like: Why are animals often "nice" to each other? How useful is the nature/nurture dichotomy? And, if human behavior is adaptive, what is it adapted to?

ALTRUISM IS AN EVOLUTIONARY PUZZLE

The genes that populate our bodies today are the genes that were good at getting passed on to the next generation. After all, genes that were not good at getting passed on would have been replaced by alternative alleles that were. They wouldn't be sitting in our cell nuclei today because they would already have lost the evolutionary game. This way of thinking helps us understand much of human and animal behavior. Genes shape the organs of behavior, for example, neural and endocrine architecture. Those genes that built the right kind of architecture found themselves in bodies that behaved adaptively and therefore got passed to the next generation. Of course they didn't build the right kind of architecture because they were clever. Every single adaptation began as a mutation. They built the right architecture, ultimately, because of a mistake, a gene-copying error, that turned out to be better than the original at getting into the next generation.

All this we know. But a knotty problem here seriously confused many evolutionists for several decades in the middle of the twentieth century. The problem is that our simple logical idea about what kinds of genes should have survived into the present cannot explain certain kinds of behavior. The kind of behavior it most conspicuously fails to explain is *altruism* or self-sacrifice, behavior where one individual accepts some sort of cost in order to provide a benefit for another individual.

Trail Marker: Darwin's original theory does not predict altruism.

This is a serious problem because altruism is not at all rare. For example, in some mammals (e.g., Cape hunting dogs, *Lycaon pictus*) and many birds (e.g., Florida scrub jays, *Aphelocoma coerulescens*) a significant proportion of adults do not attempt to breed but instead help others rear more offspring than they ever could without such help. This kind of reproductive altruism reaches extremes in many social insect species such as ants, bees, and wasps. In some cases, their colonies consist of a single reproducing female aided by tens of thousands of nonreproductive helpers. Alarm calls provide another example of altruistic behavior. In many group-living species (e.g., vervet monkeys, *Cercopithecus aethiops*) individuals give distinctive calls that warn their associates of an approaching predator. Such calls presumably benefit those who are warned but may attract the predator's attention to the caller, which can be very costly. (See Box 4–1 for a discussion of the four basic kinds of traits.)

Behavioral biologists categorize traits in terms of how they affect the the fitness of the individual who has the trait (self) and in terms of how they affect the fitness of neighbors. A trait could increase (+) or decrease (–) the fitness of the individual who has it, the self; these effects are shown on the horizontal axis. And it could increase or decrease (again, + or –) the fitness of neighboring individuals; these effects are shown on the vertical axis.

Since each of the two effects (self and neighbors) can be positive or negative, there are four possible kinds of traits. Evolutionists have borrowed names for these four from everyday life. For example, *selfish* traits increase the fitness of the self but decrease the fitness of neighbors. *Altruistic* traits do the opposite, decreasing the fitness of the self but adding to the fitness of neighbors. To detail the remaining two, *cooperative* traits are good for both the self and neighbors; *spiteful* traits are bad for both. You should remember that these four everyday words are being used as technical terms in the context of evolutionary psychology, because they refer to the fitness effects of traits.

What kinds of traits does Darwin's theory of evolution by natural selection predict? The answer is, only selfish and cooperative traits because these

Box 4–1. Four Kinds of Traits.

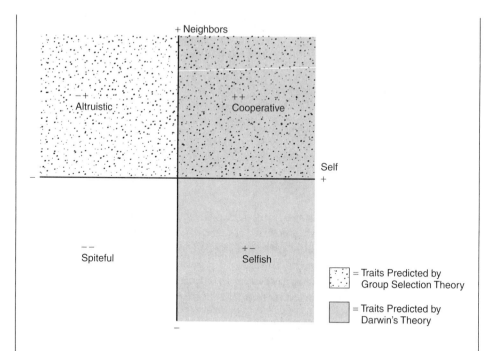

traits increase the fitness of the individual who carries them and therefore both would be passed on to the next generation at a high rate. Altruistic and spiteful traits decrease the fitness of their carriers and would thus tend not to be passed on.

Note that the theory of group selection makes different predictions. It predicts that the effects on the group as a whole ("neighbors" in the graph) determine what will spread. Thus, according to group selection, altruistic and cooperative traits should have spread and selfish and spiteful traits should have been weeded out.

Interestingly, neither set of predictions is entirely accurate, since selfish, cooperative and altruistic traits are all relatively common. (In Chapter 12 we will discuss how spiteful traits might evolve.) Return to the text and Figure 4–2 to see how the combination of natural selection and kin selection solves the problem.

Box 4–1. Continued.

Altruistic behavior is admirable, and we may wish there were more of it, but it contradicts our basic evolutionary model. As long as the costs to the altruist are genuine fitness costs, no matter how small, ordinary natural selection should weed out any altruistic tendencies. If there were genes that led individuals to decrease their own fitness and increase the fitness of their competitors, such genes would surely have been eliminated by selection long ago. Yet altruism, serious reproductive altruism, is a prominent feature of the behavior of humans and many other animals from monkeys to ants. Can the theory and the facts be reconciled?

GROUP SELECTION IS A POOR EXPLANATION FOR ALTRUISM

Curiously, for a long time no one saw any contradiction between theory and fact, because they were thinking about evolution much too uncritically. They mistakenly assumed that "if it's good, it will spread." But this summary of evolution is too vague. Good for whom? This is the key question. If A has a trait that leads her to decrease her own fitness in order to increase B's, it certainly is good for B; no doubt about that. But what will be the evolutionary fate of the genes that triggered A's altruism? What will happen to the gene that leads a scrub jay to feed the nestlings of its competitor? How will vervet genes for alarm calling spread if they end up in predators' stomachs? The costs that altruism inflicts on the altruists themselves prevent the spread of altruistic genes no matter how great the benefits to neighbors. Why? Because a selfish individual who withholds altruism will leave more descendants than an altruistic one who accepts costs and distributes benefits to everyone she meets.

THE FAR SIDE   By GARY LARSON

Figure 4–1. *Group selection's fatal flaw.* Cartoonist Gary Larson pokes fun at an old myth and at group selection. At one time it was believed that lemmings engaged in mass suicide by drowning when their populations grew too large. (Of course they don't; they do migrate out of areas of high population density looking for food and some inevitably die during the migration). Here, Larson poses the key question: if most lemmings did commit suicide, wouldn't a mutant type that refrained from suicide quickly spread through the population? (The Far Side © 1980 FarWorks, Inc. Used by permission. All rights reserved.)

Although group selection is currently rejected by a large majority of evolutionists, it does have some advocates today among qualified biologists (e.g., Sober and Wilson 1998). As discussed in the text, the basic problem is that selfish genes get passed on more often than altruistic genes. The advocates of group selection admit this; but they argue that, under certain conditions, groups that contain only altruists will outcompete groups that include selfish individuals. What are the conditions? John Maynard Smith (1976) has given a clear answer.

Consider the three possible kinds of groups: groups made up exclusively of altruists (A's), groups made up exclusively of selfish nonaltruists (S's), and mixed groups that include both kinds of individuals (A's and S's). For reasons already discussed, selfish individuals outcompete altruists within the mixed groups. Thus, mixed groups are slowly converted into pure selfish groups.

On the other hand, because their members help one another, pure altruistic groups are less likely to go extinct than pure selfish groups. Thus it seems that selfish individuals will win in the short term, but eventually lose out in competition with altruistic groups. However, one factor is still missing. Maynard Smith emphasized that any model of group selection must include migration. After all, how are groups ever formed in the first place except by migrants from other groups?

Note that when selfish individuals migrate from a selfish or mixed group to a pure altruistic group they "infect" it. This is called infection because it converts an altruistic group into a mixed group, and we know what happens to mixed groups: They become pure selfish groups.

So whether altruism can spread by group selection depends on whether selfish groups die off faster than their members infect altruistic groups. For group selection to cause the spread of altruism, every infection must be balanced by the prompt extinction of the infected group. If this does not happen, selfish groups will be created by infection faster than they are eliminated by extinction, and selfishness, not altruism, will spread. The high rates of group extinction and low rates of migration that would allow group selection to operate are rare in nature, so we should consider group-selection explanations only when their very special preconditions are met.

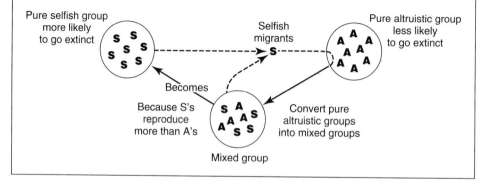

Box 4–2.   A Model of Group Selection.

This seems obvious (see Figure 4–1). Nevertheless in the 1950s and early 1960s (and even today to a much lesser degree), some biologists advocated an idea that came to be called *group selection* (Wynne-Edwards, 1962). They believed that altruism would be perpetuated because it is good for the group (or society) as a whole. Dissect the previous sentence carefully; it contains two ideas. The first is that altruism is good for the group as a whole. The second is that this good-for-the-group effect will cause the genes for altruism to spread. The first idea is generally correct: You will do better in a group that includes many altruists. But what about the second idea? Remember, a trait will spread only if the genes that shape it are good at getting into the next generation. Unfortunately, because of the costs of altruism, altruistic genes are bad at getting into the next generation. And to make matters worse, at the same time they decrease the fitness of the body that carries them they add to the fitness of competing bodies. This is about the worst an allele can do! In groups that include both altruists and nonaltruists, the nonaltruists would clearly prosper, accepting benefits at the expense of the altruists. By the very definition of altruism, altruists will be selected against.

> **Trail Marker:** Advantages for the group are generally not sufficient to spread a trait.

So why do humans and other animals ever behave altruistically? Why haven't the genes that underlie altruistic tendencies been completely eliminated by selection? This is a major puzzle because altruism is real and widespread. As we have seen, benefit to the group as a whole is insufficient to spread altruistic genes (except in rather special circumstances; see Box 4–2). There must be some other explanation for altruism.

KIN SELECTION OFFERS ONE VALID EXPLANATION FOR ALTRUISM

In 1964, in some of the most original and penetrating work since Darwin's, the British biologist W. D. Hamilton discovered a solution to the problem of altruism by thinking about evolution from the gene's perspective. He essentially pointed out that genes have two routes to the next generation, one direct and the other indirect. The direct one you already know: A gene that somehow makes its surrounding body more fit is more likely to be copied than one that does not. But, as we have seen, the fundamental problem with altruism is that it makes the surrounding body *less* fit. Hamilton (1964a, 1964b) suggested that a gene for altruism could get into the next generation via an indirect route: by inducing altruism in one individual, and aiming the benefits of that altruism at another individual who, by virtue of common ancestry, carries *the very same gene.*

This is a powerful idea. If the fitness loss to the altruist was low enough and the fitness benefit to the recipient(s) was high enough, and if the recipient was likely enough to have inherited the same gene that induced the altruism, the gene would actually reap a net benefit. Such a gene would essentially be trading away a decrease in the fitness of one carrier for a larger increase in the fitness of another carrier. Biologists use the phrase *kin selection* to refer to Hamilton's idea that altruistic genes can spread by benefitting other carriers of the same gene. They use the term kin selection because kin carry many genes that are identical by descent from their common ancestor. (You may recall from Chapter 3 that all humans have identical genotypes at two-thirds of their loci. These invariant loci "cancel out" in Hamilton's calculations. The only loci that matter are the remaining one-third where there are competing alleles. By virtue of inheritance from a common ancestor, relatives will have more similar genotypes at these variable loci.)

> **Trail Marker:** Kin selection favors altruism that is selectively aimed at relatives.

Science fiction! Genes can't do that; they're too stupid! These are typical first reactions to Hamilton's theory. But genes are neither smart nor stupid. They are mere cybernetic codes for protein assembly, instructions that have been designed by evolution. Over many eons, mutations—copying errors—have occurred and selection has evaluated their phenotypic effects. If a new mutant allele is better at getting into the next generation than the allele it mutated from, the mutant allele will spread. How it gets into the next generation is irrelevant. In the trial-and-error world built by the combination of mutation and selection, many routes to the next generation have been tried and evaluated. The ones that we see today are the ones that worked. Kin-selected genes are simply alleles that take an indirect route to the next generation.

Hamilton's original papers on kin selection amount to a mathematical proof of his theory; and the proof is airtight. But a mathematical proof merely shows that an idea is logically consistent. It doesn't say anything about what actually happens in the world. Nevertheless, the idea of kin selection was so exciting that an entire generation of field biologists dedicated themselves to finding out whether animals behave in accordance with its predictions. And the well-established answer is that they clearly do. But before we can appreciate this conclusion, we have to understand exactly what the theory predicts.

A Formal Model of Kin Selection: Hamilton's Rule

In any altruistic encounter there is an altruist, who gets a cost. And there is a recipient who gets a benefit. Let's measure the size of the cost with a variable, c, and the size of the benefit with another variable, b. Only one other variable is needed to formalize the theory of kin selection. A kin-selected gene spreads, supposedly, because it confers benefits on other carriers of the same gene. Now, nothing is absolutely certain in this world; we can't say that Sally absolutely carries the same gene as her cousin, André. But we can express the *probability* that she and André share a gene by virtue of their sharing a common ancestor. Hamilton called this probability r, the *coefficient of relatedness*. This probability, r, is a fraction, some number between 0 and 1. Now we can state *Hamilton's Rule*. A gene will spread if it induces altruistic behavior when:

$$rb > c$$

Let's translate Hamilton's Rule into words. The product term on the left, rb, has to be greater than the cost to the altruist. The product term is simply the benefit to the recipient multiplied by the probability that the recipient also carries the altruistic gene (we say "also" because the altruist obviously carries the altruistic gene). Remember, r is a fraction, somewhere between 0 and 1. So when we multiply the benefit, b, times r, we are getting a product that is smaller than b. We are devaluing the benefit by r. Devaluing the benefit makes sense. The gene in the altruist is definitely getting a cost. Unless the benefit to the recipient is large enough to compensate for the fact that the recipient may not have the altruistic gene, it's not worth paying the cost. So the predictions of kin selection theory are simple to state. Kin-selected genes should induce altruism *whenever the benefit devalued by the degree of relatedness outweighs the cost*, that is, whenever $rb > c$.

> **Trail Marker:** Kin selected altruism facultatively depends on the relationship among r, b, and c.

It will be helpful to take a hypothetical example and assign values to r, b, and c. Suppose an altruist confers a benefit on his full sister, for example, by giving her a freshly killed buffalo for her and her children to eat. On average, full siblings have half of their genes identical by descent (from their parents), so in this case $r = 0.5$. Let's say the altruistic act costs 0.1 units of fitness. That means that ten such acts would reduce the altruist's reproductive success by one offspring ($10 \times 0.1 = 1$). And let's say the benefit to his sister is 0.25 units of fitness (that is, if she received four such benefits over her lifetime it would increase her reproductive success by one offspring). Is $rb > c$? Yes, in this hypothetical example it is; 0.5×0.25 equals 0.125. Thus the devalued benefit, 0.125, is greater than the cost, 0.1. An altruistic act of this type would be favored by kin selection. See Figure 4–2 for a general picture of the kinds of altruism that would be favored by kin selection.

Can Animals Do Algebra?

If the theory is correct, altruistic tendencies should facultatively depend on the relationship among r, b, and c. But it took a brilliant biologist to come up with this mathematical formula. How will animals ever be able to solve it?. Of course they won't, but that doesn't matter. To exhibit kin-selected altruism an animal doesn't have to do algebra. It simply has to behave as if it can! Selection evaluates results. If life were a math test, selection would not check your work, only your answer. Models like $rb > c$ summarize how evolution works, not how animals work.

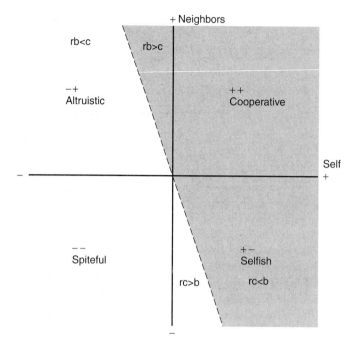

Figure 4–2. *Traits predicted by kin selection theory.* Kin selection makes two modifications to Darwin's theory. First, kin selection predicts limited, facultative altruism. In the figure these favored altruistic acts fall in the shaded wedge of the altruistic quadrant. For the majority of hypothetical altruistic acts (those in the unshaded area), *rb* < *c* because the benefit is small or the cost is large or the degree of relatedness is low. (See text for a discussion of Hamilton's Rule and the definitions of *r*, *b* and *c*.) Second, kin selection predicts a restraint on selfishness. Extreme selfishness directed at relatives can produce a net cost for the underlying genes. To be precise, in Hamilton's terms selfishness is disfavored by kin selection if *rc* > *b*. The majority of selfish acts fall outside this area and kin selection will permit them.

In terms of everything we know about animal behavior, Hamilton's Rule is a simple model. To model what birds do when they fly, we need advanced integral calculus. Nobody thinks robins actually do calculus. Yet robins regularly fly from one perch to another without missing and without crashing into anything along the way. They can do these things because selection is pragmatic. It gets the job done. If birds can't take off, or if they crash into things, or miss their landings, they won't get many genes into the next generation. Any solution that helps solve the problem of accurate flight will spread. So selection provides animals with what we call *rules of thumb*. A rule of thumb is a relatively simple, pragmatic way of solving a complicated problem. (For example, in Chapter 5 we explain a visual rule of thumb that birds use to avoid crashing.) Of course, rules of thumb are implemented by mental modules, but they're not algebra modules, they are much narrower and simpler. Let's consider what these rules of thumb might be like for kin selected altruism.

> **Trail Marker:** Evolution builds simple rules of thumb to guide behavior.

The parameters *b* and *c*, benefit and cost, are fundamentally ecological. They are things like food items, breeding opportunities, predation risks, and the like. Given this, it might seem that *b* and *c* would always be equal. If I give you five dollars you gain exactly what I lose. But the fitness effects of the transfer might not be equal.

(Remember, kin selection is an evolutionary theory, so *b* and *c* must be evaluated in units of fitness.) I might have five million dollars in the bank, and you might be starving. In that case, the five-dollar cost is practically nothing to me but the five dollar benefit could save your life. Similarly, if I'm standing next to a safe haven and see a predator coming while you're out in the open, a warning call would cost me little but benefit you a great deal. In other words, there are many circumstances in life (age, strength, location, wealth, and the like) that can make *b* and *c* quite unequal in real-world situations. (This is important: Unless *b* is a fair bit greater than *c*, then *rb* cannot be greater than *c*, because *r* is always less than 1.) So animals could behave as if they were attending to the relationship between *b* and *c* simply by responding to relatively obvious things like differences in age, strength, location, etc.

The parameter *r* should be even easier for animals to estimate. Individuals carry genes that are identical by descent because they inherit them from a common ancestor. The more recent the common ancestor, the more genes they will share. This is why the theory is called kin selection: Kin share many genes. But how can a young monkey, for example, tell who its kin are? Simple: It can cue on its mother's behavior. If Mom often grooms a particular adolescent female, it's almost certainly an older sister of the young monkey. The young monkey doesn't have to *know* this. The grooming relationship simply has to be a regular feature of monkey social life. In that case, a gene that biases altruism towards Mom's grooming partners could spread.

> **Trail Marker:** Animals can estimate *r*, *b,* and *c* by simple rules of thumb.

Other cues can also provide information about genetic similarity. Scent seems to be an important factor in many species. Genes code for proteins that interact to shape the body's physiology. Some products of these interactions are volatile (easily evaporate into the air). Thus it is possible to actually smell some very direct products of the genotype. For example, field and laboratory studies show that in the social paper wasp *Polistes fuscatus* whether or not a niece will be admitted to an unfamiliar nest by an aunt who has never met her before can be perfectly predicted from chemical data. Certain substances called alkanes were extracted from the cuticles (the hard exoskeleton that covers wasps' bodies) of both aunts and nieces. Nieces whose alkane profiles matched that of the nest they were visiting were admitted. Those whose alkane profiles did not match were driven off (Gamboa et al., 1996).

Evidence Regarding Altruism

A large number of studies show that, in humans and other animals, altruistic behavior depends on all three parameters, *r*, *b*, and *c*. The evidence for humans is discussed in Chapter 15. The work of Steven Emlen and his associates (Emlen & Wrege, 1988; Emlen et al., 1995) on white-fronted bee-eaters (*Merops bullockoides*) represents one of the best long-term animal studies. These insect-eating birds excavate nest holes in high banks along East African rivers, and these nest burrows are grouped together forming colonies of fifteen to twenty-five families. In some families just the breeding male and female tend the nestlings, but in many families nonbreeding helpers also provide additional food to the nestlings. The helpers' contributions result in better nestling survival and hence higher reproductive success for the breeding pair. But the work of helping prevents helpers from breeding at the same time. These facts added together show that helping is altruistic: Helpers get a cost in terms of their own missed breeding opportunity, and they provide a benefit in elevating the breeder's reproductive success. Now, the key question is how do bee-eater helpers distribute their aid; indiscriminately as predicted by group selection theory, or selectively in accordance with the predictions of kin selection theory? In fact, bee-eaters are very selective. They are most likely to feed nestlings with whom they share a large proportion of genes (see Table 4–1.)

As mentioned above, alarm calling constitutes another large class of altruistic behaviors. Paul Sherman and his colleagues (1981) have studied the alarm-calling behavior of Belding's ground squirrels (*Spermophilus beldingi*) in mountain meadows in the Sierra Nevada of California. These rodents also live in large colonies where the breeding burrows of many females are in close proximity. When a terrestrial predator such as a coyote or a badger approaches the colony, one or more of the squirrels often give a loud and distinctive call. (They give a different call if an

Table 4–1.   Relationship between Breeders and Helpers in White-Fronted Bee Eaters.

RELATIONSHIP OF BREEDER TO HELPER	r BETWEEN HELPER AND NESTLINGS	NUMBER OF CASES	PERCENT OF CASES	CUMULATIVE PERCENT OF CASES
Father and mother	0.50	78	44.8	44.8
Father (with new mate) Mother (with new mate) Son Brother Grandfather and grandmother	0.25	68	39.1	83.9
Half-brother Uncle Grandmother Grandson	0.13	7	4.0	87.9
Great grandfather	0.06	1	0.6	88.5
Non-relative	0.00	20	11.5	100.0

In the vast majority of cases helpers helped relatives, and they helped close relatives in preference to distant ones. (From "The Role of Kinship in Helping Decisions among White-Fronted Bee-Eaters" by S. Emlen and P. Wrege in *Behavioral Ecology and Sociobiology* (1988), 23, pp. 305–315. Reprinted by permission of Springer-Verlag New York, Inc.)

avian predator such as a hawk or eagle is approaching.) The caller stands on its hind legs and looks directly at the predator as it gives the alarm. Thus any ground squirrel hearing the alarm can simply look toward the source of the call and observe where the caller is looking to find out where the predator is. Sherman's team has shown that, relative to squirrels who remain silent, callers are at increased risk of predation. They have also demonstrated that other squirrels use the information they obtain from callers to escape to safety. And finally, Sherman's data also establish that the squirrels most likely to call are those with more living relatives in the colony and those with genetically closer relatives in the colony.

These kinds of studies make it clear that, among nonhuman animals, altruistic behavior fits the model of kin selection much better than it fits the model of group selection. Of course anthropologists will readily confirm that kinship is the most important organizing feature of every human society. More detailed analyses of the likely effects of kin selection on particular aspects of human behavior will be presented in many of the chapters that follow, and especially in Chapter 15.

RECIPROCITY PROVIDES ANOTHER VALID EXPLANATION FOR ALTRUISM

Without in any way questioning the power of kin selection, Robert Trivers (1971) offered an alternative explanation for altruism. He argued that altruism could also evolve via *reciprocity*, that is, by a you-scratch-my-back-and-I'll-scratch-yours system. In any kind of altruism, the altruist gets a cost and the recipient of the altruism gets a benefit. This means that, ordinarily, altruists are weeded out by selection. But Hamilton gave one exception, for altruism aimed at kin. Trivers (1971) essentially posed another sort of exception by adding two important conditions: 1) costs must be small compared to benefits, and 2) the altruist and recipient must regularly exchange roles. Together, these two conditions turn short-term altruism into long-term cooperation (see Box 4–1 for a definition of cooperation). To see how this works, let's consider a simple example.

How Can Reciprocal Altruism Pay?

Imagine it's half a million years ago. Enter Zug and Ord, two hunter-gatherers. If either of them has a run of poor foraging luck, he or she will starve to death. And they don't have refrigeration, so they can't store any surplus when they have a run of good luck. Suppose Zug had good luck this week and has more food than he can eat, but Ord had bad luck. At a very small cost (because what he can't eat will rot anyway), Zug can give a large, potentially life-saving benefit to Ord by giving her some food. Now, several weeks later the tables have turned; Ord was lucky and Zug unlucky. If Ord reciprocates and gives the food she can't eat to Zug, both have gotten substantial benefits but paid minimal costs. In other words, by exchanging a favor, both come out much better than if they had not.

There's just one problem with this formulation—a problem that Trivers both recognized and solved. What happens if Zug gives his surplus to Ord, but Ord fails to reciprocate when the tables are turned? Zug, the altruist, may die. And Ord, the selfish nonreciprocator, the *cheater* may thrive by grabbing benefits but never incurring any costs.

At first glance Ord seems to have a good plan. Take the benefits and run: Never pay any costs. So why don't cheaters replace altruists over evolutionary time? Trivers argues that ordinarily they will, *unless altruists discriminate against cheaters by withholding altruism.* In other words, the key to non-kin altruism is *reciprocity:* Behave altruistically towards other altruists, and withhold altruism from those who don't pay you back. Trivers did not intend this as a moral prescription. It was, and is, simply a statement about the circumstances under which altruism is expected to flourish. Remember Trivers's second condition (above): The altruist and recipient must exchange roles. If they aren't regularly paid back, altruists end up with more costs than benefits and altruistic tendencies will be eliminated by selection.

> **Trail Marker:** Reciprocal altruism can spread if altruism is withheld from cheaters.

Of course for altruist and recipient to exchange roles, they must interact more than once. And deciding who is a reciprocator and who isn't may also require repeated interactions. So reciprocal altruism isn't very likely to evolve unless individuals can recognize each other: You're not merely helping an adult female, you're helping Lucy. And it isn't very likely to evolve in large, open societies where you seldom meet the same individual twice. But the small, relatively closed societies of our hominid ancestors would have provided an appropriate environment for reciprocity to take hold (see Ancestral Environments, below).

Game Theory Provides a Formal Model of Reciprocity

Sometimes there are surprising convergences in science. The evolution of reciprocity is one example because Trivers's same conclusions have been reached by a very different route: *game theory.* Game theory is a branch of mathematics designed for studying situations where individuals have conflicting wants. It assumes players that are rational, that is, who try to maximize their "winnings." One well-studied game, the *Prisoner's Dilemma* (Luce and Raiffa, 1957), captures the essence of reciprocity. The "players" in Prisoner's Dilemma are two people charged with theft in the case of some missing jewelry. The two know that they actually did commit the crime. Beforehand they agreed that, if caught, they would cooperate (with each other, not with the police) by remaining silent about the crime. Now the police have separated them for questioning and explain the same set of alternatives to each suspect.

The police have enough evidence to convict them on a lesser charge of unlawful entry, but they do not have enough to convict them of stealing the jewels.

Thus, if both remain silent (cooperating with each other) they will receive one-year sentences for unlawful entry.

If they make it easy for the authorities by both confessing (cheating on their prior agreement to remain silent), they'll be prosecuted for the jewel theft but will get a relatively light sentence for being tractable. In this case they'll each spend five years in jail. That's a bad deal; five years in jail is obviously worse than one. Why would either of them confess?

The temptation to confess lies in the third alternative. If one confesses and testifies against his partner, he will get off scot-free (for helping the authorities close the case) and his silent partner in crime will spend ten years under lock and key for jewel theft. The situation is diagramed in Table 4–2.

The dilemma comes from the fiendish arrangement of alternatives. Let's call the two players "Self" and "Other." Look at what happens to Self as Other makes different choices. If Other is going to remain silent, then Self can improve his outcome from one year to zero by confessing. If Other is going to confess, then confessing improves Self's outcome from ten years to five. No matter what Other does, it always pays Self to confess; that is, it pays Self to cheat on his prior agreement to keep silent! (Confessing is called cheating on their prior agreement because we are considering the situation from the point of view of the partners in crime, who presumably want to minimize their jail sentences, not from society's perspective.)

The conclusion, that players should cheat rather than cooperate is a lot like the conclusion that Ord would be better off accepting Zug's altruism but not paying him back. As we saw for cases like Zug and Ord's, the only thing that can keep cheaters from coming out ahead of altruists is to punish cheaters by withholding further altruism. If players like Self and Other play Prisoner's Dilemma only once, there's no opportunity to punish a cheater. But if they play again and again (this is called *Iterated Prisoner's Dilemma*), there's plenty of opportunity; someone who cheats in one round can be punished in the next.

> **Trail Marker:** Iterated Prisoner's Dilemma provides an opportunity to punish cheaters.

Table 4–2. Outcomes of choices by Self and Other in the Prisoner's dilemma. The number before the backslash indicates Self's outcome in years in jail; likewise, the second number indicates Other's outcome.

Self's Choice	Other's Choice	
	Silence (Cooperate)	Confess (Cheat)
Silence (Cooperate)	1\1	10\0
Confess (Cheat)	0\10	5\5

Iterated Prisoner's Dilemma is the subject of much research. There are many, probably an infinite number of strategies: "always cooperate," "cheat on every third round," "cooperate unless your opponent has cheated twice in a row," and so on. So far, no one has proved conclusively that one strategy is universally the best. But some strategies are quite good, and researchers think they understand why. Robert Axelrod (1984) showed that one useful way to evaluate strategies is to stage computer tournaments among them. Each strategy is first written out as a program, and a "population" is formed by including a copy of each program. Programs are randomly selected from the population to play against each other. Then they reproduce—make copies of themselves—in proportion to their score in these pairings. Strategies that win more often become more common in the population. Strategies die when their total score drops too low. Eventually only one strategy is left. Usually this surviving strategy is something called *tit-for-tat* (Axelrod, 1984).

Tit-for-tat cooperates on the first round and then does whatever its opponent did on the previous round. Tit-for-tat, quite simply, is reciprocal. As a consequence of being reciprocal, tit-for-tat ends up being nice and forgiving, but it also reliably punishes cheating. As long as the opponent cooperates, tit-for-tat cooperates (it's nice). If the opponent cheats, tit-for-tat will cheat on the next round (it punishes cheaters). If the opponent then cooperates, tit-for-tat returns to cooperating (it's forgiving). The key to its success is thought to lie in this combination of characteristics. By punishing cheaters, tit-for-tat avoids being taken advantage of and thus keeps its losses low. And by being nice and forgiving, tit-for-tat is good at establishing bouts of cooperation; this lets it pile up gains. Like Trivers's reciprocity, tit-for-tat only cooperates with those who cooperate with it, and it punishes (withholds cooperation from) those who cheat.

Two very different approaches have led us to the same conclusion: It's a winning strategy to bestow favors on those who reciprocate, and to withhold favors from those who don't. This strategy is easiest to implement when we interact with the same individuals again and again, so that we are in a position to recognize who cheats and who reciprocates and to treat them accordingly.

> **Trail Marker:** Organisms should be designed to bestow favors
> on those who reciprocate, and to withhold favors
> from those who don't.

Trivers's (1971) original paper could be regarded as one of the cornerstones of evolutionary psychology. He explicitly noted that when selection shapes creatures to be reciprocal altruists, it must do so by shaping their psychology, that is by shaping their emotions, inclinations, and thinking abilities. Because of its wide-ranging implications for psychology, you will meet various predictions from reciprocity theory in each of three different chapters in this book. For example, we'll discuss several of the modules involved in dealing with cheaters in Chapters 8, 12, and 15.

To summarize the first major topic of this chapter, altruism is an evolutionary puzzle because altruists ordinarily would have lower fitness than nonaltruists.

Benefits to the group as a whole are generally insufficient to cause the spread of altruistic genes. On the other hand, altruistic genes could spread by either (or both) kin selection or reciprocity. Now we turn to our second major topic, the widely misunderstood matter of how genes and environment work in shaping the phenotype.

THE END OF THE NATURE-NURTURE DICHOTOMY

Nature versus nurture. Genes versus environment. Innate versus learned. Biology versus culture. These dichotomies aim at essentially the same issue. Is the trait in question shaped principally by things that happen to us over our lifetimes, or by something deeper, something that was already part of us when or even before we were born? On the surface, it seems like a reasonable and indeed interesting question. The next time you're with a group of friends, pick a trait—shyness, athletic ability, homosexuality, whatever you like—and pose the nature versus nurture question. We'll wager that your friends will find the question sensible and, moreover, will have fairly clear opinions about what the answer is. The idea that some traits are principally the result of nature and others principally the result of nurture is deeply entrenched.

This is unfortunate because this idea is simply wrong. A central message of this chapter, and an important theme of this whole book, is that the nature/nurture dichotomy is pointless and often dangerously misleading. We do not learn anything useful when we try to divide the causes of a trait into nature or nurture. And we distract ourselves from asking better, more informative questions about the trait. The argument that we will develop applies with equal force to all manifestations of the nature/nurture dichotomy (i.e., genes versus environment, innate versus learned, etc.). Our argument follows logically from the facultative model of gene–environment interaction (see Chapter 3).

Gene–environment interactions are not a matter of chance. Like other outcomes of evolution by natural selection, they are designed to improve the fit between the organism and its environment. We saw that selection favors genes with obligate effects when a single phenotype is superior over a wide range of normal environments. Alternatively, selection will favor genes with facultative effects when a single inflexible phenotype could not effectively cope with the range of prevailing environments.

On the surface, obligate traits might seem to be mainly the result of nature. But as you learned in the previous chapter, even this is an oversimplification. Selection builds obligate traits to resist environmental interference, but it does so over a particular range of normally occurring environmental conditions. If those conditions are exceeded the trait may go completely haywire. This susceptibility to environmental disruption shows that, over the course of development, obligate traits are quite dependent on environmental conditions and so have a strong nurture component.

Facultative traits present an even more interesting set of cases, especially relevant to psychology because most behavior tends to be shaped by facultative rather than obligate mechanisms. What do facultative traits have to say about the usefulness of the nature-nurture dichotomy? Let's begin with a simple example that we already understand, suntanning, even though it is not strictly a behavioral trait. Remember, when we suntan our level of melanin production is adjusted to our current levels of uv_b exposure. Thus, within limits, the more uv_b we receive the darker our skin becomes. Now ask yourself the standard question.

Is Suntanning the Result of Nature or Nurture?

Here's one way to argue: Suntanning is due to nature. The instructions for how to make the melanin molecule are written right in the genes. The specific mechanism that links the rate of melanin synthesis to uv_b exposure is also written in the genes. If the genes were different, in any way, the system would be different. Some other protein, not melanin, would be produced. Or it would be produced in response to some other environmental factor, say temperature or altitude. Or perhaps melanin production would be constant instead of variable. Maybe the norm of reaction would be different: for example, uv_b exposure could decrease, rather than increase, melanin production. Obviously, the system is the way it is because of the genes we carry. Without those genes, we would not suntan. It's all due to nature, to genes.

But here's a different way to argue: Suntanning is due to nurture, to experience. If environmental levels of uv_b were constant, nobody would suntan. Yes, people would produce melanin, but the suntanning response, the changes in skin color, would never happen if uv_b levels didn't vary. Imagine a pair of identical twins. By definition these twins have exactly the same genes. One twin lives in Buffalo, New York, one of the cloudiest places in North America; the other lives in Phoenix, Arizona, one of the sunniest. Their skin colors will be very different despite the fact that they are genetically identical. Nurture, experience, is everything.

Both of these arguments sound convincing, but they give contradictory answers. That is what happens when we ask an illogical question! We asked whether suntanning was due to nature or to nurture, and we tried to give reasons why it was one or the other. Of course suntanning is due to *both* nature and nurture. But we need to be cautious even about this answer. As stated it is open to a variety of interpretations, and some of these are naive and fail to do justice to our understanding of gene–environment interactions.

If by "due to both nature and nurture" we mean something like 40 percent nature and 60 percent nurture, or 75 percent nature and 25 percent nurture, we are still misunderstanding the logic of facultative traits. The causes of your suntanning cannot be divided up in this way because they are due not to a crude summation but to an interaction. Because genes constitute something like a recipe for phenotypes, Richard Dawkins (1982) has suggested thinking about the nature-nurture problem via an analogy with bread making. Wouldn't it be ridiculous to claim that bread is 75 percent ingredients and 25 percent heat? Bread is what happens when the right kinds of ingredients are exposed to appropriate temperatures. Either one without the other yields nothing useful at all, because bread is the product of an interaction. Similarly, the suntanning genes don't do anything very interesting without uv_b input. And uv_b doesn't do anything very interesting if there aren't any suntanning genes to respond to it. The interesting and useful thing about suntanning is how genes work *with* the environment to keep the risks of skin cancer and vitamin D deficiency low.

> **Trail Marker:** When asking about the causes of a trait, it's a mistake to separate nature and nurture.

Many social scientists operating within the framework of the SSSM (see Chapter 1) make the following kind of argument: Nature (or the genotype) sets the limits, but experience shapes the trait within these boundaries. This is a second naive meaning of the claim that "*x* is due to both nature and nurture." And it is just as mistaken as the percentage approach. The problem with this way of thinking is that it fails to address the very large problem of exactly *how* experience shapes the trait. How can it shape the trait except by rules of gene–environment interaction that are coded in the genotype? Could uv_b exposure raise IQ? Yes, if there were genes encoding such mechanisms. And no if there weren't. To say that experience shapes the trait within broad boundaries amounts to sweeping most of the interesting questions under the rug. Experience doesn't just capriciously change our skin color. It shapes it in a particular way that has been predetermined by evolution. Selection has sorted through many possible skin colors and many possible mechanisms for adjusting skin color to any number of environmental variables. And the result is suntanning: an evolved pattern that occurs because particular genes are tuned to respond in particular ways to particular environmental inputs.

> **Trail Marker:** Instead or asking "Is it nature or nurture?" ask "Why does the environment have this particular effect?"

Asking "Is suntanning due to genes or environment?" has not been very informative. Because evolution has preprogrammed an interaction between genes and environment, the question is nonsensical. But once we realize that the nature-nurture dichotomy is a false one, there are many more sensible questions we can ask about suntanning. Why isn't skin color constant? What is happening when our skin is darkening? What are the properties of the melanin molecule? Why is melanin production linked to uv_b production and not to something else? What, if any, foods contain vitamin D? These questions help us make sense of suntanning. They uncover the evolutionary logic of the trait, and help us understand why genes and environment interact in the very particular way they do during suntanning. In essence, they explain the norm of reaction for suntanning.

NATURE AND NURTURE: THE QUESTION OF VIOLENCE

By now it should be apparent that traits can be quite responsive to the environment and still have a genetic basis. Now let's take a behavioral example, one that is admittedly not so well understood as suntanning, and see how the evolutionary perspective can help us ask more sensible questions.

It has been suggested by some psychologists that violence is increasing in society because we are exposed to so much violence on television and in films, in short, that violence is the result of nurture. Of course, traditional SSSM psychology offers no basis for predicting whether violent entertainment would increase or decrease violent behavior. But they have done the empirical research to find out. The answer is clear: Viewing violence makes people more likely to be violent (e.g., Gerbner et al., 1986; Centerwall, 1989; Williams, 1986). To make sense of this an evolutionist would begin to pose a series of questions like the ones we outlined for suntanning: What is violence for? Why did we evolve a capacity for violence in the first place? If violence serves some function, why isn't there a single optimal level of violence (which might be quite low)? Why does violence vary depending on the environment? Why does seeing violence make people more likely to be violent themselves, say as opposed to being disgusted by it and therefore less likely to be violent?

Remembering the lesson of the naturalistic fallacy—when we explain something we are trying to understand it, not to justify it—let's try to answer some of these questions about violence. When we look across species, the evolved function of violence is clear. Animals use violence as a tactic to get their way, to have some contested resource or opportunity for themselves. In effect, violence works by increasing the costs to challengers. (Any resource or opportunity has some finite value in terms of how much it would contribute to fitness. And if it will cost too much to acquire, due to the violence of an opponent, it may be better to simply yield the resource.) But violence also imposes costs on the aggressor in terms of risk and energy. In strictly selfish terms, it would be better if there were some way of getting the resource without resorting to violence.

> **Trail Marker:** Violence is one tactic animals use to get disputed resources.

Clearly there are other ways to get a contested resource. Deceit is one. Maybe I can convince you that the resource is not really what you think it is, or perhaps I can get the resource without your knowing. Negotiating is another way. Let's each take half of the resource, or let's take turns so you get this one and I get the next one. Or perhaps I can offer something else you want if you'll yield the contested resource. Maybe we can work together to get more of the resource so there's plenty for both of us. These and other alternative tactics sometimes work: An individual can sometimes get the desired resource without the personal costs and risks of resorting to violence.

But these alternatives probably will not work if the opponent resorts to violence. Indeed, if your opponent resorts to violence first and you're unprepared, you may lose more than the contested resource! So natural selection should have given us a facultative violence module so that we are quicker to resort to violence when we have reason to expect that our opponents may use violence. How could this kind of facultative trait be wired up? The necessary environmental input concerns the frequency of violence in the population.

> **Trail Marker:** Violence may facultatively depend on the frequency of violence in the population.

Of course the most reliable source of this information would be direct observation: How much violence do we see? Martin Daly and Margo Wilson (1988) use this idea to explain, in part, why interpersonal violence is much more prevalent in some subcultures than in others. In essence, they argue that there is a feedback effect; each violent act observed makes the observers feel more at risk and therefore more likely to resort to preemptive violence themselves. Now, perhaps seeing violence on television or in the movies activates the same violence-estimation mechanisms as seeing real-world violence. To the extent that this is so, violent entertainment will increase people's expectations of violence and their own violent tendencies will be correspondingly elevated.

This example contains several important lessons. First, because the point cannot be overemphasized, although levels of violence may be strongly influenced by our experiences, such influences will always operate by rules that were written by evolution. If seeing violence makes people more violent, it does so *for a reason*. Second, from an SSSM perspective, experience is assumed to affect behavior, but often the SSSM is silent about the expected nature or direction of these environmental influences. Will seeing violent television programs increase or decrease violent behavior? By itself, the SSSM offers no guidance. Any relationship would have to be discovered by trial-and-error experimentation. And once the relationship was discovered, it would have to be explained *post-hoc*, since the pattern had not been predicted *a priori*. There are three conventional explanations for the positive association between violence viewing and violent behavior.

1. Violence viewing increases arousal that can spill over into behavior (e.g. Zillmann 1989).
2. Violence viewing disinhibits violence, that is, it lowers our inhibitions against violence (e.g. Berkowitz 1984).
3. Violence viewing evokes imitation.

Do you find these explanations satisfying? They certainly leave many further questions. Why does arousal spill over into violent behavior, as opposed to philanthropy or any other kind of behavior? Why should the disinhibition be limited to violence rather than to other kinds of antisocial behavior such as public nudity? Why should intentional violence evoke more imitation than accidental violence such as car crashes? The three conventional "explanations" rely on labels like disinhibition and imitation, without really saying how or why these processes work the way they do. In short, they don't really make sense of the observed facts.

The final point illustrated by this example is that, although the evolutionary approach emphasizes functional or "why" questions, it also offers useful insights about mechanistic or "how" issues. In the evolutionary approach to violence outlined on p. 83, there are several testable assumptions about how the environmental influence works. For example, we suggested that viewing violence increases our tendency to be violent because it increases our expectations of violence in our daily lives. This is a testable assumption, and Michael Morgan (1983) has tested it. He studied the association between television viewing and real-world fear. He found the predicted positive association: People who watch more television perceive themselves to be at greater risk of violence in their daily lives. But more importantly, the strength of that association depended on the demographics of violence on TV. Violence is not evenly distributed across the fictional population: Members of some age-sex-race groups are more likely to be portrayed as victims of violence than others. Morgan concluded:

> . . . viewers who see their fictional counterparts more often as victims than as victors are the ones who show the strongest links between how much they watch television and the tendency to overestimate their chances of involvement in violence (1983:155–156).

Based on Morgan's research our facultative response to observed violence seems very finely tuned. The more we see people *like ourselves* victimized by violence, the more we feel at risk of being violently attacked.

The facultative model, illustrated by suntanning and the possible effects of violent entertainment, lies behind many of the examples we will discuss in this book. It is absolutely essential to understand its logic and to appreciate why it invalidates the genes-environment (nature-nurture) dichotomy. In normal circumstances, traits respond to the environment if, and only in the way, selection designed them to respond. The response is only possible because selection in past environments has favored genes that orchestrate that particular pattern of response. The genes and the environments in which they function are inextricably woven together by evolutionary history. Thus trying to pull apart their separate effects is illogical and obscures the causes that linked them. Don't ask "Is this trait caused by genes or environment?" Instead ask why it was designed to respond to particular environmental variables in particular ways. In other words, ask why the norm of reaction takes the form it does, rather than any other imaginable form. This question is one of the fundamental contributions of evolutionary psychology.

Trail Marker: Norms of reaction provide the key to understanding the influence of environment on behavior.

A DIFFERENT KIND OF NATURE-NURTURE QUESTION

As we have seen, the causes of a facultative trait cannot be sensibly divided between genetic and environmental influences. Your present level of melanin synthesis is the result of your genotype interacting with your environment. It is the result of processes designed by natural selection in the past that express themselves in your body during your lifetime. And while that process is operating it is always genes *and* environment that jointly determine the outcome.

But psychologists sometimes ask a different sort of question. Our bread analogy will be helpful again. As we said, it makes no sense to look at a loaf of bread and argue whether its flavor was caused by ingredients or heat. The effects of ingredients and oven temperature were mingled together during the baking process. Jointly they made the bread and gave it its flavor. But, suppose we have a whole bakery full of loaves. And suppose the baker had used several different recipes and several ovens that differed slightly in baking temperature. In this case, it would be reasonable to ask about the flavor *differences* among these loaves, and in particular, whether these differences were more the result of different ingredients or more the result of baking in different ovens.

Maybe on Monday the ingredient lists were pretty similar, but the oven temperatures varied considerably. Then surely on Monday the oven "environment" will explain most of the difference in bread flavor. On the other hand, perhaps on Thursday the baker was feeling more experimental and added one unique ingredient to each loaf. On Thursday, differences in ingredients may well account for more of the difference in flavor than do any relatively small differences in baking temperature.

With this analogy in mind, let's return to the world of living things and the example of melanin production. Any *individual's* skin color is always the result of how her genes interacted with her environment. In thinking about her skin color it makes no sense, indeed it is impossible, to pull apart the effects of genes and environment. But if, instead, we ask about skin color *differences within some group of people*, then either genes or environment may account for a larger proportion of those differences.

To parallel the Monday bread scenario, let's first consider a group of Northern Europeans, say Norwegians, and let's suppose that each of them has just returned from some exotic vacation. Some have been to Iceland, some to Alaska, and some have been to tropical places like Hawaii and Tahiti. This group of people do not differ very much in their genes because they all come from one population, but they differ considerably in their recent environments—most particularly in their recent uv_b exposure. As a consequence, most of the differences in melanin synthesis among these vacationing Norwegians will be the result of their experience, not genes.

Next, to parallel the Thursday example, let's take a sample of United Nations representatives stationed at the headquarters in New York. These people come from all over the world, from areas where the average levels of uv_b exposure differ greatly. As a result, they differ in the melanin synthesis genes they carry (see Box 3–2). But currently they all are spending most of their time in the same environment, New York City. Thus among this group of UN representatives, genetic differences will undoubtedly account for more of the variation in melanin synthesis than does their recent experience.

To summarize, psychologists sometimes feel it is useful to decide whether phenotypic differences between individuals are caused more by their genetic differences or more by their unique experiences. In fact, this question defines the area of psychology known as behavior genetics, which you will meet in Chapter 9. Questions about why individuals differ are reasonable and meaningful nature-nurture questions, as long as we remember what they do, and what they do not, tell us. First, the relative contributions of genes and environment in causing differences among individuals are irrelevant to explaining the causes of the trait in any one person. For example, the measured influence of genes and environment on the social behavior of Chicago first-graders tells us nothing about why Johnny is autistic. Any single individual's phenotype is always the result of an irreducible interaction between his genes and his environment.

Second, the conclusions that we draw about the contributions of genes and environment depend greatly on the sample of people we chose to study. A group of genetically similar individuals will cause us to overestimate the environmental contribution. A group of genetically diverse individuals will lead to an underestimate of environmental influences.

NOVEL ENVIRONMENTS OFTEN CAUSE MALADAPTIVE CHANGES IN THE PHENOTYPE

We have regularly used the word "response" in talking about how genes cause the phenotype to adjust to environmental change. Thus we suggested that suntanning is an adaptive response to increases in solar radiation. But some environmentally induced changes in the phenotype are clearly not adaptive. For example sunburning is not an adaptive response. In fact it is precisely the opposite: it represents a failure to respond adequately. Sudden and large increases in the amount of solar radiation overwhelm the body's suntanning response and the result is a maladaptive change, the skin destruction of sunburn. We will use the term *susceptibility* to refer to such maladaptive failures of response.

It may seem puzzling that natural selection has not been able to design better response patterns. Why are our response patterns sometimes overwhelmed; why do things like sunburning ever happen? Of course we saw in Chapter 2 that we should not always expect natural selection to design perfect adaptations, because selection cannot create new variants; it can only spread the favorable ones that arise by chance. But more importantly, selection cannot create adaptations to very rare or nonexistent environments. Selection preserves traits that address real-world challenges; if the challenge doesn't exist natural selection can't design an adaptation to meet it.

Think about how we get sunburned. Sunburning typically occurs in the context of an abrupt increase in our exposure to solar radiation. For example, after months of indoor activity we take a summer vacation at the beach, crowding lots of sun and surf into the few available days. The suntanning response is too slow to cope with such a dramatic environmental change. This is not because facultative traits are always slow to respond; some are quite rapid. To understand any facultative response we need to look to the past, when it was designed. Clearly, our ancestors rarely if ever faced sudden and dramatic changes in their exposure to solar radiation. Living all of their lives out of doors, with only the shade of trees or rocks, they would have experienced quite gradual seasonal shifts in uv_b exposure. Hence selection built a facultative response pattern that was geared to such gradual change. Our modern lifestyles can thus overwhelm the designed facultative response.

Trail Marker: Adaptations often fail in novel environments.

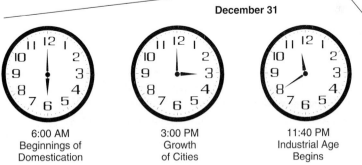

December 31				
6:00 AM		3:00 PM		11:40 PM
Beginnings of		Growth		Industrial Age
Domestication		of Cities		Begins

Figure 4–3. *The time line of human evolution compressed into one year.* The lineage leading to humans separated from the lineage leading to chimpanzees at least 5 million years ago. To help you think about this long time span, the 5 million years of human evolution has been compressed into a single year, with the human line beginning on January 1st. On that time scale, our ancestors lived exclusively by hunting and gathering wild resources for almost the entire year, until dawn on December 31st! Then, in the morning light of the last day of the year, people began to domesticate plants and animals. By afternoon some substantial cites had sprung up. Still, all work was performed by human and animal muscle until 20 minutes before midnight, when the industrial age began.

This is the general key to understanding susceptibilities. Facultative adaptations will often fail to produce an adaptive response if the environment is evolutionarily novel. And many aspects of contemporary life are evolutionarily novel. Permanent settlements, large populations, fixed work schedules, artificial lighting, rapid travel, occupational specialization, and industrial pollutants all present environmental challenges that are very recent in terms of the five to seven million years of human evolution. (See Figure 4–3 for an analogy to help you think about this time scale.) For this reason, we should expect humans to show both kinds of environmentally induced phenotypic change: adaptive facultative responses to the kinds of environmental challenges faced by our ancestors, and nonadaptive susceptibilities to relatively novel environmental conditions.

ANCESTRAL ENVIRONMENTS: THE ENVIRONMENT OF EVOLUTIONARY ADAPTEDNESS

Roughly seven million years ago, the hominid line—the evolutionary line that leads to people—diverged from the line that leads to chimpanzees. Until about ten thousand years ago, the way of life of our protohuman ancestors had much in common with that of contemporary chimpanzees. And it undoubtedly had even more in common with what we can discover about the lives of contemporary, and sadly, vanishing hunter-gatherers such as the *San* of the Kalahari Dessert and the *Ache* of the South American rain forest.

What happened ten thousand years ago was that anatomically modern peoples began to domesticate plants and animals via artificial selection. But for the 99 percent of hominid evolution that came before domestication, our ancestors had no alternative but to wrest their existence—food, shelter, clothing, medicine, and whatever else they needed to survive and reproduce—from nature. Thus, for the vast majority of human evolution, our ancestors were just like all other wild animals in that they had to secure their own well-being by harvesting what naturally occurred in their environments. Evolutionary psychologists refer to this period when all humans were hunters and gatherers of wild resources as the *environment of evolutionary adaptedness* or *EEA* (Tooby and DeVore, 1987). The EEA was the environment in which humankind evolved. Many of our adaptations are not so much designed to meet today's challenges as they are designed to solve the unique problems that confronted our ancestors in the EEA.

> **Trail Marker:** Many of our adaptations are geared more to life in the EEA than to life in the present.

The EEA reigned over human evolution for a very long time. This is where, and when, human nature (see Chapter 1) was forged. Thus, defining the EEA defines the circumstances the human psyche was designed to confront. So it is important to specify as much as we can about the EEA and the selection pressures that would have been operating in it. Unfortunately, some of what we can say about the EEA is speculative. We have no documentary footage from those days. But the fossil record, information from field studies of contemporary apes, and the ethnographic record of modern hunter-gatherers all agree in suggesting a basic outline.

Hominid life was unforgiving. Death from starvation was never more than a few weeks away. Food was generally scarce and full of danger; the plants and animals on which our ancestors depended had evolved chemical, mechanical and behavioral defenses to protect their own reproductive interests. It was impossible to store any significant quantity of food except as hard-earned and meager body fat deposits. Continued survival and the survival of dependent young required unfailing success in finding and acquiring food.

Individuals of all ages were subject to predators and to the debilitating and sometimes fatal effects of parasites and infection. All these selective forces took an even heavier toll on infants than adults. Mothers probably breast-fed their offspring for five years. Owing to the scarcity of resources, females did not ovulate, and therefore did not become pregnant again, until their previous offspring was either weaned or lost to some selective agent. Thus, for hundreds of thousands of years, the human population of the planet grew very slowly, simply because of the difficulties of finding enough food to survive and reproduce, and because of the fact that humans themselves were food for more powerful predators. Because of all these perils, a fifty-year-old individual would have been cause for marvel among our ancestors.

From the beginning, our ancestors probably were social. By this we mean that, like most primate species but unlike most mammals, hominids regularly associated with other members of their species. Their social groups were fairly small (by modern standards), consisting of fewer than one hundred individuals, and were semiclosed. As a result, hominids typically interacted with a limited set of associates whom they knew as distinct individuals. Perhaps once or twice in a lifetime, individuals successfully transferred from one social group to another. Analogy with our nearest relatives, the African great apes, suggests that it may have been females who made these transfers (Wrangham, 1987).

Within hominid groups, social interactions were complex. Members of the social group were potentially valuable allies whose favor was worth cultivating for the benefits they could provide in times of shortage or illness or when cooperative activities (e.g., stampeding prey towards a concealed partner) could increase foraging yields. But as constant companions, other members of the group were also often significant competitors for important resources like food and mates. Gaining and keeping reliable allies without forfeiting too many key resources must have presented a constantly shifting set of social challenges.

John Tooby has characterized our ancestors' existence as a lifelong camping trip. He's right, but it's not motoring over to the nearby state park for a relaxing weekend. Imagine going camping on the African savanna where lions, leopards, cheetahs, hyenas, wild dogs, and other predators are still common. As to your provisions: sorry, no high-tech gear. No sleeping bags, tents, cookstoves, pots, knives, antibiotics, or water-purification systems; no clothing either, and no transport but your naked feet. You can't bring any food and you won't be able to swing by the local 7-Eleven to reprovision. And you don't go home on Sunday afternoon. This is for life. Now you're getting the picture: camping, stone-age style.

This world of hostile predators, abundant parasites, scarce and antagonistic food resources, small social groups, and companions whose good will had to be constantly cultivated was the environment in which our ancestors, those few who became ancestors, flourished. The genes that allowed them to flourish are the genes they have passed down to the present and that lie at the root of many of our psychological adaptations. To put it plainly, our psychological adaptations are those of pleistocene hunter-gatherers. It's not surprising that these very same adaptations sometimes produce maladaptive responses in the modern world.

SUMMARY

1. Altruism poses an evolutionary problem because genes for altruistic behavior lower the fitness of their carrier.
2. Benefit to the group as a whole is unlikely to cause the spread of altruism because such indiscriminate altruism too often benefits the competing, nonaltruistic allele.
3. Kin selection, whereby altruism is systematically aimed at other carriers of the same altruistic allele, can explain altruism and is consistent with a large literature on animal behavior.
4. Kin selection theory predicts altruism when Hamilton's Rule, $rb > c$, is satisfied, and predicts altruism among blood relatives
5. Reciprocity, whereby altruists bestow benefits only on other altruists, can also explain altruism.
6. Game theory, in particular the game of Prisoners' Dilemma, provides a formal model of reciprocity.
7. The reciprocal strategy of tit-for-tat is a very successful strategy in iterated Prisoners' Dilemma.
8. Suntanning provides a simple and uncontroversial example of a facultative trait, and possible effects of observing violence represent a behavioral example.
9. Within any single individual, the causes of evolved traits cannot be assigned to genes or environments, thus the nature-nurture (genes-environment) dichotomy is unproductive and misleading.
10. Instead we need to describe norms of reaction, and explain why they take the specific forms they do.
11. Designed phenotypic responses to environmental variation are the result of facultative adaptations.
12. Unlike the traits of individuals, differences between individuals can be appropriately assigned to separate genetic and environmental influences.
13. Nonadaptive changes represent susceptibilities, not adaptations, and are most likely to occur in evolutionarily novel environments.
14. The Environment of Evolutionary Adaptedness or EEA defines the selection pressures that shaped many uniquely human psychological adaptations.

5 ◆ Sensation and Perception

No one with the slightest knowledge of cameras who takes a good look at the anatomy of the vertebrate eye needs to wonder what its purpose is. It is obviously designed to gather light and focus it on the back surface of the eyeball. The eye is for seeing. In fact, the eye is the "poster child" for evolution of organs by natural selection. As we already discussed in Chapter 2, the variety of eyes found in the animal kingdom give us considerable insight into how the eye evolved. For this reason scientists who study sensation and perception have long been convinced that the senses are the products of evolution. They have not always, however, considered the implications of this fact for perception.

PERCEPTION IS FOR ACTION

If the purpose of the eye is seeing, what is the purpose of seeing? The obvious answer to many is *knowing*; in fact many of the early students of perception were motivated by the philosophical question of how we can gain knowledge about the world. Even today many people, including writers of textbooks on perception, assume that the purpose of perception is knowledge. Jerry Fodor (1983, p. 40), for example, says "what the perceptual system must do is to so represent the world as to make it accessible to thought. . . . The normal consequence of a perceptual transaction is the acquisition of a perceptual belief." Although it is certainly true that we gain a great deal of knowledge through the senses, that view misses the point. The main purpose of perception is not mere knowledge, but to guide *action*.

Consider our perception of visual space. For years psychologists have studied how people estimate how far away they are from objects. From these experiments it seems that we are not particularly good at judging distance. When subjects were asked instead to look at an object, close their eyes and walk up to it, they do quite well (Loomis et al., 1992). An evolutionary psychologist would conclude that perception is for moving around in space, not for judging distances.

Another example is given by how we avoid bumping into things. A great variety of animals from fiddler crabs to humans respond to a rapidly expanding visual image by withdrawing from it. Now, collision avoidance is a very important ability—for people walking around a savanna or driving a car. We could accomplish this by judging our distance from the object, our speed of approach, and then use that information to calculate the time to collision. It turns out we use different information: the rate of expansion of the visual image. Consider what happens as we approach an object on a collision course and at a steady speed: The image that the object projects onto our retina grows larger. However, it grows at a rapidly *increasing* rate as we get nearer, even when our speed stays constant (see Figure 5–1). At first it grows slowly, but as we are about to collide, the image virtually explodes on our retina. Strong evidence suggest that we use the rate of expansion to avoid colliding with objects. Drivers who are pulling up behind a car stopped at a traffic light and pilots landing helicopters maintain a *constant* rate of expansion of the image until the moment they stop (Proffit & Kaiser, 1995). This simple rule causes them to stop short of the object. (Although in principle this rule would cause one to slow down forever without stopping, in practice we reach a speed so slow we simply stop.)

You may have watched pelicans fishing. They fly around over the water until they spot a fish below them, then dive swiftly toward the water. A split second before they hit the water, just when it appears they will crash, they fold their wings and neatly enter the water. Research shows that the birds use rate of expansion to judge their maneuver, not speed and distance (Sekuler & Blake, 1994). Similar

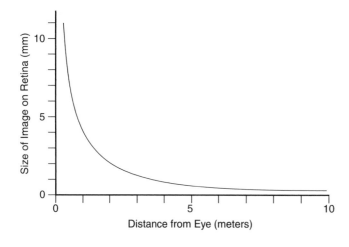

Figure 5–1. *Looming.* A given object will produce a larger image on the retina the closer it comes. For an object approaching at a constant speed, the rate at which the image grows increases markedly as the object approaches the eye.

but less spectacular feats are accomplished every time a bird lands on a branch. All of these demonstrate that perception evolved in the service of action, not knowledge.

THE ECONOMICS OF ORGANS

Whoever said there is no free lunch could have had the organs of the body in mind. Poets might claim that we have been given eyes so we can behold the beauty of the world, ears to enjoy music, noses to smell flowers, and so forth. The fact is that natural selection requires every organ in the body to pay its own way by increasing our fitness.

Building and Maintaining Organs Is Metabolically Expensive

Every organ of the body costs valuable energy to build and maintain—energy that cannot be spent growing bigger, finding a mate, tending one's offspring, or escaping a predator. Since our senses are magnificent examples of biological engineering, they must provide correspondingly valuable increases in our ability to reproduce. Consider that more than half the brain is devoted to processing sensory information, and that the brain consumes roughly 25 percent of our metabolic resources, and you will begin to understand how metabolically expensive perception is. So the purpose of perception cannot be just to gain knowledge of the world for its own sake; perception has to help us behave in ways that increase our fitness.

The economic principle that organs must provide fitness benefits to justify their costs is vividly illustrated by looking at other animals. Sessile animals (those that do not move) such as sponges lack eyes. It would make no sense to spend metabolic energy on eyes when there is nothing to be gained by seeing trouble coming. Some nematodes (round worms) have eyes in the free-swimming larval stage, but lose them as parasitic adults. With at least one animal the possession of eyes differs between the sexes: The winged male insect *Stylops* has eyes, but the parasitic female is sightless. Sir Stewart Duke-Elder (1958) says:

> It is essentially from the primitive motor response to light that vision almost certainly developed. In natural circumstances these tropisms and taxes are invariably of biological utility, and it would appear that *the essential and primary function of vision was the control of movement in order to attain an optimum environment as efficiently as possible*, a function which is eventually employed for the avoidance of obstacles, the pursuit of prey and flight from enemies. . . . It follows that the visual organs are found almost solely in actively moving animals." (p. 105, emphasis in the original)

In summary, the principle that organs are costly requires that sense organs have control of action as their first priority.

WHAT ARE THE SENSES FOR? WHAT WE ARE GOOD AT

We are really good at walking without either falling over, tripping, or bumping into things; at recognizing faces; at deciding what is good to eat; at chewing and swallowing food without biting our tongue or choking; extracting messages from complex strings of vocal sounds; and finding our way home. This is a partial list, but it illustrates that what we are good at is really important. People who can't do these things don't get to become anyone's ancestor.

Many of the things we have listed as what humans are good at no doubt seem rather unsurprising to you. We take these perceptual abilities for granted until we have trouble doing one of them. In addition, scientists discovered how much of an accomplishment perception is when they began to design robots to do tasks that requires sensory input.

There is a sturdy rumor that computer scientist Marvin Minsky once suggested to a graduate student that he "solve vision" as a summer project. Decades later, vision has still not been solved. It has proven extremely difficult to design a computer that can visually recognize objects and deal with them as well as does an insect that has only a few neurons in its brain. Yet, by virtue of millions of years of evolution, our eyes permit a major league batter to hit a ninety mile-per-hour fast ball four-tenths of a second after it leaves the pitcher's hand, and an outfielder to run one hundred feet to arrive under the ball and catch it within the five seconds it takes to travel 375 feet.

PERCEPTION IS A MIRROR OF THE WORLD

Look at Figure 5–2. It looks like a surface with a few large dents and three rows of small bumps. Now turn the book upside down and see what it looks like. (Go ahead!) When you turned the book upside down, the dents became bumps, and vice versa. This effect is compelling. (You missed a good one if you didn't follow our request!) In fact, the picture is a close-up of a water tank with some large dents and rows of rivets that stick up from the surface. When we look at the picture in its proper orientation we perceive it as it is.

Most of the time perception is *veridical;* that is, it leads to behave appropriately in the world. (The word *veridical* means truthful, or not illusory.) Indeed, perception could hardly be otherwise. An organism whose eyes led it to mistake a big round rock for a safe, hollow cave would be at a serious disadvantage in escaping from a predator. Those rare occasions when our eyes fool us cause us to scratch our heads and wonder how perception works. In fact, many perceptual phenomena became noticed, studied, and thereby understood only because of those rare instances when our eyes play tricks on us. So the study of perceptual illusions is serious science.

Why is our perception of the water tank veridical when the picture is in its proper orientation, and illusory when it is upside down? Notice that the dents are darker on top and lighter on the bottom. The bumps are just the reverse: lighter on top. Now turn the book around again (Do it this time!) and notice the patterns

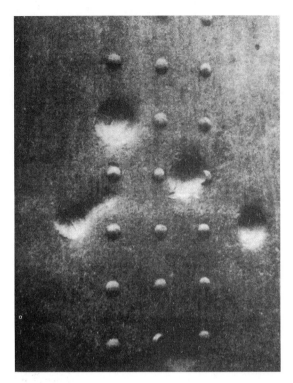

Figure 5–2. *Dents and bumps.* The shading determines whether we see dents or bumps. Compare the appearance of the features when the picture is viewed right side up and upside down. (From *Sensation and Perception* by H.R. Schiffman © 1996. Reprinted by permission of John Wiley & Sons, Inc.)

of light and dark. The things that looked like dents, and that now look like bumps, are lighter on top—just like the (real) bumps did before. Now we have isolated a rule that explains the appearance of dents and bumps: Bumps are lighter on top and darker on the bottom; dents are just the reverse.

This rule makes use of a regularity of the natural world. Light normally comes from above because the sun is in the sky. Under normal conditions more light will strike the top of a convex object (bump, ball, or head) than the bottom of it. In contrast, more light would strike the lower portion of concave objects (dents, hollow gourds, or cupped hands). We have evolved a mechanism that mirrors this rule: If something is lighter on top, it is convex; if it is darker on top, it is concave. This rule works almost all the time. The rare occasions when it doesn't work involve light coming from below—unusual circumstances before the invention of fire—and camouflage, a form of deception. Hence the creepy effect of holding a flashlight under your face to spice up a ghost story told around a campfire.

Depth Perception as a Mirror of the World

Perception in general is a remarkable achievement. But depth perception is especially interesting, considering that we see in three dimensions when the information on the retina is only two dimensional. (Even though the retina is curved, it is equivalent in all essentials to the flat film in a camera.) In this section, we will consider the ability to perceive depth monocularly (with only one eye). You may be aware that having two eyes contributes to depth perception. But depth perception is excellent even with only one eye, a point borne out by the fact that there have been major league baseball and football players who were blind in one eye.

What are the monocular cues to depth? Perception books list over a half dozen cues to depth. Each cue is based on a regularity of the physical world that the brain uses to tell depth. We have already discussed one: shading. Another important one is linear perspective: Parallel lines converge to a point on the horizon. See Figure 5–3. Many people who take art classes find it very hard to draw objects in linear perspective, even though they use the cues effortlessly to see every day. In fact, it took artists many centuries to figure out how to do this. It was not until 1435 that Leon Batista Alberti described the procedure illustrated in Figure 5–3 (Goldstein, 1999). In the method called Alberti's window, the artist stands still in front of a pane of glass and draws right on the glass exactly what he or she sees behind it. The disconnect between our ability to see in depth and to draw it on paper illustrates our earlier point that perception is for action, not knowledge—in this case knowledge of the rules of geometry.

Figure 5–3. *Alberti's window.* An artist can recreate the scene outside the window by tracing the scene on the window (while keeping his or her eye in a fixed position) and copying it to the canvas. Picture illustrates the pictorial depth cue of convergence.

Sensory Ecology

This section is an extension of the previous one. There we argued that visual perception takes advantage of regularities in the world. Here we will extend that discussion to all the senses, each of which is adapted to take advantage of some physical energy in the environment. What physical energies are there in the world that animals can use to find food and mates and avoid predators? Consideration of the sources of energy available to the major senses helps us understand what they were designed to do.

Vision. What we know as light is a small part of the electromagnetic spectrum. See Figure 5–4. Because electromagnetic energy travels extremely fast (at the speed of light!), and in a straight line, it can provide information about the geometric properties of objects—it permits us to see shapes. And because air allows light to pass without scattering it very much, it can carry information over great distances, much farther than sound, for example. Vision is one of the distance senses.

There is an abundance of light in the world, thanks to the sun. Although there is no reason in principle why our eyes couldn't have evolved to sense other portions of the electromagnetic spectrum, there are some practical reasons why they didn't. The sun provides plenty of energy in the visible range. Because wavelengths shorter than visible light (ultraviolet, x rays and gamma rays) tend to be filtered by the atmosphere, not very much reaches the ground. In addition, wavelengths either shorter or longer than the visible spectrum tend to pass through objects rather than bounce off them, and so would not provide as much information about them to our eye as visible light does.

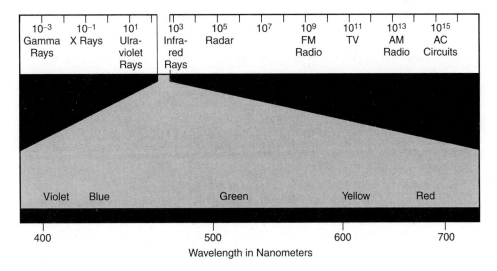

Figure 5–4. *Electromagnetic spectrum.* The visible wavelengths are a small part of the electromagnetic spectrum.

Figure 5–5. *Picture of a forest.* The absence of color in this photo makes it harder to identify individual trees, and to see depth.

The visible portion of the electromagnetic spectrum given off by the sun contains a range of wavelengths that are differentially reflected by various objects, giving us a way of identifying objects by their color. Color gives us a reliable way of distinguishing ripe from unripe fruit, for example. Color also makes it easier to recognize objects in general. If you compare a black and white photo with a color picture of a forest scene you will see how much easier it is to tell individual trees apart in the color picture (see Figure 5–5).

Hearing. Many objects produce vibrations that carry through air, water, or even solids. Sound has the advantage over light in that it is useful in the dark and goes around corners. Recall the many and varied sounds of the woods at night on a camping trip and you will begin to appreciate how useful ears can be in hunting prey and avoiding predators. Although sound waves weaken rapidly with distance from the source and interact with objects in complex ways, causing echoes for example, this complexity becomes a source of information about distance and space. Because low frequencies travel farther than high tones, we can judge our distance from a sound source by pitch. You may have listened to a marching band approach from a distance. When it was far away you could only hear the low instruments such as the bass drums and tubas. As the band came near you heard the high instruments such as the flutes and piccolos. Loudness, pitch, and echoes allow us to judge how near we are to a friend or foe in the dark.

Physical principles shape the capacities of all the senses. Nowhere is this more apparent than with sound. Large animals generally are capable of making lower pitch sounds, for the much the same reason that a tuba makes low tones, and a trumpet makes high tones. Thus elephants produce frequencies that are lower than humans can hear, known to us as infrasound. These sounds travel over great distances, permitting elephants to communicate with each other over many miles. Tiny insects, on the other hand, are capable of producing only high frequencies, which do not travel very far. Thus when insects need to communicate over long distances—for example, to attract a mate—they use chemical signals.

Whereas the production of sound is limited by physical principles, the reception of sound is an adaptation; that is, the range of frequencies an animal can hear is expected to be a consequence of selection. The perception of infrasound by elephants is an adaptation to the great distances over which they travel, and thus need to communicate. But the homing pigeon, a small animal, also responds to infrasound, produced, not by other pigeons, but by such natural phenomena as thunderstorms, jet streams, and wind blowing through mountain ranges thousands of kilometers away. It is believed that homing pigeons use infrasound to navigate (Kreithen & Quine, 1979). Most really small animals don't respond to low frequencies because they couldn't do much about getting out of the way of a big animal such as an elephant stomping toward them. The very tiniest insects (which don't fly) do not have any ears at all because they could not crawl away from anything that is big enough to make a sound (see Figure 5–6).

The Chemical Senses. The air we breathe contains chemicals given off by many objects of interest to us: other people, predators, prey, edible and inedible plants, and so forth. Aquatic animals are similarly bathed by a chemical soup. Organisms as simple as single-celled bacteria approach sources of food and avoid harmful chemicals. In addition, the foods we put in our mouths contain chemicals that help us identify them. Chemical sensitivity is undoubtedly the most important of all sensory abilities and must have been the first to evolve, because it is seen in every animal, even those that lack vision and hearing.

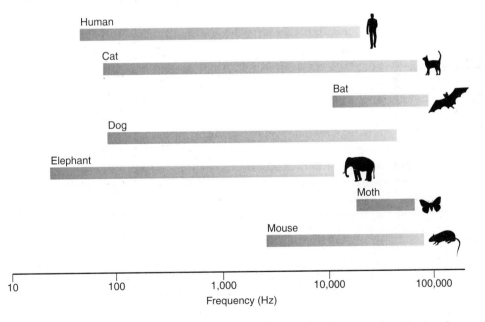

Figure 5–6. *The audible range of frequencies for various animals.* Note that larger animals tend to hear lower frequencies, and smaller animals hear higher ones. (Derived from "Audition in Spring Species of Arctiid Moths as a Possible Response to Differential Levels of Insectivorous Bat Predation" by J. H. Fullard and R. M. R. Barclay in *Canadian Journal of Zoology,* 58, pp. 1745–1750 and "Hearing in Mammals: The Least Weasel" by R. S. Heffner and H. E. Heffner in *Journal of Mammalogy,* 66, pp. 745–755.)

The two main chemical senses are smell and taste. Smell is both a distance sense, as when we catch a whiff of a nearby pig farm, and a contact sense, as when we taste an apple. Without the sense of smell, an apple tastes exactly like a potato, as you may have discovered when you had a cold that caused foods to "taste" bland. Actually, colds cause a loss of smell by blocking the odors of food from reaching your nose via the back of your mouth. It is the nose that permits us to "taste" many foods.

Smell is vital to the mating behavior of many animals. Many animals give off chemical messengers known as *pheromones* that govern sexual behavior. The pheromones of the female cabbage moth attract males over many miles. Pheromones are important in the sexual behavior of many mammals, as many a cat or dog owner knows well. Evidence is rapidly accumulating that humans also communicate with pheromones (e.g., Grammar, 1997; Stern & McClintock, 1998; Weller, 1998; Weller, & Weller, 1997).

It is often said that human smell is a vestigial sense—a leftover from the evolutionary past. This is far from the case. It is true that we are about a hundred times less sensitive to odor than a dog is. But we still can detect certain chemicals in the range of one part of chemical per 10 billion of air. This is less than one drop of chemical dispersed throughout an entire house. And if you think odor is not important to us, consider the amount of money spent on deodorants and perfumes. Think of how unpleasant it is to be near someone with a serious hygiene problem. Only people who live in middle-class western societies, bathe regularly and get their food from supermarkets can afford to think smell is unimportant. Although this question has been given relatively little attention, it is clear that odors produced by humans play an important role in social interaction (Levine & McBurney, 1986). Recent work shows that women judge the body odor of more symmetrical males to be more attractive than that of less symmetrical men (Thornhill & Gangestad, 1999a). (Symmetrical males are also judged more visually attractive.) We discuss the evolutionary significance of symmetry in Chapter 10.

Although smell is partly a distance sense and partly a contact sense, taste is entirely a contact sense. We must bring something into our mouths or lick it in order to taste it. Another difference between taste and smell is the number of qualities of sensation we experience. The different types of smells defy counting, let alone organization into a small number of categories, despite many years of effort. Taste, on the other hand, can be described by the four names: salty, sweet, sour, and bitter. Each of these taste qualities corresponds to an important environmental stimulus.

For many animals, salt is both a scarce commodity and essential to life. This was true for humans in the EEA, but today salt is both cheap and widely available. In fact there is far more salt in prepared food than is either necessary or good for us (see Chapter 13.) Many animals, including humans, show a finely tuned specific hunger for salt. For other animals, the main problem is avoiding too much salt, which is lethal at high concentrations. In either case, it is important to be able to detect salt. The sweet taste signals sugar, which is a reliable indicator of high-energy foods such as ripe fruit. Sour is caused by acids, which are corrosive to living tissue and also indicate bacterial action, which renders food unfit for consumption. Finally, many bitter substances are biologically active plant products. In the interests of not being eaten, plants have evolved an amazing array of chemicals that are toxic to their would-be consumers. Many of them in low concentrations function as medicines for humans. Animals, for their part, have evolved the ability to taste these chemicals, and thus are able to avoid them. Humans find these same compounds bitter and for the most part unpleasant. Although we don't know what animals experience when they taste things that are bitter to us, their behavior is consistent with ours.

Other Senses. The notion that there are five senses—vision, hearing, taste, smell, and touch—is only a convenient fiction. Touch alone may be thought of as consisting of many senses: warmth, cold, light touch, pressure, itch, tickle, pain, and so forth. Each of these can be seen as a way of coping with environmental challenges. Warmth and cold represent the response to the problem of maintaining body temperature within the narrow limits that permit life. Many animals must move from place to place carefully throughout the day—out of the broiling midday sun into the shade to keep from overheating, only to crawl back to the sun the next morning to warm up.

Even tickle can be seen as an adaptation. Anyone who has ever touched the long hairs inside a cat's ears knows that the cat finds this annoying. A sleeping cat will twitch its ear in response to each touch of these particular hairs, ignoring similar stimulation of hairs on other parts of the body. Continued touching of these hairs will eventually wake up the cat, which will shake its head irritably and walk off somewhere else to continue its nap. This response is an adaptation that makes it difficult for any organism that might try to take up residence in this inviting location. If you lightly touch the inside of your ear with a hair (no sharp objects, please!) you will find the experience to be unpleasant compared to similar contact with other parts of your skin. The general matter of pain is important enough to give its own section, below.

The Blessing of Pain

Every day millions of people take medication to alleviate common aches and pains; clinics in every major hospital serve patients who live with chronic pain, sometimes with no apparent cause. Everyone has wished that a pain would go away so that he or she could enjoy life. Theologians have written books with titles such as *The Problem of Pain*. Wouldn't life be better without it?

If you are tempted to say yes, consider the case of F. C., a young woman who was born without any sensitivity to pain (Baxter and Olszewsi, 1960). Her parents noticed that as a baby she would bang her head on the floor during temper tantrums until she raised bruises. When she was three years old, she caused third-degree burns on her leg by kneeling on a hot radiator while watching other children play outside the window. She bit her tongue so often that it became deformed, and eventually she bit the end off. She did not experience toothache, headache, or nausea.

Because her father was a physician, her condition received early attention. Careful investigation revealed that she had above average intelligence and her other senses were normal. Nevertheless she did not experience pain when her hand was placed in ice water, something that normal people find exquisitely painful. Nor was she fazed by heat sufficient to raise blisters, or by needles stuck into her flesh, among other things.

Cuts, bruises, and sunburn were not her most serious problem. At age seventeen she complained that she had "loose particles around her left knee that bothered her and she wanted them removed." (Baxter and Olszewsi, 1960, p. 384) These and other joint problems arose because she did not feel discomfort while standing in one position or lying still in bed. Because she failed to make the normal postural adjustments that prevent tissue damage, her joints deteriorated, the same way failure to roll over in bed can cause the skin lesions known as bed sores. Eventually the breakdown in her hip joints led to a massive infection that took her life at age twenty-nine. Curiously she complained of pain at the end, which was relieved by medication. A careful autopsy found no evidence of anatomical abnormality. The cause of her total congenital insensitivity to pain remains a mystery.

Although quite rare, the case of F. C. is not unique. There are a number of other documented cases of congenital insensitivity to pain. Lack of pain can also result from injury to a nerve and from disease, as in Hansen's disease (leprosy).

Cases like that of F. C. demonstrate vividly that pain is on balance a blessing, not a curse. It is an evolved mechanism that prevents us from damaging our bodies by our actions or inaction. Pain also demonstrates the point that natural selection does not have our happiness as a goal, only our survival and reproduction.

> **Trail Marker:** Evolution does not have our happiness as a goal, only our reproductive success.

Any mechanism that helps us survive and reproduce will be selected for, even the mechanism of pain, which causes so much suffering to so many. Looked at this way, pain can be seen as a vital part of a motivational system that is essential to our reproductive success. To be sure there are many sensations, as well as thoughts and actions, that cause us pleasure, not pain. Because natural selection has built us so that we seek them out, these behaviors must increase our fitness. We will consider other examples of both pleasant and unpleasant feelings in Chapter 12.

SENSORY ADAPTATION IS AN EVOLUTIONARY ADAPTATION

When we step into a bathtub that is just a little too hot we feel uncomfortably warm at first, but the sensation decreases with time. We smell the bacon, eggs, and coffee when we come downstairs in the morning for breakfast (if we are lucky enough to have someone else cooking for us!), but the sensation decreases over the next minute to the point that we no longer notice the smells. There are many examples of this phenomenon of *sensory adaptation,* because it occurs in all the senses. The loss of sensation to a steady stimulus is so impressive that most books imply that this is all there is to sensory adaptation. There is actually much more. Many books point out that sensory adaptation permits us to ignore stimuli that are not informative—stimuli that don't change don't provide any new information to help us cope with the environment. That is all well and good. But what these books do not point out is that sensory adaptation not only allows us to ignore unchanging stimuli, it makes us *more sensitive* to changes that do occur.

The reduction in response to steady stimuli is only part of the sensory adaptation picture. There are a number of related phenomena that fall under the heading of sensory adaptation. They are all consequences of the fact that the sensory systems are biological mechanisms that do not follow the stimulus perfectly over time (McBurney et al., 1997).

What are some of these other effects of adaptation? The most important may be *range shifting*, which permits us to adjust our sensitivity over a tremendous range of stimulus intensities that we experience at different times (Shapley, & Enroth-Cugell, 1984). You have no doubt had occasion to go into a darkened building such as a movie theater from the bright sunlight. At first you were unable to see, and stumbled to your seat in what seemed like near-total darkness. After a while your eyes adjusted to the darkness and you could see clearly the people who stumbled over your feet as they found their seats. Then when you went outside after the movie, you were temporarily blinded by the daylight. After a few moments, you could see normally once again. What you experienced during your change from daylight to dim light and back again was range shifting (see Figure 5–7).

At any one time we are able to deal with a range of intensities of about 100 to 1. Lights outside this range will either be too dazzling or quite invisible. Our limitation in range of intensities that we can deal with at a given time works fine as long as the light doesn't change too much, because most real-world scenes contain differences in light that vary over about the same 100-to-1 range of intensity. But

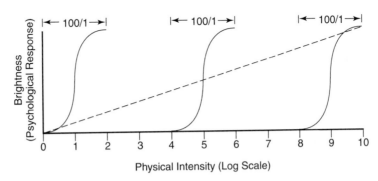

Figure 5–7. *Range shifting.* A major function of sensory adaptation is to permit a sensory system to adjust its sensitivity to ambient stimulus intensities. The eye must deal with light intensities that vary over a range of 10^{15} to 1 (1,000,000,000,000,000 to 1. 10^{10} to 1 is shown here.) Each S-shaped curve shows the response of the visual system when adapted to a particular intensity (0, 4, and 8 log units of light, respectively). This gives the visual system a much greater range of psychological response than would be the case without adaptation (dotted line).

the amount of light varies enormously from one scene or situation to another. For example, there is about a thousand times as much light inside a typical room as outdoors in moonlight. And there is about a thousand times as much light outdoors on a bright day as indoors. In fact, our eye must cope with variation in light intensities over a range of more than ten trillion to one! That is, the most intense light we experience is ten trillion times as intense as the weakest light we can see.

Range shifting helps us do that. You can think of range shifting as something like a magnifying glass that, at any one time, enlarges just a small portion of the entire visual field to increase your ability to see fine detail. A nonbiological example of range shifting is given by automatic gain control on video camcorders. You may have noticed the following: If you are using a camcorder indoors and then aim it out the window the picture briefly washes out until the camera adjusts to the increased light. The camcorder has an automatic gain control that accomplishes range shifting, much as our eye does.

Without range shifting our eye would be forced to try to spread its limited sensitivity evenly over the entire range of intensities at one time. The result of this would be that objects in the world that now look white and black to us would appear as barely discriminable shades of grey. Thus the same mechanism that causes a *decrease in response* to a stimulus intensity causes an *increase in sensitivity* to differences in intensities around that intensity. So sensory adaptation is much more than a decrease in response. It is also an *increase in responsiveness.*

Other consequences of sensory adaptation include an increase in response to certain *other* stimuli after adaptation. You have no doubt noticed after you stepped out of that initially too-hot bathtub that the air in the room felt cool, even though it felt fine when you stepped into the tub. (This is above and beyond any cooling caused by evaporation from your wet skin.) You may have noticed that a yellow patch of wall looked even more yellow after staring at a patch of blue material. You may have noticed that your orange juice tasted especially sour after a bite of sugary cereal. Sensory adaptation potentiates the response to certain other stimuli. So, once again, sensory adaptation is much more than a decrease in response, and it isn't even a decrease in *responsiveness*; it sometimes *increases* responsiveness to certain stimuli.

We see sensory adaptation as an evolutionary adaptation that improves our ability to cope with a highly variable sensory world. As such it is very similar in its effects to phenomena that are generally considered to be quite different, such as habituation and learning (McBurney et al., 1997). We see sensory adaptation as one of a number of biological adaptations that improve fitness.

COEVOLUTION AND THE SENSES

Selection pressures on an organism frequently come from other organisms. For example, some moths have evolved the ability to hear the ultrasonic cries of the bats that prey on them. When two or more species influence the course each other's evolution, we speak of *coevolution.* There are many examples of coevolution. It is proposed (Ridley, 1996) that prey species have gotten larger in response to pressures of predation, and the predators have gotten larger in turn. The brain sizes of both predators and prey have gotten larger in relation to body size as well. Because the predator and the prey each respond to the other's latest models, they enter into an *evolutionary arms race,* with each new adaptation of the one spurring further evolution of the other. We will see many examples of evolutionary arms races throughout this book.

> **Trail Marker:** Coevolution leads to evolutionary arms races, resulting in a spiral of adaptation and counter-adaptation.

In this chapter, we are interested in coevolution of the senses. We have already mentioned one of the most striking examples. Bats hunt at night using sonar to catch insects such as moths (Popper & Fay, 1995). This itself is an adaptation to the nocturnal nature of their prey. Their ability to navigate in total darkness using only their sonar is quite remarkable (see Figure 5–8). By interpreting the echos of their own ultrasonic cries, some kinds of bats are able to track and capture insects smaller than a mosquito (Roeder, 1965).

Predation by the bat causes selection pressure on the moth to evolve ways of sensing that a bat is closing in. Selection solved the problem in an obvious way. Closing bats are invariably using ultrasound to echolocate their prey; if moths could hear the bats' ultrasonic vocalizations they would be able to take evasive action. As you would expect from the principle of sensory economy, species of moths that are preyed on by bats have evolved the ability to hear the bat's sonar, but species of moths not subject to bat predation do not (Fullard, 1984).

Of course, to effectively evade the bat the moth must make the right move. The wrong one could land it right in the jaws it is trying to escape. Thus moths do not only sense the existence of a bat in the neighborhood. If the bat is far away, and the sonar pulse is therefore weak, the moth flies directly away from the bat. If the bat is close the moth has several options; it may fold its wings and drop passively, make a power dive, or go into a confusing set of loops and spirals. The moth flies upward if the bat is below it and down if the bat is above (Roeder, 1965). The coevolutionary arms race between the bat and moth has resulted in ever more sophisticated adaptations. Some

Figure 5–8. *Bat in flight.* The bat has evolved a sophisticated sonar system that allows it to fly without crashing and catch insects in total darkness.

moths even emit sonar. For a while, scientists thought that the moth might be trying to jam the bat's sonar, but recent evidence suggests that the moth's sonar serves as a warning to the bat that it is unpalatable (Popper & Fay, 1995).

The milky sap of the milkweed plant contains a number of chemicals that are both highly toxic to animals and extremely bitter (Brower, 1984). The Monarch butterfly, however, has evolved an immunity to the poisons in the milkweed sap. It lays its eggs on the milkweed plant, and the larvae (caterpillars) feed on the plant, ingesting the poison, which remains in the larvae's bodies when they pupate and then turn into butterflies. The poison is even present in the eggs that the butterfly lays, protecting the Monarch against predation at every stage of life.

Birds learn that the distinctive appearance of the adult Monarch butterfly means "Warning: I am poisonous!" A bluejay that tries to eat a Monarch butterfly will retch, vomit, wipe its bill and generally act as though the experience is extremely unpleasant.

Many poisonous creatures have evolved distinctive markings that serve as warnings to their would-be predators. The distinctive appearance of the Monarch not only warns off predators, but has permitted a nonpoisonous mimic butterfly (the Viceroy) to take advantage of the Monarch's poison by evolving to look much like the Monarch. So this example involves coevolution of four different species (actually groups of species—many birds avoid the Monarch): The milkweed evolved a chemical defense; the Monarch butterfly evolved the ability to withstand the poison as well as the sensory capacity to locate the milkweed plant and lay its eggs there; various birds evolved the chemical and visual senses to taste the poison and associate it with the appearance of the Monarch; and the Viceroy evolved to look like the Monarch.

THE MODULARITY OF PERCEPTION

The problems that the senses evolved to solve tend to be distinct: Is that fruit ripe? (color) Is that a predator? (form) Is it coming my way? (motion) For this reason, we should expect that perception would tend to operate via a number of specialized modules, rather than a single general purpose mechanism. Remember the analogy of anatomy and physiology. The need for respiration has given us the lungs, the requirements of digestion the stomach, and so forth. We tend to have specialized organs for specialized tasks. We would expect, then, that the brain would consist of a number of specialized "organs," corresponding to particular perceptual tasks. Considerable evidence exists for such modularity of perception (Fodor, 1983). As mentioned above, vision is specialized to detect certain kinds of energies and hearing specialized for others. But modularity is apparent even within each major sense.

Take vision as an example. The retina of the eye contains two distinctly different types of receptors: cones and rods. The cones permit us to see color, but their operation requires daylight (or daytime-light levels such as can be provided nowadays by artificial illumination). The rods function in low light (when there is less light than that provided by the full moon), but they are unable to sort out colors. For all practical purposes we have two different retinas, one for daylight, and one for night vision.

Some creatures that function only in the daytime, such as some birds, have only cones in their eyes. You may have noticed the flurry of activity as evening approaches and many birds return to their roosts. By dusk, these birds are totally blind. Farmers make use of this fact to catch a chicken for dinner, because the bird will sit there stupidly as the farmer picks it off the roost in the dim light, clearly visible to the farmer. In contrast, some nocturnal birds such as the great horned owl have mostly rods in their eyes (Fite, 1973) and so they have traded color vision for the ability to see better at night.

Another distinction in vision is between *focal vision* and *ambient vision*. Focal vision is the system we use to see objects, read, and so forth. Focal vision uses only the center of our visual field, but has the ability to see fine detail. Ambient vision is what we use to move around in the world. Ambient vision makes use of the entire visual field, especially the periphery. Ambient vision does not see fine detail, but is better at seeing motion. You can demonstrate ambient vision by having someone wave some small object around in the periphery of your field of view while you look straight ahead. You will be able to see movement easily but unable to tell what is moving.

The distinction between focal and ambient vision has great practical importance when it comes to night driving (Leibowitz et al., 1982). One reason there are so many nighttime accidents is that focal vision is seriously impaired at night; we don't see detail well at all in the dark. But our ambient vision is practically unaffected by low illumination. Because we use our ambient vision to steer and stay on the road, we drive much too fast for the conditions because our ambient vision leads us to be overconfident. Needless to say, we did not evolve to drive cars at night.

The processing of visual information by the brain also shows much evidence of modularity. For many years scientists have known that information from the eye goes to an area of the brain called the *striate cortex*.

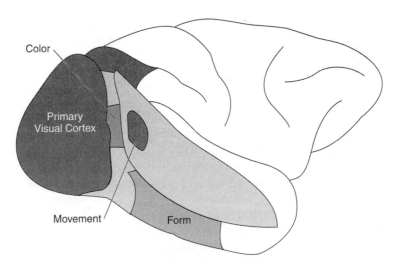

Figure 5–9. *Visual cortex of the monkey.* Each area is specialized for a particular visual function.

Neighboring locations of the retina project to neighboring locations in the striate cortex, yielding a kind of map of the retina on the visual cortex. Scientists have learned a great deal about how the striate cortex responds to visual input. Recently, however, scientists have discovered that many other parts of the cortex— more than half, in fact—respond to visual input. Why these extra areas? Surprisingly one of these other areas responds to *color*, one responds to *where* an object is, one responds to *what* the object is, another to *movement* (see Figure 5–9). Damage to these *extrastriatal visual areas* causes some surprising results.

Whereas damage to striatal cortex leaves a person blind, damage to one extrastriatal area leaves a person unable to recognize faces, the condition of *prosopagnosia*, previously mentioned in Chapter 2. Damage to another renders a person unable to perceive movement. Thus a patient with *motion agnosia* found that she:

> had difficulty . . . pouring tea or coffee into a cup because the fluid appeared to be frozen, like a glacier. In addition, she could not stop pouring at the right time since she was unable to perceive the movement in the cup . . . when the fluid rose. . . . In a room where more than two other people were walking she felt very insecure . . . because "people were suddenly here or there but I have not seen them moving." Zihl et al., 1983, quoted by Goldstein, 1999, p. 273)

These are only a few examples of many different modules that have been found in the visual cortex.

We will discuss one more example of modularity, this time from hearing. One of the most important uses of the auditory system is to perceive speech. Not surprisingly, many features of the auditory system appear to be adaptations for speech. The most important sound frequencies for speech are between 1,000 and 4,000 hertz (cycles per second). The auditory canal that carries sound from the pinna (the visible outer ear) to the eardrum (the place you were taught not to stick sharp objects into) is shaped like a tube. The physics of sound dictate that a tube will resonate to a particular frequency, selectively reinforcing that frequency. The resonant frequency of this canal is right in the middle of the speech frequencies, about 3,000 hertz. The human ear is selectively tuned to the speech frequencies. It is much less sensitive to higher or lower tones.

Some scientists believe that there are actually two distinct modes of hearing, one for speech, and the other for everything else (Liberman & Mattingly, 1989). This idea is still controversial, but considerable evidence supports it. For example when we listen to speech we are able to make finer distinctions in the timing of sounds than we can make when the sounds are clicks or tones, but not speech. One such distinction is called *voice onset time*. Voice onset time is the difference in time between when you start to make a sound with your voice and when you make a sound with your teeth and tongue. When you say "duh" you start to voice the "uh" sound before the consonant, /d/. When you say "tuh," however, the /t/ is said before the voicing of the "uh." This discrimination of voice onset time requires finer distinctions than people can make between to two nonspeech sounds, such as pure tones.

Other evidence for the special nature of speech comes from brain localization. The first example of localization of function in the brain was that of the speech area by Broca in 1861. Since that time, many different areas have been found for speech and language functions, some of them remarkably specialized. Sometimes a stroke victim with damage to a particular part of the brain will lose the ability to name living things, but can still name nonliving things, or vice versa (Pinker, 1994).

This discussion of the modularity of perception may have led you to wonder how it is that we perceive a unified world if we have all these separate modules. Somehow all these different parts of the brain work together to provide us with a coherent experience. We will discuss this problem in Chapter 6.

SUMMARY

1. Although perception gives us knowledge of the world, its primary purpose is for action.
2. Because building and maintaining organs is metabolically expensive, senses evolve only when they add to the fitness of an organism.
3. The senses make possible many functions that we normally take for granted, such as avoiding collision, but are vitally important.
4. Perception normally provides us with accurate information about the world.
5. Depth perception makes use of regularities in the visual world.
6. Vision makes use of a limited part of the electromagnetic spectrum that is both plentiful and does not pass through objects. The fact that light waves travel extremely fast and in a straight line makes them informative.
7. Sound waves provide useful information about the sources and distances of objects. Physical principles dictate that large animals make low frequencies, and small animals make high frequencies.
8. Taste and smell respond to chemicals in the environment that had significance for survival in the EEA.
9. The sense of touch is actually a collection of senses, including pressure, heat, cold, tickle and pain.
10. The case of F. C. illustrates the importance of the sense of pain for fitness. It also shows that evolution does not have our happiness as a goal, only our reproductive success.
11. Sensory adaptation is an evolutionary adaptation. The most important function of sensory adaptation is to permit range shifting, which allows us to adjust our limited range of instantaneous sensitivity over a very wide range of ambient stimulus intensities.
12. The senses frequently demonstrate coevolution, as in the case of the moth and bat, and the butterfly, the milkweed plant, and bluejay.
13. Perception illustrates the principle of modularity, whereby dedicated processes have evolved to solve particular problems, such as the rods and cones in vision, and speech versus nonspeech modes of hearing.

6 Consciousness

Consciousness is one of the most mysterious aspects of being human. Every normal person is aware of being alive and of having a mental life. On the other hand, most of us do not believe that things like rocks and machines are conscious; we wonder about which animals may have consciousness, and what sort they may have.

We all know what consciousness means until we try to study it. We are reminded of Supreme Court Justice Potter Stewart who said that he couldn't define pornography, but he knew it when he saw it. When we try to define *consciousness* we find that the term is used in several distinct, albeit related, senses (Farthing, 1992):

1. *Consciousness as voluntary action.* We say that certain actions are conscious in the sense of voluntary, as when we say that we consciously reach for a bite of food; our digestion of that food, however, will not require conscious attention.
2. *Consciousness as awareness.* We speak of being conscious of something, as you are conscious of the fact that you are reading a book that is in front of you right now, or that you have a mosquito bite on your left hand.
3. *Consciousness as wakefulness.* We speak of being conscious as opposed to unconscious, distinguishing wakefulness from sleep or coma.

Any unabridged dictionary will list other uses of the term consciousness; but we can see from this list that consciousness is used to refer to a number of different features of our behavior and experience.

We won't spend any more time trying to define consciousness, because it is a mistake to suppose that we need to have a complete definition of something in order to study it. In fact, one of the reasons we study something is so we can make a better definition of it. Biologists study life without worrying too much about exactly what constitutes life. Following normal scientific practice, we will discuss some aspects of consciousness about which we can make testable predictions.

> **Trail Marker:** Scientists are able to study consciousness even though they don't have a complete definition of it.

We will consider examples of each of the above three senses of consciousness.

CONSCIOUSNESS AS VOLUNTARY ACTION

The simple fact that we are conscious and generally in control of our actions causes most of us to assume that consciousness plays the primary role in everyday life. Most of us assume that our behavior is largely controlled by conscious mechanisms and that our thought processes are constantly available to consciousness. In fact, this assumption underlies much of ordinary human social interaction. If a man strikes us with his fist, we assume he was not only aware of what he did but did it on purpose. You may recall an obnoxious kid in grade school who bumped into you in the hallway, causing you to drop your books, and then said in mock innocence, "Oops, sorry—it was just an accident—no hard feelings." You did your own calculation of whether he did it on purpose.

Our legal system is based on the same sort of calculation; it makes conscious intent the basis for distinguishing between accidental homicide and murder. The difference means freedom or a life spent in jail. These experiences make it difficult for us to accept the fact that consciousness is but the tip of our psychological iceberg. Laypersons are not alone in overestimating the role of consciousness in the control of behavior. As John Bargh and Tanya Chartrand say, "Much of contemporary psychological research is based on the assumption that people are consciously and systematically processing incoming information in order to construe and interpret their world and to plan and engage in courses of action. . . . the authors [of this quote] question this assumption." (Bargh & Chartrand, 1999, p. 462).

Not Everything We Do or Think Involves Consciousness

One of the main functions of consciousness is to permit us to focus neural resources on novel problems and let routine ones be handled automatically. As we have already discussed, organs and functions incur metabolic costs. We would expect to find conscious control of behavior only when its benefits outweigh its costs. When something can be done automatically, without consciousness, it should be.

> The unconscious operations of the mind frequently far transcend the conscious ones in intellectual importance. . . . [The position of consciousness] appears to be that of a helpless spectator of but a minute fraction of a huge amount of brain work." (Francis Galton, quoted by Karl Pearson, 1924, p. 236.)

What are some things we do without engaging our consciousness? Recall our discussion in Chapter 5 that the purpose of perception is to guide action. One action that is of great importance, and which we do a lot of, is walking. Walking without falling down requires our sense of balance, which is largely mediated by our *vestibular system,* an organ closely associated with the sense of hearing. It is well established that the vestibular system operates mostly outside of consciousness; it ordinarily works by means of reflexes. We walk and do all sorts of things without any conscious awareness of the whereabouts and actions of our limbs. So here we have a sense that does not usually involve any conscious sensations!

> **Trail Marker:** Voluntary behavior does not always operate by way of conscious sensations.

We generally become conscious of the details of our motor movements only under certain circumstances. One such situation is when our reflexes fail us, as when our leg "goes to sleep," when we are intoxicated, when we become dizzy by spinning around, or from diseases such as Meniere's. We also pay attention to our motor movements when we must perform unfamiliar tasks, try to learn new ones, or we are self-conscious about them, as when we walk into a room of people who are watching our every move. The rest of the time we have better things to do with our limited consciousness.

In fact, the single most common voluntary human behavior is the eye movements we make as we look around (e.g., Monty, 1976). Until only about 130 years ago, when scientists first began recording eye movements, people thought we move our eyes smoothly from place to place as we look around, the way a camera pans a scene. Instead *saccadic eye movements,* as they are known, have a particular, stereotyped form: a fast, ballistic movement to a location, followed by a fixation. So the most basic facts about the most common thing we do were completely unknown to anyone until fairly recently. In other words, while we may consciously look at something, we are not conscious of the actions we perform in doing so.

For another example, how do you turn right on a bicycle? Over the years we have asked thousands of students in dozens of classes this question. Without fail they tell me that you turn the handlebars to the right. When we point out that this will cause the rider to fall off the bike to the left, they suggest you first lean to the right and then turn right. Of all those thousands of students, no one has ever correctly described the correct maneuver, which is to first turn to the *left,* causing you to lean to the right (see Figure 6–1). Only then is it possible to turn to the right, bringing the bike under you as you make the turn to the right. Believe me, you can't turn right on a bicycle without first turning left. Better yet, try it for yourself (but be careful!). This fact is what makes it so hard to stay on the pavement when you are riding on the very edge of it, for example.

I assume that all of those students who couldn't describe how to turn right on a bicycle could actually ride a bike perfectly well. They could turn right on a bicycle, but they couldn't *describe* how to turn right. This maneuver, although well learned, does not require consciousness, and may not be available to it. There are countless other examples.

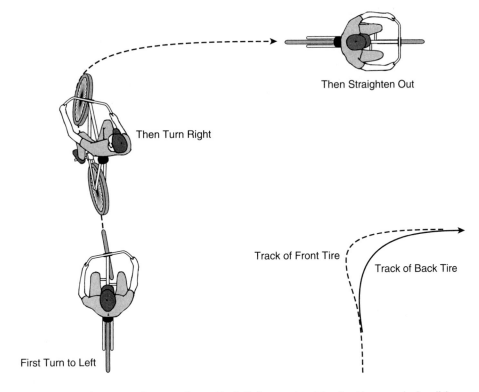

Then Straighten Out

Then Turn Right

Track of Front Tire

Track of Back Tire

First Turn to Left

Figure 6-1. *Bird's eye view of turning right on a bicycle.* Before turning right, the rider turns the handlebars to the left, causing the bike to lean, and permitting the rider to execute the turn without falling off. Inset shows the tracks made by the front (dashed line) and rear (solid line) tires.

Some Behaviors Are Conscious While They Are Being Learned, but Become Lost to Consciousness

It is possible (although we doubt it) that people are consciously aware they need to turn left before turning right on a bicycle while they are learning to ride, and lose awareness of this as they become more skilled. Nevertheless, some actions are conscious when we are learning them only to be lost when they become automatic. As I (DMcB) sit and type this sentence I am totally unable to say which letters are located on either side of the *r* on the keyboard. Yet I am a skilled typist; I can type any word containing the letter *r* effortlessly. It is likely that when I was learning to type I memorized the layout of the keyboard and could tell you that *r* lies between *e* and *t*. (I just peeked.)

Psychologists distinguish between *controlled* and *automatic* processing (Schneider & Shiffrin, 1977; Shiffrin & Schneider, 1977). Controlled processes require our conscious attention and we perform them slowly and effortfully. Further, we are easily distracted while engaged in controlled processing. Controlled processing is typical of tasks that we are only beginning to learn, such as our first efforts at typing or driving a car. You may recall that when you first learned to drive a car, whenever you changed stations on the radio the car seemed to wander off the road, because you couldn't concentrate on steering and tuning at the same time.

After considerable practice, these tasks become automatic: We do them rapidly, effortlessly, and simultaneously with other tasks. A skilled driver can drive while carrying on a conversation and listening to the news on the radio. Driving even becomes so automatic that most drivers have occasionally realized that they have driven for several miles without being aware of driving at all. Similarly, I have known typists so skilled they could engage in complicated conversations at the same time they were transcribing a manuscript.

We save enormous amounts of time and effort by routinizing the tasks we do every day. Let's see, do I put on my socks before or after I put on my shirt? Where did I leave my keys?

Consciousness Is Not Required for Learning to Take Place

So conscious attention is required to master some tasks like typing or driving a car; but you should not assume that this is always true. One of many examples of this point is given by the work of Ralph Hefferline and others (Hefferline et al., 1959) who had human subjects learn to turn off an annoying noise that interfered with their listening to music. They placed recording electrodes several places on their body, but didn't tell subjects what it was they could do to turn off the noise. What actually turned off the noise was a tiny twitch of the thumb so small that subjects couldn't even do it on purpose. If they so much as thought about it, they made too big a twitch to count. Nevertheless subjects learned to turn off the noise. Some subjects were not even told they could turn off the noise and they learned to do it anyway. One subject thought that he (or she—we aren't told which) was controlling the noise by doing various actually irrelevant things such as wriggling his ankles, holding his jaw in a certain position, making subtle rowing motions with his wrists, and breathing carefully. All the subjects learned to turn off the noise except for those who tried to move their thumbs—they couldn't make a small enough response. This classic experiment illustrates vividly that learning can take place outside of consciousness.

> **Trail Marker:** Learning can take place outside of consciousness.

Arthur Reber (1992) makes a strong case that a considerable amount of *implicit learning* takes place outside of awareness, when we are not even conscious that we are learning anything. Implicit learning can be thought of roughly as learning *how* rather than *what*. It is more like learning a skill than a set of facts. It is more like learning to ride a bicycle than learning the laws of physics that the bicycle obeys.

We learn our native tongue effortlessly and speak it without giving a thought to the rules of grammar. Young children (three to five years old) say that a monster that eats mice is a *mice eater,* but one that eats rats is a *rat eater,* not *rats eater* (Gordon, 1986). It is extremely unlikely that kids learn this rule by imitating adults who talk about rat eaters. Nevertheless kids unconsciously follow a rule that is so subtle that neither they nor adults can articulate: It is ungrammatical in English to form compounds with *regular* plurals (e.g., "cats-breeder" or " wines-collector") but it is perfectly grammatical to do so with *irregular* plurals (e.g., "men-hater" or "cattle-farmer").

We learn innumerable practical skills:

which way to turn the key in the front door

which way to turn the faucet

how hard to step on the brake

how to swing a golf club

how far to lower yourself before putting your weight on the sofa

how fast to pour the milk from the carton

how to turn right on a bicycle

We also learn innumerable social skills and attitudes:

how and when to flirt

how close to stand to someone we are talking with

how to take turns in conversation

when to talk to strangers

how loud to converse in public places

when to use bad words

political opinions

prejudices toward outgroups

We learn all of these things without the slightest awareness that we are doing so. We are not even aware that we have learned the feel of the brake until we have trouble driving a different car. We are not aware of how the faucet works until we scald ourselves on a different model. We are not aware that we have learned how to sit down until we drop too far into a different sofa. Similarly we don't realize we have learned the social skills, attitudes, and prejudices until we embarrass ourselves by blurting out something inappropriate.

Implicit learning is particularly important in many kinds of expertise. A physician ordinarily makes a diagnosis quickly and effortlessly without consciously thinking through all the possibilities and ruling out the alternatives. In one study (Carmody et al., 1984, as cited by Reber, 1992), radiologists were observed while they taught medical students how to read chest x rays. The experts gave the students clear and explicit instructions on how to locate tumors. A camera that recorded the experts' eye movements, however, revealed that the experts were basing their own judgments on other criteria, of which they were totally unaware. The students, of course, remained ignorant of these criteria.

To be fair, we should mention that some psychologists believe that awareness *is* required for learning (e.g., Shanks, 1996). They base their belief on classical conditioning experiments in which people learn a connection between two stimuli, such as a tone and a puff of air to the eyeball. In these experiments, it is sometimes found that only those subjects who realized there was a connection between the two stimuli actually learned the task. We will not review the debate here, but simply note that recent evidence favors the position that awareness is not necessary in classical conditioning (Papka, Ivry, & Woodruff-Pak, 1997).

Evolutionary considerations make it highly improbable that consciousness is required for learning. For one thing, it drives a wedge between learning in humans and other organisms. We do not assume that the consciousness of planaria (worms) and digger wasps approaches that of humans, but they learn nevertheless. Second, it pays too much attention to what we are conscious of, and ignores the host of processes that take place without benefit of consciousness.

Many Cognitive Processes Are Unavailable to Consciousness

Finally, some cognitive processes plainly are unavailable to consciousness under any circumstance. What was your mother's maiden name? The answer to this question just popped into your head without your having the slightest clue as to *how* you accomplished it. It doesn't matter whether you imagine your memory to be like a filing cabinet, a computer network, or a giant laundry pile. Your belief about the matter has no effect whatever on the way your memory works.

A great deal of our mental life takes place without the benefit of consciousness. We perceive speech, see colors, judge depth and distance, and solve many kinds of problems using the *cognitive unconscious* (Kihlstrom, 1987). (This term has nothing to do with Freudian notions of the unconscious; it simply refers to cognitive processes that are not available to consciousness.) Processes that are part of the cognitive unconscious are not only unavailable to consciousness, they are not affected in any way by what we believe—about the world, the brain, or how it works.

> **Trail Marker:** Scientists use the term unconscious in a way that has nothing to do with Freudian notions.

Consider the famous Müller-Lyer illusion, shown in Figure 6–2. Although the two horizontal lines are identical in length, they look considerably different. Even after you know the lines are the same length—even if you measure them with a ruler, which I hope you do—even if you have known about this illusion for forty years, as we have—the two lines still look unequal. All those processes that take place in the cognitive unconscious including the Müller-Lyer illusion, have the property of *cognitive impenetrability;* they are inaccessible to consciousness, and are unaffected by it. (In case you are wondering why evolution would build a mechanism that fools us about the world, the leading theory of this illusion is that it is a quirk of the mechanism by which we normally, and accurately, perceive size and depth.)

In summary, evolutionary thinking leads us to expect that we should make use of consciousness only when its benefits outweigh its costs. This explains why a

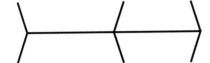

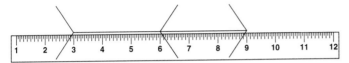

Figure 6–2. *Müller-Lyer Illusion.* Knowledge that the two horizontal lines are actually the same length does not affect the illusion.

host of behaviors take place outside of consciousness, including chewing without biting our tongues and swallowing without choking. You are reading this book without paying the slightest attention to staying upright, swallowing your saliva, and blinking your eyes. Behavior should not be equated with consciousness.

CONSCIOUSNESS AS AWARENESS

The previous section has given us one answer to the question of what consciousness is for: It permits us to focus attention on novel problems and lets routine ones be handled outside of consciousness. Considering consciousness as awareness gives us another evolutionary insight into consciousness. As we said in Chapter 5, perception couldn't have evolved just to provide useless knowledge. Similarly consciousness couldn't have evolved just to permit us to ponder the meaning of life, the universe, and everything. Selection would have weeded out any genes that caused us to waste energy on such pursuits when alternative alleles were causing our competitors to search for food and mates, and avoid predators.

The Unity of Consciousness

We become aware of many psychological processes only when they fail. Examples we have mentioned already in this book include our sense of balance and the ability to recognize faces. We don't give them a thought unless we get dizzy, or suffer from prosopagnosia. The unity of consciousness is another ability we take for granted. We assume that we are a single person, not a collection of independent modules. We also assume that the world we live in is one world, not a different, parallel universe for each sense.

The unity of consciousness, although seldom a problem in everyday life, is a problem for psychology. Recall that we have emphasized a number of times that evolution crafts adaptations, which operate as separate brain modules. How do these modules work together? We will consider the problem in two parts: the unity of the world, and the unity of the self.

When you take a bite of a barbecued potato chip, you see the golden brown color, taste the saltiness, smell the spices, feel the crispness, hear the crunch, and experience the pain from the red pepper. (Red pepper stimulates pain, not taste.) Eating food is a multisensory experience; yet you perceive a potato chip, not six (or more) separate sensory experiences. Change any one attribute of the potato chip and it will "taste" different. How do we integrate all of that information into a single, unified percept? This is known as the *binding problem,* and has bothered thinkers since the time of the ancient Greek philosophers. Aristotle's solution to the binding problem was to postulate the existence of *the common sense.* Aristotle's idea of common sense is not what keeps us from trying to roast a marshmallow by holding it in the fire with our bare hands. The common sense is a super sense that unifies all the information from the different senses. We can perceive a big dog because it looks big, makes a big noise when it barks, feels big to our hands, or because it is heavy to lift.

> It matters little through which sense I realize that in the dark I have blundered into a pig-sty. (Hornbostel, 1925, as cited by Marks, 1978, p. 5)

We can say that no organ of common sense has been located in the brain. There are, to be sure, places in the brain that respond to more than one type of sensory input. But there is no super sense where information from all the other senses goes. We do, however, have some hints about how the brain accomplishes the astonishing task of unifying the input from different senses.

For many years, some philosophers held that touch is the fundamental sense because it is in actual contact with the world. When we look at a stone, our only contact with it is by the light rays that bounce off it to our eyes. But when we stub our toe on the rock our body comes into direct physical contact with it. For this reason these philosophers held that "touch educates vision." They thought we learned to see things according to how they felt to touch. The case is actually the reverse, however.

It is easy to put vision and touch into conflict, although everyday examples are few. When we look through prism lenses, straight lines look curved. Surprisingly, if we feel a straight edge while looking through the distorting prisms, it feels distinctly curved. This phenomenon is called *visual dominance,* or *visual capture.* You may get some idea of this by feeling some object while looking at it through the wrong end of binoculars. Vision dominates other senses besides touch. Any time you watch a movie, you experience visual dominance over audition if you perceive the sound to be coming from the actors' mouths. Of course, the sound is actually coming from the speakers, which are many inches to several feet away from where the voices appear to emanate. (This is the basis of ventriloquism. The ventriloquist doesn't "throw" his voice. The dummy captures it.)

It appears that evolution has solved the problem of the unity of the senses in large part by the mechanism of visual dominance, suppressing any information that conflicts with vision, even when vision is wrong. Of course in the real world conflicts between vision and the other senses seldom arise, so evolution has solved the problem of the unity of the senses in a manner that seldom causes us problems.

We will deal with the other half of the question of the unity of awareness—unity of the self—after we have discussed self-awareness, to which we turn next.

Self-Awareness

One of the most important things that we humans are conscious of is ourselves. We are aware that we are distinct from the rest of the world:

> It hurts when you bite yourself but not someone else.
> Wherever you go, there you are.
> Other people act as if you do things on purpose.

You are admonished to do unto others as you would have them do unto you. Richard Dawkins (1989) suggests that self-awareness evolved because it is helpful for us to make ourselves the objects of our thought. For example: What did I do to make my neighbor angry at me? Is that tree branch strong enough to hold me?

In fact, Daniel Povinelli and John Cant (1995) propose it was exactly the problem of swinging through the branches that led to the evolution of consciousness in the larger primates. Consider the fact that differences in physical size have important consequences for the way animals interact with the environment. A spider that drops twenty feet floats to the ground; a squirrel bounces; an elephant splats. Further, a very small animal is supported by almost any surface, but a larger one will cause many objects to bend or break.

Povinelli and Cant note that smaller primates such as monkeys run on all fours through the forest canopy in a stereotyped manner that suggests they do not pay much attention to the strength of the branches and vines that support them (see Figure 6–3). Larger primates such as orangutans, however, show much more variability in their behavior. They generally clamber rather than run through the canopy—hanging from branches, bridging from one limb to the next, and causing the tree to sway so as to bring them closer to their next means of support (see Figure 6–4).

Figure 6–3. *Monkey running through tree.*

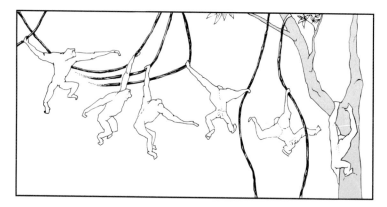

Figure 6–4.   *Ape clambering through tree.*

Povinelli and Cant propose that the demands of locomotion through the canopy led to the development in the larger primates of the ability to think of themselves as an object that interacts with the world. This notion is admittedly speculative, but it has the advantage of making testable predictions. It predicts that orangutans and chimpanzees will pass certain tests for self-awareness that monkeys will fail.

One such test is the mirror test. A wide variety of animals react to mirrors. Some animals, including fish and birds, will attack their image, as if it were a rival, suggesting they are unaware they are looking at themselves. After a while these animals may come to ignore the mirror. Some primates, on the other hand, will gaze raptly into a mirror. What are they thinking? An orangutan or a chimp that has looked at a mirror for a while begins to use it to examine parts of the body that they can't normally see, such as their teeth and their hindquarters. This behavior suggests strongly that they are aware they are looking at themselves (see Figure 6–5).

Gordon Gallup (1977, 1991) tested this hypothesis by painting a red dot on the forehead and ear of primates while they were anesthetized, so they would not have any way of knowing the dot was there. When they came to, chimps and orangutans showed great interest in the dots while looking in the mirror, touching them and rubbing at them. Monkeys, however, did not.

The one large ape that fails the mirror test for self-awareness is the gorilla. Consistent with Povinelli and Cant's hypothesis, the gorilla is terrestrial and does not ordinarily climb more than a foot or two off the ground.

It may have occurred to you that humans do not swing through trees on a regular basis outside of Tarzan movies. Does Povinelli and Cant's hypothesis have any relevance to humans? It is important to realize that organs that evolve for one purpose are often taken over later for another purpose. For example, according to one popular theory, wings of insects evolved from structures that originally served in thermoregulation (Kingsolver and Koehl, 1985). Similarly, the three little bones in the middle ear of mammals that transmit sound to the inner ear evolved from the jaw bones of fish.

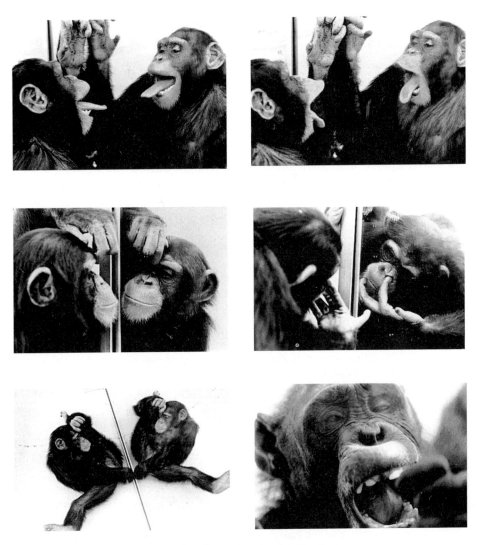

Figure 6–5. *Chimp using mirror for self-exploration.*

Trail Marker: Organs that evolve for one purpose are often later adapted for an entirely different purpose.

So once self-awareness evolved to serve some purpose in a hominid ancestor it could have been further adapted for other purposes. Because humans are highly social creatures, it is likely that self-awareness was then turned to serve functions such as asking questions like, "Why does my neighbor refuse to share meat with me? Is it because I failed to share my last kill with him?" The complex social life of humans creates many situations in which self-awareness would be useful.

Unity of the Self, Deception, and Self-Deception

We discussed the unity of the world earlier. Here we discuss the conviction that we each have that we are a unified person, which is the other half of the concept of the unity of consciousness. (We are talking about normal people, not those with personality disorders.) But normal people often behave in ways that make us wonder whether they are aware of how they appear. A middle-aged man who is spreading at the waist dyes what is left of his hair and wears a muscle shirt. A middle-aged woman dresses like a teenager. How could they look in the mirror and not cringe? Such human foibles prompted the Scottish poet, Robert Burns, to exclaim,

> Oh wad some power the giftie gie us
> To see ourselves as others see us!

The puzzle of self-deception has intrigued psychologists as well as poets. Much research and theorizing on the matter has been based on Freudian psychodynamics. Perhaps this is the reason psychologists have made little progress in understanding self-deception! A classic paper was entitled, "Self deception: A concept in search of a phenomenon" (Gur & Sackeim, 1979). The problem with the concept of self-deception is that the deceiver and the deceived are the same person. How can a person logically believe two opposite things at the same time? The Freudian answer is that one belief is conscious and the other is relegated to the unconscious. Attempts to demonstrate the presence of the two beliefs at the same time in the same person, however, have not been persuasive.

Evolutionary thinking suggests that psychologists may have been barking up the wrong tree. For one thing, the concept of a unitary self as a single, integrated entity should not be taken for granted. Although our consciousness tells us that we are a unitary self, we may well be mistaken. Remember that consciousness doesn't have access to everything; we can ride a bicycle but can't say how we do it. And there are clear examples of inner disharmony. We have all said things like, "I have half a mind to dye my hair," or "half of me wants to shave my beard and the other half doesn't." These remarks reflect a reality about the human mind. The fact that the mind is modular should suggest that different modules may well have different, and conflicting, goals. Further, the existence of the cognitive unconscious implies that we will not always be aware of these conflicting inclinations.

In a telling example, Michael Gazzaniga and Joseph LeDoux (1978) describe the case of a patient, P. S., a young boy who had the two halves of his brain surgically separated to alleviate a serious medical condition. In most split-brain patients, the left hemisphere is in control of speech, whereas the right hemisphere is unable to speak. P. S. was unusual in that his right hemisphere, although mute, was able to read and write. When Gazzaniga asked P. S. what he wanted to be when he grew up, he said "draftsman." When he presented the written question to the right hemisphere of P. S.'s brain only, P. S. spelled out "race car driver."

The fact that P. S.'s two different hemispheres have different thoughts and actions is only half the story. His speaking, left hemisphere often made up explanations for the actions of his right hemisphere. In one experiment, a picture of a winter snow scene was shown to his nonspeaking right hemisphere while the speaking hemisphere saw a chicken foot. The hand controlled by the speaking hemisphere correctly matched a chicken to the chicken foot; the hand controlled by the nonspeaking hemisphere correctly matched a snow shovel to the snow scene. When Gazzaniga asked P. S. what he saw, he said, "I saw a claw and picked the chicken, and you have to clean out the chicken shed with a shovel" (p. 148). Time after time, P. S. instantly made up stories like this to explain what he saw his two hands doing. The term for this sort of behavior is *confabulation,* which means filling in gaps in memory or knowledge by fabrication. It is not the same as lying, because the confabulator is unaware that the story is anything other than factual. Confabulation is common in certain psychiatric disorders. Other examples from Gazzaniga and LeDoux's study include a split-brain patient whose nonspeaking hemisphere was given the command to laugh. When asked why she had laughed, she said without hesitation, "Oh, you guys really are something!" (p. 146).

Split-brain patients are not normal, of course. But the sobering implication of the split-brain research is that we all confabulate constantly. Gazzaniga and LeDoux argue that all people contain a set of selves, or modules, each with its own desires and motives. Marvin Minsky (1986) has called this idea the Society of Mind. Gazzaniga and LeDoux say that in all normal people the verbal system gains control over the other mental processes to the extent that it becomes the only self that we are aware of. In other words, the self that we know is the verbal self. Other selves exist outside of our ability to verbalize. According to this view, the unity of the self is an achievement, not a given. More recently Gazzaniga has called this system the interpreter mechanism (Gazzaniga, 1998). We find ourselves yawning, and we say, "I'm really tired." Or we eat a big meal and say, "I was really hungry." We explain or interpret our own behavior, both to ourselves and to others. We are doing far too many things at once to monitor them all consciously. We (our interpreter mechanism, that is!) freely make up stories that give our actions consistency.

> **Trail Marker:** The unity of the self is an accomplishment, not a necessity.

Anthony Greenwald (1988) takes a different approach to solving the problem of self-deception. He agrees that the Freudian approach involves a paradox: The same person both knows and doesn't know at the same time. But he believes that giving up the concept of unity of the self is too drastic. How can we get around that problem? He suggests that the Freudian approach sees the unconscious as having the same ability to understand, except of course that it is unconscious. Instead, Greenwald proposes that unconscious processes (there are many of them) have very limited abilities. They do only a preliminary analysis of information and pass the results on to later, more conscious, processes. They can reject information without analyzing it completely. He calls this the junk-mail model of self-deception. We receive a great deal of junk mail along with important mail. Although advertisers are very clever in disguising junk mail as important information (You are guaranteed to be a winner!), we discard junk mail without reading it by relying on clues such as a lack of first-class postage.

According to the junk-mail model, we first analyze the message according to low-level clues (e.g., presence of a first-class stamp). If it passes these criteria, we open it and read the message. The junk-mail model explains how the middle-aged man can wear the muscle shirt. (Don't look in the mirror.) It explains how we can ignore signs of serious illness. (It's probably just a cold.) We believe the junk-mail model avoids the problems of the Freudian model, which must assume two intelligent processes, one conscious and the other unconscious. At the same time, however, we believe that the Society-of-Mind model is supported by a wide range of cognitive phenomena.

A second idea about self-deception suggested by evolutionary thinking is that accurate perception of ourselves is not always the best thing. To be sure, our perceptions must be close to reality. A ninety-five pound weakling who thinks he can beat up a linebacker doesn't become anyone's ancestor. But maybe there is an advantage to be gained by seeing yourself as a little better than you are. That middle-aged man in his inappropriately youthful clothes might just get lucky with the right woman. If two women of similar attractiveness are competing for the same man, the one whose ego is inflated the right amount may try enough harder and persist enough longer to win out.

Psychologists use the term *self-serving bias* to describe the fact that we have a strong tendency to see ourselves as above average. A large body of social psychological findings presents a consistent pattern: We consistently think of ourselves as above average on many dimensions. The average person rates himself or herself more ethical, more persistent, more original, a better driver (even those who have been hospitalized for automobile accidents!), and more intelligent than average (Myers, 1996). Now, by definition, the average person is average. But we all tend to act like we live in Garrison Keillor's mythical Lake Wobegone, where "all the women are strong, all the men are good looking, and all the children are above average."

A little reflection reveals that deception is widespread among living things. Some insects look like sticks, and so avoid being eaten; some fish have wormlike projections on their heads, and so attract unwary prey (see Figure 6–6). Some flowers smell like rotting flesh, and so attract flies to pollinate them. In Chapter 5, we discussed the butterfly that mimics the poisonous Monarch to avoid predation. It is clear that organisms (plants as well as animals) will evolve to present themselves in ways that augment their fitness, even if these ways are deceptive.

Trail Marker: Deception is a predictable outcome of natural selection.

In humans, the best deception could be self-deception. The suitor says with all his heart, "I love you more than anyone else in the whole world. I will be faithful

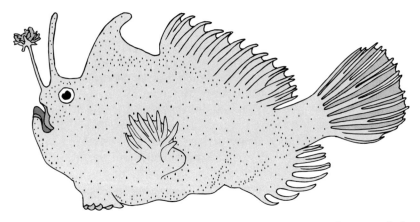

Figure 6–6. *Animal deception.* The angler fish uses its appearance to lure prey; in this species the lure is luminescent. Animals will present themselves in any way that advances their survival and reproduction. Consciousness is not essential for effective deception. (From *Feeding Ecology of Fish* by Shelby D. Gerking. Copyright © 1994 by Academic Press, Inc.)

to you for the rest of my life." And this kind of message will be all the more convincing if he can conveniently forget that he said the same to someone else last year! Evolutionary thinking suggests that the man who really believes that he will never leave his love will make the most convincing suitor, something that ordinarily would increase fitness. It also suggests that the married man who really believes that the troubles in the marriage are all his wife's fault will more easily rationalize his search for another partner. It is totally unnecessary to assume that one belief is conscious while the other is unconscious according to some Freudian process. Mechanisms evolve when they further reproductive success. These mechanisms may not fit very well into our existing theories, especially when they concern something so complicated as consciousness.

CONSCIOUSNESS AS WAKEFULNESS: WHY DO WE SLEEP?

> Why we sleep has puzzled thinkers at least since the time of Aristotle. Lab shelves sag beneath volumes of data, yet no one has discerned that sleep has any clear biological function. Then what evolutionary pressure selected this curious behavior that forces us to spend a third of our lives unconscious? Sleeping animals. . . . have less time to search for food, to eat, to find mates, to procreate, to feed their young. As Victorian parents told their children, sleepy-heads fall behind—in life and evolution. (Chet Raymo, 1988, as quoted by Dennett, 1995, p. 339)

One evolutionary clue to the function of sleep is provided by the fact that night and day divide any piece of real estate into very different ecological niches. There is a big difference in the amount of light, obviously, but also in temperature and humidity. An evolutionist would expect different animals to evolve to fill these different niches. A hypothetical animal that was designed to function equally well in the day and at night would be outcompeted in the daytime by animals with better vision or better ability to withstand heat; it would be outcompeted at night by animals with better hearing or better adapted to dampness. One logical idea, then, is that sleep functions to keep animals quiet and out of harm's way during the part of the twenty-four-hour cycle to which they are not adapted, the part that constitutes a different ecological niche occupied by another organism.

A testable prediction is that diurnal (daytime) creatures should sleep more in the winter and less in the summer. This effect is well known for many animals but has only recently been demonstrated in humans. Studies of people going about their normal routines show small and inconsistent results, probably because electric lighting permits us to escape the limitations of sunshine. A controlled study in which volunteers remained in the laboratory under controlled light conditions showed that they slept three hours longer when there were fourteen hours of darkness and ten of light, compared to when there were eight hours of darkness and sixteen of light (Wehr et al., 1993). Consistent with this explanation is the fact that blind cave fish, adapted to living completely inside dark caves, do not sleep (Pitcher, 1993).

But Daniel Dennett (1995) turns the question of why we sleep on its head. In the light of evolution the real question, he says, is why are we ever awake? Being awake is costly: Even when resting, an awake person consumes about 10 to 30 percent more calories per hour than when asleep (Carskadon, 1993). We need to be awake to find food and to mate and do many other essential tasks, some of which can increase our energy consumption up to ten times resting level; but otherwise we should sleep to conserve energy. "Powering down" by 25 percent for eight hours a day can be the difference between life and death, or between fertility and infertility, for hunter-gatherers when food is scarce.

We are familiar with the phenomenon of hibernation by which certain animals drastically reduce their metabolism during the winter when food is scarce and being active is metabolically very expensive. Other animals use a similar strategy

Figure 6–7. *Lion sleeping.* Predators sleep more than prey animals.

during hot or dry spells. Some desert frogs, toads, and fish lie buried in mud during the dry season in a state of estivation for most of the year. They become active and reproduce during the brief wet season, only to estivate until the next rainy season. During droughts they may estivate for several years. Even squirrels estivate when it is hot and dry.

The percent of time spent sleeping varies widely among animals. Because small animals have higher metabolic rates, they pay a relatively heavier price than larger animals do for being active. Thus, it is not surprising that small animals sleep more than large animals (Carskadon, 1993).

Predators, such as cats, tend to eat very large meals when they make a kill, and sleep much of the rest of the time. Moreover, predators can sleep deeply because they are relatively safe when asleep (see Figure 6–7). Grazers, who are among the prey of large cats, sleep little and lightly. Woody Allen said that "the lion and the lamb shall lie down together, but the lamb will not be very sleepy." (*Love and Death*, 1975, as cited by Myers, 1998, p. 216)

In summary, this chapter takes an evolutionary approach to a subject that is not usually looked at from this perspective. We found that we began asking questions that are usually ignored. In the case of sleep, we found that we turn the usual question on its head, thereby explaining a number of puzzling features of sleep. Perhaps the most important lesson from this chapter is that because consciousness incurs metabolic costs it should be used sparingly, only when we cannot function as well without it.

SUMMARY

1. The concept of consciousness is used in a number of distinct ways, including: voluntary action, awareness, and wakefulness.
2. Laypersons, and much of contemporary psychology, assumes that most behavior is under direct, conscious control
3. Even voluntary behavior involves many mechanisms of which we have no conscious awareness.
4. Some behaviors are conscious while they are being learned, but later become lost to consciousness.
5. Controlled processes require conscious attention, and are performed slowly and effortfully; automatic processes, on the other hand, are rapid, effortless, and may be performed simultaneously with other tasks.
6. Learning can take place without consciousness.
7. Learning a skill, called implicit learning, takes place outside of consciousness to a considerable extent.
8. Many cognitive processes are unavailable to consciousness and take place in the cognitive unconscious.
9. The problem of perceiving a unified world via distinct sensory systems is called the binding problem.
10. Conflict between sensory systems is generally settled in favor of vision.

11. Richard Dawkins suggests that self-awareness evolved to permit making ourselves the object of thought.
12. Daniel Povinelli suggests that locomotion through trees by larger primates led to the evolution of consciousness.
13. Gallup showed that certain apes, but not monkeys, show self-awareness, as defined by showing interest in their altered image in a mirror.
14. Evolutionary psychology approaches the problem of self-deception by recognizing that it can be an aid in survival and reproduction.
15. Work on split-brain patients suggests that the unity of the self is an accomplishment, not a given.
16. Dennett suggests that the question why we sleep should be, rather, why we are ever awake.
17. Sleep may have evolved to save energy during periods when activity was unlikely to be advantageous, and to keep animals out of harms way.
18. Humans sleep more during the winter than the summer.
19. Smaller animals (which have higher metabolic rates) sleep more than larger ones, predators sleep more than prey, and blind cave fish do not sleep at all.

7 Learning: How Experience Modifies Behavior

Niko Tinbergen, one of the winners of the 1973 Nobel Prize in medicine and physiology was selected for his pioneering studies of animal behavior. One of Tinbergen's early experimental studies focused on insect learning (Tinbergen, 1958). His subjects were "bee wolves" (*Philanthus triangulum*). These predatory wasps capture bees to feed their young.

Unlike some more familiar wasps, bee wolves are solitary. Each female bee wolf digs a two-foot burrow with several side chambers. In each chamber, she lays a single egg and provisions the egg with two bees, paralyzed by her sting. Digging a burrow takes a lot of time and energy so a completed burrow is valuable to her. Unfortunately, the female must leave her precious burrow repeatedly to find and capture bees, sometimes a mile or more away. Any female who could not find her burrow after a hunting trip would have wasted a great deal of time and effort. Tinbergen wondered how female bee wolves relocate their burrows after hunting.

He noticed that when a bee wolf left her burrow she flew over the area, in a progressively expanding set of loops, and he hypothesized that she was studying the local landscape. He also noticed that cold, rainy weather kept the wasps in their burrows for days, and such confinements were followed by especially long "locality studies." Tinbergen suspected that stormy weather often shifted many small landmarks, necessitating careful restudy by the departing female.

Tinbergen tested his ideas in a number of ways. To begin, he found a wasp emerging from her burrow after a storm and placed a ring of pine cones around her burrow. The wasp made a long inspection flight and then flew off. While the wasp was away Tinbergen moved the ring of pine cones a few feet to the south.

When the female returned, what do you think she did? She landed at the center of the ring of pine cones and of course did not find her burrow until Tinbergen chased her off and replaced the pine cones around her nest, as they had been when she departed. This experiment and variations of it were performed many times. They left no doubt that female wasps were learning, and relearning when necessary, the detailed features of the landscape around their nests.

You may not ordinarily think that insects are capable of much learning. But clearly there are some kinds of problems, like the location of one's burrow, that are very important to reproductive success but could not possibly be coded in the genes simply because every individual has its own unique burrow. In this chapter, we will explore the various kinds of learning mechanisms that have evolved.

LEARNING MECHANISMS ARE PRODUCTS OF EVOLUTION

In this chapter, you will discover that learning is not independent of evolution. Instead, learning mechanisms are evolved adaptations to the organism's natural environment. Like any adaptation, they are specialized to solve particular kinds of real-world problems.

Although we will criticize this dichotomy, it is important to understand that many psychologists believe there are two kinds of behaviors: innate and learned. According to this view, innate behaviors represent adaptations designed by natural selection. *Innate* behaviors are said to be instinctive, that is, they have been preprogrammed over the history of the species by natural or sexual selection and are coded in the genes. Innate or instinctive behaviors are supposedly fixed and stereotyped, not showing much variation from one individual to another or from one occasion to another. And, importantly, they are said to develop spontaneously, independent of experience.

In contrast, *learned* behaviors are much more variable and are shaped by various kinds of experiences over the lifetimes of individuals. As a matter of definition, we could say that learning occurs when behavior is modified by experience. This gives us a useful definition of learning that will include a wide array of cases: children's mastery of language, rats' solution of mazes, Pavlov's salivating dogs, the bee wolf's unerring return to its burrow, and others discussed in this chapter.

> **Trail Marker:** Learning occurs when behavior is modified by experience.

So what is wrong with the traditional distinction between innate (or instinctive) and learned behaviors? Basically, it is another manifestation of the nature-nurture or genes-environment dichotomy, which we soundly criticized in Chapter 4. First, it suggests that selection has shaped innate behaviors but that, because learning results from each individual's experience, evolution has nothing to do with learning. This idea is outdated and wrong. We know that there is a very important class of evolved traits, facultative adaptations, that always depend on ex-perience. So claiming an important role for experience does *not* rule out the influ-ence of selection in shaping learned behaviors. Remember that suntanning, our evolved response to solar radiation, depends on experience.

Second, as we saw in Chapters 3 and 4, the phenotype is a result of interac-tions between genes and environment. Thus it turns out that even supposedly in-nate behaviors depend on experience. The classic method for showing that a behavior is innate is the deprivation experiment: deprive the animal of normal ex-perience and show that the behavior occurs anyway. But the logic of this approach highlights the central problem with the notion of innateness. You already know that even obligate traits depend on experience. If the environment is too novel, they will not develop normally. So deprivation experiments end up showing that *all* behavior depends on experience. To think through this problem consider how bird song develops.

Failure of the Innate/Learned Dichotomy: The Example of Bird Song

In many bird species, song learning seems to depend on certain early experiences. Yearling males (in most songbird species only males sing) master their species-typical songs by matching their own vocal output to the songs they heard their fa-ther sing when they were young (Catchpole and Slater, 1995). This has of course been revealed by deprivation experiments. Take young birds from their nests and rear them by hand in soundproof chambers where they cannot hear adults of their species sing and, sure enough, they fail to develop anything like a normal song (e.g., Marler, 1970). So far there is no problem. This story fits the conventional de-finition of learning: The singing behavior is clearly modified by the experience of hearing (or not hearing) normal adult song.

Now let's consider the case of the brown-headed cowbird (*Molothrus ater*), a brood parasite. Brood parasites don't build nests or care for their own young. In-stead, they lay their eggs in the nests of unsuspecting birds of other species who un-wittingly rear these interlopers. Because young cowbirds have no contact with their parents they do not have the opportunity to learn their father's song. Thus their normal development involves a "deprivation experiment." Yet young male cow-birds grow up to sing good renditions of cowbird song anyway. So is cowbird song innate? Using the criteria of the deprivation experiment you would have to con-clude that it is. But an interesting set of experiments by King and West (West and King, 1988) suggest that many other experiences are important to the develop-ment of cowbirds' song. For example, young males refine their songs by retaining elements that female cowbirds respond to and deleting those females ignore.

This example makes an important point. When we perform a deprivation ex-periment we are assuming that we know *which* experiences matter. For example, let's make the reasonable assumption that song development depends on hearing the father's song—as it does in many species. Since male cowbirds develop their song without this experience, we conclude that their song is innate—independent of experience. But, in fact, King and West showed that it isn't!

Ironically then, deprivation experiments have provided some of the best evidence *against* innateness, as this concept is traditionally understood. The point of a deprivation experiment is to show that the behavior emerges in the absence of experience. But it will always be possible to find some type of deprivation that *does* disrupt the behavior. Dividing up behaviors based on their responsiveness to experience turns out to yield only one category—because *all* behavior depends on some kind of experience.

> **Trail Marker:** All behavior depends on some kind of experience.

The scientists who developed the notion of instinct were bright and dedicated people. They greatly advanced our understanding of behavior. But they were studying at a time when the nature-nurture dichotomy was unquestioned, because much less was understood about what genes actually do. Given our present understanding of developmental genetics it makes more sense to think about these issues in terms of the two kinds of gene-environment interaction, obligate and facultative. To the extent that instinctive or innate behaviors exist, they must be shaped by genes that have relatively obligate effects, genes that resist environmental interference. They thus produce a more or less fixed and definite outcome—in this case a fixed and definite behavior—over the entire range of normal environments. But, of course, even obligate traits can be disrupted in novel environments.

> **Trail Marker:** Instinctive (or innate) behaviors are relatively obligate; but even they can be perturbed by novel environments.

To see why, remember how selection works. Selection simply retains those genes that are good at getting into the next generation. There are just two possible outcomes for genes. They either produce phenotypes that meet the tests of the environment and are therefore passed on. Or they fail these tests and are weeded out. But note that genes are only tested for their ability to cope with the environments they actually encounter; they may have unpredictable effects when they encounter new environments. This highlights another logical fallacy of the deprivation experiment. Even obligate traits are designed with a certain set of built-in "expectations" based on the kinds of environments in which they were designed. Perturb the environment enough by eliminating certain normal inputs (for example, prevent the young cowbird from testing its song on females) and you will inevitably perturb the trait.

LEARNING MECHANISMS ARE FACULTATIVE ADAPTATIONS

If so-called innate (or instinctive) behaviors are relatively obligate, then learned behaviors can be usefully viewed as facultative adaptations, designed by selection to track the environment and adjust the phenotype accordingly. Like the physiological adjustment of melanin synthesis to match uv_b exposure, learning involves adjustments of the behavioral phenotype in response to environmental input. To make sense of the suntanning response, we had to discover the separate effects of uv_b and melanin. This allowed us to reconstruct how selection must have operated and to explain why the melanin norm of reaction has the particular form it does. Likewise, to understand the modes of learning that have evolved we have to ask the same kinds of questions. What is the nature of the environmental inputs and what are their likely fitness effects? What aspects of behavior are modified by this experience and why? The key point is that selection designs what can be learned and how it is learned in the same way that it designs other facultative adaptations, by building mechanisms that produce specialized patterns of responsiveness.

> **Trail Marker:** Learning mechanisms are facultative adaptations.

LEARNING IS NOT A SINGLE ADAPTATION, BUT MANY

The definition we have given—learning is the modification of behavior by experience—is general enough to satisfy almost everyone who studies learning. But it is so general that it hides an important fact: Learning happens in many different ways (Gallistel, 1995). The problem is that the kinds of things that people and other animals learn are incredibly varied. Consider this list. Most people learn to walk, talk, and assess the motives of others. Birds learn to sing their courtship songs and to fly north and south with the seasons. Animals learn what to eat: They learn what's nutritious, what's dangerous, and what's just not worth pursuing. They master the local geography, learn to find the resources they need, and how to get home when their needs are satisfied. In many species, parents learn to distinguish their own young, and in some species the recognition is reciprocal. Could all these outcomes be the result of one learning process? Or would learning be more effective and efficient if a series of specialized learning modules were each finely tuned to particular tasks?

> **Trail Marker:** Like all adaptations, learning mechanisms are designed to solve particular real-world problems; hence learning mechanisms are specialized.

A body is a complex self-perpetuating system. It harvests and processes a wide range of resources necessary for maintenance and for the all-important function of reproduction. But each of the steps in these processes is accomplished by some specialized organ, designed by evolution for efficiency in a particular function. Everywhere we look in the body we see specialized designs. The heart pumps blood, and the lungs aerate it. It would be ridiculous, in fact fatal, to ask them to exchange roles. Organs are specialized because specialization allows them to do their job better. And "better" is what selection is always creating. For this reason, specialization is the rule in biology. As we saw in Chapter 5, the eye is designed to see (to be sensitive to light in a narrow range of wavelengths), and the ear is designed to hear (to be similarly sensitive to pressure waves in the air). Unless selection had designed the necessary specialized mechanisms (as it has in bats), we could not hope to "see" with our ears what we easily perceive with our eyes. For the very same reason, selection has designed a variety of specialized learning mechanisms each of which is efficient at solving a particular class of problems, but relatively useless for others.

Psychologists have been slow to appreciate the idea that evolution builds specialized mechanisms. In fact, under the influence of B. F. Skinner and other behaviorists, many psychologists have believed that all learning was a single process, governed by a single mechanism. For this reason much research on learning has focused on how rats or pigeons learn. If learning depends on a single mechanism, we can observe the same mechanism no matter whose learning we study.

But there are easy ways to show that the behaviorists were wrong. Specialization can be demonstrated in at least two ways. It is visible within any given species, where we see an array of organs each shaped for a particular function. And it is also apparent when we compare species. Each species faces a unique set of environmental challenges and thus tends to evolve different kinds of organs to meet those challenges. Thus one of the simplest ways to show that there are many learning mechanisms, not one, is to show that different species learn very different sorts of things in very different ways.

THE DIVERSITY OF LEARNING MECHANISMS

Most people believe much of the behavior of animals is governed by instinct, whereas human behavior is learned. Ants find their way back to their nests by instinct. Birds fly south for the winter by instinct. But people learn language. In fact, the behavior of birds and ants, often regarded as instinctive, critically depends on experience—on learning. And our learning of language is no more and no less instinctive than either the homing of ants or the migration of birds. Understanding how and why each depends on learning helps us appreciate how specialized learning mechanisms evolve.

The Learned "Star Compass" of Migratory Birds

Many songbirds that breed in North America during the summer escape our winter, when food is scarce and the weather is harsh, by migrating to tropical areas in Central and South America. They make their migration twice a year, northbound in the spring and southbound in the autumn. Researchers mark (with numbered bands) many thousands of these migrants every year, and this technique allows us to recognize individuals. From this evidence, we know that migrants orient very precisely, because known individuals regularly return to the same areas year after year. How do they do it?

Many of these migrant species do their long-distance flying at night, so they are unlikely to be using landmarks (as the bee wolves do) to guide their route. One possibility is that they use some type of compass-based orientation, flying a particular northerly heading in the spring and the complementary southerly heading back to the wintering grounds. To do this the birds must have a reference heading, such as true north. Anyone can easily tell up from down because the force of gravity puts a natural polarity on this dimension: Down is where things fall to. But where is north? Suppose your life depended on walking north. Without a compass how could you do it?

Here's a possibility. As the earth spins on its axis, virtually all celestial objects (e.g., the sun, other stars, galaxies) appear to rotate across the sky. From our perspective in the northern hemisphere, the center point of that rotation, the only point that stays put while everything else turns around it, will always be directly to the north. To see why, picture a rod straight through the earth's axis of rotation and aiming out into space (Figure 7–1). The point in space at which this rod is aiming will be directly north of you, no matter where you are in the northern

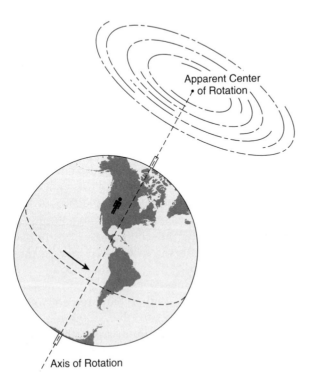

Apparent Center of Rotation

Axis of Rotation

Figure 7–1. *The earth in space.* As the earth spins on its axis, the heavens appear to rotate. The apparent center of rotation is true north.

hemisphere. And as the earth turns, that point in space will also be the center around which celestial objects seem to be rotating. If you, or a bird, could visually locate this apparent center of rotation you could go north simply by heading towards it. Of course the center of rotation is not obvious at a glance because the earth spins slowly, one rotation every twenty-four hours.

The birds face another complication: The center of rotation changes. Just as a child's top wobbles as it spins, the earth wobbles cyclically as it turns on its axis. Of course this wobble changes the point in space at which its axis is aiming, and thus changes the appropriate sighting line for true north. Each one of these cycles, referred to as the precession of the equinoxes, lasts about 25,800 years (Payne-Gaposchkin and Haramundanis, 1970). The star Polaris is close to the center of rotation now and thus provides a good sighting line for north. In another 25,800 years Polaris will again approximate the center of rotation, but in the intervening time it will be as much as 47 degrees away from north! This precession is slow enough that it does not make any difference over the ten-year life spans of individual birds. But an obligate mechanism specifying "Polaris equals north" would begin sending birds well off course within a few thousand years. Selection would favor any better solution that came along. Because many migratory species have been making their annual round trips for millions of years, they must already have a better solution.

> **Trail marker:** Migratory birds learn a star compass suited to the earth's tilt during their lifetimes.

Indeed they do; each young bird learns a "star compass" appropriate to the current phase in the precession of the equinoxes! Let's begin by reviewing the evidence that birds use stars to orient. Migratory birds become restless at night in the spring and again in the autumn. And their restlessness shows a strong directional bias. For example, when held in cages where they cannot fly these migratory birds hop instead. A cage with a slippery conical floor requires the bird to start each hop from the same location, the depressed center of the cone. And placing an ink pad in the center yields a discrete ink mark indicating the end point of each hop (Figure 7–2). Thus the marks on the cone tell what direction the bird is trying to go. These cages can be placed outdoors during the migratory season. On clear cloudless nights when the stars are visible, wild-caught birds hop in a seasonally appropriate direction; but on cloudy nights when the stars are hidden the birds hop at random (Emlen, 1975). Birds must be using the stars to orient, but how do they learn to do so?

Steve Emlen's experiments with indigo buntings (*Passerina cyanea*) provide clear evidence (Emlen, 1969a, 1969b). To begin, Emlen hand-reared young buntings indoors, making sure they had no opportunity to observe the night sky while growing up. Later, during their first autumn migration season, these birds were tested under a stationary (nonrotating) planetarium projection of the normal night sky. Under these conditions the birds showed no southerly orienta-

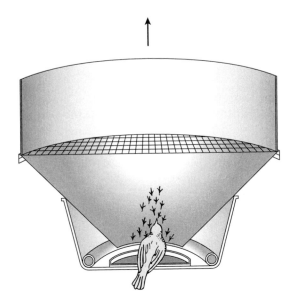

Figure 7–2. *A conical orientation cage.* The ink pad causes the bird to leave footprints that indicate its flight direction. ("Circular Test Cage" illustration by Adolph E. Brotman from p. 105 in "The Stellar-Orientation System of a Migratory Bird" by S. Emlen in *Scientific American,* 233, August 1975. Reprinted by permission of Adolph E. Brotman.)

tion; but this result has at least two interpretations. Perhaps, because they had no prior experience with the night sky these birds had not learned to orient by the stars. Alternatively, they might have failed to orient properly because the non-rotating planetarium sky under which they were tested was too artificial to evoke the normal southerly response. The next experiment eliminates the second hypothesis.

In this experiment, two groups of young buntings were reared indoors. These birds were given nightly exposure to a planetarium projection of the northern-hemisphere constellations which rotated at the normal speed (i.e., once in 24 hours). The only difference between the two groups was the apparent center of rotation. For one group the sky projection was rotated around Polaris, similar to what young indigo buntings would see in the wild. For the other group, the constellations were rotated around Betelgeuse, a bright star in Orion. Both groups were subsequently tested under a stationary planetarium projection of the northern-hemisphere constellations. The Polaris-trained group oriented south as defined by Polaris. The Betelgeuse-trained group oriented to what would be south if Betelgeuse were the pole star! The pattern of rotation they had seen as young birds had "defined" a different north-south axis for these two groups of birds.

The Betelgeuse-trained birds were permanently affected by their early experience. After testing they were moved to outdoor cages where they regularly saw a normally rotating night sky for the next year. Nevertheless, when tested in the planetarium during their second autumn migration season these birds continued to orient toward a Betelgeuse-defined south. This kind of learning, which occurs during a defined window of the life span and then resists revision, is called *critical period* learning. Below we discuss another example of critical period learning, human language learning.

> **Trail marker:** Critical-period learning is specialized to happen once, usually early in life, and then be resistant to revision.

Let's summarize. Indigo buntings clearly use the stars to orient their travels because they are disoriented when clouds hide the stars. They *learn* to use the stars because young birds that have not previously seen the sky are just as disoriented as birds whose view of the sky is hidden by clouds. When young birds do see the night sky, they learn two related things. First, from long gazes or from a series of gazes they learn the center of rotation, as shown by the comparison between the Polaris-trained and Betelgeuse-trained birds. Second, they learn to recognize stars or star clusters in a way that allows them to locate the center of rotation later, even in the absence of rotation. (Although trained under a rotating planetarium projection, the buntings were tested under a stationary one, so they could not have determined the north-south axis by watching the stars rotate during the test.) Finally, once they have learned the center of rotation, they resist revising this knowledge, as evidenced by the performance of the Betelgeuse-trained birds during their second migration season.

Every aspect of this learning mechanism makes adaptive sense. The center of rotation is an abstract notion, even to us, yet nestling birds are designed to extract it from the vast array of celestial (and other) stimuli because it is the *only* reliable clue to true north, or, for that matter, to any compass direction. (Other cues are unreliable: For example, in many places magnetic north and true north disagree by many degrees.) The center of rotation shifts fairly rapidly in evolutionary time but is stable over the short life spans of individuals. Thus, birds must initially learn where the center happens to be during their lifetimes, but have no further need for that learning mechanism once the task is accomplished (hence the resistance to retraining by the Betelgeuse-trained birds). And birds must not only learn where the center is but also learn to recognize the pattern of stars that define it because, in nature, the rotation is slow. A migrating bird would either waste a significant part of each night or risk flying significantly off course if it had to wait for rotation to redefine the center each evening. The star compass provides an example of a highly specialized learning mechanism. A very specific set of behaviors is precisely adjusted by exposure to a particular kind of experience. The pattern of responsiveness must have been designed by natural selection because of its usefulness in orienting migration.

How Desert Ants Find Their Way Home

The Tunisian desert is hot, dry, and relatively featureless. There, long-legged, fast-moving ants (*Cataglyphis bicolor*) live in underground colonies and make a living by finding and eating dead insects and other arthropods that have succumbed to the harsh environment. Most species of ants that feed on large patches of food work in teams to bring home their finds bit by bit; and to facilitate the many necessary trips they lay a trail of smelly pheromones to mark the route between the nest and the food patch. But the food items of *C. bicolor* are small and widely scattered. Thus this desert ant usually forages alone. A typical forager leaves the nest on a relatively straight course, but after twenty or more meters she begins searching, turning every meter or two. (We say "she" because all of the workers in all known ant species are females.) When she eventually finds a dead insect, she picks up the food item and, remarkably, heads straight for home. She is able to accomplish this straight-line homing from distances of more than one hundred meters. How does she do it?

These ants are not following pheromonal highways because every individual forager follows an independent path in searching for food. And because each forager eventually finds a separate prey item, when she turns for home she will be in a unique geographic position in reference to the home nest. Thus, every ant faces a new orientation problem on each foraging trip.

Perhaps individual *C. bicolor* learn the detailed landmarks surrounding their nests. In this way, they might grab their tasty find, rear up and look around, spot the nest, and haul their prey directly home. A simple experiment shows that this is not how they solve the problem. If a forager is picked up as she leaves the nest and moved a mere two meters away she is unable to find her way home by visual landmarks (Wehner and Flatt, 1972). What other way-finding strategies are left to explain their long-distance homing? Dead reckoning is a possibility.

In dead reckoning, or vector summing as it is sometimes called, the animal must keep track of headings and distances traveled and sum the resulting vectors to continually update its position in relation to the starting point. Is there an experiment to test for dead reckoning ability? Absolutely, and it's simple. When an ant finds a prey item at some location far from the nest, immediately pick her up and move her. If she has been using pheromonally marked trails she will wander aimlessly, having been displaced from the trail. If she can use landmarks, she will run toward her actual nest because the landmarks will provide a beacon. If she has been summing vectors she will run to the spot where the nest would have been had she not been moved.

Wehner and Srinivasan (1981) performed these displacements with individual *C. bicolor*, transporting them half a kilometer to an experimental area where one-meter grid lines had been marked on the desert floor. This grid allowed detailed plotting of the ants' movements. The ants behaved as if they had not been moved at all. That is, they ran the compass heading that would have linked the spot where they found food with their nest (Figure 7–3). And they ran this heading for a distance that equaled, within a few percent, the distance between the food and the nest. At that point they began a tight search pattern, apparently looking for the missing nest. There is no explanation for this result but dead reckoning, and no way for the ants to do it except by vector summing.

> **Trail Marker:** Desert ants constantly learn where they are by vector summing.

The way finding of these desert ants clearly involves learning. If deprived of the experience of their outward journey—for example, if they are picked up as they leave

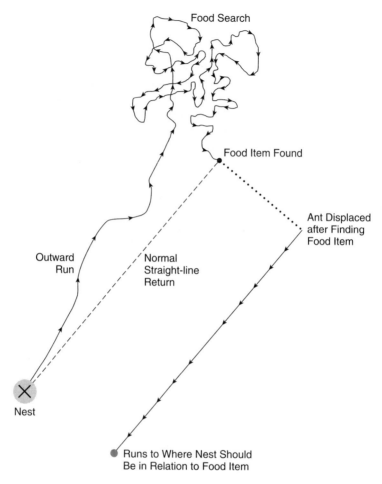

Figure 7–3. *An experiment to test for dead reckoning.* Desert ants ordinarily run straight back to their nests after finding a food item. If moved as they begin their homeward run, they travel the heading and distance that would have taken them home had they not been moved.

the nest—they find their nests only after much random searching. But if allowed to run out from the nest on their own, then even after quite long and convoluted journeys they select the correct heading and distance for a straight-line return. The crucial heading and distance information is being extracted from the experience gained in that outward run. This is an admirably specialized learning mechanism.

How Babies Learn Language

No matter whether you learn calculus, or learn how to fly a 747, or become a chess master, the most amazing learning task that you ever accomplish will be one that you essentially completed by the time you were seven years old. In those first few years of life you learned a language, and you learned it from scratch. During much of the process no instruction was possible because words were meaningless to you! You had to deduce everything, just as buntings have to deduce the center of rotation out of the mass of stimuli around them. How did you do it? Steven Pinker (1994) has summarized the process in his engaging book *The Language Instinct*. He calls it an instinct because, just like star-compass learning, it depends on preprogrammed modules designed by evolution to respond to very particular kinds of input from the environment.

Let's start with newborns. One thing babies do very well is sucking, because this is how they get the nutrients they need. It turns out that their sucking rate is correlated with shifts in their attention. Researchers have taken advantage of this fact, putting an electronic switch inside a plastic nipple so sucking rates can be monitored (e.g., Eimas et al., 1971). A lot has been learned in this way.

For example, babies systematically attend to language; they devote more attention to speech than to other sounds like ringing telephones or barking dogs. And, from birth, they attend to the sound of their parents' language more than to foreign languages (Mehler et al., 1988). This is apparently because they can hear from inside their mother's uterus and have already learned to recognize the distinctive melody of their mother's language.

After birth, infants continue gathering information about their parents' language. Research shows that by two months of age, they can discriminate between similar speech sounds. If infants are played the same sound over and over (for example the sound of the initial "d" in den), they habituate to it and their sucking rate decreases. If another, similar sound is then presented (say, the initial "t" in ten) the baby sucks harder and more often. The baby must have heard the difference because it reacted to the change from one sound to another (Eimas et al., 1971)

The next phase is fascinating. To understand it you will have to appreciate a subtle fact about language. Each language relies on the kind of sound contrasts that babies recognize ("t" versus "d") to do the important job of marking unique meanings. The sounds that make a difference in meaning in a given language are its *phonemes*. In English "d" and "t" are phonemes because our language contains words like "den" and "ten" that have different meanings; substituting "t" for "d" changes the meaning. Now, one of the ways in which languages differ is that they have different sets of phonemes. Depending on your dialect, American English has about thirty-eight phonemes. It is difficult for you to distinguish the sounds that do not represent contrasting phonemes in your language, for reasons that will be clear shortly. But you do notice when native speakers of another language speak your own, because they tend to use their phoneme system. For example "r" and "l" are phonemes in English (rake and lake have different meanings), but they are not in Japanese. Substituting the "r" sound for the "l" sound does not change the meaning of any Japanese word. Japanese speakers tend to use "r" and "l" indiscriminately when they speak English. Here's why all this happens.

Babies initially distinguish a wide array of linguistic sounds. But by the age of six months or so they begin ignoring, as shown by the habituated sucking response, the sounds that do *not* represent phonemic contrasts in their language. In other words, babies in both English-speaking and Japanese-speaking families initially distinguish "r" and "l" but babies in the Japanese-speaking families learn not to. That's why you find it difficult to distinguish sounds that aren't phonemes in your native language—you learned to ignore them even before you could talk.

> **Trail Marker:** Human infants learn which sounds signal a difference in meaning.

Also around six months of age, babies begin their efforts at sound production with what we call babbling. During this phase, the baby experiments and practices with the organs of articulation (the lips and tongue) and the organs of voice (the larynx and nose), working to coordinate the many muscles involved so as to produce the same phonemes as those noisy adults. The typical "talking" parrot is just as likely to imitate a telephone or a dog as a human, but babies imitation efforts are focused on speech sounds. Their mastery proceeds through single syllables ("ba," "ga") to the repeated syllables of their typical first words ("dada," "mama") to more phonetically complex words ("baby").

Language is not mere sounds, and it is not mere words. Language is a coherent, ordered system for conveying meaning. Perhaps even more amazing than the infant's knack for phoneme recognition and imitation is its gift for grammar. Again, this is something that is learned largely without instruction. Your high school English teacher was trying to get you to think consciously about rules you followed unconsciously, even as a young child. By the time they are eighteen months to two years old, normal children are producing simple two- and three-word sentences and the vast majority of these have the grammatically correct word order.

In addition children also extract and generalize other grammatical rules from the stream of language they hear around them. And the best evidence, oddly enough, comes from certain kinds of common mistakes. For example, a three-year-old might say "we buyed it." "Buyed" demonstrates the overgeneralization of a rule the child has deduced—add "d" to the action word to say it already happened. We say overgeneralize because the rule is being extended to a situation where it does not apply, because "buy" has an irregular past participle, "bought." Mere imitation can not account for overgeneralization because adults don't say "buyed." The child is extracting rules from the patterns of speech it hears and can use these rules to join and modify words to express novel ideas.

This is at least as impressive as deducing the center of celestial rotation, but it is profoundly different, and certainly accomplished by quite distinct mental modules. Indeed, as you have seen, language learning itself involves learning many separate systems—sound differentiation, sound production, word ordering, grammatical elements such as the past tense. And each of these kinds of learning is likely to depend on its own specialized set of modules. For example, Myrna Gopnik (1990) has described an inherited disorder that interferes with the ability to grasp grammatical rules (such as, add *s* to form the plural) but has minimal effects on other linguistic abilities.

> **Trail Marker:** Overgeneralization shows that children do not merely imitate; they deduce the rules of grammar.

Like axis-of-rotation learning, language learning has a rather marked critical period. Many of us have had painful experiences in trying to learn a second language. But being second is not the problem. It's not that some sort of language storage space is occupied by the first language with no room for the second. In fact, a second language can usually be learned as painlessly as the first, if it is learned early enough, typically before puberty. It seems that the relevant learning mechanisms, such as those that allow recognition of phonemic distinctions, tuning of the articulatory apparatus and deduction of grammatical rules, progressively shut down in the post-pubertal years. Indeed those elements learned first seem hardest to revise. For example, if you learn a language after puberty you will almost certainly retain a "foreign" accent; you will render that new language using the phoneme system of your native language. Indigo buntings have a critical period for axis-of-rotation learning because the axis does not change significantly during their lifetime. The critical period in language learning suggests that, in the EEA (see Chapter 4), our ancestors did not encounter new languages after their first ten or fifteen years of life.

Language acquisition is just one area where humans exhibit a set of specialized learning modules. There are many other such areas. For example, numerous studies suggest that infants manifest a quite distinct set of modules that helps them learn about the properties and movement of three-dimensional objects (e.g., Baillargeon, 1994; Spelke, 1994).

LEARNING DIFFERS AMONG CLOSELY RELATED SPECIES

In the previous examples, we saw how each of three quite different species had evolved a unique and specialized learning mechanism suited to a particular environmental challenge. Learning specializations can also be clearly demonstrated by comparing the different adaptations of closely related species. In these cases, animals that are similar to each other in many respects show variations in their learning abilities which match the demands of their environments.

In any species with parental care, there is strong natural selection to give that care to one's own offspring. Obviously, a parent who was indiscriminate in her rearing efforts—say by feeding any young individual she met—would reduce her fitness two ways. She would benefit the young of competitors and deprive her own young of any care she directed at others. For these reasons, evolution typically designs a recognition mechanism that prevents the waste of parental effort. For example, parents might learn to recognize their young or the place where they put their young.

Michael and Inger Beecher and their colleagues have compared offspring recognition abilities among several species of swallows. Both bank swallows

(*Riparia riparia*) and rough-winged swallows (*Stelgidopteryx serripennis*) nest in holes they excavate in river banks. Bank swallows are highly gregarious, nesting in large, closely spaced colonies, but rough-wings are solitary. Offspring recognition is a much more serious problem for bank swallows where the offspring of many different couples all fly together. But as you might expect, by the time young bank swallows emerge from the nest, mom and dad have learned the distinctive begging calls of their own young and reject all others seeking their parental generosity. The evolutionary context has been quite different in rough-winged swallows. Because of their solitary habits, parents who learned to recognize their own young got no special benefit. Thus rough-winged swallows are currently very indiscriminate. They do not learn to recognize the begging calls of their own young and, under experimental conditions, will even feed young bank swallows (Beecher et al., 1981, 1986).

> **Trail Marker:** Selection favors individual recognition where the young of many parents mix.

Another pair of swallow species provides a more detailed comparison. Like bank swallows, cliff swallows (*Hirundo pyrrhonota*) nest in large dense colonies. Barn swallows (*Hirundo rustica*) are much less gregarious but not as consistently solitary as rough-wings. Here again we predict that the more social species will be better at learning to discriminate among young. Field experiments confirm this: In cliff swallows, parents reliably recognized their own young on the basis of distinctive vocalizations, but barn swallows were unable to discriminate the calls of their own young from those of unrelated chicks (Stoddard and Beecher, 1983; Medvin and Beecher, 1986). For this pair of species a controlled laboratory experiment provides further evidence. Cliff swallows and barn swallows were rewarded with food for making discriminations among prerecorded swallow begging calls. To provide a fair test, an equal number of cliff and barn swallow vocal comparisons were presented. Cliff swallows mastered the task more quickly, suggesting that they had evolved better mechanisms for learning auditory distinctions (Loesche et al., 1991).

AN EVOLUTIONARY ANALYSIS OF CLASSICAL AND INSTRUMENTAL CONDITIONING

We have argued that each learning mechanism is designed to be efficient at solving some particular real-world problem. Because a mechanism specialized for a particular task tends to do a better job than a general, open-ended one, evolution has built many separate learning modules. The previous examples show that the detailed design of each module can be best understood in terms of the ecological context that defines both the problem and the cues or environmental inputs available to solve it. The problem of how to find north is different from the problem of how to recognize your offspring. Why would we expect the two to be solved with a single general-purpose mechanism? Surely a general solution would not be as good as a series of specialized mechanisms or modules, each an expert at its own job.

On the other hand, selection might build general-purpose learning mechanisms if animals faced any general problems. But, do they? Psychology has focused a great deal of study on classical and instrumental conditioning in the hope that these general-purpose learning mechanisms could explain much if not all of learned behavior. The examples we have already discussed—homing ants, migrating birds, and language-deducing infants—are unlikely to be explained by conditioning. Nevertheless, conditioning may be a general learning mechanism that, while it cannot account for migration and language, does account for a wide range of other learned behaviors. Let's find out. We'll begin by explaining the standard view of conditioning, and then we'll show how this view is incomplete and oversimplified. In the process, it will become apparent that even these supposedly general learning mechanisms are specialized in ways that adapt them to real-world situations.

Classical Conditioning: Does One Event Cause Another?

Classical conditioning is described in every introductory psychology textbook. The process begins with a natural relationship between a stimulus and a response. For example, an *unconditioned stimulus* (US) such as food produces an *unconditioned response* (UR) such as salivation. The connection between the unconditioned stimulus and response is taken as an intrinsic feature of the organism (although, as an evolutionist, you now know that this relationship also requires explanation). What is learned in classical conditioning is the connection between a new, arbitrary stimulus and the normal US. This conditioning happens when some other, previously neutral stimulus becomes associated with the US.

For example, in the classic Pavlovian experiment (Figure 7–4), if a bell is rung when food is offered, the bell becomes a *conditioned stimulus* (CS) in that the dog will eventually salivate whenever it hears the bell, even if no food is offered. The response of salivation to the bell alone is the *conditioned response* (CR). This is the essence of classical conditioning: The initial triggering effects of one stimulus are transferred to another because of a repeated pairing of the unconditioned and conditioned stimuli.

The standard view is that classical conditioning works because of—in fact, depends on—the tight temporal contiguity between the US and the CS. For example, food must be presented when the bell is rung (temporal contiguity between US and CS) in order for the bell to eventually trigger salivation. But this formulation is being reevaluated, primarily because of the discoveries by psychologists such as Robert Rescorla and John Garcia that contiguity is neither necessary nor sufficient to produce learning.

Let's imagine an experiment in which, whenever a bell is rung, food is presented. Will the animal learn the association between the bell and food and eventually salivate in response to the bell alone? If you understand the conventional view of classical conditioning you will say "yes." But, as it turns out the more correct answer is "it depends on how often food is presented *without* the bell." In other words it depends on what Rescorla (1988) calls the *background rate* of food

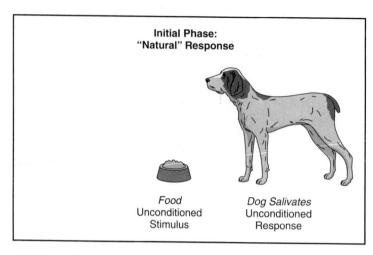

Initial Phase:
"Natural" Response

Food
Unconditioned
Stimulus

Dog Salivates
Unconditioned
Response

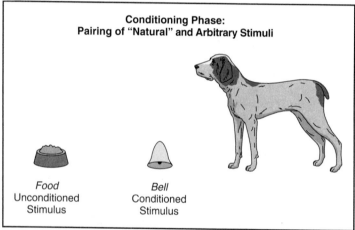

Conditioning Phase:
Pairing of "Natural" and Arbitrary Stimuli

Food
Unconditioned
Stimulus

Bell
Conditioned
Stimulus

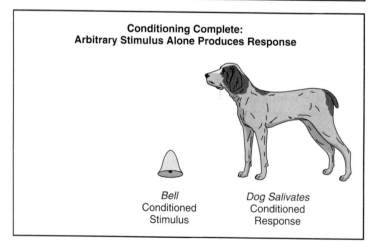

Conditioning Complete:
Arbitrary Stimulus Alone Produces Response

Bell
Conditioned
Stimulus

Dog Salivates
Conditioned
Response

Figure 7–4. *The standard picture of classical conditioning.* After repeated pairings of the unconditioned and conditioned stimulus, the original effects of the unconditioned stimulus are transferred to the conditioned stimulus.

Conditioning Phase with Low Background Rate: Good Learning

Bell (cs)   b   b   b   b

Food (us)   f   f   f f   f

Time ————————➤

Conditioning Phase with High Background Rate: No Learning

Bell (cs)   b   b   b   b

Food (us)   f f f   f f f f   f f   f   f f

Time ————————➤

Figure 7–5. *Low and high background rates compared.* For this comparison all variables are held constant except the background rate. Note that for "low" and "high" background rates the bell is rung an equal number of times, and every time the bell is rung food is presented. The difference lies in how often food is presented without the bell.

presentation. The background rate refers to how often the US, in this case food, is presented without the CS, the bell. If food is offered every single time the bell is rung and seldom or never offered without the bell (a low background rate) the animal will learn the association and begin to salivate in response to the bell alone. But if food is offered not only when the bell is rung but also on many occasions without the bell (a high background rate) there will be no learning at all (Figure 7–5)!

Rescorla believes that the importance of background rates in classical conditioning reveals the true task confronting the learning animal:

> I favor an analogy between animals showing Pavlovian conditioning and a scientist identifying the cause of a phenomenon. If one thinks of Pavlovian conditioning as developing between a CS and a US under just those conditions that would lead a scientist to conclude that the CS causes the US, one has a surprisingly successful heuristic [rule] for remembering the facts of what it takes to produce Pavlovian associative learning. (Rescorla 1988, p. 154)

If food regularly followed a bell and never appeared without the bell (low background rate), it would be reasonable to conclude that the bell caused food. If on the other hand, food regularly followed a bell but also appeared on many bell-less occasions (high background rate) no one would imagine that the bell caused food. Animals could be expected to have higher fitness if they were able to learn about the true causal relationships in their world, and to avoid forming associations between causally unrelated events. Rescorla's studies suggest that, while classical conditioning is more general than any of the learning mechanisms we have discussed previously, it is specialized for a particular task: identifying causation.

Trail Marker: Temporal contiguity alone does not produce learning.

Now we see why contiguity is not sufficient to promote classical conditioning. A high background rate causes the animal to discount the association between the US and CS. Because food is as likely without as with the bell, there is no reason to behave as if food is causally linked to the bell. But why, as we claimed above, is contiguity not even necessary for classical conditioning?

The justly famous research of John Garcia and his colleagues provides a clear example. Garcia studied food-aversion learning in rats. The general outline of the experiments is that rats were fed foods that were paired with certain novel stimuli and then the rats were punished in some way for consuming the foods. The question was, could the rats learn to associate the novel stimuli with the punishment? The answer is yes for some stimulus-punishment pairs, and no for others (Garcia and Ervin 1968).

In one version of the experiment, rats were offered a food with a novel taste. Overall, the taste was neither good nor bad, it was just different from anything the rats had previously experienced. After eating the unusual-tasting food the rats were made nauseous, either by exposure to x rays or by injection of a toxin. Surprisingly, from the viewpoint of classical conditioning theory, the rats learned this association on a single trial of the experiment, they learned it permanently, and they learned it even if they were made ill up to seven hours after tasting the novel food! Translate back to the classic Pavlovian experiment. Would you expect a dog to salivate on hearing a bell if the bell had only been paired with food on a single occasion? Would you expect the dog to learn the association between bell and food if it were fed seven hours after hearing the bell? Garcia's work showed that at least some kinds of classical conditioning do not require temporal contiguity. And there were further surprising results.

> **Trail Marker:** Temporal contiguity is not even necessary for learning.

On the basis of the taste experiments one might argue that nausea is an especially strong stimulus and thus leads to rapid learning. But other versions of the experiment show that nausea alone is not the key. For example, in some experiments a particular food was associated with novel visual or auditory stimuli, instead of novel flavors. Rats made sick after consuming such "noisy" or "bright" foods were completely unable to learn the association, and continued eating these clearly distinguishable foods no matter how many times they were made ill. The evidence that the rats could recognize the uniqueness of these foods is that other groups of subjects who were punished with electric foot shocks instead of nausea quickly learned to avoid "noisy" and "bright" foods. There is one more available pairing, between novel flavor and foot shock, and this also could not be learned by the rats despite repeated punishment (Figure 7–6).

Garcia and Ervin argued that these seemingly inconsistent results were perfectly understandable if viewed from an evolutionary perspective. First, taste is a chemical sense located at the site of ingestion. It provides a preliminary laboratory analysis of what is eaten. Nausea is a physiological state that could have several causes but may often result from mistaken food choices. Novel flavors—indicating novel foods—are especially good candidates for causing unusual physiological states. Moreover, digestion requires time so the physiological consequences of a novel food might not be immediately apparent. All this suggests that, if you were

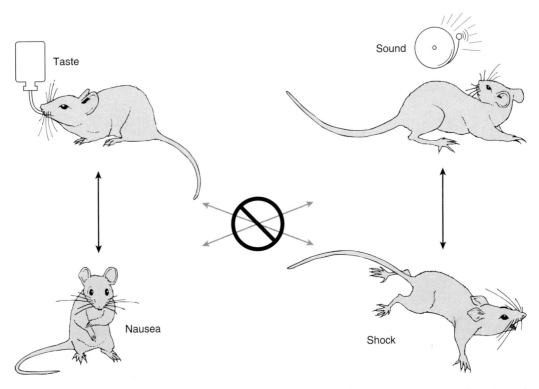

Figure 7–6. *Results of Garcia's food-aversion studies.* Some stimulus-consequence pairs could be learned easily; others could not be learned at all. See text to understand why these findings make adaptive sense. (Data for this drawing from "Gustatory-Visceral and Telereceptor-cutaneous Conditioning: Adaptation in Internal and External Milieus" by J. Garcia and F. Ervin in *Communication in Behavioral Biology,* Series A 1, (1968). Drawing from *Animal Behavior,* 6th ed. by J. Alcock. Copyright © 1998 by John Alcock. Sunderland, MA; Sinauer Associates.)

designing an animal you would wire it up to associate usual tastes with any unusual physiological states occurring in the near future. In contrast, because they provide few chemical cues about food content, visual or acoustic stimuli should not be treated as if they can predict subsequent physiological states. Surface pain, whether resulting from electric shock or predator attack, is not likely to be preceded by a particular taste experience, but it might well be signaled by an unusual sight or sound. In other words, Garcia's rats show clear predisposition to associate certain stimuli with certain outcomes and these predispositions are entirely sensible given the normal patterns of cause and effect in their environments.

Instrumental Conditioning: Did I Do That?

We have argued that the learning that goes on during classical conditioning is specialized to collect information about causation. Instrumental conditioning goes one step further, to the realm of control. An animal that can learn about causal patterns may be able to use those patterns to its own advantage. If food follows the pressing of a lever, perhaps more food could be obtained by more presses. Learning how to manipulate the environment might be a general problem. Here are some experiments that explore that issue.

Hummingbirds are tiny, glittering birds that feed on the nectar of flowers. Nectar is calorically rich, but each flower produces very small amounts and takes time to replenish its supply after a hummingbird feeds. For this reason, hummingbirds must visit many flowers to feed themselves and would do better if they avoided flowers they had recently visited.

Researchers can maintain hummingbirds in captivity by providing synthetic nectar—sugar, vitamins, and minerals dissolved in water—in plastic tubes fitted with artificial flowers at the tips. Susan Cole and her associates have used synthetic nectar as a reward in learning experiments with hungry hummingbirds. Each trial of their experiment had two brief phases, an "information" phase followed within ten to twelve seconds by a "choice" phase. In the information phase, the bird was presented with a single artificial flower and allowed to feed from it briefly before it was withdrawn. In the following choice phase, the same bird was presented with two identical artificial flowers, one in the same position as the information-phase flower, and one twenty-five centimeters to the right or left. In the choice phase, only one of the two flowers had nectar. If the bird chose the wrong flower, it did not get any nectar reward during the choice phase.

Using this technique, the birds were trained to solve two different problems, called "stay learning" and "shift learning." In stay learning, the flower that was in the same position as the information-phase flower had the nectar, so the bird had to choose the position where it had just fed to get the reward. In shift learning, the flower in the novel position had the nectar, so the bird had to choose a new location to get the reward. The experimenters wanted to know if the birds would learn shift learning and stay learning with equal ease. Traditional learning theory would predict that, because the birds are getting the same reward in each case, they should perform equally well on the two tasks. What do you predict?

Cole and her associates found that all three of the hummingbird species they tested were much better at shift learning than stay learning (Cole et al., 1982). In fact, even the slowest birds mastered shift learning in many fewer trials and with many fewer errors than any bird needed to master stay learning. Given what you know about the natural food of hummingbirds, can you form a hypothesis about why hummingbirds are better at shift learning than they are at stay learning? Do you think animals will generally be better at shift learning than stay learning?

Trail Marker: The ease of learning a task depends on how well it matches a real-world situation.

Here's an elegant experiment that answers that question. Take six dozen male rats and randomly divide them into two groups. For a defined period withhold water from one group and food from the other. Then, give each animal the opportunity to find the withheld substance (food for the hungry rats, water for the thirsty rats) in a T-maze. A T-maze has a long straightaway, where the animal starts its run, plus a right arm and a left arm, one of which contains the reward. There are several ways to place the reward. For example, you might use a "fixed" site, always placing the reward in the same arm.

Lew Petrinovich and Robert Bolles (1954) performed this experiment and found that, when rewarded at a fixed site, thirsty rats learn faster and make fewer errors than hungry rats. Perhaps thirsty rats are more motivated to solve the problem than hungry rats. To test this explanation, Petrinovich and Bolles repeated their experiment exactly as before but used a different reward placement rule. Instead of placing the withheld substance in the same arm on every trial they systematically alternated its placement—right, left, right, left—on successive trials. This change in reward placement produced an entirely different result. When the reward is alternated between the right and left arms, hungry rats learn faster and make fewer errors that thirsty rats. In fact, most of the thirsty rats never learned the alternation task, despite the fact that the same level of deprivation allowed them to learn the "fixed" task faster than hungry rats (Figure 7–7). How can we make sense of this apparent contradiction?

Petrinovich and Bolles argued that motivation could not be the explanation because it was the same in the two experiments. Instead the rats seemed to have a natural bias about where food and water would be found. They were more likely to look for water where they had previously found it, but seemed willing to look for food in areas where they had not recently fed. These biases are ecologically sensible. Water systematically occurs in certain areas such as valleys and ditches, and these reservoirs typically hold much more than one animal could drink. Once you have learned

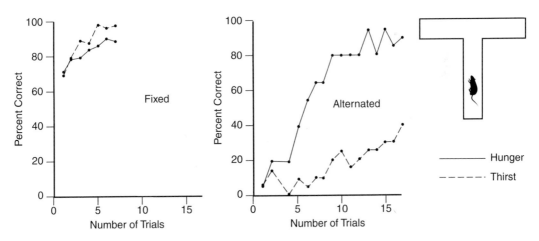

Figure 7–7. *T-maze learning of hungry and thirsty rats depends on reward placement.* Rats learn the location of water more easily than they learn the location of food, as long as the location is constant. However, if the location is alternated, they learn the location of food easily and have great difficulty learning the location of water. This learning bias matches the natural distribution of food and water for wild rats (see text).

where these reservoirs are, you should store the information permanently so you can retrieve it any time you are thirsty. Food on the other hand is much less predictable, both because some food items are themselves mobile and because it often occurs in small packets that are quickly used up. Unlike water, food might be here today and somewhere else tomorrow. About the only thing certain about food is that if you've eaten a particular food item, it's gone. Given all this, animals should not be designed to behave as if an area that once held food always will.

This example provides a useful contrast with the hummingbird experiments discussed above. The hummingbirds were much quicker to learn which artificial flower had food in "shift learning" experiments, when they had to choose a new location to get a reward. Some psychologists have suggested that switching to a new location after receiving a reward is a general rule that animals apply to any learning situation. But as Petrinovich and Bolles showed, the very same animal might use a "switch" strategy for some kinds of resources and a "stay" strategy for others, depending on how the resource is distributed in nature. How do you predict thirsty hummingbirds would perform on switch and stay learning where they were rewarded with the opportunity to drink water?

These examples suggest that even for the supposedly most general kind of learning mechanisms, classical and instrumental conditioning, animals exhibit clear adaptive specializations.

SOME CONCLUSIONS ABOUT LEARNING

We began with a discussion of innate and learned behavior, arguing that the distinction no longer matches our modern emphasis on the interaction between genes and environment. Behavioral traits are the most facultative aspects of the phenotype. We have suggested that learning occurs when behavior is modified by experience; and the examples we have discussed make it clear that selection has favored a wide array of learning mechanisms. In other words, selection has designed a large set of ways for experience to influence behavior. In many cases, a very precise sort of environmental input is required and a very narrow aspect of the behavioral phenotype is modified. For buntings, stellar rotation defines migratory orientation; for ants, locomotion updates the vector record; for human infants, adult speech marks out distinctive phonemes; for cliff and bank swallows, begging calls trigger acoustic discriminations; for rats, food and water prime different searching strategies. The examples could be multiplied endlessly. The essential point is that in each case clear benefits can be had by learning (such as avoiding the harsh winter, or returning to the refuge of the nest), and clear ecological constraints limit how the learning could be accomplished (the pole shifts with the precession of the equinoxes, the desert has few landmarks). Thus in each case, selection has produced a unique learning mechanism suited to the opportunities and constraints of the situation.

Like other evolved adaptations, the learning mechanisms we have discussed in this chapter are species-typical traits; barring some genetic or developmental accident, they are likely to emerge in all normal members of the species in question. All normal ants of the species *C. bicolor* will possess the ability to sum vectors, and all normal human infants will have the ability to deduce phonemic and grammatical rules from the speech they hear. But individual ants will follow different homeward courses because they will have had unique experiences and hence computed unique vector sums on their outward journeys. And individual human children will grow up speaking different languages because they will have extracted different sets of rules depending on the language their parents spoke. Thus, the behaviors that result from these learning mechanisms are highly facultative, highly responsive to experience.

A final point concerns the role of practice in learning. Often we assume that for something to be learned there must be a period during which less-than-perfect performance improves until it matches some ideal standard. While this may be true for some kinds of learning, it is not a general rule. An infant may require practice to master the production of certain speech sounds. And a dog will have to experience repeated pairings before it will associate a bell with food. But an ant cannot practice its return run from a foraging expedition because each return run is different. On each outward run, it must continuously learn its location by constantly updating its vector record (Gallistel 1995). In general, practice *cannot* be a feature of learning if there are severe penalties for error. This can be shown even in the realm of conditioning. Psychology texts all emphasize that both classical and instrumental conditioning require repeated trials. Phrased in our terms, they would argue that the animal cannot learn about causation unless it has many opportunities to evaluate contiguity and background rate. This is often true, but Garcia has shown that in some cases one-trial conditioning is the rule. When the pairing is ecologically salient—e.g., novel flavors and subsequent nausea—a single exposure produces a permanent change in behavior. Thus the role of practice is yet another dimension on which learning mechanisms differ from one another.

In conclusion then, the most useful way to think about learning is not as an alternative to evolved behavior patterns. Learning occurs not because evolution has left some behavior to chance, but because some kinds of behavior lead to higher fitness if they are molded to fit current environmental conditions. What we call learning includes many very specific kinds of processes by which particular kinds of behavior are shaped to fit particular aspects of the environment. Each learning mechanism embodies facultative rules implemented by modules that were crafted by natural selection to meet the ecological opportunities and constraints of the environment where they evolved.

SUMMARY

1. Behavior is not usefully divided into innate and learned because learning itself is a result of evolution, and because all behavior depends on certain kinds of experience.
2. Learning mechanisms are best understood as facultative adaptations.

3. There are no general problems for animals to solve, only specific ones; hence there would be little use for a general-purpose learning mechanism.
4. Thus, learning is not a single process, but many processes, each specialized for particular kinds of problems.
5. The means by which birds learn to migrate, ants learn their way home, and infants learn language are all very different.
6. Different species have evolved different learning mechanisms because they face different challenges and opportunities.
7. Despite the predictions of conditioning theory, animals learn relationships that "make sense" in terms of their natural ecology much more easily than they learn relationships that don't make sense.

8 ◆ Cognition

Thinking—cognition—consists largely of mental processes we take for granted. As you walk across campus, you consider that if you don't step up your pace you will be late for class, whether you can get tickets to the concert this weekend, a clever topic sentence for next week's writing assignment, (that car is moving fast, better wait for the walk signal), why your roommate's been in a bad mood lately, and more. We think constantly, take it for granted and seldom analyze the process itself. At one level, it's easy to understand thought: Our cognitive processes must have evolved to solve the kinds of problems our ancestors faced every day. As Douglas Kenrick and his associates have put it, "cognitive modules are designed not for cool rationality, but for hot cognition, to respond to crucial events related to survival and reproduction" (Kenrick, Sadalla and Keefe (1998, p. 488.). It stands to reason that we can better understand thought if we ask what those events and problems were.

CATEGORIZATION

One fundamental aspect of thought is that we do not treat everything we encounter as unique. Instead, we group things and places and situations, even people into categories. Psychologists have done quite a bit of research on how people recognize underlying concepts and form categories. Table 8–1 contains several two-character items, some of which are members of a certain category and some are not. Try to discover the rule that determines category membership.

Table 8–1.   Members and nonmembers of a category.*

ITEM	CATEGORY MEMBER?
t4	yes
3H	no
Rs	no
9k	no
P2	yes
m8	yes
4Y	no
d3	no
J7	no
36	yes

*Category members have an even number on the right.

Kintsch (1970) reviewed an extensive literature on this topic. Not surprisingly, the ability to learn concepts is affected by the number of relevant and irrelevant dimensions there are. In the above example, note that upper- and lowercase are irrelevant. Similarly, it makes no difference whether the left-hand element is a number or a letter.

But in the 1970s, Eleanor Rosch began to suggest that much of this research was itself irrelevant! She claimed that the abstract shapes, letters, and numbers used in these experiments bore no relation to real-world stimuli. Thus there was no particular reason to assume that these experiments revealed much about how people form, recognize, and use real-world categories. One of her key lines of evidence was that many natural categories—categories people spontaneously form outside the psychology laboratory—have an internal structure (Rosch 1973, 1975; Rosch and Mervis 1975). This is demonstrated by a phenomenon that Rosch called "typicality."

Typicality

Reconsider the category exemplified above, "even number on the right." Is "t4" a better example of the category than "P2" is? Of course not. They fit the rule equally well and are therefore both full members. To begin to grasp Rosch's point, let's contrast this artificial example with a natural category like "bird." Is "robin" a better example of a bird than a "penguin" is? Most people say "yes." In other words, in most of the artificial concept-formation experiments (like the example in Table 8–1), items either belong to a category or they don't. But in the case of many real-world categories, items exhibit different degrees of membership. Thus real-world categories are *fuzzy*: Some items like "robin" are typical or central members of their category and others like "penguin" are peripheral, at or near the category boundary. Rosch argued that natural categories are structured by typicality, that is, by a recognition that some items are more and some items less central to the category. She and her colleagues demonstrated the influence of typicality on many aspects of cognition. For example, typicality must affect how items are stored in memory because reaction time depends on typicality. Thus, subjects take less time to decide that a sparrow is a bird than they do to decide that a chicken is a bird. (Rips, Shoben and Smith 1973).

> **Trail Marker:** Many natural categories seem to be organized by typicality.

At least as importantly from our perspective, typicality affects not only how items are stored and retrieved but also what we think about them. For example, members that are typical of a category share more features than do members that are atypical. Sparrows and robins share more features—they hop, fly, rear their young in grassy nests—than penguins and chickens do. Moreover, typical category members share fewer features with members of other categories than atypical members do. Sparrows and robins don't swim, but penguins share their aquatic habits with fish and dolphins. Why should this all be so? Why did the tendency to categorize evolve in the first place? Rosch suggested an answer by focusing on natural categories.

The tree of life has a branching structure. One species splits into two, each of which may later divide, *ad infinitum.* Thus living things really do form a nested hierarchy. Several species of baboons are nested within a single genus (*Papio*); at the next level baboons, vervets, and guenons are grouped together to form a single family; and so on, up to the highest levels. Because of the way traits are added and deleted by selection, a pair of species with a more recent common ancestor (species whose branches have separated only recently) share more characteristics than a pair of species whose common ancestor lies farther in the past (see Figure 1–2). A creature will almost always be more similar to the species on adjacent branches. And for this same reason, what is true of one kind of animal or plant is likely to be true of closely related ones as well. Thus, it seems that our fuzzy categorization is very good at recognizing natural kinds—that is, the kinds that evolution creates.

> **Trail Marker:** Typicality-based categories reflect the nested hierarchy of relatedness among living things.

One source of evidence on this point comes from studies of how people perform when directly asked about natural kinds. For example, Boster and D'Andrade (1989) asked people to group museum specimens of stuffed birds. Despite the fact that the subjects included professional ornithologists, college students with no ornithology training, and members of the South American Jivaro Indian tribe, they showed a high level of agreement. Not only did they produce similar groupings, but they agreed on their choice of grouping criteria, while at the same time selecting different criteria for different subgroups of birds. Of course evolution has produced a collection of bird species linked in a web of closer and more distant relatedness. There is little choice except to conclude that Boster and D'Andrade's subjects were in fact recognizing that pattern of relatedness.

In another study also using birds as stimulus material, Boster (1988) asked what factors influence typicality judgments. If typicality is a reflection of the tree of life, then people should regard species with many closely related species as the most typical. That's exactly what he found: Typicality is better predicted by the number of closely related species than it is by how common the bird is (either in the subjects' environment or in written materials such as prose or poetry).

> **Trail Marker:** "Typical" species are those with many close relatives.

So here is one of cognition's little "quirks": We think in categories. But this is not the whole story. Our categories are special; they have a nested structure including typical and progressively more atypical representatives. This category structure is highly correlated with the actual structure of evolutionary relatedness among living things, so this cognitive architecture may well have evolved to reflect the world around us. But why? What is so important about the ability to sort creatures by how close or far apart they are on the tree of life?

We said in Chapter 5 that perception is for action, not mere knowledge, and the same is true for categorization. The adaptive advantages of simple categorization are fairly obvious. Dealing with everything we encounter as an entirely unique item would be a waste of time and effort, not to mention impossible. Most things we've seen before. If we recognize them as such, we'll know how to deal with them. But typicality-based categories go a step further. Remember, natural kinds share properties depending on how closely related they are. If you know what to expect of a typical category member like a robin, then you'll have a good idea what to expect from another typical category member, like a sparrow. But the less typical a category member is, the less we should expect it to share properties with more central members of the category. In other words, typicality-based categories could give us an evolutionarily appropriate way of using our experience to anticipate the properties of living things. But do they? Do we use typicality judgments to make predictions?

In an early and elegant experiment, Rips (1975) showed that we do. He asked subjects to read a story and then make some predictions. The story involved an island with just eight kinds of inhabitants: robins, sparrows, hawks, eagles, ducks, geese, ostriches, and bats. (Of course bats aren't birds at all; they were included because they fly and might be imagined to represent a very peripheral member of the category.) Subjects were told that one of the species was infected by a highly contagious disease. Some subjects were told the sparrows were infected, others were told the eagles were, others the geese. Then the subjects were asked to predict what proportion of each other species would contract the disease. Their predictions showed a strong influence of typicality. Subjects said that typical species like sparrows and robins would infect most of the other species, but that atypical ones like geese would infect only other similarly atypical ones, such as ducks.

> **Trail Marker:** It remains to be seen whether all categories are
> organized by typicality.

Like so many other topics in this text, this is fertile ground for further research. Another domain that is very important to fitness is kinship and our responses to it (see Chapters 4 and 15). Here also the branching tree of reproduction means that the true structure of categories is a nested hierarchy. You are more related to your mother than to your grandmother, and so on. So the use of typicality-based judgments in this arena also provides a good match to reality. But it's not clear that *all* natural categories represent nested hierarchies. For example, nothing about the tree of life implies that the category "dangerous stranger" is automatically a nested hierarchy. In other words, there may be some domains where typicality-based judgment would be incorrect and hence produce maladaptive results. It would be interesting then to examine whether people classify, for example, allies and potential mates differently from the way they classify plants, animals, and kin. So far as we know, this remains to be studied.

MEMORY

The fundamental problem of memory is data management and retrieval. From some points of view, human memory is frustratingly inefficient. Just think back to that recent test when you simply could not remember material that you had studied several times! Why hasn't evolution designed us to have ready access to all of our memories, all of our past experience? The simple answer is that such a system would be both prohibitively expensive and not especially useful.

In viewing a single scene, we are exposed to millions of bits of information. Multiply this by the thousands of scenes we view every day of our lives. Add the equal amounts of information flowing in through our other senses and we have information overload! Storing a lifetime of such information in a quickly retrievable form is beyond the management capacities of even the largest and most efficient supercomputers. Besides, what good is all this information? What does it matter whether your cousin Betsy wore a blue or green sweater two Thanksgivings ago? For our memories to function efficiently, we *have to forget* much of our experience (or ignore it in the first place).

> **Trail Marker:** An efficient memory would forget
> the less useful items.

Of course, an optimal memory system wouldn't forget at random. Some bits of information are useful. We should forget what is less useful in order to provide efficient storage and access to what is more useful. In other words, at some level, there ought be a sorting of information by its likely usefulness. If those sorting decisions required conscious judgment that too would be very expensive. Imagine sorting every bit of information in a scene: "I'll need that, but not that or that . . ." Is there a way to get this sorting done more cheaply? John Anderson and Lael Schooler (1991) have advanced a theory of memory that suggests we use simple and automatic rules that match the demands placed on our memory by the environment. Let's begin by considering some baseline facts about how our memory actually performs. Then we'll go on to explore whether these facts seem well-suited to the challenges posed for our memory by the environment.

Practice and Retention Effects

Several features of memory are well understood. For example, people find it easier to retrieve information they have been exposed to many times. You are more likely to remember the stores along your regular route to school than the ones along the route to a less frequent destination, such as your Aunt Martha's house. This is called the *practice effect*. You have more practice with the more frequently traveled route and so can more easily remember what lies along it. A second well-known memory phenomenon is called the *retention effect*. This refers to the fact that we are better able to recall recent information. You may know who is Secretary of State, but you probably don't remember who held the post previously, even though there was a time when you heard the name equally often.

Neither the practice nor the retention effect is startling; you probably realized both of the effects were true without ever assigning them a special name. But psychologists have studied these effects much more closely and we will need to do likewise to follow Anderson and Schooler's argument. What is the precise pattern of forgetting? Will doubling the amount of practice double your recall? Waiting three days to report a conversation will decrease your accuracy, but by how much? These are quantitative questions best answered mathematically or graphically. When we examine practice and retention carefully, both the effects seem to be best described by power functions. Memories decay rapidly at first and then more and more slowly, as a function of time taken to a negative power. (We will not go into the details of the mathematics.)

Spacing Effects

A third and less familiar aspect of memory is called the spacing effect. Imagine you can practice something a limited number of times, say four. What practice pattern do you think would produce the best recall? Since the number of practice sessions is set at four, only the retention effect should matter; so group the practice sessions close to the test, right? That works well under some conditions. In particular, when the interval from the last practice session to the test is short, concentrated practice yields better recall (Case 1 in Figure 8–1). But if the interval from the last practice session to the test is long (Case 2), then recall is actually better if the preceding

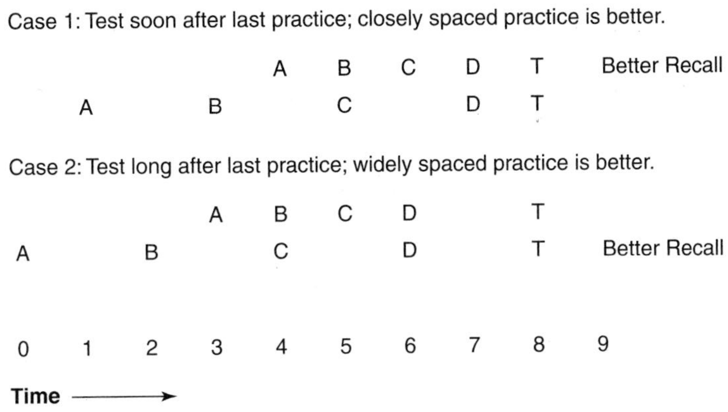

Case 1: Test soon after last practice; closely spaced practice is better.

| | | | | A | B | C | D | T | Better Recall |
| A | | | B | | C | | D | T | |

Case 2: Test long after last practice; widely spaced practice is better.

| | | | | A | B | C | D | | T | |
| A | | B | | | C | | D | | T | Better Recall |

| 0 | 1 | 2 | 3 | 4 | 5 | 6 | 7 | 8 | 9 |

Time ⟶

Figure 8–1. *The spacing effect.* The horizontal axis is time. A, B, C, and D, are four episodes of practice; T is the test, when recall is measured. The spacing effect refers to the fact that recall is better when the interval between the last practice episode and the test approximates the interval between the practice episodes.

practice sessions were also at longer intervals. Yes, this partly overshadows the retention effect because it means that recall can sometimes be better when the earlier practice episodes occurred longer ago.

Anderson and Schooler (1991) wanted to know why memory works the way it does. They asked why the practice and retention effects are power functions (instead of linear functions or exponential functions, for example) and why there is a spacing effect—why recall is better when the test interval is similar to the practice interval.

Their premise is, like ours, that it would be impossible to store for quick access all of the information that we receive. We would be better served by a memory system that made items available in proportion to how likely they were to be needed. We should store little-used memories in progressively less accessible ways (perhaps eventually forgetting them completely), but keep the frequently needed ones readily accessible. This makes sense. But remember, the results of memory experiments tell us that retention curves have a particular (power function) shape. Does this pattern of retention serve the goal of making the most needed memories the most accessible? The answer depends on the pattern of real-world experience. What's the schedule on which memories are needed? Anderson and Schooler wanted to know if this schedule fits a power function. If the demands placed on our memory fit a power function that would explain why our memory systems are built on power functions.

Modeling the Demands on Memory

In order to explore this question, Anderson and Schooler selected three sources of real-world information flow: *New York Times* headlines, utterances by parents to their children (MacWhinney and Snow 1990), and the authors of e-mail sent to

John Anderson over a four-and-a-half year period. The idea is that each time a word is used (in a headline or in a parent's speech) it represents a demand on the reader or listener to recall the meaning of the word. And similarly, each time e-mail is received it requires the recipient to recall who the sender is. If you have grasped the notion that our psychological adaptations are matched to the demands of life in the EEA, you may worry about Anderson and Schooler's choice of data sets. Surely parents talked to their children in the EEA, but there were certainly no newspapers or computers. Nevertheless, there was "news" (events) that people must have talked about, and people did interact with others even if these interactions were face-to-face rather than electronic.

> **Trail Marker:** To see what an ideal memory would have to do, Anderson and Schooler studied the pattern of events in the world.

With these reservations in mind, let's consider the retention function specified by these data. For example, how likely is a particular word (such as "north") to appear in the *New York Times* headline on a particular day? (Think about how you would try to predict such a thing if a friend proposed a bet. Would you think of asking how many days had elapsed since it last appeared in the headline?) It turns out that a word's probability of appearing is an ever-decreasing function of the number of days since the word last appeared in the headline. If the word appeared the previous day, its probability of occurrence is at its maximum value, about .17. If it occurred five days ago, its probability of occurrence drops dramatically to .04, less than one-fourth of what it was for a one-day interval. For words that last appeared ten and twenty days ago, the probability of occurrence drops again, but far less precipitously, to .025 and .017, respectively. The key point is that the curve that relates probability of occurrence to the number of days since the last occurrence is a power function!

Anderson and Schooler took essentially the same approach to the parental speech data and the e-mail data. It turns out that the probability that a word will appear in a parental utterance is a power function of the number of utterances since it last appeared. And the probability that you will get e-mail from a particular person is a power function of the number of days since you last got e-mail from him or her. These results suggest that our memory decays in the power-function way that it does, because this pattern of decay matches the likelihood that we will need to recall it! These same authors used similar techniques to model the practice function for their three real-world information sources and again found power-function relationships.

Finally Anderson and Schooler tried to model the spacing effect. Remember, in the spacing effect, items that are tested soon after their last presentation are recalled more accurately if the series of presentations was at short intervals, but items that are tested longer after the last presentation are recalled more accurately when the presentations were at longer intervals (see Figure 8–1). To see if real-world experiences cluster in this same way Anderson and Schooler needed to measure two things: 1) the "presentation interval" between two prior occurrences of the same word or name and 2) the "test interval," that is, the number of days since its most recent occurrence. And they needed to assess how these two measures affect the probability that a word or name would appear in the next headline (or utterance or e-mail message). They found, for all three data sets, a pattern that strongly paralleled the spacing effect. Words or names that had occurred recently were more likely to appear if their previous appearances were at short intervals. But items that had not appeared recently were more likely to appear if their previous occurrences were at long intervals. Thus, here again Anderson and Schooler found a good match between our ability to recall items and their real-world patterns of occurrence. It seems that the detailed features of memory systems are calibrated to mirror the pattern of events in the world. To the extent that further evidence continues to support these findings, they suggest that memory consists of a set of very precisely tuned cognitive adaptations.

> **Trail Marker:** The practice, retention, and spacing effects seem to match the pattern of real-world events.

As we noted in our concluding remarks about typicality, considerable work remains to be done in the area of memory. Anderson and Schooler have pointed the way: What we want to know is, does memory performance match the demands placed on memory by the real world. However, the question remains whether these demands differ from one cognitive domain to another. In that case, we should expect our memories to perform differently with different kinds of subject matter. Some tantalizing data from the study of animal memory suggests that this is a promising line for future research (Healy, (1992). For example, the study of t-maze learning (Petrinovch and Bolles, 1954) discussed at the end of Chapter 7 suggests that rats have separate memory modules for the location of food and the location of water.

ARE WE DESIGNED TO THINK LOGICALLY?

Logic formalizes the rules of valid inference. The subject is taught in every college and university and most students find it mind-bending. Why don't we learn the rules of logic in infancy the way we learn the arcane grammatical rules (see Chapter 7) of our parents' language?

Leda Cosmides and John Tooby have used a procedure called the Wason Selection Task to examine our logical skills, and they have found some revealing strengths and weaknesses. You can best appreciate what they learned by trying a few Wason selection tasks. Here's an example that you should try to solve.

Example 8.1

You have been hired as a clerk. Your job is to make sure that a set of documents is marked correctly, according to the following rule:

"If the document has a D rating, then it must be marked code 3."

You have been told that there are some errors in the coding of the documents, and that you need to find the errors. Each document has a letter rating on one side and a numerical code on the other. Here are four documents. Which document(s) do you need to turn over to check for errors?

| D | F | 3 | 7 |

Before we give you the correct answer to this problem let's try another example of the Wason Selection Task.

Example 8.2

You have been hired as a bouncer in a bar and you must enforce the following rule:

"If a person is drinking beer, then he must be over twenty years old."

The cards below have information about four people in the bar. One side of each card lists a person's age and the other side shows what he's drinking. Which card(s) do you need to turn over to be sure no one is breaking the law?

| beer | coke | 25 yrs | 16 yrs |

The bouncer problem is easy, isn't it? Obviously the answer is just two cards: "beer" to make sure the person is over twenty, and "16 yrs" to make sure the person isn't drinking beer. You don't care what the twenty-five year old is drinking, and anybody can drink coke. Was the clerical problem harder for you?

It turns out that these two problems have the very same logical structure. Thus, the answer to the clerical problem is just two cards: "D" and "7." "D" must be turned over to make sure it is marked 3, as required. And "7" must be turned over to make sure it does not have a D on the other side, in which case the 7 would be an error. Our rule says nothing about how F's should be coded (they might also be

Rule: D-rated documents must be marked code 3.	Rule: Beer drinkers must be over twenty years old.
Step 1: Check D-rated documents to see if they meet the coding criterion.	Step 1: Check beer drinkers to see if they meet the age criterion.
Step 2: Check any documents not matching the coding criterion (e.g., code 7) to see if they are D-rated.	Step 2: Check anyone who does not meet the age criterion (e.g., 16 years old) to see if they are drinking beer.
No more checking necessary:	No more checking necessary:
F ratings (paired with any code) could not violate the rule.	Coke drinking (at any age) could not violate the rule.
Code 3 documents do not have to be D-rated.	People over twenty do not have to drink beer.

code 3, or code 17 or code 15,000; we just don't know), so "F" does not need to be checked. Similarly, we have not been told that all code-3 documents have a D rating, only that all D-rated documents should be marked code 3.

Let's compare these two logical problems side by side. Even after you see that these two problems have exactly the same logical content, you probably still find the clerical problem harder than the bouncer problem. You are not alone. Less than 25 percent of college students solve the clerical problem correctly, but roughly 75 percent give the correct answer to the bouncer task. Why are some logical problems easier than others, even when they are essentially the same problem? Perhaps the difference in difficulty is a matter of familiarity. The clerical problem is novel, whereas the bouncer problem is likely to be familiar to most college students. Your own abilities can be used to test this hypothesis. Let's consider another pair of examples.

Example 8.3

In the Wiki-wiki tribe, married men live west of the mountains where casava root is common, and unmarried men live east of the mountains where mola nuts are more common. Cassava roots and mola nuts are equally nutritious and equally tasty. Among the Wiki-wiki married men wear tattoos and unmarried men do not. An anthropologist has told you that:

"Among the Wiki-wiki, if a man eats cassava root, he has tattoos."

The following four cards tell what a man eats on one side and whether he has tattoos on the other. Which card(s) do you need to turn over to check the anthropologist's claim?

Eats cassava root	eats mola nuts	tattoos	no tattoos

Here's another example with identical structure but a different story.

Example 8.4

Among the Beri-beri people cassava root is thought to be a potent aphrodisiac. Because the Beri-beri are concerned about sexual mores, only married men are allowed to eat cassava root. Unmarried men can get the same nutrients without any aphrodisiac effects by eating mola nuts. The Beri-Beri can monitor whether men cheat because married men wear tattoos and unmarried ones do not. Thus they enforce the rule:

"Among the Beri-beri, if a man eats cassava root, he has tattoos."

Now look back at the four cards from the preceding example. Which card(s) do you need to turn over to make sure no one is breaking the rule?

These two problems again have the same logical content, and both represent unfamiliar rules. In fact, note that the rules are exactly the same (except for the names of the imaginary tribes). If familiarity is the key that helps us unlock logical problems then, because they both are based on unfamiliar stories, these two tattoo problems should be equally difficult. But if you are like most college students, you found the second one noticeably easier. Familiarity is apparently not the most important factor. What then might make some logical problems easier than others?

Cheater-Detection Problems are Easy

After testing people's ability to solve many different Wason selection problems, Cosmides and Tooby have argued in favor of an interesting generalization. If the problem involves what they call *cheater detection*, then most people can solve it; when the very same problem is structured in a way that does not involve cheater detection, most people cannot solve it. A cheater is a person who takes a benefit to which he is not entitled, for example because he has not paid the associated cost. Cheater detection, then, is the ability to see who has undeservedly taken a benefit.

> **Trail Marker:** Our evolved tendencies toward reciprocity help us solve certain logical problems, but not others.

As did Robert Trivers (1971), Cosmides and Tooby argue that reciprocal altruism has been important in the evolution of our species (see Chapter 4). In particular, they suggest that selection arising out of the advantages and risks of exchanging favors with our fellows has shaped not only our social behavior but also our reasoning abilities. Remember that for reciprocally altruistic tendencies to spread through the population individuals must be able to recognize nonreciprocators and withhold benefits from them. In other words, individuals must be able to spot (and punish) cheaters. Cosmides and Tooby thus argue that we should have evolved a specialized mental ability to recognize when someone has taken a benefit to which he is not entitled. Behaving in this way is called cheating, or violating a social contract.

The examples presented so far support this view. In the bouncer problem the social contract concerns the drinking age. In the Beri-beri version of the tattoo problem there is a similar social contact. You can consume the aphrodisiac only if you are married (and thus have tattoos). These are the problems that most people can solve. In the clerical problem and in the Wiki-wiki version of the tattoo problem there is no social contract, no benefit to be stolen, only a descriptive rule. The majority of college students cannot solve these problems when they are phrased in descriptive form.

Note that the clerical problem in Example 8.1 could be converted into cheater-detection problem. The story might go something like this.

Example 8.5

The draft board uses medical records to assign ratings. People with a "D" rating are exempt from the draft and will not have to risk their lives. But only people who have a code-3 medical record are entitled to a "D" rating. Unfortunately, the former clerk of the draft board accepted bribes to change people's ratings; some people who did not have code-3 medical records were given exemptions. You have been hired to check the ratings. The rule is just as it was before:

"If the document has a D rating, then it must be marked code 3."

The person's rating is shown on one side of the card and his medical record is shown on the other. Which card(s) do you have to turn over to be sure that no healthy people are avoiding the draft?

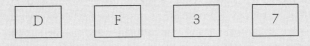

The answer is two cards. You must check "D" to make sure that the person really has a code 3 disease. And you also need to check "7" to make sure this person, who does not have a debilitating disease, has not been unfairly exempted (given a D-rating to which he is not entitled).

This kind of change, converting the problem to one in which some individuals might be taking a benefit they do not deserve, typically makes the problem much easier. Averaged over many such studies (Cosmides and Tooby, 1992; Gigerenzer and Hug, 1992), between 10 percent and 30 percent of college students correctly solve Wason selection tasks that involve a simple descriptive rule. But 65 percent to 90 percent of college students solve the task correctly if the rule is a social contract *where someone may be cheating*. The possibility of cheating is critical. For example, if we delete the idea that the former clerk accepted bribes and simply say that he was sloppy or absent-minded the percentage of correct responses declines sharply.

Gigerenzer and Hug (1992) showed this effect in another clever way. They gave subjects very similar Wason selection tasks, matched for their logical structure and much of their content. In fact, each task described a social contract, for example, "if you stay overnight in a mountain shelter you must help out by carrying up some firewood to add to the supply." In some versions of the task, subjects were asked to look for violations of the rule to determine if anyone was cheating. In other versions, subjects were asked to look for violations of the rule as a way of deciding whether the rule was in effect or not, rather like the Wiki-wiki example, above. Between 78 percent and 90 percent of subjects solved the cheater-detection version correctly. Converting to the rule-verification format roughly halved the percentage of subjects who answered correctly. In other words, the mere inclusion of a social contract rule is not sufficient to trigger good logical analysis. Again, the possibility of cheating is the key difference between logical problems that are easy to solve and ones that are difficult.

By using hand puppets and other age-appropriate materials, Denise Cummins (1999) explored these issues with young children, averaging just over two years old. She contrasted the children's performance on two different sorts of tasks. In one kind of task, the child was simply asked to check the truth or falsehood of a statement. For example, the child is shown a sketch of three children, two of whom are touching their heads. A puppet ("Big Bird") says "All the children in this picture have their hands on their heads." Then the experimenter asks "Is Big Bird right?" In the second kind of task, the child was shown the same picture but told "Big Bird says all the children must put their hands on the their heads," and asked "Is anyone doing anything wrong?" As predicted, the children were much better at detecting rule violations than falsehoods.

A plausible claim from this literature is that our brains are not designed to solve logic problems in general, any more than they are designed for reading. For this reason, we must have considerable formal training to learn to read or to master the general principles of logic. On the other hand, we spontaneously learn the monumentally complicated task of decoding our native language. And similarly, we seem especially competent at solving logic problems when a cheater lurks within. The argument is simple. The cognitive tasks that come easily and naturally to us are ones we were designed for. Those that require extensive training were not important to our ancestors. The cheater-detection literature is especially convincing because, by the use of ever-more-similar control tasks, it shows how narrow the cognitive specialization is.

COGNITIVE HEURISTICS: ARE WE INTUITIVE STATISTICIANS?

Our cognitive strengths and weaknesses provide numerous other windows into what our brains have been designed to do. For example, try this problem. How many seven-letter words in this chapter have the form "- - - - -n-" that is, how many have "n" as the next-to-last letter? Write down your estimate. Now, in contrast, how many seven-letter words in this chapter have the form "- - - - -ing"? Again, write down your estimate. If you're like most people you wrote a higher estimate for "- - - - -ing" than for "- - - - -n-" but does that make sense? Every single -ing word also has n as the next-to-last letter. And quite a number of seven-letter words like "content" and "present" and "confine" also have n as their next-to-last letter without being "- - - - -ing" words. So if you estimated that there were more "- - - - -ing" words than "- - - - -n-" words you were almost certainly wrong. Why do people tend to make this mistake?

Heuristics

According to Amos Tversky and Daniel Kahneman, we make mental errors and give biased estimates because our minds operate on the basis of what they call *heuristics* (e.g. Kahneman, Slovic and Tversky, 1982; Tversky and Kahneman, 1974). Heuristics are mental "rules of thumb." One example is the so-called *availability heuristic,* a rule of thumb that emphasizes the first thing that comes to mind. The availability heuristic leads us to overestimate the frequency of things that come easily to mind. For example, in the "- - - - -ing" versus "- - - - -n-" problem, "- - - - -ing" words are easier to think of (are more available to memory) than are words that have n as the next-to-last letter (Tversky and Kahneman 1983). The problem, as you can see, is that using the availability heuristic can give you the wrong answer. In other words, using heuristics to solve problems can produce biases.

According to Tversky and Kahneman, other mental heuristics can cloud our judgment; the *representativeness heuristic* is another example from this literature. This heuristic supposedly leads us to make judgments based on perceived similarity. Try this problem. Jennifer is a student at a major Midwestern university. She is attractive, athletic, and infectiously enthusiastic. Do you think it's more likely that Jennifer is an English major or a cheerleader?

If you answered "cheerleader," you may have used the representativeness heuristic. Let's think through the problem. How many female cheerleaders do you think there are at Midwestern U.? No more than a dozen. What proportion are attractive, athletic, and infectiously enthusiastic? A majority no doubt; let's generously say ten of the twelve fit all three criteria. Now, how many female English majors are there? Perhaps five hundred. And what proportion of them are attractive, athletic, and infectiously enthusiastic? Even judging harshly, we would still have to say at least 10 percent. This leaves us with fifty English majors who fit the criteria as compared to just ten cheerleaders. Once we dissect the problem, it turns out that Jennifer is five times more likely (50/10) to be an English major!

> **Trail Marker:** According to Kahneman and Tversky, "availability" and "representativeness" may bias our judgments.

What went wrong? According to Kahneman and Tversky, the description of Jennifer resembles our idea of a cheerleader more than it resembles our idea of an

English major. Jennifer seems more representative of a cheerleader. This representativeness allegedly leads us to overlook large differences in what are called *base rates*. In other words, we overlook the fact that there simply are many more English majors than cheerleaders. Thus, in this example, representativeness supposedly causes a kind of bias called *base-rate neglect*.

Do Heuristics Cause Bias, and If So, How?

There has been considerable debate over heuristics and the kinds of biases they supposedly cause. You learned earlier in this chapter that recall is very responsive to practice. Put in heuristic terms, more frequent events should be more available to memory. And we learned that availability also depends on the retention and spacing effects. But if availability mirrors real-world patterns of occurrence (as Anderson and Schooler argued that it does), availability should not produce biased judgments. In other words, exactly how does the availability heuristic work? What factors (beyond practice, retention, and spacing) make one kind of memory more available than another? What determines the strength of the representativeness and availability effects. Could one ever overshadow the other? We don't have answers to these questions because, at present, these heuristics are poorly defined. This is problematic. Poorly defined ideas are difficult to test and can actually slow scientific progress because it is hard to say exactly what experimental result would falsify them (Grigerenzer, 1996).

> **Trail Marker:** No one has yet described how the availability and representativeness heuristics work.

There is another reason why claims about mental heuristics and biases deserve careful examination. If heuristics consistently produce incorrect judgments, they are puzzling from an evolutionary perspective. If these thinking rules give us wrong answers why have they become part of the mind's standard equipment? Perhaps heuristics produced more accurate judgment in the EEA. In other words, the tasks currently used to evaluate heuristics may be artificial in terms of what the heuristic was designed to do.

In some cases, that is clearly true. Estimating the frequency of "- - - - -n-" versus "- - - - -ing" words is an artificial task at a number of levels. Obviously, spelling is not something that preoccupied our Pleistocene ancestors. And even in the modern literate world, normal adults do not process words letter by letter, but in larger, more meaningful chunks. In English, "ing" carries grammatical meaning (it forms the present participle of a verb), whereas "n" by itself has no such meaning. Perhaps it's this difference in meaningfulness that explains the availability effect in the word-estimating task.

Here's a visual analogy. Computer screens and printers represent images with arrays of differently colored dots or "pixels." Our brain interprets the pattern of pixels as a real scene: a baby taking its first steps, an abandoned house in a sea of long grass, a coiled rattlesnake. You would probably remember these meaningful scenes, but you would not remember which one had a green pixel at some particular location, because, all by itself, the green pixel is meaningless. The look on the baby's face, the broken windows of the house and the snake's rattle are, like the "ing" ending, final or near-final output from complex information-processing modules. We need final output to be accessible. But we're probably better off if lower levels of this processing—such as the green pixel and the "n"—are kept from cluttering up our consciousness.

Of course this idea—that higher levels in the processing hierarchy are more available to memory—may be wrong. But at least it's specific enough to be testable. We mention it simply to illustrate the kind of refinement that must be proposed and tested in order to learn what mental processes are actually responsible for availability and representativeness effects.

Information Formats

Gigerenzer and Hoffrage (1995) have argued that there is another important artificiality in many of the tests used to study heuristics: the notion of probability. Their argument has both philosophical and adaptive components, but we will concentrate on the latter. Gigerenzer and Hoffrage were motivated to study this problem because of the widely reported result that people are poor intuitive statisticians (Kahneman and Tversky, 1972, 1973; Bar-Hillel, 1980). In the EEA, our ancestors would have had to make many judgments without the benefit of complete information. And their fitness may have depended on their ability to make the right judgment. Statistics is all about this kind of judgment under uncertainty, so why aren't we good at it? Once again, to help you understand the issues involved, we'll invite you to solve some problems (Example 8.6).

This is a difficult problem, isn't it?. But note that the question is obviously important; and this type of question must come up again and again in medical diagnosis. If it's any consolation (and it probably won't be!), physicians (Eddy, 1982), including the staff of the Harvard Medical School (Casscells, Schoenberger and

Example 8.6

The probability of breast cancer is 1 percent for a woman of age forty who has a routine mammography exam. If such a woman has breast cancer, the probability is 80 percent that her mammography result will be positive. If a woman does not have breast cancer, the probability is 9.6 percent that her mammography result will be positive. A forty-year-old woman has just received a positive result in routine mammography. What is the probability that she actually has breast cancer?

Grayboys, 1978), find it difficult also. As shown in Box 8–1, the correct answer is 7.8 percent. But in Eddy's (1982) sample, most physicians estimated the probability to be between 70 percent and 80 percent. In other words, the vast majority of physicians, a group who should be especially practiced with this sort of problem, gave estimates that were ten times too high! Notice that the physicians' answers to this problem show the same kind of bias as typical answers to the "Jennifer" problem (see above): base rate neglect.

Gigerenzer believes this kind of problem is difficult because probability is an evolutionarily novel concept, one that has really only been developed by a few highly trained mathematicians, and only in the last hundred years. It's true that our ancestors had to make judgments under uncertainty. But the data they used to make these judgments were not probability estimates. They were frequency data. Before thinking about probabilities and frequencies in detail, let's see, in principle, why the kind of data we use might make a difference.

> **Trail Marker:** Probability is an evolutionarily novel concept.

Gigerenzer and Hoffrage (1995) offered the analogy of a calculator. The calculator can perform various operations like addition, subtraction and multiplication because programmers have built certain algorithms into its circuits. Of course, there are many ways to represent numbers, for example, the Arabic system we use, Roman numerals, or the binary numbers used by computers. Table 8–2 is a short table of Arabic numbers and their corresponding binary equivalents.

What would happen if you entered binary instead of Arabic numbers into a standard hand calculator and tried to add them? For example, add 2 plus 3 but enter the 2 and the 3 as binary numbers, 0010 plus 0011. The calculator will give the answer, 21, which is clearly wrong. (Obviously 5 is the correct arabic answer;

Let C = cancer, –C = no cancer; T = positive mammography result; P = probability. These terms can be combined. Thus $P(T|C)$ = probability of a positive mammography result given that the woman has cancer. We need to solve for $P(C|T)$, the probability of cancer given a positive mammography result. The solution is given by the following equation:

$$P(C|T) = \frac{P(C) \times P(T|C)}{P(C) \times P(T|C) + P(-C) \times P(T|-C)}$$

$$= \frac{(.01)\,(.80)}{(.01)\,(.80) + (.99)\,(.096)} = .078$$

Box 8–1.   Solution to the mammography problem.

Table 8–2. Arabic and binary equivalents

ARABIC	BINARY
1	0001
2	0010
3	0011
4	0100
5	0101
6	0110
7	0111
8	1000

0101 is the correct binary answer). The mistake did not happen because the calculator has no addition algorithm. It happened because its addition algorithm was built to "expect" a certain kind of input data. The calculator would add perfectly if the data were entered in the (Arabic) form it was designed to handle.

This analogy is intended to suggest that human thought is also based on algorithms, algorithms that have been built by a history of selection in particular environments. And like the algorithms of your calculator, your evolved algorithms work correctly only when they receive input in the appropriate form.

Probability Data versus Frequency Data

What information would our ancestors have had to help them make judgments under uncertainty? How could they get information about what kinds of things were likely to happen? Obviously, from how often they did happen, from their natural frequencies, not from abstract probabilities. To accumulate information on natural frequencies we simply need to update an event counter each time a relevant event occurs. Studies of the foraging behavior of animals suggest that they accurately monitor frequencies of various types of prey and adjust their behavior accordingly (Gallistel 1990, Real 1991). A large body of literature suggests that people are likewise sensitive to event frequencies and may acquire such information more or less automatically (Hasher and Zacks 1984). If Gigerenzer is right, our mental module for making judgments under uncertainty was designed to receive frequency data, not probability data. The obvious prediction is that we would perform better on such problems if they were phrased in terms of frequencies than if they were phased in probability terms. Let's consider the disease problem in a frequency format (modified from Gigerenzer and Hoffrage 1995). (See Example 8.7.) Natural frequency data make this a much simpler problem. A total of 103 (= 8 + 95) have shown the symptom. Of these 103 only 8 had the disease. Thus the likelihood that the new patient also has the disease is simply 8/103 or 7.8 percent. Does the answer sound familiar? In fact this problem is identical to the mammography problem, but expressed in frequencies instead of probabilities! Even if you did not get the exact answer, do you think you would have estimated the patient's chance of having the disease at 70

Example 8.7

You are an experienced "physician" in a preliterate society. You have no books or surveys, only your own accumulated experience. A severe disease is plaguing your people. You have discovered a symptom that signals the disease, but not with certainty. Over the years you have seen many people, most of whom did not have the disease. Of those who had the disease, eight had the symptom. Of those who did not have the disease, ninety-five had the symptom. Now you meet a new "patient" who has the symptom; what is the chance she has the disease?

percent or 80 percent, as the physicians did for the mammography problem? Surely you would have noticed that most of the people who had the symptom did not have the disease, and therefore said the patient's chance of having the disease was low.

Gigerenzer and Hoffrage (1995) draw a number of conclusions based on a comparison between probability formats and frequency formats. First, a reliable algorithm for making judgments under uncertainty is much simpler when the data are expressed as frequencies. By simpler, we mean fewer steps are required and the operations can be performed on natural numbers rather than fractions or percentages. To convince yourself of this compare the contents of Box 8–1 with the solution to the preliterate physician problem given above. Second, there are fewer attentional demands for the frequency format. For the frequency format only two numbers are relevant: the number of people who had the symptom plus the disease, and the number of people who had the symptom without the disease (or, instead of the second, the total number of people who had the symptom regardless of whether they had the disease or not). Note that base rates are irrelevant in the frequency format. We do not need to know how common the disease is in the population to solve the problem. We can get the correct answer while completely neglecting base rates—something that Tversky and Kahneman consider a "bias."

> **Trail Marker:** People are much better intuitive statisticians when they are given frequency data in place of probability data.

Gigerenzer and Hoffrage (1995) used probability and frequency versions of the same problems to test people's judgment under uncertainty. They found that conversion to frequency formats roughly tripled the proportion of subjects who answered correctly. Cosmides and Tooby (1996) used a design in which they converted, one by one, the relevant bits of information from probability format to frequency format, and found that their subjects' performance improved in parallel. People might be better intuitive statisticians than we think. Presenting data in terms of natural frequencies, the way it would have been available to our ancestors, seems to dramatically improve performance.

The Gambler's Fallacy

The gambler's fallacy is often cited as further evidence that humans are poor intuitive statisticians. Consider the following scenario. A coin has just come up "heads" four times in a row. Is it more likely to come up "heads" or "tails" on the next flip? People who say "tails" are falling prey to what is called the gambler's fallacy. Fair coins, roulette wheels, dice, and other such objects are supposed to produce fully independent outcomes. Each time a fair coin is flipped it has a 50:50 chance of coming up heads or tails, *regardless of how it came up the last time.* Its past performance tells us nothing about its future behavior. The belief that these sequential flips are not independent is the gambler's fallacy. Why do so many people subscribe to a fallacy?

As Steven Pinker (1997) has pointed out, fair coins, dice, roulette wheels and other gambling devices are very specially engineered. Without quite precise machining they would not be fair. A die that comes up "6" more often than you expect might be slightly unbalanced, and in that case, its past performance *would* be a clue to its future behavior. The fact that we have to work so hard to produce fair gambling devices suggests that, in the natural world, events are typically not independent.

There's an old truism about weather forecasting: If you simply predict that tomorrow will be like today, you'll be right as often as the professional meteorologists in the short run. If it's raining today, the chances are good it will rain tomorrow too. Why is that? Because today's weather and tomorrow's weather are linked by a shared set of causes. More or less the same forces are at work. Events that share causes are naturally linked, and we would be ignoring important sources of information if we acted as if they were independent. In addition, many events are linked by the simple playing out of a regular process. The longer I gather in this food patch, the more likely it is to be used up. The longer I've been out hunting, the fewer hours of daylight remain. The longer I've been pregnant, the sooner I'll be a mother. The longer the dry spell, the closer we are to the monsoon season.

> **Trail Marker:** In the real world, the gambler's fallacy is seldom a fallacy!

Because so much of what goes on in the world involves processes with more-or-less regular time courses or events with shared causes, future events often strongly depend on past ones. Consequently, in most real-world situations, the gambler's fallacy is not a fallacy at all. If humans had evolved in casinos where their winnings translated into reproductive success, selection probably would have eliminated the gambler's fallacy. But in the real world it often pays to behave as if the past and future are not independent.

SEX DIFFERENCES IN COGNITION

Sexual selection seems to have produced differences in the mating psychologies of women and men (see Chapter 10). But could it have produced sex differences in cognition? Some theory and data suggest that it has. For the most part, SSSM psychology has doubted and attempted to disprove reported sex differences on cognitive traits. But there are a few areas where these sex differences won't go away. Women and girls are better at an array of verbal tasks, and men and boys are better on a range of spatial tasks. No one seriously contests this. In fact, the differences are so well-known that they are taken into account in the design of IQ tests. Test designers know they must balance the number of verbal and spatial questions to avoid producing a test that yields higher IQ's for one sex or the other!

> **Trail Marker:** Sex differences in verbal and spatial ability are well documented.

One problem in studying the sex difference in verbal performance is that there are no other verbal species for comparison. But many species solve spatial problems so we have a basis for comparison on this dimension. In general, males of other species also seem to perform better on spatial tasks, and experimental manipulation shows that this sex difference depends on the effects of sex hormones acting during development (Kimura and Hampson, 1993; Gaulin, 1995). Clinical evidence from children with hormone disorders suggests the same is true for humans. For example, girls are ordinarily exposed to low doses of male hormones (androgens) during development. But girls with a syndrome called congenital adrenal hyperplasia (CAH) are exposed to unusually high androgen levels. Compared to matched, same-sex controls these girls have elevated spatial ability (Resnick et al. 1986). It seems that evolution has designed a facultative mechanism linking the development of spatial skills to androgen levels. But why?

There are several ideas, but only one is presently supported by comparative evidence. In many polygynous species, males and females have different ranging patterns. Females travel relatively short distances, but males range more widely in an attempt to meet and mate with many females. Selection favors the ability to acquire, store, process, and retrieve spatial information more strongly in the more mobile sex. This idea is testable: There are closely related sets of species where some species are polygynous with wide-ranging males, and others are monogamous with males and females that always travel together. The theory predicts a male advantage on spatial tasks in the polygynous species, but not in the monogamous ones—where selection has not favored wanderlust. As you can see in Figure 8–2, this is exactly what the data show (Gaulin and FitzGerald, 1986, 1989).

> **Trail Marker:** Sex differences in ranging behavior lead to the evolution of sex differences in spatial ability.

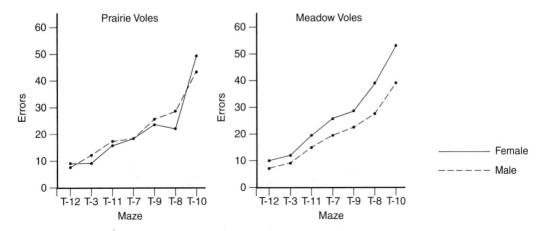

Figure 8–2. *Maze performance in two species of voles.* Meadow voles are polygynous and male meadow voles solve the mazes with consistently fewer errors than females. Prairie voles are monogamous and show no consistent sex difference in maze performance. (Data from "Sexual Selection for Spatial Learning Ability" by S. Gaulin and R. Fitzgerald in *Animal Behavior,* (1989), 37.)

There are neural correlates of these sex differences. Many studies suggest that, at least in nonhuman animals, the hippocampus is a brain region critically important to processing spatial information (Sherry and Vaccarino, 1989; Sherry et al., 1992). As you might predict, males have a larger hippocampus in species where males range more widely; but in species where the sexes have ranges of similar size there are no sex differences in the size of the hippocampus (Jacobs et al., 1990). Interestingly, sex itself is not the key variable; what matters is the relative spatial demands placed on females and males. Therefore we would expect that the difference would not always be in favor of males. In the brown-headed cowbird, females are subject to more intense selection for spatial problem solving than males are, and in this species it's the females that have a larger hippocampus (Sherry et al., 1993).

By now, none of this should strike you as very surprising. Selection builds cognitive systems to solve particular real-world problems. These problems will differ from species to species, and sometimes, between the sexes within species. Hence species (and sex) differences in cognitive abilities, algorithms and equipment are a normal product of evolution.

SUMMARY

1. Our cognitive processes were designed by selection to solve particular problems that faced our ancestors in the EEA.
2. We spontaneously categorize our experience.
3. The categories have an internal structure (based on typicality), with some example being regarded as more, and other less, typical of the category.
4. Typicality generally reflects the natural organization of world.

5. Our ability to remember things is tempered by three well-known effects: a practice and a retention effect that each are power functions, and a spacing effect, by which items are best remembered when the test interval matches the practice interval.

6. Each of these three effects seems to match the pattern of demands placed on our memory by naturally occurring events.

7. Humans seem to perform poorly at solving logic problems unless the problem involves possible violations of a social contract.

8. Humans have been alleged to use certain cognitive heuristics (e.g., availability) that can produce biased judgments.

9. But this conclusion may be premature because many of the experiments are unnatural.

10. For example, although probability and risk estimates are difficult for people, they become much easier if the data are presented as frequencies, as they would have been in the EEA.

11. The "gambler's fallacy" is not a fallacy in many real-world situations.

12. Sexual selection can produce sex differences in cognition if female and male reproductive success depend on solving different problems.

13. Cross-species comparison suggests that male/female differences in spatial problem solving may constitute an example of evolved cognitive sex differences.

9

Individuality: Intelligence and Personality

Evolutionary psychology is interested for the most part in those things people have in common, not their differences. We are interested in adaptations: mechanisms that evolved to solve problems for our ancestors in the EEA. Those mechanisms will be basically the same from one person to another because people who didn't have them left few offspring. The more important a mechanism is, the less variation we expect in it. All humans have four-chambered hearts because variations from that design didn't work as well in humans, if indeed they worked at all. This is the reason that we have not discussed individual differences in the book up to now.

People differ on many dimensions, of course: height and weight, eye and hair color, and so forth. Some of the dimensions that we vary on are behavioral: musical ability, friendliness, and the like. And we are not surprised that some of these differences are influenced by genes. But the genetic basis of differences is not the main interest of evolutionary psychology. There is a specialty in psychology known as *behavior genetics* that is concerned with assessing the genetic contributions to differences in behavior. Think back to our discussions on genes and environment in Chapter 4. An individual's traits cannot be attributed either to her genes or her environment because of the way genes and environment interact during her development. But *differences* between individuals can logically be attributed either to genetic *differences* between them or to their different experiences.

It is important to realize the difference between the fields of behavior genetics and evolutionary psychology because people commonly confuse the two. Behavior genetics focuses on the genetic basis of differences between people, whereas evolutionary psychology focuses on the (presumably genetic) mechanisms that are common to all people. Evolutionary psychology does not deny that there are differences among people, or that these differences have a genetic basis. It is just more interested in the adaptations that we all have. Behavior genetics and evolutionary psychology overlap, however, when we consider an evolutionary basis for differences.

> **Trail Marker:** Evolutionary psychology mainly focuses on adaptations that are common to all people, not on differences.

WHY IS THERE VARIABILITY IN INTELLIGENCE AND PERSONALITY?

There is a big evolutionary puzzle here. If intelligence and personality are important, why do people have different personalities and different levels of intelligence? Why aren't we all smart, creative, reliable, and so forth? After all, we don't differ on the really important things, as we noted above. There are several reasons for variability in these behavioral traits. Some of them apply to both intelligence and personality. We will discuss those here. Other reasons are specific to one or the other, and so we will discuss them in the appropriate section.

Normal Variation around an Optimum

It is likely that, just as for height, much variability in human intelligence and personality is simply a byproduct of sexual reproduction. Recall from Chapter 3 that polygenic traits tend to exhibit a normal distribution. The mean of this distribution tends to be near the optimum value. Thus, values above and below the mean are non-optimal, by definition. But such non-optimal values are created every generation by the genetic shuffling that goes on in sexual reproduction. See *Effects of sexual reproduction on polygenic traits* in Chapter 3 for a review of the reasons.

The Optimum Value of a Trait May Vary over Time

Consider a sparrow that is foraging for food. It interrupts its eating frequently to look around for predators. If it eats steadily without ever looking up, it is certain to become dinner for a hawk or other predator. If it spends all its time scanning the horizon, however, it will starve to death. Consider Figure 9–1, which shows hypothetical data on the probability of dying as a function of the proportion of time spent feeding versus scanning. The probability of dying by predation goes down steadily as the time spent scanning increases. But the probability of starving to death increases over the same range. At some point the lines cross, and the overall probability of death is lowest. This is the optimal allocation of time between the two tasks.

This is all well and good. But, why doesn't natural selection reduce the variability and fix the population at the optimum as it does with vital traits like the number of chambers in the heart? One reason is that the optimum value of some

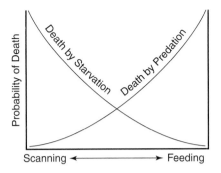

Figure 9–1. *Probability of dying as a function of the time spent feeding versus scanning for predators.* These two activities compete for an animal's time yet both are important to fitness.

traits can vary from time to time. One year may be dry and there is little food to eat, favoring those sparrows that tend to feed more. Another year there may be plenty of food, favoring the vigilant individuals. If conditions vary, selection will not drive the trait to a narrow range of expression. Spatial variation in food supply or predator density would similarly maintain variation in vigilance.

It is important to note that the variation in the environment must be slow relative to the lifetime of the individual for selection to maintain genetic variants in the population. In our example of the sparrow, a few dry decades may be followed by several with adequate rain. For a few decades birds that fed more would be favored, but another time the more vigilant birds would prosper. But suppose conditions varied markedly within the lifetime of an individual. In that case, individuals whose vigilance levels were obligately fixed would inevitably be mismatched to their environment during some phases. Under this kind of more rapid fluctuation, natural selection would favor the evolution of facultative mechanisms to monitor the current environment and adjust behavior appropriately.

Frequency-Dependent Selection

It is possible that frequency-dependent selection helps maintain the psychological variation in the population. Recall our discussion in Chapter 3 of scorpion flies, where males have two strategies to attract mates: hunting males who offer nuptial gifts to the female, and deceiver males who pretend to be females so as to steal another male's gift. Which strategy is better for an individual to adopt depends on the relative frequency of the two strategies in the population.

Many Psychological Traits Are Facultative

We have seen many times throughout this book that psychological mechanisms are highly responsive to the environment. We will see below that personality is likely to be facultative. The optimal value of various personality traits may vary with the social landscape.

Thus, there are several reasons why people may vary on important psychological traits. We will return to consider them in more detail later in the chapter.

PEOPLE REPRESENT SOCIAL RESOURCES FOR EACH OTHER

All organisms harvest resources from the environment. We harvest food, of course, but there are many more kinds of resources. Many of these resources come in the form of other people. When we mate we harvest the resources of the opposite sex. Both females and males not only harvest the genes of the opposite sex, but also the investment that the partner will make in the resulting offspring. Also, relatives, friends and allies represent social resources. It is crucial for our fitness to be able to size up other people as potential resources. We consider the case of mating in detail in Chapter 10.

Because humans are such a highly social species, social skills are required to harvest many of those resources we get from others. But one of the most important of those social skills is the ability to size up other people as potential cooperators or competitors: members of the opposite sex as potential partners; newcomers to a group for their potential as leaders, workers, or troublemakers. What can this new person do for me, for good or ill? Intelligence and personality are concepts that describe important features of individuals as potential resources for us.

> **Trail Marker:** The concepts of intelligence and personality reflect our evaluation of others as potential resources.

In this light it is not surprising that the concepts of intelligence and personality are built into our language and culture. Allport and Odbert (1936) found 4,504 words describing enduring, public aspects of personality in *Webster's New International Dictionary*. Considering that there are about 100,000 words in such a dictionary, this means that almost 5 percent of them describe personality. Clearly the concepts of intelligence and personality are dominant aspects of folk psychology.

INTELLIGENCE

Although the concept of intelligence has been around for thousands of years, scientists only began trying to measure it about one hundred years ago. Then it became necessary to think more carefully about just what intelligence is. You may be surprised to find out that there is no agreed upon definition of intelligence. An old, and often quoted, quip has it that "intelligence is whatever the intelligence test tests." This saying is true. It is also the key to understanding why psychologists have trouble defining intelligence. Intelligence tests were originally designed to predict success in school, and they are still used primarily for that purpose. The developers of intelligence tests included whatever tasks predicted success in school, without any theoretical consideration. So modern intelligence tests have sections that test verbal ability, memory for facts, spatial ability, and so forth. All of these are skills needed to succeed in school.

Why would we expect the set of skills needed for success in school to make up a single ability? One skill needed for success in school is the ability to follow directions. One can argue that this skill is actually tested by intelligence tests, albeit indirectly, because you can't do well on any test that requires paying attention to verbal instructions (whether written or oral) without it. Psychologist Robert Sternberg once sat observing a large, noisy, multi-grade classroom in Jamaica. Straining to hear the teacher, Sternberg thought that if Alfred Binet (author of the first modern IQ test) were in his place wondering what should go into an IQ test, he might well include a hearing exam (Sternberg, 1998).

What insights does evolutionary psychology have to offer in this discussion of intelligence? There were no schools in the EEA, to the best of our knowledge. And the fact that schools are an evolutionary novel institution leads us to be suspect that the concept of intelligence that developed in the service of education may not match very well the one that has served since the EEA to describe smart people.

> **Trail Marker:** Because modern intelligence tests were developed to predict success in school, an evolutionarily novel setting, we should not be surprised if they neglect many abilities that are obviously intelligent.

Therefore we are not surprised that there has been much debate about the nature of intelligence.

Is Intelligence One Ability or Many?

Both sides of this matter have been argued. Charles Spearman and others hold that there is a general or overarching intelligence, known as g, that underlies and promotes various special abilities, such as verbal, spatial, and so forth. This concept of g is supposed to correspond with what most people mean when they describe a person as "smart," or "intelligent" in the everyday sense. All intelligence tests measure g to a greater or lesser extent. Evidence for Spearman's position comes from a sophisticated statistical methodology called factor analysis. Essentially it rests on discovering whether a person who is good at one type of item, say spatial ability, tends also to be good at another type, say, verbal ability. The fact that the same person tends to perform similarly on many different types of items gives evidence for g.

On the other hand, some people can do well on certain groups of items, such as spatial visualization, and poorly on another type, such as verbal fluency. This situation gives us evidence for separate primary mental abilities. Louis Thurstone championed the idea that intelligence consists of seven separate and independent factors, or primary mental abilities: verbal comprehension, verbal fluency, inductive reasoning, spatial visualization, number, memory, and perceptual speed.

Some theorists combine Spearman's and Thurstone's notions in a hierarchical model. (See Figure 9–2.) They believe there are separate abilities, but that g underlies all of them. A person can have special talents in one area more than another, but someone who is high in g will tend to do well in all the separate

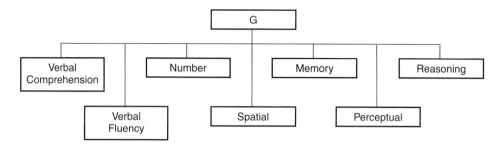

Figure 9–2. A model of intelligence that views *g* as an overarching factor influencing separate abilities.

abilities. An analogy may be several boats of various sizes representing different abilities. But they all rise or fall together with the tide, which represents *g*.

It is important to realize that most scientists now believe the concept of *g* to be well established. John Carroll (1997) says, "At the present time the evidence for a general factor [*g*] is overwhelming" (p. 32). In what follows, we are not denying the existence of *g*. Nor do we equate *g* with intelligence. Rather, we follow the spirit of the hierarchical model that combines Spearman's and Thurstone's ideas.

If *g* exists, what is it? Since the time of Darwin's cousin and contemporary Francis Galton, scientists have tried to find a simple physical or physiological measure of intelligence. For example, Galton tried unsuccessfully to correlate intelligence with head size, reaction time, sensory acuity, and the like. More recent efforts have found modest correlations between intelligence and brain size (after taking into account the fact that larger people have larger brains) and certain measures of brain activity (Jensen, 1998). Intelligence may be a measure of efficiency of brain function. But, at present we cannot say exactly what differs about the brains of more and less intelligent people.

Successful Intelligence

Robert Sternberg (1998) suggests that the conventional "g-ocentric" view of intelligence takes too narrow a view of what we mean by intelligent behavior. He suggests that current intelligence tests focus on analytical skills and ignore creative and practical intelligence. Probably everyone has known someone who was a whiz at school work but a complete failure at social skills. Everyone can think of unkind terms commonly used to describe such people.

Sternberg reviews both his own work and that of others who studied behavior in practical situations that required considerable intelligence. In one study, Steven Ceci and Jeffrey Liker studied expert racetrack handicappers. These people make a living predicting the outcomes of horse races, taking into account an enormous number of factors. Their ability to perform these complex reasoning tasks, however, was not related to differences in their IQs.

Another group investigated Brazilian street children who operate businesses that require them to make sophisticated price calculations. The children, however, generally did poorly at tests of school mathematics. Similar studies have found that ability to comparison shop in a grocery store (before the days of per-ounce pricing information) did not predict ability to do the same problems in a classroom setting. Sternberg's group studied Kenyan children's knowledge of traditional herbal remedies. Their expertise was either unrelated or *negatively* correlated to standard measures of intelligence.

Sternberg is working to develop tests of these other aspects of intelligence. Meanwhile it appears clear that standard tests of IQ that were developed to predict success in school have less relevance outside the classroom.

Multiple Intelligences

Howard Gardner (1983, 1993) takes a different approach to intelligence in his widely influential theory of multiple intelligences. Although he is primarily interested in predicting school performance, he takes a broader view of intelligence than previous workers. He believes that there are several different intelligences, not just abilities within a single intelligence. He lists:

1. Linguistic intelligence. Reading a book, writing a poem, understanding spoken words.
2. Musical intelligence. The ability to appreciate music, to sing, play instruments, and compose, and so forth.
3. Logical-mathematical intelligence. Solving math problems using formal symbols, balancing a checkbook, logical reasoning.
4. Spatial. Getting from place to place, reading a map, packing suitcases into the trunk of a car.
5. Bodily-kinesthetic. Sports, dancing.
6. Interpersonal. The ability to understand other people and their moods and motivations.
7. Intrapersonal. The ability to know one's self and one's feelings.

Gardner proposes a number of criteria for a skill to be considered an intelligence. Three of the most significant for our purposes are:

1. The ability can be affected selectively by brain damage, as injury can produce aphasia (problems in speaking and understanding speech) without affecting facial recognition.
2. There should be prodigies and *idiots savants* who display highly uneven distribution of skills. For example, we should expect to find musical prodigies, or retarded persons who are nevertheless computationally adept and can say, for example, on which day of the week the 10th of March, 2017 will fall.
3. (Most important for our purpose) A plausible evolutionary basis.

Gardner's work is a step in the right direction to an evolutionary perspective on intelligence. It recognizes the fact that people act intelligently in situations other than school, and therefore in ways not tested by traditional intelligence tests. In particular, musical ability, bodily-kinesthetic ability, and the personal intelligences are not well tested by standard intelligence tests.

Sternberg (unpublished) criticizes Gardner's theory because it has not led to any research that would test its validity. Without such tests it remains only a suggestive idea. We believe, however, that it highlights the narrow focus of much present research and discussion of intelligence.

In fact, we suggest that even Gardner's list of intelligences is too narrow. Several abilities, such as face recognition, meet those of Gardner's criteria we listed above (but not some of his we didn't list). We have already discussed the condition of prosopagnosia (in Chapter 2), in which people are unable to recognize faces after localized brain damage. It is also likely that some people are better at this task than others. And face recognition has a plausible evolutionary basis. But Gardner rejects face recognition as an intelligence because it is not acknowledged across many cultures as a valued skill, with individuals recognized as novices and experts, and a standardized way of discussing the ability in a symbol system. Similarly there are people who are recognized in our culture as wine tasters, or perfumers, with outstanding ability to identify flavors or smells. But Gardner rejects these abilities because they are too specialized to be acknowledged across many cultures.

We believe that the list of potential intelligences is quite large, and would include face recognition, recognition of emotions in faces, ability to deceive, detection of cheaters, imitation, planning for the future, diagnosing disease, making art works, storytelling, tracking and hunting animals (see Figure 9–3), deciding what is edible, and identification of medicinal plants. For each problem to be solved in the EEA we would expect a skill to evolve as an adaptation. At present, however, this is only a suggestion for future research.

Figure 9–3. *Hunters tracking prey.* Hunting may require kinds of intelligence not captured by IQ tests.

> **Trail Marker:** An intelligence test designed for hunter-gatherers would probably test different skills than ones designed to predict school success.

It is entirely possible that these intelligences would never be found using the statistical methods that psychologists have employed to date. Remember that the factors, or mental abilities, are found from statistical analysis of correlations between pairs of test items. In order to compute a correlation, some people have to do well on an item and others poorly. If there were little variability among people in their scores on an item it could never turn up as a factor, or separate ability. So if everyone did equally well on a test of facial recognition, it could never show up as a mental ability, because it wouldn't correlate with anything else. Recall that there is little variability among people on the really important traits: two eyes, one nose, four-chambered heart. Number of chambers in the heart would not correlate with verbal fluency, or anything else.

Second, it is necessary to include the item on the test in the first place. Facial recognition, tracking animals, or diagnosing diseases have never been used as intelligence test items, to our knowledge.

In summary, the scientific concept of intelligence originated in the need to describe ability to do school work, which is an evolutionarily novel situation. We suggest that there are many specialized abilities that could be considered intelligent. Some of these are useful in school and others are not; but they exist because they were useful skills in the EEA.

Why Do Humans Have Such Large Brains?

Among species of animals there is a strong relationship between body size and brain size. Humans, however, have a larger brain than can be accounted for by this relationship, although we are rivaled by dolphins. The human brain is so large that it causes significant problems in the birth process. The female pelvis, through which the birth canal passes, has become large enough to be an impediment to optimal locomotion. And the human brain must continue to grow after birth, rendering the newborn quite immature by mammalian standards. Why do we pay the cost of large brains?

It is generally assumed that the answer is, to give us our great intelligence. It is well established that there is a modest, but significant, relation between brain size and intelligence (Jensen, 1998). John Skoyles (1999), however, notes that a number of people with normal or even higher IQ have very small brains, even small enough to be considered microcephalic. If it is possible to have normal intelligence with a 30 percent smaller brain, why did we pay the price? Skoyles proposes that the human brain grew to its present size to make possible the accumulation of expertise, not intelligence per se. Humans develop skills over many years. Hunters continue to learn tracking skills for many years, so that !Kung bushmen in their fifties or sixties might accompany a son on the hunt to interpret sign (Skoyles, and references therein).

Skoyles's suggestion is too new to have generated research that would test its implications. Nevertheless it should be apparent that it fits with Sternberg's theory of successful intelligence. It has been known for many years that cognitive factors (IQ) contribute more to differences in performance in the early stages of learning than they do later on (Cronbach, 1984). It seems clear that the theory of intelligence is far from settled.

Differences in Intelligence

We have said that we don't vary on really important things like number of chambers in the heart. Yet people clearly differ on intelligence. People who are in the top 10 percent of intelligence are readily distinguishable in ordinary behavior from the bottom 10 percent. Isn't intelligence really important? We suggest two possibilities.

Variation in intelligence follows a normal (bell-shaped) curve, indicating that it is influenced by a large number of independent factors. Because it is clear that intelligence is influenced by genes, we can expect that a large number of genes all contribute to intelligence, as is the case with many traits such as height and skin color. In fact, a recent study has identified one gene for intelligence out of the many that presumably influence it (Chorney and others, 1998). This gene is believed to contribute about four points to IQ score. Polygenic traits such as height and intelligence show variation as a consequence of the reshuffling that takes place in the process of sexual reproduction. Intelligence simply follows the pattern of polygenic traits.

A second reason intelligence may vary is the effect of developmental challenges. Every individual is subject to disease, parasites, and teratogens (substances that disrupt development in various ways) during the course of development, both before and after birth. In addition, physical and social deprivation are sources of developmental difficulty.

It is well documented that developmental challenges reduce intelligence. A number of diseases that the mother may contract during pregnancy, including rubella (German measles) and chicken pox, can cause mental retardation. In addition many teratogens have documented effects on intelligence, including drugs such as alcohol and nicotine, and environmental pollutants, such as lead and PCBs (polychlorinated biphenyls) (Kail, 1998). You may note that the teratogens we list are primarily available in modern society, and may not have been a risk in the EEA. Obviously, research has focused on those teratogens that are particularly common hazards to development in our contemporary environment. But the list of teratogenic substances present in the EEA would be quite long and would include a wide array of naturally occurring plant compounds.

Social deprivation has known effects on intelligence. For example, Robert Bradley and Bettye Caldwell (1984) measured the quality of home environment during the first two years of life. They observed such things as the mother's responsiveness to the child, whether there was a predictable household routine, and the availability of stimulating activities for the child. Bradley and Caldwell found that quality of home environment predicted children's intelligence scores a couple of years later. It is certain, then, that considerable variation in intelligence among people results from the accidents of growing up in an uncertain world. Further, individuals may vary in how well they are able to fend off these challenges.

A third reason for variation in intelligence follows from the expensive tissue principle. Although the brain makes up only 2 percent of the human body by weight, it consumes about 25 percent of its energy budget. Energy put into building and fueling the brain cannot be put into other tissues and their functions. Although intelligence is very important, it is not all-important. Consider the peacock. Peahens choose to mate with the peacock who has the most magnificent tail. A peacock that grew a larger brain at the expense of a magnificent tail would probably not fare well in the mating game. Many traits besides intelligence contribute to human fitness, including dominance (for males), for which size is important. It is possible that a trade-off between investing in a powerful brain and investing in other fitness-enhancing traits may contribute to some of the variability among people.

IMPLICATIONS OF AN EVOLUTIONARY VIEW OF INTELLIGENCE

Once we realize that intelligence did not evolve to help us earn high grades or be admitted to medical school, a variety of implications follow. Many of these implications are relevant to understanding why the educational system often falls short of its objectives, and to explaining why many students have a difficult time mastering many of the standard subjects.

Why We Have to Go to School

Traditionally, school meant the three R's: Reading, 'Riting, and 'Rithmetic. Why do we have to go to school to learn to read, write, and calculate, but not to talk, recognize when someone is angry, or find our way home? An evolutionary perspective recognizes that reading, writing, and arithmetic are evolutionarily novel tasks for which we have not evolved specialized modules. Writing began about eight thousand years ago, and mathematics about five thousand years ago. Decimal fractions were invented only about four hundred years ago, and calculus about three hundred years ago. These are but an eye blink in evolutionary time. By contrast, it is believed that spoken language began at least 100,000 years ago (Pinker, 1994). Because we don't have modules designed for these evolutionarily novel tasks, we need formal schooling to master them. In school, we learn to use modules designed for the challenges of the EEA to master these novel tasks.

> **Trail Marker:** The things we go to school to learn make use of modules that evolved for other purposes.

Why Suzy and Johnny Can't Read

There is abundant evidence for specialized modules underlying the production and recognition of speech. For example, the ear is most sensitive to sounds in the range of frequencies most important for speech. Much of the coding and decoding of the meaning of speech sounds occurs at a level of processing completely unavailable to consciousness. Thus, it could never be learned by any process requiring conscious attention, because conscious attention would be useless for the purpose. Furthermore speech is learned effortlessly by two-year-olds. By contrast, the eye shows little evidence of specialization for reading (Rozin & Gleitman, 1977), and reading requires effortful learning of the connections between squiggles on paper, sounds, and meanings.

Of course reading is an invention of humans, and as such, is a product of the human mind, and thus indirectly, of evolution. But the process has placed new demands on a brain whose structure was designed for other purposes. What is it about reading that makes it so difficult that roughly 10 percent of Americans fail to learn to read in spite of years of education?

Lila Gleitman and Paul Rozin (Gleitman & Rozin, 1973; Gleitman & Rozin, 1977; Rozin & Gleitman, 1977) have taken an evolutionary approach to reading, and to the teaching of reading. They find it significant that all systems of writing are not equally difficult to learn. Systems in which there is one symbol for each word (Chinese) are easier to get started learning than systems that have one symbol for each syllable (Japanese, in part), which in turn are easier than systems based on an alphabet (English, Hindi). The tables turn later in the learning process. Word-based systems are harder to master because one must learn tens of thousands of different characters. Alphabetic systems are easier to master, because all words use the same small set of letters. So there is a trade-off between ease of initial learning and ease of mastery.

Alphabetic systems require fewer symbols than syllabic systems, which in turn require fewer symbols than word-based systems. The gain in efficiency that results is considerable. A language might have 100,000 words, 500 syllables, but only about two dozen letters. Clearly an alphabetic language makes much more economic use of written symbols. Try to imagine building a Chinese typewriter! Over the course of time, ease of mastery has won out over ease of initial learning. The history of writing systems shows a general trend from systems based on one symbol for one word (Egyptian and Mayan hieroglyphics, for example), to one symbol for one syllable, to alphabetic systems.

But the task of the reader becomes increasingly abstract and more difficult as one goes from systems based on words, to syllables, to letters. The reader of an alphabetic language must make connections between letters and sounds that are much more complicated than in the case of the syllable or word-based system. (Roughly they need to learn that the sequence of letters corresponds to a sequence of sounds—the letters b-a-t correspond to the sounds buh–aa–tuh.) The problem is made even worse in English by the fact that the mapping of sounds to letters is more complicated than in many other languages (compare: cough, through, though, and tough.) But irregular rules for mapping letters to sounds is not the main problem: It is the idea of mapping letters to sounds itself.

Gleitman and Rozin (1973) demonstrated that children who had difficulty learning to read English could more easily begin to read Chinese. They also had little trouble with English when it was presented in a syllabic format: WILL|Y WILL YELL FOR YELL|O CAN|DY (Gleitman & Rozin, 1973, p. 471). Gleitman and Rozin argue that children with trouble reading could benefit from a teaching method explicitly based on an evolutionary analysis of what is difficult about reading.

Why Johnny and Suzy Avoid Math

Not only do we have to go to school to learn math, many of us have to be forced to study it. Even highly educated people who are proud of their breadth of knowledge often willingly admit their ignorance of math, and sometimes even boast about it. As with reading, mathematics is an evolutionarily novel invention that makes use of modules that must have evolved for other purposes. As we discussed in Chapter 8, thinking evolved to deal with social and physical events in the world of experience. A module that evolved to detect cheaters deals poorly with abstract logic. A module that evolved to deal with events in the world of everyday experience makes it hard to do statistics, which is based on randomness, a process seldom encountered outside of casinos. Like logic and statistics, mathematics requires the manipulation of abstract symbols. We are not surprised that math is difficult.

David Geary (1995) notes that certain numerical concepts are adaptations and others are recent inventions. Here are some adaptations: the ability to determine quantity (up to some small limit) without counting, an understanding of more and less, counting up to three or four, and realization that adding increases quantity and subtracting decreases it. These adaptations for numerical concepts are present in infants and so do not require training (Strauss & Curtis, 1984; Haith & Benson, 1998). They operate largely below the level of consciousness, and children are motivated to practice and master them.

Other mathematical abilities are more recent inventions: Counting in base 10, addition and subtraction with carrying, fractions, exponents, and the like. Evolution has not provided us with these modules. They must be learned with effort, and with instruction in the rules. Most people are not inclined to do addition, subtraction, multiplication, or division of three-digit numbers just for fun. (Those who do enjoy math are generally very high in intelligence and treat math problems like puzzles.) People develop the skills required for these recent inventions only in societies with an educational system and a system of commerce that depends on accurate records about large quantities.

Implications for Educational Practice

Geary (1995) draws on his evolutionary analysis to make recommendations for educational practice. He notes that American students are among the worst at mathematics in the entire industrialized world. Geary blames this situation on an educational strategy that emphasizes understanding over skill practice. He argues that children are not required to do enough of the practice that is necessary to make mathematical skills automatic. He does not downplay the need for understanding the concepts, but calls for a better balance between conceptualization and skill. Precisely because mathematics skills do not build on adaptations but on cultural inventions, most students are not intrinsically motivated to practice them sufficiently.

> **Trail Marker:** Children are not intrinsically motivated to practice math and reading skills because these tasks are not the natural products of adaptations.

We believe that the same prescription goes for reading and writing as well. Students are not motivated to read unless the material is intrinsically interesting. They are not motivated to write unless it accomplishes a valuable goal. If reading were intrinsically interesting, people would sit down and read the telephone book for fun. It appears that education would be improved by a blend of conceptualization and skill practice.

Hyperactivity

About 10 percent of school-age boys and 3 percent of girls have Attention Deficit Hyperactivity Disorder (ADHD). These children have trouble remaining in their seats, are easily distracted, interrupt other children's activities, and have difficulty following through on instructions (Gaddes & Edgell, 1994). Not surprisingly they have trouble in school. ADHD has a strong hereditary (probably largely genetic) component.

A clue to understanding ADHD may come from the facts that it is mainly a problem in school, and that children tend to outgrow it to some extent. Because school is an evolutionarily novel situation, it is possible that the traits that make up ADHD were either neutral or even beneficial in the EEA (Panskepp, 1998; Pomerleau, 1997). Life in the EEA did not require young children to learn to sit still in one spot for several hours a day. A child who was easily distractible may have been more likely to notice a predator's approach. Jaak Panskepp asks whether "'acting without regard for consequences' [(which characterizes ADHD) instead of being viewed as a problem] might not reflect a greater 'willingness to take risks and face dangers.'" (p. 93). He suggests that rough-and-tumble play is a normal and beneficial part of development. He believes that schools may be making a mistake by not providing more opportunity for children to engage in active play. He notes that few U.S. states still require physical education for all children in kindergarten through twelfth grade.

In summary, evolutionary considerations lead to a number of suggestions for improving modern education based on the differences between the EEA and the school setting.

PERSONALITY

Our personality is the face we present to the world. It represents our style of interacting with others, and confronting challenges and opportunities. Like most psychologists, we will follow what is called the "trait" approach to personality. The traits are the various dimensions of our interaction style. Personality traits are considered to be inherently continuous. The trait approach assumes that there is more than one dimension of personality and therefore tries to measure where people lie along each of these continua. That way people can be characterized by a location in multidimensional space, much as the location of an object anywhere in a room can be uniquely specified in three dimensions.

The scientific study of personality, like all scientific enterprise, seeks to "carve nature at the joints." But this effort is complicated by the fact that the personality traits we have come up with are based on how people perceive each other. The basic methodology that led to our personality theories was to ask people to describe others. In other words, our personality theories are based on folk psychology —what people with no training in psychology believe about human behavior. Folk psychology is not necessarily correct, or we could skip doing the hard work of scientific psychology and just take a poll to find out how people perceive, learn, and so forth. On the other hand, folk psychology isn't always wrong, or we would have to get a Ph.D. in psychology just to carry out the activities of daily life. Evolutionary considerations suggest that those individuals who could accurately assess others as resources and threats would leave more descendants. Thus there is reason to hope that folk psychology would carve nature at the joints in this case.

How many personality traits are there? This is similar to asking how many types of intelligence there are. In the 1940s, Raymond Cattell took those thousands of words in the English language that describe personality and weeded out the obvious synonyms. Then he used factor analysis to see how the terms clustered together. That way he narrowed them down to sixteen "source traits." Over the years workers refined their techniques and did many more studies. Eventually workers settled on what we call the "Big Five" model of personality (McCrae & Costa, 1990; Segal & MacDonald, 1998), because five traits consistently account for so much of the variation among people. The Big Five personality traits are:

> *Openness to experience/Intelligence:* curious, broad interests, creative (vs. closed: stupid, boorish, conventional, narrow interests, unartistic)
>
> *Conscientiousness:* organized, reliable, hard-working (vs. irresponsible: aimless, unreliable, lazy)
>
> *Extraversion (surgency):* bold, forceful, active, talkative (vs. introversion: reserved, sober, quiet)
>
> *Agreeableness:* good-natured, trusting, helpful (vs. disagreeable: cynical, rude, uncooperative)
>
> *Neuroticism:* Worrying, nervous, emotional (vs. emotional stability: calm, relaxed, secure)

You can remember these terms because their initial letters spell out OCEAN. (We have listed them in the order that makes them easiest to remember, not necessarily in their order of importance. In fact, extraversion and agreeableness are the biggest of the Big Five because they turn up in just about every study.)

Buss (1991) suggests that each of these five dimensions represents an adaptation to a particular problem presented by the social landscape. People can adopt extraversion or introversion as strategies for survival, for example. An extraverted person can be successful through her forcefulness in many situations, if she can pull it off. An introverted person may succeed by being more reserved in those same situations. Buss suggests that there are clear reasons to attend to each of the Big Five in our social relationships.

Openness/intelligence: Who will be innovative or astute? An open person will make wise decisions and give good advice.

Conscientiousness: Who will complete a task? You can put a conscientious person in charge of a task because you can be sure it will get done.

Extraversion: Who is likely to become powerful or high in status? Human societies are all hierarchical to some degree, even those that seem less so than ours. We need to know who the "movers and shakers" are. A person high in surgency will become a leader. You had better know what she thinks, and either become an ally or not antagonize her.

Agreeableness: Who will make a good cooperator? Can you trust him, or do you need to handle him with kid gloves?

Neuroticism: Who can handle stress? Will he stand up in difficult situations, or will he break down?

In support of his hypothesis that personality terms reflect the usefulness of people as social resources, Buss (1997) notes that the vast majority of everyday terms used to describe personality are clearly positive or negative; that is, they are evaluative. This goes for the Big Five, as well. We like people who are creative, reliable, active, helpful, and calm. We dislike those who are stupid, lazy, passive, rude, and nervous.

Differences in Personality

We have previously listed some reasons why people might differ on personality and intelligence. Here we return to discuss some of them further.

The optimal combination of personality traits could plausibly vary from time to time, or place to place. Following our earlier example of the sparrow, the usefulness of being anxious could vary over time or space. At one time (or place), a more vigilant person may have a reproductive advantage; at another, a more trusting individual may succeed better. If the environmental changes were slow then anxiousness may be favored in one generation, and trustingness could be favored in another. This situation would prevent selection from eliminating variability in personality. Likewise it is possible that human groups have less need for leadership under conditions of peace and plenty, but need stronger leaders when conditions are less benign. The niche for extraverts could expand and contract as conditions fluctuate. Similar arguments can be made for the other major traits.

Frequency-dependent selection is another possible mechanism to maintain personality variability in the population. Perhaps if there are many extraverts, then introverts will succeed because they gain an advantage simply by staying in the background and avoiding conflicts. The problem is that this mechanism is hard to test in the case of personality for reasons that are fairly complicated (Tooby & Cosmides, 1990). For this reason, we will not consider that mechanism further.

As we have seen a number of times throughout the book, variability in the environment can lead to the evolution of facultative adaptations. Some personality traits may result from a module that monitors the environment and adjusts behavior accordingly. Many facultative modules vary their output over fairly short time periods, as in suntanning; others, such as the star orientation of the bunting, are set once and for all in the life of an individual.

Consider mating systems. Although all societies recognize some form of marriage, the degree of involvement of men in rearing the children varies widely. In father-present societies the fathers play a crucial role in provisioning the family. In father-absent societies the mothers rear the children on their own. Draper and Belsky (1990; Belsky, 1997) propose that children have a critical period during which they develop attitudes about marriage and families that shape their later style of relating to the opposite sex. They review studies that show that if the father is present, children develop more favorable attitudes toward the opposite sex and delay their sexual activity. If, however, they grow up in a father-absent home, they have more antagonistic attitudes toward the opposite sex, form less durable bonds with a mate, and begin sexual activity earlier. Children of divorce marry earlier, have children earlier, and have shorter marriages. They are more impulsive, aggressive, and antisocial. Some of the facultative responses are physiological as well as behavioral. For example, girls in father-absent households reach puberty six months earlier than others on average.

Draper and Belsky propose that these personality traits (as well as the physiological process of puberty) are part of a facultative mating module. This module scans the early environment to see whether men can be counted on to support women and children. When mating relationships are likely to be long-term partnerships both men and women benefit by taking their time to find the best possible mate. (See Chapter 10 for a detailed discussion of the evolution of mate-choice criteria.) But if men cannot be counted on as stable partners then there is little advantage to cautious pair formation.

While Draper and Belsky's argument is internally consistent, an alternative explanation can be given for their results. It is possible that different styles of parental investment and the personality patterns that go with them are the result of genetic differences between individuals. It is entirely possible that people whose personalities incline them to form stable mating relationships convey genes for these personality traits to their children, who also therefore tend to grow up in father-present homes (Cleveland, 1997). At the present time, it seems likely that both genetic factors and early environment make some contribution. This is not surprising to an evolutionary psychologist, however. We expect a certain amount of variability in many adaptations because of reasons we have discussed above: variation about an optimum because of sexual reproduction, unpredictable differences in the optimum value of a trait from time to time, and frequency-dependent selection. What is clear, however, is that an evolutionary approach suggests reasons for differences in personality.

Effects of Birth Order on Personality

More than a thousand different studies have looked for effects of birth order on personality. Most researchers, in reviewing the conflicting results, conclude that the effects are minimal. Yet if the effects are so small, why have there been hundreds of studies, and why is a belief in them so widespread? Frank Sulloway subjected this enormous literature to a procedure called *meta analysis*. This technique effectively combines the results of many studies as if they were actually one very large study. It is particularly useful in cases where the individual studies failed to find effects because they used too few subjects. In his meta analysis, he considered only the 196 studies that used proper controls for variables that are related to birth order, such as family size and social class.

When he did so, his meta analysis indicated that birth order was related to the Big Five personality factors: Firstborns tend to be less open to experience, more conscientious, less agreeable, more neurotic, and more extraverted.

Convinced that there was an effect of birth order on personality, Sulloway proceeded to design his own study. One reason the earlier studies disagreed among themselves was that birth order is only one of many factors that influence personality, resulting in a small effect of birth order. One way to increase the effect of a variable is to consider extreme cases (see Figure 9–4). Consider this analogy. Although men are six inches taller than women on the average, it is not particularly unusual for an individual woman to be taller than an individual man. In fact roughly 35 percent of adults taller than 5'4" (the average height of women) are women. But only about 2 percent of adults taller than 5'10" (the average for men) are women. And virtually no adults taller than 7'0" are women. So if you wanted to find the biggest sex effect for height you would sample only very tall (or very short) people.

Following this line of thinking, Sulloway chose to study people who had made outstanding contributions to fields such as science and politics. He asked a panel of historians to classify the contributions as liberal or conservative: Did the contribution go against the status quo, or did it support it? For example, Charles Darwin's theory of evolution challenged the status quo by questioning prevailing religious teaching. Sulloway found a large birth-order effect in this sample of conservative and liberal movers-and-shakers. Firstborns tended to make conservative contributions, whereas laterborns made liberal contributions. (Darwin was a laterborn, fitting the pattern.) Sulloway finds laterborns disproportionately represented among supporters of Darwin's theory of evolution, the Protestant Reformation, and the early stages of the French Revolution. The magnitude of the birth-order effect can be dramatic: Laterborns were forty-eight times more likely to die as martyrs in the Protestant Reformation than their firstborn siblings. Laterborns have been eighteen times more likely to die as radical political revolutionaries. Sulloway sums up his findings in the title of his book: *Born to Rebel* (1996).

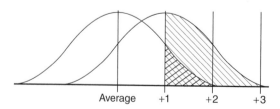

Figure 9–4. *Two similar but non-identical distributions.* When two populations differ, as indicated by the two curves, they overlap most near their means and least near their extremes.

Average   +1   +2   +3

What can be an evolutionary origin of a tendency for laterborns to rebel? It is important to realize that there can be no gene for birth order. The same parental genes are shuffled anew for each birth. Any birth order effect must arise from a facultative mechanism that responds to the family environment. Essentially, Sulloway's model postulates a mechanism that scans the family environment and decides: If a firstborn, then be conservative; if a laterborn, be rebellious. Sulloway considers the family to be a system that contains ecological niches. All ecological niches are ways of gaining resources. The most obvious way of gaining resources in a family is to please one's parents. This niche is generally taken by the firstborn, which forces the laterborns to adopt different strategies, or to claim different niches. The way to do that is to be somewhat rebellious. Martin Lalumiere and colleagues (1996) make a similar suggestion. They propose that competition for parental resources drives siblings to differentiate themselves from each other. The process is very much like a well-known ecological phenomenon called "character displacement": Pairs of similar species are more different where they live near one another than they are where they live in separate areas.

Sulloway's idea of the family as an environment with different niches fits with recent findings in behavior genetics. Studies that consider the inheritance of traits such as intelligence and personality must try to separate out the effects of differing genes and differing environments. Two siblings may be similar in intelligence either because they share genes or because they share a common upbringing—the latter is their *shared environment.* Clever studies have been done to see how heredity and environment contribute to differences in behavioral traits. But many studies have found, surprisingly, that siblings are not much more alike in their personalities than randomly selected unrelated individuals. [Siblings correlate about .10 in personality, and even this is owing to genetics, not environment (Plomin, 1987).] This finding is counterintuitive because we see obvious family resemblances in physical traits. Even more surprising is the fact that siblings are more alike on behavioral traits later in life—when they typically live apart—than they are when they live in the same family. Current thinking is that members of the same family also have a *nonshared environment*—different friends, different teachers, different life events. But competition among siblings for parental investment would additionally cause them to be forced apart to coexist in the same family. If this nonshared environment is systematically different for siblings as a function of variables such as birth order then siblings would differ systematically in personality.

Sulloway's book is too new for us to know how his ideas will be accepted by the scientific community. He has clearly amassed a prodigious amount of evidence in support of his conclusion, and his statistics are compelling. One note of caution comes from the fact that he published his results in a book intended for the general public. Therefore it lacks some of the details that would permit thorough scientific evaluation. We cannot say whether his conclusions will stand the test of time.

SUMMARY

1. Behavior genetics focuses on the genetic and environmental bases of differences between people, whereas evolutionary psychology focuses on mechanisms that are common to all people.

2. Reasons for variability in intelligence and personality include: normal variation around an optimum, change in optimum value of a trait over time (or space), frequency-dependent selection, and facultative mechanisms.

3. Intelligence and personality are concepts that describe important features of individuals as potential resources for us.

4. Because intelligence tests were developed to predict school success they may not measure all traits that make people smart in other contexts.

5. Spearman held that intelligence is best characterized by *g*, or general intelligence. Thurstone, on the other hand, believed that there were seven separate primary abilities.

6. Sternberg holds that current intelligence tests ignore creative and practical intelligence.

7. Gardner believes that there are at least seven intelligences, including some not tested by any current intelligence tests.

8. An evolutionary view suggests that there are many separate abilities that make up intelligence besides those tested by current tests.

9. Skoyles suggests that the large brains of humans evolved to permit acquisition of expertise, not intelligence, per se.

10. Variation in intelligence could arise as a consequence of genetic recombination, or, given the expensive-tissue principle, from different life strategies.

11. We have to go to school to learn abilities for which specialized modules have not evolved.

12. Gleitman and Rozin suggest that reading places new demands on a brain that was designed for other purposes.

13. Geary proposes that humans have adaptations for certain numerical concepts, such as more and less, but not for others, such as counting in base 10.

14. Geary suggests that, because children are not intrinsically motivated to practice skills for which we lack adaptations, schools need to provide a balance between mastering concepts and practicing skills.

15. Hyperactivity is mainly a problem in the school context, and may have been adaptively neutral, or even beneficial, in the EEA.

16. The Big Five personality traits are: Openness to experience, Conscientiousness, Extraversion, Agreeableness, and Neuroticism.

17. Buss proposes that each personality trait represents an adaptation by which we evaluate how people deal with a problem presented by the social landscape.

18. Differences in personality may arise from the fact that the optimal combination of traits varies from time to time, from frequency-dependent selection, and facultative adaptations.

19. Sulloway proposes that differences in birth order result in different family niches. He finds evidence that laterborns are more rebellious.

10 The Psychology of Human Mating

The military was able to fulfill congressional and popular demands for ethnic and skin-colour integration with notable success. But trying to do the same with women has been a major intellectual failure, because the military has operated on the incorrect assumption that skin colour and sex are equally important classifications. They are not. There is nothing we can know about a person's nature by knowing his skin colour. Sexuality, on the other hand, is an all-important, all-pervasive force in the lives of people, especially the 19- to 30-year-olds who predominate in military life. (Tiger 1997, p. A15).

There are many differences between men and women, a fact that traditional psychology overlooks to a remarkable degree. Consider the following experiment. Male and female confederates approached strangers of the opposite sex and, after a brief introductory conversation, asked one of the following questions: "Would you go out with me tonight?" "Would you come over to my apartment tonight?" "Would you go to bed with me tonight?" The experimenters were interested in how people would respond to these invitations. Do you think men and women responded similarly? To all of the questions?

As it turns out, men and women seem to be about equally interested in dating. About 50 percent of each sex agreed to a date with the person they had just met. But the sexes differed greatly in their interest in the other two activities. Only 6 percent of women accepted the invitation to visit the confederate's apartment, whereas 69 percent of men did so. And not a single woman said she would have sex with the confederate but 75 percent of the men accepted this invitation (Clark and Hatfield 1989). How can we explain such a divergence in their responses? In this chapter, we will consider the results of this and other experiments that illuminate human mating strategies. In the process, we will be asking how sexual selection has shaped the psychologies of women and men.

REPRODUCTIVE RATES OF WOMEN AND MEN

As you will recall from Chapter 2, sexual selection is caused by sex differences in reproductive rates. Obviously, then, the first question is: Do men and women differ in reproductive rates? This question deserves more than a simple yes or no answer because the situation is complicated.

Let's consider women first. Except in the relatively rare cases of twinning, a woman can produce only one child per year. This is because her commitment to gestation and preparing her body for another pregnancy would require about a year. In fact, over most of human evolution, when breast milk was the only suitable food for infants and young children, her minimal commitment might have been more like four to five years. This estimate is based on what we know of reproduction in chimpanzees (Tutin and McGinnis, 1981), our closest relatives among the nonhuman primates, and on contemporary hunter-gatherers like the !Kung San of Botswana (Howell, 1979: see Figure 10–1). Notice that having multiple mating partners would do little to increase a woman's reproductive rate. This is because her fertility is limited by the constraints of gestation and lactation, not by any shortage of mates.

Figure 10–1.   *Late weaning is the norm in hunter-gatherer societies.* Photo shows a !Kung San woman nursing her child.

Trail Marker: A woman's reproduction is limited by her physiological investment capacity.

How does this compare with male reproductive rates in humans? If a man made little commitment to rearing the children, and if he could have multiple partners, he could reproduce much more rapidly than a woman ever could. Each of his partners could, in principle, produce one offspring per year, so his reproductive rate would just be the sum of the rates of his partners. Unlike a woman's, a man's fertility *is* limited by access to mates. The more partners he had, the higher his reproductive rate could be. Consider a well-documented example. Moulay Ismail, who lived from 1672 to 1727, was the last Sharifian emperor of Morocco. By 1703 (when he was 31 years old) he had produced 525 sons and 342 daughters; his 700th son was born in 1721 (McFarlan et al., 1992), and he presumably continued to produce children for the remaining six years of his life. Of course this high reproductive output was only possible because Moulay Ismail had hundreds of wives.

Trail Marker: A man's reproduction is limited by his access to fertile women.

Moulay Ismail is fact, not fantasy, but his reproductive output is highly unusual; in fact it rates him a citation in the *Guinness Book of Records* (McFarlan et al., 1992), although his total number of children has recently been called into question (Einon, 1998). For at least two reasons, men will seldom be able to reproduce much more quickly than women. First, among contemporary humans everywhere, men do invest in offspring. How much they invest varies from society to society, but men are seldom like the deer we discussed in Chapter 2 who simply copulate and depart. Men's paternal investment slows down their reproduction. Paternal investment takes time and resources that might otherwise be spent on courting additional mates. Second, human mating practices also impose limits on men's reproductive rate. In a perfectly monogamous system, the sexes would have identical reproductive rates. Moulay Ismail could not have fathered hundreds of offspring if he were monogamous. If all of a man's children were produced with his one monogamous partner, his reproductive rate would necessarily be the same as hers. This idea provides a baseline. We would not want to naively claim that human mating systems are perfectly monogamous. But, to the degree that they approach monogamy, they tend to reduce the sex difference in reproductive rate.

So what are human mating systems actually like? Is monogamy the norm? Marriage practices offer one sort of evidence, and these practices vary quite a lot from one society to the next. North Americans are often surprised to learn that 85 percent of well-described human societies allow polygyny—the practice of one man marrying several women (Murdock, 1967). The reason this surprises people is that most of the large, modern nation-states that readily come to mind prohibit polygyny. And most of the more than one thousand societies that permit polygyny are smaller tribal groups. But anthropological and historical records suggest that prohibitions on polygyny are, evolutionarily speaking, very recent, nowhere dating back more than five hundred years (e.g., MacFarlane, 1986).

Trail Marker: Monogamy is evolutionarily novel in humans.

Of course marriage practices are not a perfect reflection of mating practices. Even societies that prohibit and punish polygyny are not fully monogamous for two reasons: marital infidelity and the combination of divorce and remarriage. Marital infidelity results in defacto polygyny because, as we saw above, having multiple partners raises a man's reproductive rate more than it raises a woman's. In principle, a man's wife and his lover could be pregnant simultaneously. But having a lover will not help a married woman produce more children; how could it? Through in-depth interviews, Susan Essock-Vitale and Michael McGuire (1985) studied the sexual and reproductive histories of a random sample of thirty-five to forty-five year-old, middle-class white women living in Los Angeles. Of the 283 women who had been married at some time in their lives 23 percent reported having at least one extramarital affair. But having more than one mate had not increased their reproductive success. Those who reported having affairs had an average of 2.2 children; those who did not averaged 2.3 children.

Trail Marker: Even in monogamous societies, infidelity, divorce, and remarriage allow effective polygyny.

Divorce and remarriage also affect the reproductive rates of men and women. The important fact is that, regardless of age, men are more likely to remarry than are women. And the difference between the sexes in their prospects of remarriage increases with age. For example, among people in the United States who divorce between the ages of twenty-five and twenty-nine, men are 30 percent more likely to remarry than are the women they divorce. For partners divorcing between the ages of fifty and fifty-four, men are four times (400 percent) more likely to remarry! These patterns are not unique to North America. A study of remarriage patterns based on data from forty-seven countries showed that, on a worldwide basis, men are more likely to remarry after divorce than are women, often much more likely (Chamie and Nsuly, 1981). Further, when men divorce and remarry they tend to marry women younger than their previous wife (Mackey, 1980). In this way, they exploit the fertile years of more than one woman. The effect of remarriage on fertility is potentially large; by 1980 nearly 40 percent of all marriages in the United States involved one partner who was remarrying (Chamie and Nsuly,

1981). The conclusion is that both infidelity and divorce and remarriage turn nominally monogamous societies like our own into at least mildly polygynous ones.

SEXUAL SELECTION IN HUMANS

What we have said so far is that human mating systems are not perfectly monogamous, but neither are they as polygynous as those of many nonhuman mammals. Men are much more committed and investing fathers than most of their mammalian counterparts. And this involvement limits their opportunities for polygyny, and thus slows down their reproductive rate. In Chapter 2 you saw that members of the fast sex compete while members of the slow sex choose. In perfectly monogamous species, where reproductive rates are equal, sexual selection favors similar traits in females and males. Thus, in monogamous species females and males tend to be equally competitive, and they tend to be equally choosy. Given what we know about the reproductive rates of men and women, how will sexual selection have acted in humans?

> **Trail Marker:** Because of a tendency toward weak polygyny, women are expected to be somewhat choosier, men somewhat more competitive.

The human situation, neither strongly polygynous nor fully monogamous, leads to an interesting prediction about the effects of sexual selection on human mating psychology. Because women have somewhat lower reproductive rates than men, they should have evolved to be quite choosy, but also somewhat competitive. Because men have somewhat higher reproductive rates but do typically invest in their offspring, they should have evolved to be quite competitive and somewhat choosy. This might seem like a prediction that can accommodate any finding, but it can not. For example, it predicts a clear sex difference on both choosiness (women choosier) and competitiveness (men more competitive). And it predicts that, relative to what we see in polygynous mammals such as chimpanzees and gorillas, human females will be more competitive and human males more choosy.

Choosiness

Reticence to initiate sexual relations is one clear indicator of choosiness. Sex partners are potential co-parents. Individuals who are relatively indiscriminate about their sex partners are not being very choosy. Thus the Clark and Hatfield (1989) study discussed at the beginning of this chapter is clear evidence for a sex difference in choosiness. Women were just as eager as men to go on a date with the person they had just met. But men were eleven times more likely than women to agree to visit this person's apartment. And not a single woman agreed to sexual relations, while 75 percent of the men did. This study is especially relevant because the participants presumably thought the solicitations were genuine, and that their answers would have real consequences. Either they would or would not find themselves in bed with their new acquaintance. Men generally found the idea appealing whereas women did not.

Note however that one-quarter of the men declined the sexual proposition. Such a rejection would be very unlikely in the vast majority of mammalian species. Unless a more dominant male were standing by, ready to punish the transgressor, a male deer, male baboon, or male chimpanzee would seize virtually any opportunity to mate with a fertile female. David Buss and David Schmitt (1993) have provided a variety of evidence showing that, while men are less choosy than women, men are not indiscriminate when it comes to mating. Buss and Schmitt asked women and men to rate how likely they would be to consent to sexual intercourse with someone they viewed as desirable, given that they had known the person for various periods of time from one hour to five years. Participants rated their willingness on a scale from −3 (definitely not) to +3 (definitely yes). The data are shown in Figure 10–2. Men consistently indicate a greater willingness to engage in sexual intercourse than women do; the gap does not close until they have known each other for five years. So men are clearly less choosy than women. But note also that men do not have a flat response at +3. For relationships of less than one week duration

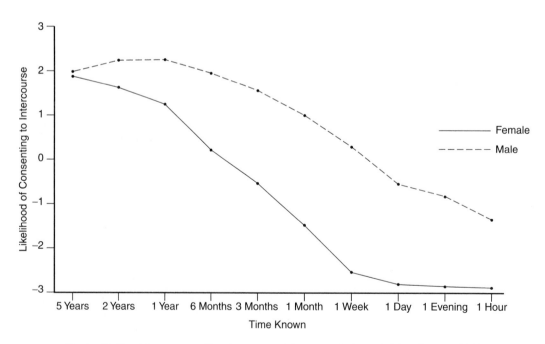

Figure 10–2. *Men are more willing than women.* Subjects rated the probability they would be willing to have sexual intercourse with an attractive partner they had know for various periods of time. (From "Sexual Strategies Theory: An Evolutionary Perspective on Human Mating" by D. Buss and D. Schmitt in *Psychological Review,* (1993), 100. Copyright © 1993 by American Psychological Association. Reprinted by permission of the American Psychological Association, Washington, DC.)

they also rate their willingness as on the negative side of neutral; and they reach a plateau closer to +2 than to +3.

Trail Marker: On average, women are choosier about their sex partners, but men are not wholly indiscriminate.

In a seminal book on evolutionary psychology, Donald Symons (1979) pointed out that homosexuals provide an interesting window on the sexual inclinations of men and women. As we have just outlined, men are more interested in having a large number of sex partners than women are. From a heterosexual man's viewpoint that creates a problem: The people with whom he must negotiate his sexual desires are women, whose desires differ! Homosexual men, on the other hand, negotiate their sexual activity with other men, whose desires are presumably more coincident. Thus we would expect that homosexual men would be more successful in achieving large numbers of sexual partners than are heterosexual men. Indeed this seems to be the case; homosexual males often report having hundreds or even thousands of partners. Fear of dangerous sexually transmitted diseases such as AIDS may have narrowed the gap somewhat. But even as late as the early 1990s homosexual men were still reporting significantly more sexual partners than were heterosexual men.

J. Michael Bailey and his collaborators have explored this issue in more detail. For example, this difference in promiscuity is not the result of differences in underlying interest. Homosexual and heterosexual men show no difference in their self-reported desire for uncommitted sex, only in their success in satisfying this desire. As it turns out, lesbians are slightly less interested in uncommitted sex than are heterosexual females. And among women sexual orientation makes no difference in the number of actual sexual partners (Bailey et al., 1994).

With respect to their eagerness to copulate, it seems that men behave as if they constitute the fast sex, the sex with the potentially higher reproductive rate. We will present more evidence on these matters a little later in this chapter. But first we need to detail several other aspects of human mating systems.

HUMAN PARENTAL INVESTMENT

Parental investment (Trivers, 1972) is actually a technical concept in evolutionary biology. It includes anything that a parent does for a particular offspring that helps the offspring (reproductively of course) and reduces the parent's ability to invest in other offspring. It is a limited resource, just like your income or allowance. What you spend on one purchase is unavailable for something else. Gestation and lactation are clear examples of parental investment. So are groceries, medical fees, clothing, and time and money spent preparing the child to compete effectively in the world. As we noted above, both women and men contribute significant amounts of parental investment. This pattern, which we can call *biparental investment,* is rather rare among mammals (but quite common among birds).

The Evolution of Biparental Investment

Why, if males could accelerate their reproductive rate by acquiring more mates, do they slow themselves down by investing? The answer is that, under some circumstances, offspring who receive investment from two parents do much better than offspring who receive it from only one. Now consider two hypothetical kinds of males. One who merely fertilizes females and then departs to seek additional mates, and one who gives up some mating opportunities to stay around and help rear his offspring. If offspring who receive biparental investment have a big enough advantage, then investing males might end up with more grandchildren than males who fail to help.

> **Trail Marker:** Biparental investment is most likely to evolve in species with helpless young.

This is sensible enough, but biparental care is rare among mammals (Kleiman, 1977). Is there anything special about humans that might have made the additional investment of a dad especially valuable? Yes; human infants are very helpless and take a very long time to grow to adulthood. Perhaps in protohuman populations of several million years ago, males who abandoned their mates had fewer surviving children than males who stuck around to help. In this way, the extreme dependence of human infants and children may have favored the evolution of biparental investment in our species. This idea is speculative of course; we cannot answer this kind of (pre-)historical question with great confidence. But what is clear is that if some women received reproductively useful help from their mates and others did not, the former would be favored by selection. Under these conditions, any trait that helped a woman get material assistance from her partner would spread.

Sex Differences in Parental Investment

There are some underlying asymmetries in *how* women and men invest. For example, some very important components of female parental investment—gestation and lactation—are physiological. At least in this early phase of child rearing, women in better physiological condition will be better parents, and therefore better choices as mates.

In contrast, men's parental investment is not physiological but economic, in the broadest sense of this word. Men are involved in harvesting resources from the environment which they may channel to offspring (or to courtship). This is not to say that women never harvest resources. They clearly provide for their (older) children in this way too. The key point is that men *only* harvest resources. They never commit their own bodily resources to children. So a man's "economic" well being may provide a better indication of his value as a mate than does his physiological state.

> **Trail Marker:** Both sexes invest economically in offspring; only women invest physiologically.

These differences in how men and women invest in offspring have implications for the kinds of mates they are expected to prefer. Try to predict men's and women's mating preference based on what you have just learned. Much of the rest of this chapter presents evidence that will allow you to test your predictions, but first we turn to the important issue of physical attractiveness.

THE EVOLUTION OF MATING PREFERENCES: PHYSICAL ATTRACTIVENESS

A brief analogy will be helpful in thinking about how we judge attractiveness. Recall our discussion of evolved dietary preferences. There is nothing inherently tasty about sugar or fat. But they do taste good to us: Why? Our taste preferences have been shaped by selection. In the EEA, sweetness and fattiness consistently signalled nutritious foods. Those protohumans who were attracted to and ate sweet and fatty foods ended up being better nourished and were thus more likely to be ancestors than those who rejected these foods. The key principle here is that attraction is not simply caused by intrinsic features of the "attractive" object. Nothing is automatically attractive. True, we experience attraction as a result of certain sensory input. But our sensory systems are not passive receptors; they have been designed by selection with particular built-in biases. Simply put, we perceive certain stimuli as attractive because those stimuli were reliable signals of fitness-enhancing situations.

Now, let's consider physical attractiveness. Physical attractiveness has long been known to be an important variable in mate choice (Berscheid and Walster, 1974). And contrary to some popular notions, criteria of physical attractiveness are not all that variable from one culture to another (e.g., Jones, 1996). For example, Nancy Anderson and her colleagues showed facial photographs of Asian women to a sample that included Japanese-, Korean-, Chinese- and European-derived Americans. She asked these judges to rate the attractiveness of each face, and to say whether it was most likely to be Japanese, Korean, or Chinese. While the various groups of judges focused on quite different facial features in rating the ethnicity of the faces, they agreed closely on which faces were the most and least attractive and on the particular facial dimensions that contributed to attractiveness (Anderson et al., 1999).

But traditional SSSM psychology has begged the question of what constitutes attractiveness. Why do we see some people as attractive and others as less so? EP would approach this question by asking: What phenotypic features have been reliably correlated with fitness? Those are the features that we will have evolved to see as attractive As Donald Symons (1995) has stressed, "Beauty is in the adaptations of the beholder." We can suggest several correlates of fitness that seem to shape our attractiveness judgments.

> **Trail Marker:** "Beauty is in the adaptations of the beholder."
> (Symons 1995).

Youth is a clear example. Other things being equal, young people have more of their reproductive careers ahead of them and thus would make better mates. Not surprisingly then, youthfulness is an essential component of attractiveness. Nowhere are wrinkles and sagging skin viewed as attractive. Of course the correlates of male and female fitness are not necessarily identical. For example, female fertility declines more dramatically with age than does male fertility. Thus an evolutionary view would suggest that apparent youthfulness is a more essential feature of female attractiveness than male attractiveness. In fact, women spend billions of dollars to reduce the signs of age with cosmetics and surgery.

By its very nature, youth is transient. All of us are young once, and, with good luck, we'll all be old, too. So this aspect of our attractiveness varies over our lifetime. But some of our attributes—such as our genotypes—do not change over our lifetimes. This is relevant because one thing partners offer to each other is genes for their offspring. Of course, potential mates inevitably differ in terms of the quality of the genes they offer. Wouldn't it be helpful if we could "see" those differences? In fact evolutionists believe that, to a large degree, we see them when we make attractiveness judgments!

The arguments and evidence on this point are complicated but fascinating. To begin to understand them you should first read Box 10–1, if you have not already done so. The key points there are as follows. At present, it seems that slowly reproducing species like humans use sexual (as opposed to asexual) reproduction as a defense against parasites and pathogens. Organisms should choose mates based on the reasons they engage in sex. If avoiding parasites and pathogens is the reason for sex, then mates should be chosen, first and foremost, for parasite and pathogen resistence.

Some of the ways of doing this are fairly obvious and some aren't. On the obvious side, a parasite- and pathogen-resistant individual will show clear signs of health and vigor. Thus we should have evolved to value signs of health and vigor in our attractiveness judgments. And as with age, many signs of health are visible in the face. Clear skin, bright eyes, and shiny hair all suggest an individual in good physiological condition, one not too stressed by parasites. You know this is so because, if one of your friends is not well, a mere glance at his face reveals this fact.

Here's the less obvious part. The face provides not only a report of current health but also a lifelong medical record. The reason is that, because they drain the body's resources, parasites and pathogens disturb normal processes of growth and development. Such disturbances leave a permanent, though often small, trace. How can we see these traces?

Evolutionary biologists have long wondered why so many organisms reproduce sexually. Think about it. Asexual forms pass on all their genes each time they reproduce, whereas sexual forms pass on only half. And sexual reproduction carries with it other significant costs, such as the cost of finding mates and the cost of producing offspring with previously untested genotypes. Despite these costs, there are reasonable explanations for sexuality in organisms that produce very large numbers of progeny. But in low-fertility organisms like ourselves there is currently only one plausible reason for sexual reproduction: to cope with the parasites and pathogens that make us sick (Hamilton and Zuk, 1982; Tooby, 1982).

Parasites and pathogens are small, rapidly reproducing organisms that eat us from the inside out. They can kill us or seriously reduce our fitness. Because they reproduce rapidly, they can evolve and adapt rapidly. Their environment is their host's body and thus, over time, they get better and better at exploiting that host. Of course hosts evolve defenses, too. But, because hosts have much longer generation times than these "micropredators" do, parasites and pathogens have the upper hand in this evolutionary arms race (see Chapter 2 to remind yourself why generation time affects the rate of evolution).

By the time a typical host reaches reproductive age, he or she will have provided a stable environment for tens of thousands of generations of parasites and pathogens. If hosts reproduce asexually, they pass an identical copy of their whole genotype to their offspring. Since their own parasites and pathogens have already become adapted to that very genotype over the host's lifetime, this burdens the offspring with many well-adapted enemies. Wouldn't the offspring have a better start in life if it had a new and different genotype? According to Hamilton and Zuk (1982), this is why we mix our genes with our mate's: to change the rules of the game for our parasites and pathogens. Their additional insight was that, if we have sex to help our offspring escape pathogens, shouldn't we choose mates who have the most pathogen-resistant genes? In other words, shouldn't the evolutionary reason for sex have shaped the way we choose mates? If Hamilton and Zuk are correct we should have evolved to view signs of consistent good health as attractive.

Box 10–1.   Sexual Reproduction: A Race to Stay Ahead of Our Parasites.

Like many other animals, humans are bilaterally symmetrical. Viewed from the outside at least, our right side is nearly a mirror image of the left. However, the disruptions of growth and development caused by parasites and pathogens perturb the symmetry and leave a permanent trace in terms of slight right-left differences. For this reason, deviations from right-left symmetry constitute a lifelong medical history that is also a matter of public record since any potential mate can read it at a glance.

Trail Marker: Youth, health, vigor and symmetry are key components of attractiveness.

Of course no face is perfectly symmetrical (see Figure 10–3). However, a number of recent studies indicate that, the less the deviation from perfect symmetry, the more attractive the face is judged to be. This is true for both men's and women's faces (Grammar and Thornhill, 1994). Using a computer "morphing" technique, Hume and Montgomerie (1999) were able to increase the symmetry of digital photographs of normal faces. They found a clear-cut relationship: The more a face was modified to approach perfect symmetry, the more attractive it was judged to be.

In a particularly intriguing study, Steve Gangestad, Randy Thornhill, and Ronald Yeo (1994) computed right-left asymmetry of nonfacial features (for example, elbow, ankle, and wrist diameters) for seventy-two undergraduates and then took standardized facial photographs of these same volunteers. The facial

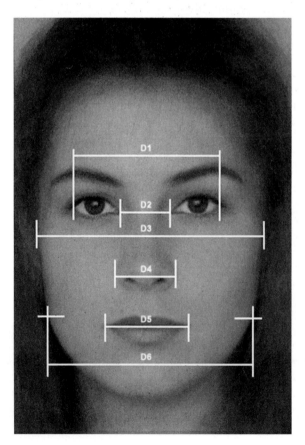

Figure 10–3. *How is facial symmetry measured?* Here's one technique. First, the distance between right and left facial landmarks is measured. Then the midpoint of each measurement is computed. On the most symmetrical faces these midpoints line up.

photographs were then rated for attractiveness by another group of subjects. Those individuals who were more symmetrical on the basis of nonfacial measurements were judged to have more attractive faces. This is presumably because the kind of developmental insults that produce asymmetry affect all parts of the body: those with nonfacial asymmetries also had less symmetrical faces. Recent work also suggests that, among males, the most symmetrical individuals have first sexual intercourse at younger ages and have more sex partners over their lifetimes (Thornhill and Gangestad, 1994). Women even seem to prefer the scent of symmetrical men. When asked to smell t-shirts that had been worn by men for several days, women rated those worn by more symmetrical men as more sexy and more attractive (Thornhill and Gangestad, 1999a, 1999b). Interestingly, this discrimination ability is limited to women who are in the most fertile phase of their monthly cycles. We will return to the issue of physical attractiveness below.

THE EVOLUTION OF MATING PREFERENCES: PARENTAL INVESTMENT

We have seen that women are more selective, for example requiring a longer friendship before copulating. Perhaps women and men use exactly the same mate-choice criteria, but women simply set a higher standard or cut-off. Alternatively, the two sexes may use different yardsticks in judging potential mates. Thinking in terms of sexual selection, what would you predict?

Women and men have evolved similar dietary preferences because we have similar nutritional needs. But men and women need somewhat different things in a mate, because of their different investment patterns. Remember that women invest physiologically in offspring whereas men invest only through the resources they provide. Thus, a mate with lots of resources could enhance a woman's fitness, so women may have evolved a preference for resource-rich partners. Men, on the other hand, may attend more to a woman's physiological investment potential. Of course these are matters of degree, matters of relative emphasis, not absolutes. For example, a man in poor health might die, in which case much of his economic potential would be lost.

What data are available on the mate-choice criteria of women and men? As a first intuition you might think of looking at people's marriage choices. Aren't they a conspicuous behavioral indication of mating preferences? In fact, actual marriages may not accurately reflect evolved mating preferences. Let's briefly return to the dietary analogy. If you crave a particular food, then, within very wide bounds, you can just eat it. The food on the supermarket shelves has no strategies of its own. For this reason the stuff that modern humans actually eat is probably a reasonable indicator of what we have evolved to find appetizing. But in the realm of mating, our cravings can be frustrated by the rather different cravings of our intended. Marriage is the result of a successful negotiation between two partners, and it is reasonable to assume that each has made some compromises in reaching the agreement. Realizing this, some researchers have tried to assess what people want in a mate, rather than what they are willing to accept.

Women's Preferences

In a series of studies reaching back to the 1930s, researchers have asked North American women and men about the characteristics they find important in potential mates. For example, Reuben Hill (1945) asked participants to rate a series of eighteen different traits in terms of how indispensable they were in a marriage partner. Women's and men's preferences are, overall, quite similar. For example, both sexes rate a sense of humor and various personality characteristics at the top of their list. Of course this is to be expected, on commonsense grounds, but also because, unless sexual selection is favoring differences between the sexes, natural selection will keep them quite similar. Because we are exploring the effects of sexual selection, we will concentrate on the areas where men's and women's preferences differ.

Hill (1945) found that women rate financial status as about twice as important as do men, despite the fact that the sexes differed little in the importance they placed on many other attributes. David Buss (1989a) used the same methodology with a sample of about fifteen hundred North Americans in the mid-1980s and obtained the same result, as did studies in the intervening decades (Hudson and Henze 1969, McGinnis, 1958). More recently, a representative sample of unmarried Americans between the ages of nineteen and thirty-five confirmed that this sex difference is not limited to college students and seems to be stable despite a growing emphasis on similar socialization for boys and girls (Sprecher et al., 1994).

Analysis of personal advertisements in newspapers leads to a similar conclusion. In a sample of more than eleven hundred heterosexually oriented advertisements (Wiederman 1993), both sexes indicated that they were seeking financial resources in a prospective mate, but for every man who mentioned this criterion, eleven women did! In another study of one thousand such advertisements that appeared in a British newspaper women mentioned financial criteria 3.7 times as often as men did (Greenlees and McGrew, 1994).

> **Trail Marker:** Women prefer partners with good economic potential.

At least one more line of evidence is relevant here. Many of us have a clear idea of what we want in a mate. But to the extent that we agree with members of our own sex, we will be thrown into competition for the most desirable members of the opposite sex. Publically criticizing or putting down rivals can be an effective tactic in this sort of competition. Of course the put-downs will only be effective if they criticize aspects of the competitor that matter to the opposite sex. David Buss and Lisa Dedden (1990) studied the use of such derogation tactics among both undergraduates and newlyweds. They found that men are significantly more likely to denigrate other men's resources or resource acquisition potential than women are to criticize women in this way.

But perhaps this sex difference is just a response to the modern Western socioeconomic scene. After all, don't mate-choice criteria vary widely from one culture to another? This is an empirical question, and fortunately there are plenty of cross-cultural data. With a large number of collaborators David Buss (1989a) undertook a study of mating preferences in thirty-seven cultures from thirty-three different countries. The study included over ten thousand participants representing "a tremendous diversity of geographic, cultural, political, ethnic, religious, racial and economic groups" (Buss 1989b). Buss and his collaborators asked participants to rate or rank the importance of various criteria in their choice of a mate. Some of these were "distractor" variables, that is, mate-choice criteria on which the sexes were not expected to differ. Others were "target" variables—criteria expected to be of greater importance to one sex than to the other. Distractors included such items as "sociable," "intelligent," and "dependable character." Target variables included items like "good financial prospect" and "good looking."

In every one of the thirty-seven cultures, women scored "good financial prospect" as a more important criterion of mate choice than men did, and the difference between women's and men's rankings was statistically significant in thirty-six of the thirty-seven cultures (Table 10–1). This is a striking regularity considering the diversity of cultures sampled. Could this be an evolved sex difference, universal among contemporary humans?

The Structural Powerlessness Hypothesis

Before drawing that conclusion, you may want to consider other hypotheses. Perhaps women value economic potential not because men have invested that way for several million years. Instead, they may value it because, being largely excluded from the economic arena by men, women only have access to economic resources through their mates. This idea is called the "structural powerlessness hypothesis" (Buss and Barnes, 1986). According to this view:

> . . . women's relative preferences for economic resources in a mate may be byproducts of the culturally determined differential economic status of men versus women. If women are typically excluded from power . . . then women may seek mates possessing characteristics associated with power and resource acquisition skills (e.g. earning capacity). . . . In short, the structural powerlessness hypothesis implies that as economic differences between men and women diminish, men and women become more alike in their mate selection preferences" (Wiederman and Allgeier, 1992:117).

So do women with relatively good access to economic resources relax their standards with respect to the earning potential of prospective mates, as the structural powerlessness hypothesis predicts? In short, the answer is "no." Let's look at the data.

Table 10–1. Emphasis Placed on Financial Prospects of Potential Mates by Men and Women in Thirty-Seven Cultures (data from Buss 1989a).

SAMPLE	MEN	WOMEN
African		
Nigeria	1.37	2.30
S. Africa (whites)	0.94	1.73
S. Africa (Zulu)	0.70	1.14
Zambia	1.46	2.33
Asian		
China	1.10	1.56
India	1.60	2.00
Indonesia	1.42	2.55
Iran	1.25	2.04
Israel (Jewish)	1.31	1.82
Israel (Palestinian)	1.28	1.67
Japan	0.92	2.29
Taiwan	1.25	2.21
European-Eastern		
Bulgaria	1.16	1.64
Estonian S.S.R.	1.31	1.51
Poland	1.09	1.74
Yugoslavia	1.27	1.66
European-Western		
Belgium	0.95	1.36
France	1.22	1.68
Finland	0.65	1.18
Germany-West	1.14	1.81
Great Britain	0.67	1.16
Greece	1.16	1.92
Ireland	0.82	1.67
Italy	0.87	1.33
Netherlands	0.69	0.94
Norway	1.10	1.42
Spain	1.25	1.39
Sweden	1.18	1.75
North American		
Canada (English)	1.02	1.91
Canada (French)	1.47	1.94
USA (Mainland)	1.08	1.96
USA (Hawaii)	1.50	2.10
Oceanian		
Australia	0.69	1.54
New Zealand	1.35	1.63
South American		
Brazil	1.24	1.91
Colombia	1.72	2.21
Venezuela	1.66	2.26

(From "Sex Differences in Human Mate Preferences" by D. Buss in *Behavioral & Brain Sciences,*
(1989), 12. Copyright © 1989 by D. Buss. Reprinted by permission of Cambridge University Press.)

> **Trail Marker:** Structural powerlessness does not explain women's preference for economically promising partners.

In a study of one hundred newlywed couples, Buss (1989b) collected data on both income and mate-choice priorities. Among the men in his sample, Buss found no association between income and the importance placed on the partner's income. But among women a positive correlation was observed: Women with higher incomes placed a *greater* emphasis on a mate's earning potential than did women with lower incomes. Similarly, John Townsend (1989) found that in a sample of twenty female medical students, each of whom expected a very good salary of her own, all stressed earning potential as an important criterion of mate choice.

Michael Wiederman and Elizabeth Allgeier (1992) pursued the same question with nearly 1000 college students and a sample of 282 individuals from the wider community. In neither sample did men's expected earnings affect their own mate preferences. In the college sample, women again showed a significant positive correlation: Those who expected to earn more placed more, not less, emphasis on a potential mate's income. In the broader community sample, there was no relationship between earnings and women's mate-choice priorities. Remember, the structural powerlessness hypothesis predicts a negative correlation: If women prefer men with good earning potential because women in general have poor financial prospects, those women with the best financial prospects should care less about the earning potential of suitors. But no study has reported this negative relationship. Most report a significant positive relationship and one sample suggests no relationship. Thus, the structural powerlessness hypothesis has received no support and its usefulness as an explanation for the sex difference in mating preferences is therefore in doubt.

You may wonder why women with considerable resources of their own still emphasize the resource potential of prospective mates. Why women don't exhibit a facultative response, decreasing their emphasis on partner wealth when they themselves are wealthy. In other words, couldn't the structural powerlessness hypothesis be an evolutionary hypothesis after all? Perhaps. But remember, facultative responses will reflect the range of environmental variation that has prevailed during evolution. Here's an analogy. At African savanna temperatures of 110 degrees, your body will exhibit some helpful facultative response such as sweating. But we have no useful response to temperatures such as 500 degrees, simply because that's not an environment in which humans have ever competed for reproductive success. The point of the analogy is that ancestral women did not differ in wealth nearly as much as their modern descendants do, and probably none were so well off that they would be better served by ignoring their suitors' resource provisioning ability. Like the rest of our adaptations, our mate choice modules were crafted in the EEA.

Men's Preferences

What does an evolutionary approach predict about men's preferences? Given that a significant fraction of a woman's parental investment is physiological, men are expected to value signs of good physiological (rather than financial) condition. You often can't tell how rich someone is by looking at them. But you can tell how healthy and vigorous they are. Men should have evolved to pay attention to signs of physiological well being. Any such signs will surely be physical. So, unlike women, men will have evolved to attend disproportionately to the physical attributes of potential mates, and to see as attractive those features most strongly correlated with physiological investment capacity.

> **Trail Marker:** Men prefer physically attractive partners.

The first prediction is abundantly verified. The same series of studies that examined the importance of financial status in mate choice also evaluated the extent to which men and women value physical attractiveness in their mates (Buss, 1989a; Hill, 1945; Hudson and Henze, 1969; McGinnis, 1958). Men consistently rate physical attractiveness as significantly more important in a mate than women do. This is not to say that the emphasis placed on physical attractiveness is unmodifiable. Over the fifty years spanned by these studies, both men and women have shifted in the direction of placing more emphasis on physical attractiveness (an interesting observation that will be discussed in Chapter 16). But, throughout this period the magnitude of the difference between the sexes has been essentially unchanged (Buss, 1994; Sprecher et al., 1994). By a steady margin, men rate physical attractiveness as more important in potential partners than women do.

Personal advertisements support these findings. In a large North American sample of such solicitations men were 3.7 times as likely as women to be explicitly seeking a physically attractive partner (Weiderman, 1994). Cross-cultural data match the North American pattern. In every one of the thirty-seven cultures studied by Buss (1989a), men rated physical attractiveness as a more indispensable trait of potential mates than women did, and the difference between men's and women's ratings was statistically significant in all but three cultures (Table 10–2). Derogation tactics exhibit the same sex bias. Women are much more likely to put down a rival's physical appearance than are men (Buss and Dedden, 1990).

After puberty, a woman's physiological investment capacity declines with age. Women are less fertile at thirty years of age than at twenty, and less fertile at forty than at thirty. On the other hand, economic investment capacity may, for a time at least, increase with age as experience and social influence grow. These patterns may underlie the consistently divergent age preferences expressed by men and women. In Buss's (1989a) cross-cultural study, men preferred mates younger than themselves and women preferred mates older than themselves in every culture, and the difference was statistically significant in all thirty-seven cases.

Table 10–2.   Emphasis Placed on Physical Attractiveness of Potential Mates by Men and Women in Thirty-Seven Cultures (data from Buss 1989a).

SAMPLE	MEN	WOMEN
African		
Nigeria	2.24	1.82
S. Africa (Whites)	1.58	1.22
S. Africa (Zulu)	1.17	0.88
Zambia	2.23	1.65
Asian		
China	2.06	1.59
India	2.03	1.97
Indonesia	1.81	1.36
Iran	2.07	1.69
Israel (Jewish)	1.77	1.56
Israel (Palestinian)	2.38	1.47
Japan	1.50	1.09
Taiwan	1.76	1.28
European-Eastern		
Bulgaria	2.39	1.95
Estonian S.S.R.	2.27	1.63
Poland	1.93	1.77
Yugoslavia	2.20	1.74
European-Western		
Belgium	1.78	1.28
France	2.08	1.76
Finland	1.56	0.99
Germany-West	1.92	1.32
Great Britain	1.96	1.36
Greece	2.22	1.94
Ireland	1.87	1.22
Italy	2.00	1.64
Netherlands	1.76	1.21
Norway	1.87	1.32
Spain	1.91	1.24
Sweden	1.65	1.46
North American		
Canada (English)	1.96	1.64
Canada (French)	1.68	1.41
USA (Mainland)	2.11	1.67
USA (Hawaii)	2.06	1.49
Oceanian		
Australia	1.65	1.24
New Zealand	1.99	1.29
South American		
Brazil	1.89	1.68
Colombia	1.56	1.22
Venezuela	1.76	1.27

(From "Sex Differences in Human Mate Preferences" by D. Buss in *Behavioral & Brain Sciences,* (1989), 12. Copyright © 1989 by D. Buss. Reprinted by permission of Cambridge University Press.)

Trail Marker: Men prefer youthful partners.

Of the three variables we have examined so far—financial capacity, physical attractiveness, and age—we have been able to predict, and verify, the direction of the expected sex difference. It turns out that an evolutionary view also allows a more precise prediction with respect to age criteria. Averaged across the thirty-seven cultures studied by Buss, men preferred a wife who was about 2.7 years younger than themselves. But what does that tell us? Are males expected to prefer a mate because she is x years younger than him or because she is y years old? Clearly, a woman's fertility is related to her own age, not to how much younger she is than her husband. This suggests that as men age they are expected to prefer a progressively greater age difference between themselves and their partners.

Data from disparate societies support this prediction (Kenrick and Keefe, 1992). Men younger than twenty years of age tend to marry women their same age. In their twenties men marry women three to four years younger. Men marrying in their thirties select wives who average six to eight years younger. And the trend continues. The wives of men marrying in the forties, fifties, and sixties are thirteen, fifteen, and sixteen to nineteen years younger, respectively. The data for women marrying at progressively later ages show no such pattern. In fact, regardless of their age at marriage, women tend to marry men who are one to six years older than themselves.

Are men attending to any other traits in their attractiveness judgments? Devendra Singh (1993) has an interesting answer. As a consequence of sex hormone regimes, men and women deposit body fat differently. Estrogen, a reproductively important female hormone, inhibits fat deposition in the abdominal region and fosters its deposition on the hips, thighs, and buttocks, producing the so-called "gynoid" fat distribution. In contrast, male hormones, called androgens, foster fat deposits that are concentrated abdominally and on the upper body, the "android" fat distribution. The difference between gynoid and android patterns is immediately clear from a simple ratio of waist to hip measurements. Healthy premenopausal women have waist-hip ratios in the range of 0.67 to 0.80, whereas healthy men typically have waist-hip ratios between 0.85 and 0.95. The distributions of healthy women and men do not even overlap on this trait! Most important is the fact that, among women, high (that is, android) waist-hip ratios are correlated with low fertility and higher susceptibility to a range of degenerative diseases. In other words, a woman's waist-hip ratio honestly reveals her reproductively relevant hormone profile.

Trail Marker: Men prefer partners with a low waist-hip ratio.

Given this, and given the negative fitness consequences of high waist-hip ratios in women, men should have evolved to prefer mates with low waist-hip ratios.

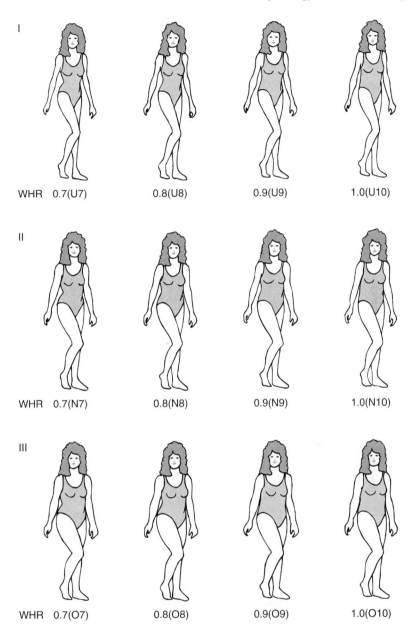

Figure 10–4. *Stimuli used to assess male preferences with respect to female body shape.* Men consistently prefer the leftmost figure in the second row; this figure depicts a women of normal weight with a waist/hip ratio of 0.7. (From "Adaptive Significance of Female Physical Attractiveness: Role of Waist-to-Hip Ratio" by D. Singh in *Journal of Personality and Social Psychology*, (1993), 65. Copyright © 1993 by American Psychological Association. Reprinted by permission of American Psychological Association, Washington, DC.)

In personal advertisements, men are 9.5 times more likely than women to mention body shape in describing the kind of partner they seek (Wiederman, 1993). But this test is indirect. Using a range of methods, Singh has explicitly examined the effects of waist-hip ratio on men's evaluation of female attractiveness (see Figure 10–4). Low waist-hip ratios are consistently preferred not only in North America (Singh 1993) but across a range of cultures (Singh and Luis, 1995).

To sum up, women provide large amounts of physiological investment for their offspring whereas men's investment emphasizes the provision of resources. An evolutionary view predicts that women's and men's mate-choice criteria would reflect these different patterns of investment. The available data support this view. Compared to men, women focus on the resources a potential mate might provide. And women seem to emphasize this criterion more when they are relatively well-off, so their preference is probably not motivated by a lack of access to resources. Compared to women, men look for signs of fertility in potential mates such as physical attractiveness, a low waist-hip ratio, and youth. Data from around the world suggest that these patterns are not artifacts of western culture, but rather universal features of male and female mating psychology. Even in the realm of their sexual fantasies—a domain that is presumably little influenced by arbitrary social conventions—women and men exhibit this same pattern of differences (Ellis and Symons, 1990).

MIXED REPRODUCTIVE STRATEGIES

When we choose a reproductive partner we can recruit two things for our offspring: the partner's genes and the partner's parental investment. Up to a point at least, a woman's genes and her investment necessarily flow to the same offspring. This is because (barring the evolutionarily novel technique of egg transplantation) she will invariably gestate only offspring that carry her genes. But a man's investment is not automatically linked to his genetic progeny.

Another way of stating this asymmetry is that a woman's child definitely bears her genes, but man's child . . . well, that's just the point: who is a man's child? His wife's children are not automatically his own. Thus there is a large sex difference in what evolutionists call *parental confidence,* the ability to accurately identify one's own offspring. A great deal follows from this sex difference. Because a man's investment and his genes are not automatically linked, women could recruit the two separately. Some males may offer better genes than investment and others may offer the reverse. In the final analysis, selection would favor women who get the best possible genes and the best possible investment, even if they come from different sources. And likewise, because a man's investment and his genes are not automatically linked, men can separate their contributions, giving only genes to some of their offspring. The male's potential to achieve higher reproductive rates means that there is at least some selection on men to desert their partners and children and seek additional mates.

These opportunities define what evolutionary biologists call *mixed reproductive strategies.* In playing a mixed reproductive strategy an individual tries to "get the best of both worlds." Without falling prey to the naturalistic fallacy—in other words, remembering that what's natural is not necessarily virtuous—let's explore the mixed reproductive strategies open to men and women.

A woman's reproductive ends would be best served if she had a reliable partner able and willing to invest lots of resources in her offspring and if she could recruit the very best genes for those offspring as well. (The notion of good genes is discussed above under the heading Evolution of Mating Preferences: Physical Attractiveness.) The amount of resources a man has to invest may be partly related to his genotype; men with good genes may be somewhat better at getting resources. But luck and historical accident affect a man's resources too. So the men with the best genes are not always the ones with the most resources. Thus women will sometimes find themselves with a difficult choice: recruit a mate with good genes or one with good resources. Either of these "pure" strategies may deprive a woman of some of the benefits men can provide. The mixed strategy is to recruit genes and investment separately, choosing the best source of each.

> **Trail Marker:** Women playing a mixed reproductive strategy would accept genes and investment from different men.

Similarly, males also face conflicting reproductive goals. A man can benefit by having a fertile mate capable of high-quality maternal investment. But men also can raise their reproductive rates by having multiple mates. Should they settle down or play the field? Whichever they choose they sacrifice something. For a male the best of both worlds—the mixed reproductive strategy—is to have one fertile partner and invest in her offspring, but to also commit just enough resources to gain reproductive access to a number of other women.

> **Trail Marker:** Men playing a mixed reproductive strategy would invest heavily in one partner but still attempt to attract additional mates.

Obviously, these mixed reproductive strategies violate the ideal of marital fidelity for both sexes. But we know that marital infidelity occurs. Estimates of the actual rate of adultery vary greatly, from 26 percent to 70 percent for women and from 33 percent to 75 percent for men (Buss and Schmitt, 1993 and contained references). Of course some of this may just be sexual bragging, and some of the estimates have come from self-selected samples (e.g., readers of *Playboy* or *Cosmopolitan*). But even very careful studies based on random samples make it clear that true rates of infidelity are likely to be well above zero. For example, remember that in Essock-Vitale and McGuire's (1985) random sample, 23 percent of ever-married Los Angeles women reported extramarital affairs. That said, does extramarital sex seem to be motivated by the evolutionary incentives of mixed reproductive strategies?

Douglas Kenrick and his associates used an innovative technique to assess whether people change their level of choosiness when seeking different kinds of relationships. Other studies have asked which characteristics of a potential partner are important and which are unimportant. For example, from Buss's studies we know that men prefer attractive mates, but we do not know what level of attractiveness they would find acceptable: We do not know how selective they are. Kenrick et al. (1993) studied selectivity. Basically, they asked people to specify the minimum ranking of an acceptable partner on a series of characteristics, such as status, agreeableness and attractiveness. (They explained that, for example, a person at the sixtieth percentile of status would be above 60 percent of other people but below 39 percent on this trait.) And they asked about these minimum percentile rankings for several levels of involvement including a single date, steady dating, one-night stands, and marriage. Figure 10–5 shows their data for four characteristics. There are several points you should notice.

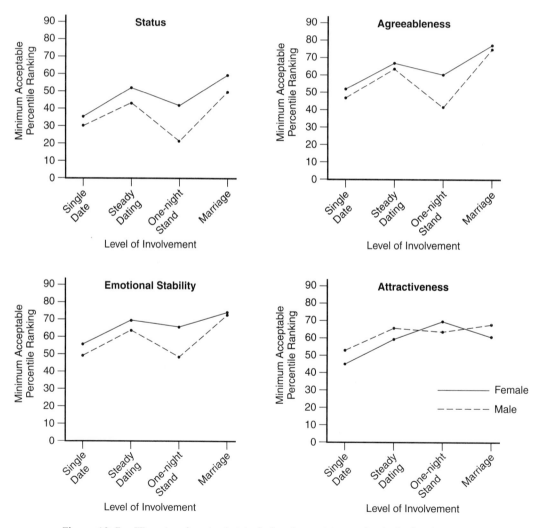

Figure 10–5. *Women's and men's selectivity for four characteristics over four levels of involvement.* See text for a discussion of the data.

The Kenrick team found that, for most levels of involvement and for most characteristics, women set higher standards—they specified higher minimum percentile rankings—than men did. (The only exception here is that, in agreement with previous findings, men tend to set higher standards for the physical attractiveness of their partners.) Men's generally lower standards could be predicted from what we have said about male reproductive strategy. Remember, men's mixed reproductive strategy involves gaining access to multiple partners. In comparison to women, men are expected to emphasize partner number more and partner quality less. Setting high standards eliminates potential mates. Thus, relaxed standards function to increase the size of the potential mate pool for men.

> **Trail Marker:** Women are especially selective about the physical attractiveness of their one-night-stand partners.

Overall, and for most individual traits, both men and women set the highest standards for marriage partners. The greater the commitment, the more people insist on a high-quality partner. But there is one notable exception: Women set even higher standards for the attractiveness (and only for attractiveness) of their one-night-stand partners than they do for their marriage partners. (For comparison, men exhibit the more typical pattern of lowered standards for all the characteristics of one-night-stand partners, including attractiveness.) Since attractiveness is the best proxy measure for assessing genetic quality, the Kenrick team's findings have an obvious evolutionary interpretation. When women marry and thus expect to get investment as well as genes they are willing to compromise somewhat on genetic quality. But in the context where they can expect to get nothing but genes (the one-night stand) they set maximal standards for genetic quality and relax all other criteria. These patterns would be difficult to explain without the guidance of an evolutionary framework.

COUNTER-STRATEGIES

Selection has favored these mixed reproductive strategies because, on average, they increased the fitness of the women and men who displayed them. But how do mixed reproductive strategies affect the fitness of partners? The answer is obvious: negatively. When a man forms a union with a woman and invests in her children, he suffers serious fitness costs if those children are not his.

To see why this is so, again imagine two kinds of males: one who invests selectively, by aiding only his own (genetic) offspring, and one who invests indiscriminately in anyone's offspring. By targeting his investment at his own offspring, the selective investor helps his own genes spread. In comparison, the indiscriminate investor suffers two fitness costs. First, any genetic offspring he might have will suffer because much of his investment goes elsewhere. And second, his investment is not just wasted; it aids the offspring of his competitors. There is a word for being duped into investing in another man's children: *cuckoldry*. Obviously, genes for in-discriminate investment would lose out in competition with genes for investing in one's own children. Precisely because women can sometimes gain by drawing genes and investment from different men, men are expected to have evolved de-fenses against giving only investment, against being cuckolded. (If this argument starts you wondering about adoption, see Box 10–2).

Likewise, women should have evolved counter-strategies to men's mixed re-productive strategies. A woman might sometimes opt to mate with a male who will give her little investment, if he demonstrates sufficient evidence of high genetic qual-ity. But she pays a price if her husband plays the same role to other women. The price can take several forms. First, because women are generally selective in their mating, any mating will require the male to make some investment in courtship. The time and other resources spent on this courtship necessarily reduce what he has available for parental investment. Second, women are favored by selection to get as many re-sources as they can from their partners. When a man's extramarital partner captures some of his resources, she depletes what is available to his wife's children. Finally, a husband might completely desert his wife and commit all of his resources to a woman who initially was an extramarital partner. In short, women stand to lose at least some and possibly all of their husband's investment when he takes a lover. And women are expected to have evolved defenses against losing this valuable resource.

> **Trail Marker:** Both women and men are expected to guard against the mixed reproductive strategies of their partner.

What form do these male and female counter-strategies take? The male's problem is cuckoldry, and he has two lines of defense. He can attempt to secure a sexually faithful mate; if he fails at that he can divorce his partner and minimize his investment in her offspring. We'll address these in turn.

In two separate studies Buss and Schmitt, 1993, asked men to rate over sixty characteristics of long-term mates (that is, wives) and short-term mates (for exam-ple, casual sex partners). From the array of characteristics men rated sexual fidelity as the single most important characteristic of a long-term mate and sexual infi-delity as the most negative possible trait of such a partner. Indeed the positive and negative ratings of these two traits closely approached the limits of the rating scale. In contrast, in the short-term mating context where men expect to invest few re-sources they rated both fidelity and infidelity much more neutrally.

Women seem to use men's sensitivity to the risk of cuckoldry in competing for mates. For example women attempt to make their competitors less attractive to men by stressing the competitors' promiscuity:

> Calling a rival a tramp, saying that the rival is loose, or telling others that a rival sleeps around a lot emerge in the top 10 percent of effective derogation tactics for women. Newlywed couples also maintain that women are significantly more likely than men to derogate their rival's promiscuity (Buss, 1994; 114–115).

If selection disfavors investing in other people's offspring, why does anyone ever adopt? This is an interesting question. The first thing to note about adoption is that our practices in the modern West are unusual. On a world-wide basis, most adoptions involve relatives (Silk, 1990). If the parents die or are otherwise unable to care for children, the children are typically adopted by a closely related individual. This pattern matches the predictions of kin-selection theory (Hamilton, 1964a, 1964b; see Chapter 4). If my sister is able to raise her offspring (my nieces and nephews), then I should let her. But suppose she is incapacitated in some way, then my choice could be between letting her children die and taking them in. Under some circumstances, the costs of adopting them may be compensated by their increased chance of reproducing genes we share. So the general pattern of kin adoption fits with our expectations from modern evolutionary theory.

But in countries like the United States a large number of adoptions are by non-kin. How can these be explained? There are two kinds of cases. First, a step-parent may adopt his or her stepchildren (Kirk, 1981). This, too, is fairly easy to understand. If you marry someone who has children by a previous union (your stepchildren), you can help cement your new marriage and signal a common purpose by adopting your mate's children. Assuming the marriage can produce genetic progeny for you, the benefits of adoption may again outweigh the costs.

The second kind of case is even more interesting. Here, a married couple adopt a child to whom neither is related. Such adoptions are regular in the United States, accounting for almost half of all adoptions in the 1950s and 1960s (Silk, 1990), and they might seem to defy evolutionary explanation. But remember, neither human beings nor any other animal is designed to consciously compute the likely fitness outcomes of alternative strategies. We are simply designed to respond to a system of internal and external rewards that ordinarily signal high fitness.

To take a pragmatic example we might ask, why does sex feel good? Presumably because individuals who found sex unpleasant avoided it and thus left few offspring. What does this have to do with non-kin adoption? Sex is just one step in reproduction. Selection designed us to enjoy the other phases as well. Most people find parenting genuinely rewarding and feel some degree of dissatisfaction when they are deprived of those rewards. Adoption provides an outlet for these motivations. This predicts that the majority of non-kin adoptions would be by people who have tried to reproduce and been unsuccessful, a prediction which accords well with the available data (Bonham, 1977).

One way to think about whether this analysis makes sense is to consider the following social experiment. When a woman leaves the hospital after giving birth she is given an infant to take home—the one most ready to be discharged in the opinion of the medical staff—without regard to whose infant it actually is. Do you think parents would, in general, be happy with this arrangement?

Box 10–2. Adoption.

Men are much more likely than women to engage in physical aggression over potential mates (Daly and Wilson, 1988). But physical aggression is not uncommon among teenage girls of low socioeconomic status. In this group, one of the surest ways to trigger violence is to call a rival promiscuous (Campbell, 1995; Marsh and Patton, 1986). Girls are willing to fight to protect their sexual reputations.

Even if a man finds he has been cuckolded there are some available strategies. About thirteen hundred men living in or near Albuquerque, New Mexico, in the early 1990s were interviewed about a wide range of reproductive issues. Of the 2952 children born to the partners of these men, the men identified thirty-six (1.2 percent) as low paternity confidence children. The point is not that this is a large percentage (it isn't); the point is how the men responded. Men were roughly ten times more likely to divorce women who bore them low paternity confidence children and invested much less in these particular children after divorce (Anderson et al., 1999).

When their mates play a mixed reproductive strategy, women need to guard against a loss of resources. In other words, the cuckoldry risk that men face and the resource threats that women face are both triggered by infidelity. Is there any evidence that men and women have different sexual psychologies, tracking the different risks that infidelity poses for the two sexes? The most relevant studies focus on sex differences in jealousy (Buss et al., 1992). They asked men and women to picture themselves in a serious, committed romantic relationship and then presented two alternative scenarios: (A) Their romantic partner forming a deep emotional attachment to someone else, or (B) their partner having sexual intercourse with someone else. You might try imagining these two situations yourself. Do you find one more upsetting than the other?

> **Trail Marker:** Patterns of sexual jealousy reflect the different risks that men and women face.

Buss and his colleagues expected that men would find sexual infidelity more threatening because, over human evolution, sexual infidelity would have signaled a significant risk of cuckoldry. And they predicted that women would find emotional infidelity more threatening because this would signal a weakening in the commitment of her partner, and therefore the potential loss of some or all of his paternal investment. The magnitude of sexual jealousy was measured in three different ways. First subjects were asked to report which of the two scenarios would upset or distress them more. Second, a set of physiological measurements were also taken. These included two indicators of autonomic arousal: pulse rate, and skin conductance, (measured with a standard polygraph or "lie-detector" test). In addition, brow muscle contraction was measured (electromyographically) because this muscle is typically contracted in facial displays of unpleasant emotion (Fridlund, Ekman and Oster, 1987).

Buss and his associates found large sex differences in self-reported distress. Only 17 percent of women reported that sexual infidelity of a partner was more distressing than emotional infidelity. But 60 percent of males selected this alternative. And physiological measurements matched these self-reports. Men showed consistently stronger physiological responses to the sexual-infidelity scenario than to the emotional-infidelity scenario. Women showed the reverse pattern, responding more strongly to the prospect of emotional infidelity.

FACULTATIVE INFLUENCES ON REPRODUCTIVE STRATEGY

What shapes the reproductive strategies of individuals? Some men are faithful investors, while others seek as many partners as they can. Some women remain faithful to a single mate while others have children by several different men. Are these differences in any way predictable? One key factor may be expectations about the frequency of these strategies in the population (Draper and Harpending, 1982; Cashdan, 1993, 1996; see Chapter 3 for an explanation of frequency-dependent selection).

For example, imagine that the population includes many men who are both able and willing to invest in offspring. Under these circumstances it would pay a female to secure an investing mate. In such a population many offspring will receive biparental care; and those who do not will therefore be at a competitive disadvantage. Thus, a woman who secures an investing mate avoids handicapping her offspring. Because of the risks of cuckoldry, even investing men are expected to withhold resources when there are significant threats to their paternity. Hence when investing males are sufficiently common, women are expected to offer the sexual fidelity that fosters male investment.

In contrast, when investing men are scarce different female strategies may be favored. Short-term investment can be extracted from men in return for sexual access. In this case, a woman might increase the amount of investment she harvests by increasing her number of sexual partners. This strategy would surely decrease her attractiveness to marital partners but could be her best option where few males are willing or able to provide long-term investment.

There are parallel alternatives facing men. If investing males are common, women can reasonably expect to attract one. Women should evolve to recognize the difference between investing and non-investing males because mistaking the latter for the former is very costly. Once women evolve this capacity to discriminate, non-investing males might expend considerable time and effort on courtship with very limited success. Better to be an investing male and produce offspring with one female than to be rejected by all.

Conversely, if there are few investing males in the population men may have higher reproductive success simply by maximizing the number of sexual partners they have. If most offspring receive only maternal investment a male handicaps his offspring little when he abandons them to seek additional matings. And with few investing males in the population women could not expect to secure such a mate and hence will not be in a position to categorically reject non-investors. This will mean that at least some attempts at courtship will bear reproductive fruit.

These scenarios suggest that the local availability of paternal investment is a key environmental variable. Just as the level of uv_b predicts the costs and benefits of melanin production (see chapter 3), the abundance of investing men predicts the payoffs of alternative reproductive strategies. In a groundbreaking paper, Patricia Draper and Henry Harpending (1982) argued that children show lasting, critical-period responses to the presence or absence of an investing father during their early years. It seems that children read the absence of a father as an indication that investing males are scarce. Males who grow up in father-absent homes engage in more interpersonal manipulation and dominance striving; women reared in father-absent homes engage in sexual activity at earlier ages and more indiscriminately, and form less stable bonds with their mates.

> **Trail Marker:** Both men and women adjust their mating strategies to their expectations about the availability of male investment.

Elizabeth Cashdan (1993) has tested a critical assumption of this model. She investigated the relationship between people's own reproductive strategy and their beliefs about the need for and likelihood of securing male parental investment. First she examined the paternal investment expectations of her subjects. Here's a sample item from the men's questionnaire:

> Bob says "A woman can raise children successfully on her own." Don says "Children need to have their father present when they are growing up." (Cashdan, 1993: 10).

Subjects were asked to locate their beliefs along a continuum between Don's and Bob's views. A series of these scales probed several related beliefs, about men's willingness to support children, the stability of marriage, and economic factors affecting men's ability to invest. Similar items presented from a female perspective made up the women's questionnaire. Then, each participant was asked to rate, on a five-point scale, how often they used particular mate-attraction tactics, such as "showed I wasn't interested in dating anyone else," "wore sexy clothes," or "paid for dinner at a nice restaurant."

Cashdan found that the subjects' own expectations about the necessity and likelihood of male parental investment were correlated with their mate-attraction tactics. Women who believed investing males to be scarce were significantly more likely to use overtly sexual mate-attraction tactics such as wearing sexy clothes and copulating. In contrast, women who expected considerable male parental investment downplayed their sexuality and were reluctant to copulate, instead offering higher sexual fidelity and thus greater assurances of paternity. Men too seemed to adjust their mating tactics to their own parental investment expectations. Like women, men who downplayed the importance of male parental investment relied on overtly sexual mate-attraction tactics. And men who thought high levels of male parental investment were the norm were significantly more likely to attract mates by displaying both their ability and willingness to invest. In other words, each sex responded to their beliefs about the kind of mating arena in which they were competing. When they assume male investment to be rare, both men and women show mate-attraction behaviors that reduce the likelihood of long-term bonding. When they perceive long-term bonding between an investing man and woman to be the norm, they behave in ways that maximize their chances of securing such a relationship.

In summary, although men and women are very similar in many respects, they approach dating, mating, and marriage somewhat differently. They emphasize different traits in choosing partners, and they compete for partners using different tactics. These sex differences seem to be universal, in that they are present across a very wide range of cultures. And these differences are predictable from a consideration of sex differences in parental investment.

Monogamy is an evolutionary novelty for humans, because polygyny was permitted everywhere until the last few hundred years. For this reason, both men and women often exhibit mixed reproductive strategies. That is, women and men have been designed by selection to form cooperating reproductive pairs, but also to monitor—and sometimes seize—opportunities for extra-pair copulation. Mixed reproductive strategies have in turn selected for counter strategies in both sexes.

Over the course of development, culture seems to shape our expectations about the durability of pair bonds and the opportunities for extra-pair copulations. This facultative effect seems to shape the reproductive strategies of both sexes, leading them to behave in ways that maximize their chances of success, given their beliefs about prevailing mating patterns.

SUMMARY

1. Sex differences generally evolve in species where females and males can reproduce at different rates.
2. Despite considerable male parental investment, humans exhibit sex differences in reproductive rate: females are the slower sex. Hence humans are likely to have evolved reproductively important sex differences.
3. Among humans, as among other mammals, females are generally more selective about their sexual partners.
4. Women invest physiologically (as well as economically) in offspring, whereas men's investment is never physiological.
5. This difference in parental investment leads to sex differences in mate choice criteria.
6. Compared to women, men place more emphasis on physical attractiveness of potential partners, and in this regard they seem to value indicators of high fertility, such as youth, health, absence of asymmetry, and a low waist/hip ratio.
7. Compared to men, women place more emphasis on the resources and social dominance of potential partners.
8. These findings are cross-culturally valid.
9. These patterns are not due to economic inequities between the sexes. For example, when women have high earning potential they show no tendency to relax their standards; in fact they raise them, insisting on even wealthier partners.
10. Both women and men have the option of using mixed reproductive strategies.

11. For a woman this would involve recruiting genes for her progeny from one man and parental investment from another.

12. For a man this would involve having a primary mate, in whose offspring he invests considerably, and one or more secondary mates in whom he invests just enough to gain or maintain reproductive access.

13. Patterns of jealousy, patterns of derogation of competitors, and patterns of mating selectivity all support the idea that mixed strategies have been important during human evolution.

14. Both men and women should have evolved to guard against the mixed reproductive strategies of the opposite sex.

15. Women are expected to guard against the loss of male parental investment to competitors.

16. Men are expected to guard against cuckoldry.

17. Sex differences in jealousy support these predictions.

18. When women derogate their same-sex competitors they tend to stress the rival's promiscuity.

19. When man derogate their same-sex competitors they tend to stress the rival's low status and lack of resources.

20. Both men and women set higher standards for marriage partners than for mere sex partners, with one exception: Women set higher physical-attractiveness standards for one-night-stand partners (when they can expect nothing but genes) than they do for husbands.

21. The tactics men and women use in competing for mates seem to be facultatively dependent on local levels of male parental investment.

11

Families and Development

The typical psychology book gives scant indication that humans pay any attention to family relationships other than father, mother, and child. Second-degree relatives (grandparents, aunts/uncles) and third-degree relatives (cousins, for example) are nearly invisible to SSSM psychology. If these relatives are really as unimportant as psychologists make them seem, how do you explain the fact that sickness and death of grandparents are among the leading reasons college students give for missing tests?

It Takes a Village (of Kin) to Raise a Child

By contrast the African proverb, "It takes a village to raise a child," has gained some recent acceptance. This saying captures a reality of human family life that the American psychological community has tended to overlook: Parents are generally only the leading actors in a family drama with a large supporting cast. But the African saying doesn't make explicit a fact of life in the EEA that is still true in most traditional societies: The people our ancestors knew and interacted with the most were kin, who shared a fitness interest in them and their children. EP gives a theoretical basis for considering extended family ties.

WHAT IS A FAMILY?

The subject of families is one that arouses strong feelings. Most of us believe in the importance of families and the roles of mother and father in child rearing. But when we approach the study of family interactions from an evolutionary standpoint, we must start with principles. It is necessary to step back and ask a basic question. What is a family?

We generally think of a family as one or two parents with dependent children. Stephen Emlen suggests a somewhat different approach based on his work with birds. Emlen starts from the concept of kin selection (Hamilton, 1964a, 1964b; see Chapter 4): Animals can further the success of the genes they carry by aiding other individuals who are likely to have inherited the same genes from a common ancestor—close relatives. This idea leads Emlen to consider how individuals other than the parents may offer aid to their kin. For purposes of his research, he (e.g., Emlen, 1994) defines a family as a group in which there is continued interaction between sexually mature offspring and their parents. This interaction takes place when the offspring do not go off to seek their fortune, but stick around the natal home.

Families: An Avian Example

The species studied by Emlen and his colleagues (e.g., Emlen et al., 1995) is the white-fronted bee-eater, a highly social species of African bird. Bee-eaters nest in tunnels dug into sandy cliffs. Up to twenty-five families make their tunnels near each other, forming a colony.

A striking feature of bee-eater breeding is that it generally involves more individuals than just a male and female pair. A typical bee-eater family contains a breeding pair plus one or more nonbreeding relatives (a parent, offspring, or sibling of one member of the pair)—it is a family by Emlen's definition. The nonbreeding family members typically function as helpers at the nest: They help dig the tunnel, incubate the eggs, forage for food for the nestlings, and defend them from would-be predators. In short, they do everything except breed. Why? For one thing, the offspring need the help: Half of all nestlings starve to death before fledging. Emlen's group found that families with only two adults were able to fledge 0.5 offspring on the average, but those with six adults fledged three. But that is not enough to explain helping, because helping by definition takes place at the expense of the helper's own breeding. The key to helping comes from the fact that helpers overwhelmingly aid their close relatives. When bee-eaters work as helpers, they help unrelated individuals less than 12 percent of the time and help their closest relatives almost 85 percent (see Table 4–1). Helpers contribute to the spread of their own genes when they aid the reproductive efforts of kin.

What Keeps Bee-Eater Families Together?

Emlen's analysis of family interaction considers the variables that go into the decision of an offspring to leave the natal home. He makes more than a dozen predictions about families from his evolutionary analysis of bee-eaters. We have already considered evidence for one of them: Helping should be greatest among families made up of closely related individuals. We will consider two more of the most interesting predictions. Perhaps the most significant is that families will be unstable, disintegrating when individuals can further their fitness better by forming their own families. The reason behind this prediction is that families form only when individuals delay their own reproductive efforts in favor of supporting those of relatives. This prediction is supported by studies in which experimenters created new breeding opportunities by physically removing a nearby family. As soon as the space opened up, helpers left the family and started their own (Emlen, 1994, and references therein).

The second prediction is that families with access to many resources will be more stable than poorer families. An individual in a rich family will not be attracted to marginal territories that would seem good to one from a poorer family. Animal families that control high-quality resources form dynasties that stick together, much as human dynasties do. These predictions are all well supported by animal data, as are the others that we do not discuss only for lack of space.

Are Human Families Similar to Bee-Eater Families?

Parallel effects occur in human families. When times are good, children leave home and start their own families. During harder times they stay home longer and delay marriage. This effect has frequently been explained simply on the basis of economics. Recently, however, Beverly Strassmann and Alice Clarke (1998) studied marriage patterns in rural Ireland, a country where farm land is scarce and people commonly marry late in life. The likelihood of remaining celibate on the family farm after sexual maturity depended on the wealth of the farm and the availability of other farms, in parallel to the bird literature. To be sure, some of the effects they found can be understood in purely economic terms. But they found evidence that decisions were sensitive to expected reproductive consequences and not just economic ones. For example, people who emigrated to another country had a much higher probability of marrying, but their standard of living was often lower than the one they left behind.

We should note that Emlen's definition of the family is not the only useful one. We are definitely *not* saying that the presence of a helper is necessary to have a true family. Rather we wish to point out the advantages of considering the family from an evolutionary point of view. In Emlen's case this emphasizes the role of nonparental kin in support of offspring. Other evolutionary approaches to the family may well take a different approach. Finally, Jennifer Davis and Martin Daly (1997) suggest that Emlen's predictions need to be modified to account for important differences between humans and nonhuman animals. Among other things, they propose that the complex nature of human sociality, including reciprocal altruism, and the existence of menopause increases the stability of human families.

EVOLUTIONARY THEORY PREDICTS
CONFLICT WITHIN FAMILIES

Traditional psychology describes families as either functional, meaning relatively harmonious, or dysfunctional, if they exhibit internal conflict. The problem with this view is that, while members of a family often interact with high frequency, they remain individuals whose interests are not identical. In evolutionary terms, families are collections of individuals who share many genes by common descent. Because of their genetic overlap they also have overlapping evolutionary interests. But because a family's members are not genetically identical they are bound to disagree to some extent.

Thus, evolutionary thinking suggests that we should expect a certain amount of conflict in families for the simple reason that each individual's own fitness interests inevitably conflict to some degree with those of others in the family. The fundamental reason for conflict in the family is that each individual is related to himself or herself more closely than to anyone else. A person is related to himself 100 percent; to his mother and father 50 percent, and siblings 50 percent (assuming they have the same mother and father; otherwise siblings are related 25 percent). It may sound silly to say you are related to yourself by 100 percent and to your brother by 50 percent, but what this means is simply that you are two times better (100 percent/50 percent) at spreading your genes than your brother is. This is the basis of parent-offspring conflict, which we discuss below, and for sibling rivalry; each offspring sees itself as twice as valuable, genetically speaking, as any of its full siblings.

Parent-Offspring Conflict

Robert Trivers (1974) analyzed parent-offspring conflict in a groundbreaking paper. Because the mother is equally closely related to all present and future offspring, she should want to invest equally in all. Because the offspring is related only by 50 percent to other offspring, each offspring wants mom to give it twice as much as she gives the others. For this reason the offspring should want more investment in itself than the parent is designed to make.

Conflict over Parent's Investment in the Child. Consider a mother nursing her baby. The mother's milk has a cost to the mother in fitness terms. Whatever energy the mother invests in this particular baby cannot be invested in the next one. In fact, in all but the best nourished populations, nursing functions as a contraceptive by preventing ovulation. Evolutionary considerations lead us to predict that the mother should have a mechanism that tells her to wean her child when the energetic resources could be put to better use by investing in a new baby. The child needs the milk less as it develops and becomes able to get food elsewhere. Besides, it is in the child's own interest to stop nursing at some point because it will be related by 50 percent to the next baby that mother produces. (This assumes they will have the same father; otherwise it will be 25 percent.) Those resources that it no longer needs as much can be better invested (from child's viewpoint) in a new baby that will share half of the child's genes.

At what point should the mother stop nursing the baby? Here is where the conflict arises. Consider Figure 11–1. This graph shows the cost and benefit to the two parties as a function of time. First look at the benefit to the offspring, which starts out at a very high level when the baby depends utterly on the mother, but decreases as the baby grows and is able to forage for itself. Now look at the cost to the

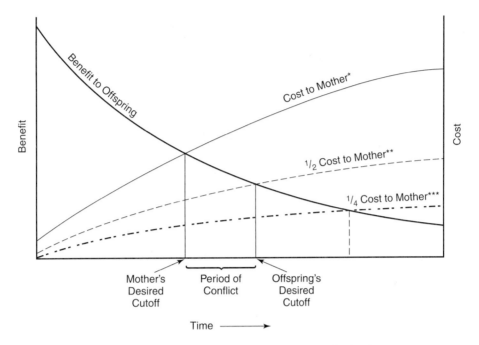

Figure 11–1. *Weaning conflict, after Trivers.* See text for details.

mother, which starts out low when the baby is tiny, but increases as the growing baby requires more and more milk to meet its nutritional needs. You might expect the mother and the offspring would mutually agree to stop nursing when the cost to the mother's future reproduction just exceeds the benefit to the offspring. But that ignores the fact that they have different interests. The mother is equally related to this and all future offspring. So she should be designed to stop investing in this offspring when her cost just exceeds the benefit to this baby, and begin investing in the next baby.

The dotted line represents the baby's view of the situation. Baby "agrees" that at some point mother's investment in it would be better spent on a new baby to which it will be related. But because baby will only be related by 50 percent to any new baby, it "wants" mother to stop investing in it when its benefit is 50 percent of the cost to mother. The problem is that these two points are different. The child wants to nurse longer than the mother wants to. The period during which there is conflict is shown in Figure 11–1.

Struggles over weaning are universal among mammals. Babies of all species will demand nursing long after mother becomes reluctant and pushes the infant away. Trivers's analysis shows that there is no "natural," that is, mutually beneficial, time for weaning to take place, because each party sees the situation differently. Books on child rearing that advise the mother to let the baby decide when to be weaned ignore the interests of the mother in the situation. Leaving the decision to the baby can lead to nursing for several years. A friend of one of the authors can remember being old enough to ask his mother to send visitors away because he wanted to nurse.

Trivers's analysis makes it clear that the child is not a passive recipient of mother's love and attention, but an active player in eliciting her investment. One way a child has of obtaining more resources than the mother wants to provide is by appearing younger, and more needy, than it really is. This explains the regression (a return to less mature behavior) that children often show when a new baby appears. The now-older child may revert to baby talk, or ask to be carried, instead of walking, as a way of getting more of the resources it is now losing to the new baby. What the child is doing is manipulating the mother's impression of where it is on the developmental curve shown in Figure 11–1. It would not be in the mother's interest to wean an insufficiently mature child.

Parent-Offspring Conflict Begins before Birth. Perhaps we should emphasize again that these mechanisms do not necessarily operate consciously. We do not suppose that a child consciously calculates when it is time to stop nursing. The nonconscious nature of these processes becomes apparent when we consider that the conflict between mother and offspring begins in the womb. The mother should be designed to weigh the value of investing in this particular fetus against the value of potential future fetuses. The fact that something like half of all fetuses are spontaneously aborted is believed to be a result of a negative maternal evaluation of the fetus. The fetus, for its part, is more interested in its own survival than the mother is. As a result the fetus has evolved hormonal means of manipulating the mother to provide more resources than are in the mother's best interests. The conflict of interests between fetus and mother causes a number of common problems that occur during pregnancy, including maternal diabetes and maternal high blood pressure (Haig, 1993).

Sibling Rivalry

Conflict in families is not limited to conflict between parents and children. Trivers's analysis of parent-offspring conflict provides the basis for considering other types of conflict as well. Here we take up the familiar example of sibling rivalry. We would expect that children would show a certain amount of concern for the welfare of their siblings because they share some of the same genes. But, here again, there will inevitably be conflict between siblings because each individual carries more of his own genes than anyone else does.

It might occur to you that identical twins should be an exception in the matter of relatedness because they both carry exactly the same genes, and so are related to each other by 100 percent. Shouldn't identical twins be completely unselfish to each other? But the occurrence of identical twins may have been too rare in human history for a special mechanism for recognizing an identical twin to evolve. There is some evidence, however, that identical twins actually are less selfish to each other than fraternal twins are (Segal, 1988; Loh & Elliott, 1998). The decreased selfishness is not necessarily because they perceive that they are identical twins. Because identical twins resemble each other more than fraternal twins, it is possible that perceived similarity is one mechanism that mediates kin altruism. This remains to be tested.

> May you grow up and have children exactly like yourself.
> —Common saying of parents to their children.

Why Parents Teach Their Children To Share. Parents spend a considerable amount of energy settling disputes between their children. They painstakingly teach their children that it is nice to share. Is this just a matter of teaching society's expectations? We will see, instead, that there is a good evolutionary rationale to teaching children to share. Let us first consider the situation from the mother's standpoint. Her fitness is served by getting as many of her genes as possible into future generations. In practical terms, this means converting her resources into grandchildren. Because she is equally related to all her children, she should invest in all of them equally, other things being equal. As we saw above, things are not always equal, and so she must sometimes temporarily divert more resources to a child with greater need, such as a helpless baby or a child with a fever. But for now we will assume that all children have equal value in furthering the mother's fitness for the simple reason that they are all equally related to her.

The child sees things differently from the mother. It is twice as valuable to itself as a full sibling is. So the child should be somewhat selfish toward siblings, but the mother should want them to be unselfish to each other. It is no wonder that *me* and *mine* are among the first words in a child's vocabulary. And it is no wonder that siblings fight over resources, not the least being food. Some families have elaborate rules to ensure sharing of resources. Such a rule in many families is that one of the sibs gets to cut up the pie, but another gets to choose the first piece. This is a fiendishly clever way to get the child doing the dividing to consider the others' point of view. One drawback is that the cutting process sometimes becomes agonizingly slow!

A mother's interest in furthering altruism extends to more distant relatives, such as cousins. The offspring is related to its cousins by one-eighth, but the offspring's mother is related to her nephews and nieces (the offspring's cousins) by one-fourth. The mother should want the offspring to be altruistic to cousins when the benefit exceeds twice the cost to the offspring (because she is twice as related to her children as she is to their cousins), not the eight times the cost that is ideal from the offspring's viewpoint. The same logic applies to more distant relatives.

Further, Trivers's analysis even explains why parents should teach their offspring to be nice to nonrelatives if there is a likelihood that the nonrelative would retaliate against one's other relatives, not just the offspring. What hurts your relatives hurts your fitness. Thus we see that there is an evolutionary basis for teaching altruism to children. It is not just a matter of culture somehow teaching us to be altruistic.

Finally, we emphasize that the parent is designed not to enforce altruism for altruism's own sake, but to advance its own interests. The fact that the parent and the children all have different interests *naturally* and *inevitably* leads to conflicts among the parties. Harmony is not to be expected. Instead, it is expected that parents will try to enforce their own self-interest, which they like to call harmony, or altruism, if they know the word.

Neglect and Infanticide

As we discuss the troubling questions of neglect and infanticide, remember the naturalistic fallacy (Chapter 1). We study this sort of behavior not to excuse or justify it, but to understand it.

The evaluation that begins in the womb continues after the child is born. The mother may deviate from equal investment in her offspring according to circumstances. A younger child needs more care than an older one, and a sick child needs more than a well one. The mother has a motive to evaluate each child as a vehicle for her fitness. Should she invest in a deformed child or one so sick that it has little prospect of making her a grandmother? Should she invest in this baby born during a famine or withhold resources in hopes that circumstances may be better when the next baby is born? There is abundant evidence that humans in many cultures practice this type of *discriminative parental solicitude* (Hausfater & Hrdy, 1984).

In many societies, babies are not named until they are several days old, when it becomes apparent that the baby is viable. Daly and Wilson (1988) propose that the postpartum blues, and the more serious postpartum depression, experienced by many women are part of a mechanism to put the mother in a frame of mind for an objective evaluation of the baby before she commits herself to years of investment. If a mother were simply euphoric at the birth of a child, she would not be as able to ask difficult but adaptive questions, "Should I continue to invest in this baby at this time? Perhaps another baby would be a better bet for my fitness, or perhaps I will have more resources available next year for a different baby."

Although infanticide is condemned in our society, its vestiges remain. As this material is being written there have been several well-publicized cases of young women killing their babies or abandoning them shortly after giving birth. In one case a high school girl gave birth in the toilet during the school prom and returned to the dance floor after disposing of the baby. It is not surprising from an evolutionary point of view that the women who kill their babies are mostly young, poor, and unmarried. These are exactly the conditions that in the EEA would predict low success in raising the infant. A woman in the EEA would have been more able to rear her child successfully if she had the help of a partner. For example, he could provision her with more food (and perhaps certain types of food, e.g., meat) than she could have harvested on her own, and helped to protect her infant from enemies and predators.

In fact, it was not so long ago that infanticide was a common practice in western societies.

> In England [in the 1700s] a retired sea captain, Thomas Coram, was so depressed by the daily sight of infant corpses thrown on the dust heaps [garbage

dumps] of London that he devoted seventeen years [to] soliciting support for a foundling hospital. Eventually a group of his supporters petitioned the King to charter a Foundling Hospital so as "to prevent the frequent murders of poor, miserable infants at the birth," and to "suppress the inhuman custom of exposing new-born infants to perish in the streets." (Langer, 1974, p. 358)

Even placing a child in a foundling home was little more than infanticide in a hidden form. It was common knowledge that 80 to 90 percent of the children given up in this way died (Rose 1986). This situation is the setting for Dickens's story of Oliver Twist. In nineteenth-century France poor parents could place their babies anonymously in orphanages by leaving them on a little turntable set behind a door in the wall of the institution.

Similar practices occur today, and not just in tribal societies. Nancy Scheper-Hughes (1992) documents dramatic examples of discriminative parental solicitude by women in a Brazilian shantytown. These women must cope with rearing children in such desperate poverty that 46 percent of their children die before age five. The high death rate leads the women to withhold resources from sickly and deformed children. Even babies who only suffered from diarrhea, and could be saved by relatively simple treatment, are thought of as

> a little winged angel, a fragile bird . . . or visitor more than as a permanent family member. . . . Eventually [Scheper-Hughes] learned to inquire warily before [trying to help]: . . . "Dona Auxiliadora, is this a child worth keeping?" And if the answer was no, as it sometimes was, [she] learned to keep [her] distance. (p. 342)

Conflict between Father and Mother

We have considered parent-offspring conflict from the mother's point of view so far, rather than the father's, because she is certainly related to her children. If humans were completely monogamous, the interests of father and mother in their children would be identical. But we have seen in Chapter 10 that humans have an evolutionary history of mild polygyny. So the degree of conflict between father and mother will depend on the father's confidence that his mate's children are his. To consider the extreme case, if he is sure his mate's children are not his, he has an interest in minimizing the investment their mother gives them, because that investment could be going to his children. (He may, however, invest in her children in order to show her that he is a good provider of resources, so as to win her affection.) In some species, it is common for a male that has taken a new female to kill all her existing dependent offspring. This is particularly true of cats, including the common house cat. The evolutionary basis for this behavior is the incentive to get the female to stop investing in another male's offspring and become pregnant with his offspring as soon as possible (Hausfater & Hrdy, 1984).

Paternal uncertainty not only leads to conflict between the parents, but also between the children. There are two reasons for an increase in sibling rivalry when paternal confidence is low. First, the less certain the father is of his paternity, the less interest he has in seeing the children receive equal resources (or any resources for that matter as we have just discussed), and he will be less interested in enforcing harmony. Second, if the children are related by only one-fourth, they will want to share only when the benefit to the sibling is four times the cost to themselves, not the one-half that full sibs should see as equitable.

Stepparent Conflict over Investment in Children. Stepparenting provides a clear case of conflict of interest because the stepparent knows for a certainty that the stepchild is unrelated. The logic of the conflict is identical to the problem of paternal uncertainty we just discussed above, with the one important difference: Both women and men can become stepparents. Evidence abounds that human stepparents disagree with the child's natural parent over the optimal investment in children. The wicked stepmother is a well-known figure in literature; Cinderella's plight has a clear evolutionary basis. And it is little wonder that problems of treatment of children in blended families is a common theme in the letters to Dear Abby.

A leading SSSM explanation of child abuse is that child abusers learned bad parenting skills from their own parents. Although this may well be true in some cases, it does not explain why stepchildren are at much greater risk than biological children. Joy Lightcap and her colleagues (Lightcap et al., 1982) studied a particularly informative subset of families that had come to the attention of the authorities because of documented child abuse. All the families they studied contained two parents and both a biological child and a stepchild. So each abuser was both a parent of at least one child and a stepparent of at least one other in the same home. If bad parenting skills were the sole explanation, then biological and stepchildren should be equally likely to be abused. Instead, the adults in their sample abused twelve out of twenty-one step children (57 percent), but 0 out of 20 (0 percent) of their biological children! The abusers may well have learned bad parenting skills from their own parents, but they displayed them in a markedly selective way—against stepchildren only.

Once again, it is instructive to consider extreme behavior to test evolutionary predictions (see Chapter 9). Daly and Wilson (1988) studied homicides of children. A child living with one natural and one stepparent is as much as one hundred times more likely to be killed than a child living with two natural parents. Although this tragic situation is fortunately rare, the huge difference in homicide rates of stepchildren compared to natural children supports the evolutionary prediction. The results cannot be explained by poverty or other social factors.

Perception of Paternity. Everyone has watched people look at a new baby and say, "He looks just like his grandpa," or "she has her daddy's eyes." Why do we comment so much on who the baby looks like? Could there be an evolutionary basis for the intense interest? Evolutionary considerations suggest that the father should be interested in determining whether the baby is his before investing in its care. The mother, for her part, has an interest in convincing a potentially investing male that it is indeed his. The male, in turn, should be designed to evaluate such claims carefully. Two studies (Daly & Wilson, 1982; Regalski & Gaulin, 1993) have examined the comments made about newborn babies' looks. Both sets of investigators found that the baby was most often said to look like the father, and that it was mostly the mothers and the mother's relatives who made the claim. Fathers often expressed doubts that the infants resembled them.

> Mama's baby; Papa's, maybe.
> —Folk saying

Treatment of Handicapped Children. Lightcap et al. (1982) tested several other evolutionary hypotheses. For example, they found that handicapped children were abused more often than nonhandicapped children. This is expected simply because children with physical handicaps would have had a difficult time competing effectively for resources in the EEA, and thus were less likely to convert maternal investment into grandchildren. This is another example of discriminative parental solicitude that may well have been adaptive for our ancestors.

> "I'll beat you like a one-legged stepchild."
> —Robert Duvall in *The Apostle*

Divorce. Conflict between husband and wife may reach a level at which one or both partners decide that being married is worse than not being married. Laura Betzig (1989) sorted through cross-cultural data from 186 societies, mostly nonindustrialized, to find the accepted grounds for divorce. All but a few recognize at least some grounds for divorce. Around the world, in every region, and in both industrialized and traditional societies, infidelity and infertility were the most common bases for divorce. These led by a wide margin over personality differences, economic problems, problems with in-laws, and all the rest. Significantly, the two major causes of divorce involve threats to the reproductive fitness of one or both partners.

Spousal infidelity poses threats to both male and female fitness. To the extent that a man expends time and other resources on extramarital courtship or on any children that result from such relationships, his wife's children suffer a parallel loss of paternal investment. Of course paternal investment is only adaptive when it goes to a man's own children. A woman's infidelity threatens this arrangement: It raises the possibility that her husband will end up rearing the children of another man.

Infertility of the couple is also a clear threat to the reproductive fitness of both partners. Without sophisticated, modern medical technology, it is often impossible to determine whether it is the husband or wife who is infertile. Thus if no children are produced after a few years, they may both be better off trying to find another partner. Around the world, divorce is more likely the fewer children a couple have (Betzig, 1989). There is truth in the popular belief that the birth of a baby helps cement a marriage, at least as measured by whether the marriage lasts.

Other Types of Family Conflict

Now we take up two particular types of conflicts between parents and children that have clear Darwinian bases. They are familiar to any parent and anyone who remembers childhood: finickiness over food, and refusing to go to bed.

Finickiness. Food likes and dislikes are very strong and hard to change. It is easy to start a lively discussion by asking people what foods they love and hate. Some of the things we like that are not popular with many are liver, tripe, tongue, okra, broccoli, and spinach. These were all served frequently at home when we were small. The lasting nature of food preferences is reflected in the fact that the last ethnic tradition to be lost by immigrants to a new country is their special foods. Long after their language, religion, and other customs have gone by the wayside, people of Norwegian, Slavic, or Scots ancestry celebrate holidays by eating ludefisk, haluski, or haggis, respectively.

The SSSM would suggest that we like to eat what we ate as a child by associative learning. But the SSSM cannot explain why all parents struggle with their children about eating. Nor can it explain why the problem is overwhelmingly one of trying get children to eat things they don't want to, whether liver or broccoli. Parents face little difficulty preventing children from eating things they want to eat that we don't consider food, such as feces, tree bark, rocks, and rotten meat. (Note that we are talking about children, not babies, who will eat the most disgusting things imaginable.)

The evolutionary approach to the problem of finickiness begins with the fact that humans are omnivores; that is, we eat a wide variety of foods, both animal and plant products. In this regard we are very unlike the panda, that exists solely on bamboo or the koala that eats only eucalyptus leaves. Omnivores face a complex set of dietary challenges. A great many plants are poisonous, having evolved chemical defenses to deter animals from eating them. Of the millions of species of both plants and animals in the world, we rely on only a few dozen of each for our food. Some of these are edible only because of domestication or because they are detoxified during preparation and cooking. Because many things are potentially edible, but also potentially poisonous, we are faced with the omnivore's dilemma (Rozin, 1990): What is edible?

We have evolved three rules that guide us in food selection. Rule number one is eat only what is familiar. If you must eat something new, take only a tiny bit. This *neophobia* is a prominent feature of the eating behavior of omnivores, such as rats and humans (Rozin, 1996). A rat that encounters a novel food will nibble a little bit of it. Over time, if the rat does not become sick, it will accept more and more. This is why it is so hard to poison rats, unless it is possible to lace a common food with a poison that doesn't have much flavor.

One way foods become familiar to babies is indirectly, while nursing. A host of chemicals in the food eaten by a lactating woman are secreted in the milk (Mennella & Beauchamp, 1993, 1996). These chemicals impart the flavor of whatever a mother has eaten to her milk. So babies are exposed to everything from asparagus to zucchini by tasting them in their mother's milk. You may have noticed that cow's milk tastes different in the spring when the cows are first put out to pasture and start eating green grass.

Rule number two is eat what mom eats. This rule is easy to follow because the mother feeds the baby. In many cultures, the mother first chews some food and then presents it to a child that is being weaned. Babies that are held by mother will reach for foods she is trying to eat herself.

Rule number three is don't eat anything that ever made you sick. We have already discussed the Garcia effect in Chapter 7. It is significant that we are designed to learn to avoid foods that make us sick after a single bad experience.

These rules lead to several predictions. Assume that finickiness evolved to prevent people from ingesting poisons—which in the EEA would have been evolved defenses of various plants and animals. In that case, babies will have no need for finickiness as long as they rely completely on breast milk. As we said above, babies will eat most anything. In the EEA, children would continue nursing for the first four or five years of life. But they would increasingly sample foods their mother ate, and be likely to ingest items they encounter as they explore away from the mother. We can predict that finickiness will increase as children become less dependent on their mother's milk. The rules predict that it will be very hard to get children to eat anything new after early childhood. According to Cashdan (1994) mothers report that their children become increasingly finicky from age two to four. And this increase in finickiness parallels the decrease in accidental poisonings recorded by poison-control centers. In other words, even in the present finickiness seems to serve its evolved function.

Young children are especially vulnerable to poisons. In addition, some chemicals, known as teratogens, cause developmental deformities. Children are most susceptible to teratogens when they are developing most rapidly. Consistent with these facts, Cashdan found some evidence that children decrease in finickiness after age eight, when they are physiologically more mature. Interestingly, teratogens and poisons tend to taste bitter. Although children hate bitter foods, adults often develop a taste for some bitter foods. It is possible that a taste for certain bitter foods develops in adulthood because they have anti-cancer or anti-oxidant properties that outweigh their costs once development is complete.

The three rules of food choice also have practical implications when it comes to getting children to eat right. First, is to teach children what to eat by example. It does no good to try to get them to eat something that you can barely choke down yourself. Second, start early with many different foods. [Exceptions to this are very spicy and "hot" foods. Even in places like Mexico, very young children don't eat hot foods (Rozin, 1990)]. Third is to present a small amount the first time and encourage them to eat just one bite. One of us can remember to this day having to eat one bite of asparagus each spring when it first came up. Then one day he took the obligatory bite of the offensive stalk, and thought to himself, "Hey, this stuff isn't half bad." Parents who force children to sit at the table until they clean their plate risk teaching them the Garcia effect—certainly not the way to get them to like new foods.

Bedtime. Another common source of conflict between parent and child concerns bedtime. Millions of parents, following the advice of psychologists and pediatricians have put babies to bed and let them "cry themselves to sleep." The crying is often more like screaming; it can be long lasting; and it is always aversive to anyone within earshot. When the baby grows older, and begins talking, there may be elaborate pleading, threats, and negotiations. Bedtime is one of the trials of parenting. At least it is for western parents, which provides a clue to the evolutionary significance of the conflict. Around the world, most babies sleep with the mother, and the evidence is that this has been true from ancestral times (McKenna, 1993). Westerners are unusual in putting babies to sleep alone—and in having conflict with them about going to bed. The Western custom is so strong that parents who sleep with their children risk strong disapproval. The disapproval can be seen by the fact that adoption agencies commonly require parents who wish to adopt children to be able to provide the child with its own bedroom.

So why might babies prefer to sleep with their parents? Pleistocene babies that were content to sleep alone were more likely to be swallowed by a python, or dragged off by hyenas, and didn't become anyone's ancestor. Babies that cried when alone in the dark were picked up and comforted by their parents. We believe that this behavior is an adaptation to Pleistocene life. The fact that babies in Western society are relatively safe sleeping alone is cold comfort to a baby's stone age adaptations. And there may be other benefits to sleeping with the mother, including more frequent nursing. We consider evidence below that sleeping with the mother may reduce the incidence of Sudden Infant Death Syndrome (SIDS).

Children also fear the dark generally, commonly including a belief in monsters (see Figure 11–2). Of course, nighttime was dangerous, with predators about, and decreased visibility. In fact, we proposed in Chapter 6 that sleep evolved so that animals could specialize as either nocturnal or diurnal creatures, rather than trying to be equally at home in the day and night environments. A belief in monsters would reinforce the tendency of humans to find shelter at night and stay there. It matters not

Figure 11–2. *Depiction of child's imagined monster.* The tendency to believe in monsters may function to keep relatively defenseless young near protective adults. (Illustration by David Rose, *There's a Monster Under My Bed* by James Rose © Simon & Schuster.)

a bit whether the belief in unseen dangers has a factual basis if believers have more offspring than nonbelievers, and if there is a genetic tendency to believe.

Sleeping Alone and Crib Death

Sudden Infant Death Syndrome (SIDS) is the name given to the tragic situation in which an apparently healthy infant dies in its sleep. SIDS is many times more likely to occur in societies where babies sleep alone (McKenna & Mosko, 1990). James McKenna and his associates considered what it is about co-sleeping that seems to protect against SIDS. For one thing, co-sleeping is more likely if the mother breast-feeds the baby. Mother's milk contains antibodies that protect the baby against pathogens. But McKenna and Mosko found that the benefits of co-sleeping extend beyond the benefits of breastfeeding. Because breast-fed babies that co-sleep nurse on demand, they awake several times during the night and suckle. Bottle-fed infants, in contrast, sleep longer between feedings. This suggested to McKenna and Mosko that co-sleeping might cause the infant to sleep less deeply. They recorded the sleep patterns of co-sleeping mothers and infants and found that the pairs tended to synchronize their sleep cycles, spent less time in deep sleep, and woke more frequently (McKenna, 1996; McKenna, Mosko, Richard, Drummon, et al., 1994). The human brain is immature at birth compared to our close relatives, as seen by the relative helplessness of newborn babies. Babies are relatively poor at thermoregulation, for example. They also sleep more deeply and are less easily aroused. McKenna and his colleagues argue that co-sleeping protects the infant against the possibility that it will sleep too deeply to respond to threats to breathing, such as suffocation. Because co-sleeping has been the norm throughout human history, it is the healthiest for the infant in the sense that infant physiology is adjusted to that environment. Thus, current Western practices may be in conflict with some of the infant's evolved adaptations.

DEVELOPMENT

Babies are not the same as teenagers, who likewise differ from adults and elderly people. In each phase of life, we seem to have different priorities and thus behave differently, in accordance with those priorities. An evolutionary perspective sheds light on why lives unfold the way they do.

It's Only a Phase

Human behavior, motivation and cognition change predictably throughout life. You may remember the moron-joke phase, the sleepover phase, the Barbie doll or superhero phase, and the driver's license phase. If you think these are less important because they occur in youth, there is the getting-a-job phase, getting-married phase, rearing-children phase, and grandparent phase, among others. Shakespeare described seven ages of man:

One man in his time plays many parts, His acts being seven ages.
At first the infant, mewling and puking in the nurse's arms;
Then the whining school-boy, with his satchel And shining morning face,
    creeping like snail unwillingly to school.
And then the lover, sighing like furnace, with a woeful ballad made to
    his mistress' eyebrow.
Then a soldier, full of strange oaths, and bearded like the pard, jealous in
    honour, sudden and quick in quarrel, seeking the bubble reputation even
    in the cannon's mouth.
And then the justice, in fair round belly with good capon lin'd, with eyes
    severe and beard of formal cut, full of wise saws and modern instances;
    and so he plays his part.
The sixth age shifts into the lean and slipper'd pantaloon, with spectacles on
    nose and pouch on side, his youthful hose, well sav'd, a world too wide
    For his shrunk shank; and his big manly voice, turning again toward
    childish treble, pipes and whistles in his sound.
Last scene of all, that ends this strange eventful history, is second
    childishness and mere oblivion; sans teeth, sans eyes, sans taste,
    sans every thing.

        —*As You Like It*, II. vii. 142–166

Notice that Shakespeare describes changes in behavior as well as physical appearance for each stage of life. Let's review these stages, in rough temporal order.

Attachment

A baby responds to the sight or sound of its mother, or other regular caregiver, with smiling, laughing, reaching, and snuggling. At first these behaviors are directed toward any person, but there is a marked change at about six months of age. The baby becomes attached specifically to the mother, is wary or fearful of strangers, and protests vigorously when the mother leaves (see Figure 11–3). This

Figure 11–3. *Fear of stranger.* Strangers have been a source of danger to babies, and fear of them may have been favored by selection.

measure of attachment, known as separation anxiety, peaks at about fifteen months of age in societies around the world (Kagan et al., 1978).

Developmental psychologists have done numerous studies of attachment, and many theories have been proposed to explain it. John Bowlby was a psycho-analyst (a medical doctor specializing in psychiatry from a Freudian perspective) who was also strongly influenced by evolutionary thinking (Bretherton, 1992). He proposed (e.g., Bowlby, 1982) that attachment developed as an aid to infant survival. The world is a dangerous place for all humans, but especially to infants, who are helpless against predators and in finding food. One thing infants are good at is harvesting resources from adults, particularly their parents—those who have a special stake in their survival. Attachment can be seen as an adaptation to keep infants near their mother, and away from strangers—who often are dangerous to infants.

Why does separation anxiety appear rather abruptly at about six months of age? This is about the time that children start to crawl, and it becomes possible for them to get out of their mother's sight. Those infants who developed separation anxiety by the age they became mobile grew up to become ancestors more frequently than those who didn't. There is no need to show separation anxiety before this age because the infant wouldn't have been out of her mother's arms much before that time. This makes a very important point: Abilities develop when they are needed and not before. Recall the expensive organ principle: Organs and abilities take metabolic resources that could be devoted to other tasks. An organism that devoted energy to abilities before they were needed would be at a competitive disadvantage to one that waited.

Trail Marker: Abilities develop when they are needed.

Visual-Motor Development: The Visual Cliff

Similarly, babies learn to fear heights at about the same age of six months, and for the same reason—they are beginning to crawl. In a classic series of studies, Eleanor Gibson and Richard Walk (e.g., 1960) placed babies of different ages on a glass table. A patterned material was located immediately under half the glass. The same material was also under the other half, but on the floor, some distance below. They found that by the time babies started to crawl they refused to cross from the "safe" side to the "deep" side (see Figure 11–4). When their mothers tried to coax them across they showed signs of conflict and distress. Similar results were found in a wide variety of animals, including chicks and goats. (It was always humans who did the coaxing.) Any animal that was mobile refused to go across. When a goat was pushed onto the deep side, it spread out its legs and refused even to stand up on the glass.

Figure 11–4. *The visual cliff.* Babies avoid crossing what appears to be a cliff about the time they begin to crawl.

What Is Childhood For?

In order to win at the evolutionary game, an individual must first survive to reproductive age and then reproduce. The reality of accidents, predation, and disease means that the longer an individual waits to reproduce, the odds of doing so go down. Then, even if an individual survives to reproduce, a faster-maturing competitor would outreproduce the slowpoke. Immaturity is an evolutionary handicap.

Why is it, then, that humans take such an extraordinarily long time to reach maturity, even compared to our primate relatives? It is not just a matter of growing, because many other animals grow to a similar adult size quite rapidly; at just one year of age a male deer can weigh as much as an adult human. One reason that has been suggested for the long human childhood is to allow time for children to learn the innumerable linguistic, social, and practical skills necessary to function in human society. Although human societies have similar structures around the world (see Chapter 4), it is necessary to learn the local language, the local edible foods, the local marriage and kinship pattern, and so forth.

Around the world people refrain from holding children to adult standards of behavior; children are indulged when they enter private spaces in homes, touch adults in private places, and ask personal questions. ("Grandpa, did you know that you have hairs growing out of your ears?") Many a parent has had to tell a child something like, "Don't punch Uncle Sid in the stomach; you're too old to be cute." The flip side of greater adult tolerance of childhood behavior is that children have fewer privileges. They can't marry, vote, drive cars, or enter into legal contracts. A standard source of conflict between parents and their children arises from their differing perspectives on the child's rate of maturity and readiness for adult rights and responsibilities. ("But *all* the kids are getting their noses pierced!")

Play. Children spend an enormous amount of time in play, an activity that is easier to recognize than to define. And psychologists have devoted a great deal of attention to play (Rubin et al., 1983). They note that children's play changes with age. Infants' play consists largely of manipulating single objects: shaking rattles, banging blocks, and mouthing dolls. Then during the second year, children begin pretend play: feeding their dolls and putting them down for naps; driving model cars around, complete with sound effects. Later stages include adoption of different social roles (playing house, or cowboys-and-Indians), and intellectual games (tick-tack-toe).

One of the earliest theories of why children play had a Darwinian basis. Groos (1901) proposed that play served the purpose of giving the child practice at skills that would be necessary as an adult. Groos's theory makes sense of the regular progression with age in the nature of children's play, and suggests that play consists in practicing those skills the child is learning at that time. For the infant, this means learning the nature of physical objects: what happens when you bang them, drop them, and put them in your mouth. Older children are learning social relations: what happens when you ask questions ("Knock knock!" "Who's there?"), and who sits in which chair at dinner. At every stage, it is possible to watch children play and see what skills they are learning. We believe that Groos's theory is essentially correct.

Immaturity Is Not All Bad. Children are not just little people who haven't learned how to be adults. They think and act differently. They are immature. Many a frustrated parent comes to think of childhood as a necessary evil that babies have to pass through to become adults.

> "Stop acting your age!"
> —Frustrated parent to child

David Bjorklund (1997), however, suggests that "immaturity . . . may play an adaptive role in a child's life and development. Some aspects of childhood . . . are designed by evolution to adapt the child to its current environment but not necessarily to a future one" (p. 153). A chick has a temporary structure on its beak, called an "egg tooth," that helps it break out of the shell in hatching, but which disappears soon afterwards. In the same way, human children may have psychological mechanisms that help them at being children.

Children are relatively oblivious to how poor they are at many tasks. They show pride in their clumsy achievements and persist in practicing them. This unawareness of their limitations may prevent them from becoming discouraged from the important task of learning many basic skills. Young children are also unaware of how they compare to other children on many skills. Even more so than adults, they think they are smarter than their peers. Bjorklund suggests that this contributes to children's optimism and willingness to compete. (We will see in Chapter 16 that they are able to compare themselves to others when it comes to social dominance.)

This lack of awareness of their inabilities may relate to the failure of young children to detect sarcasm. A child will beam with pride at an adult who looks at its sloppy coloring and says, "My, what a nice job you did of staying inside the paper!" One former child can remember the embarrassment of coming to realize later on that her mother had meant exactly the opposite of what she understood by saying, "What a *little* helper!" when she had made a mess at some attempt to help.

The Life Course and the Social Clock

Social scientists have documented changes in typical behavior with age. Bernice Neugarten and colleagues (1965) found a high degree of consensus among Americans on the ages at which it was appropriate to do a wide variety of things, from finishing school (twenty to twenty-two), marrying (nineteen to twenty-four for women, twenty to twenty-five for men), becoming a grandparent (forty-five to fifty) to retiring (sixty to sixty-five). Neugarten and her colleagues found that "men and women are aware not only of the social clocks that operate in . . . their lives, but . . . also of their own timing and readily describe themselves as 'early,' 'late,' or 'on time' with regard to family and occupational events" (p. 711). Of course, these norms will differ from one culture to another, and even over time within the same culture. Since the 1960's, when the Neugarten data were collected, the typical age of marriage has increased, for example. The work of Neugarten and her colleagues has been updated and extended by others (Settersten & Mayer, 1997, and references therein).

The Social Clock Will Differ in Response to the Environment. We have emphasized the facultative nature of psychological adaptations. We should not suppose that the social clock depends on social influences constrained only by the limits of biology. An evolutionary approach suggests that individuals will scan their environment and adjust their social clock accordingly. You may have noticed that the life events we have just discussed have a decidedly middle-class flavor to them. Poor individuals are not as likely to go to college, and so will complete their education earlier, for example. Linda Burton (1990) studied the life course considered desirable by poor, African-American women. These women wanted to start having children as teenagers and to become grandmothers in their thirties. They considered the likelihood of finding a suitable husband as low, and so saw little reason to wait for one before starting to have children. Further they believed it less likely that they would live to the age when they could serve the role of grandmother, suggesting some urgency in starting their reproductive careers.

What Is the Origin of the Social Clock? Those who operate in the SSSM describe the social clock as a set of "social norms," that influence individuals by a process called "socialization." Mayer and Tuma (1990) say, "The life course is shaped by, among other things, cultural beliefs, . . . institutionalized sequences of roles and positions, legal age restrictions, and decisions of individual actors. . . . According to the life course paradigm, the *life course of an individual is mainly a product of larger social forces* and structures." (Emphasis added, pp. 3, 5.) Surely we are familiar with parents who nag their children to get a job, marry, and have children. And legal restrictions control the timing of events such as marriage and entering the work force. But the SSSM model ignores the biological underpinning of the social clock: Nobody lives forever; you had better marry by a certain age or there will be no children. The professor we knew who remained a bachelor until age sixty-five, at which time he retired, married, and had children, is a statistical rarity—and could not have been a woman! SSSM thinking also ignores the fact that individuals follow the social clock willingly, even eagerly. It is just that other people may have a different idea of the proper age at which to achieve the particular milestones. This follows from the brute fact that different individuals have different self interests. Related individuals will have common interests in each other but the interests will only partly overlap. Related individuals from different generations may have different views of a given individual's optimal reproductive strategy because of their different experiences, or because of age-related differences in such characteristics as the value placed on risk and reward.

Grief for Lost Children Depends on Their Age

In the movie, *Sophie's Choice*, the title character is forced to make the harrowing decision which of her two children to save from death at the hands of the Nazis. The dramatic power of the movie derives from the fact that the death of a child is every parent's nightmare. Research shows that people grieve more over a child than over a spouse or parent (Sanders, 1980). This is not a surprise from an evolutionary point of view; only our own death threatens our fitness more (providing we are not past reproductive age).

What may surprise at first glance is that the intensity of grief depends on the age of the lost child. The reason lies in the concept of *reproductive value* of an individual. A person's reproductive value is the number of future children he or she can be expected to produce (see Figure 11–5). Reproductive value is not the same

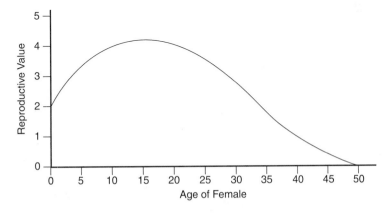

Figure 11–5. *Reproductive value as a function of age.* The graph depicts the expected number of future offspring at each age shown. The graph is lower before puberty because of the uncertainty of living to reproductive age, then falls because of the loss of fertility over time. (After data in *Demography of the Dobe ¡Kung* by N. Howell, 1979, Academic Press.)

as fertility. A child has zero fertility but has prospects of producing children in the future. It is easy to understand that reproductive value declines with age after puberty (it increases up to that point): The older you are, the fewer children you can expect to have in the future. This function is steeper for women than for men because of the fact of menopause (see below.) But reproductive value increases markedly up to about age fifteen in traditional hunter-gather societies. The reason lies in the vagaries of childhood. Before an individual can reproduce he or she must first survive to reproductive age, and that is by no means certain.

Charles Crawford and colleagues (1989) found that intensity of grief reported by parents who lost children of various ages closely matched the curve in Figure 11–6 showing change in reproductive value as a function of age. Significantly, maximum grief was reported for children who died at an age corresponding to the peak of the reproductive value for hunter-gatherers, not the current reproductive value for Canadians. Canadians have much higher reproductive value at birth than traditional societies because of low infant mortality. Further, their actual production of children occurs later because Canadians follow the pattern of industrial societies of postponing childbearing until their twenties and thirties. So the intensity of grief as a function of child age found in an industrial society follows a pattern that is tuned to the reproductive value curve that existed in the EEA, not today's existing conditions.

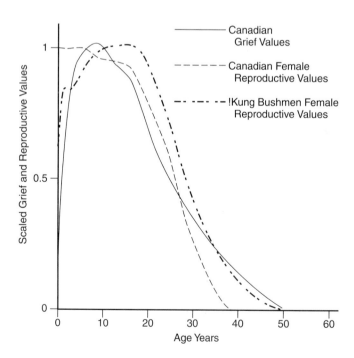

Figure 11–6. *Grief for lost child as a function of child's age.* The grief parents feel for a lost child closely matches the reproductive value that a child would have had in the EEA.

The Grandmother Hypothesis

Everyone, man or woman, loses fertility as they age. But women's loss is more abrupt and complete than men's. Why do human females, alone among our primate relatives, experience menopause, which leaves them infertile for the last years of life? The grandmother hypothesis proposes that a time comes when women can further their fitness more by investing in existing kin—especially grandchildren—than in trying to produce more children of their own. Kristen Hawkes and her colleagues studied Hadza hunter-gatherers of Tanzania (Hawkes et al., 1998; Hawkes, et al., 1997). They found that women's ability to forage took a nose dive when they had new babies. Those weaned children whose grandmothers took up the slack in foraging grew much faster than those without grandmothers, or whose grandmothers didn't help as much. Some of the grandmothers—mostly in their sixties—foraged more than the mothers did, providing a significant boost to the children's diets. Hawkes believes that menopause evolved to switch women from investing in producing children of their own to investing in kin.

The grandmother hypothesis needs further evidence and testing before it can be considered well supported. Nevertheless it helps to explain all those middle-aged women who dote on their grandchildren. Why aren't men so involved with their grandchildren? First we need to emphasize that we are talking about the relative investment by men and women, not the absolute amount. Many men—most in our society—show considerable interest in their children, grandchildren, nieces and nephews. But it is well-documented (e.g., Euler and Weitzel, 1996; Gaulin, McBurney, & Brakeman-Wartell, 1997) that men in Western societies invest less in relatives than women do (see Figure 11–7). There are two reasons. First, men in general invest less in their offspring: Since men have more to gain (in fitness terms) from having multiple partners, they have a greater tendency to skimp on parenting and use their time and resources courting. Second, a man always runs the risk that his wife's children are not his own. This paternal uncertainty

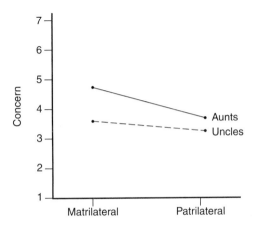

Figure 11–7. *Matrilateral biases in concern for nieces and nephews.* Matrilateral relatives show more concern than do patrilateral ones and aunts show more than uncles.

increases with grandchildren. A woman is 100 percent certain that her children are hers, and that her daughter's children are her grandchildren. But she can't be sure of her son's children. A man, by contrast, has the risk not only that his wife's children are not his but also that his supposed grandchildren may not belong to his supposed son.

Why Males Die Younger than Females

It is well known that human males live about five years less than females. Popular writing, and some psychology texts, suggest that the difference arises because men are under more stress because of "societal demands"—to be macho, work hard, and so forth. These books imply that if men would only act more like women, they would live as long as women do. Not likely. Males of many (but not all) species live shorter lives than females, including species as diverse as rats, ground squirrels, grouse, and hummingbirds, none of which are known to pursue stressful careers in business. But, even more tellingly, males have a higher mortality rate at all ages, starting with conception—long before "societal demands" begin to operate.

The reason men (and males of many species) die sooner than females stems from the fact that men have the potential to reproduce more rapidly than women. (See Chapters 2 and 10.) This potential tips the scales toward taking more risks, both biologically and behaviorally. The testosterone that makes males more masculine, and more able to attract females, also suppresses their immune system, making them more vulnerable to disease. In addition, males engage in more risky behavior than females. For example, accidents are the leading cause of death for young American males (one to twenty-four years of age). From twenty-five to forty-four years of age accidents are second to HIV, also the result of risky behavior. The rate of death from accidents for males fifteen to twenty-four is 2.8 times that of females (U.S. Bureau of the Census, 1998). Males trade shorter lives for increased reproductive success. Men literally live fast and die young in a gamble to leave more offspring.

In summary, SSSM notions about the family require serious revisions in the light of evolution. Labels like "functional" and "disfunctional" miss the essential point that family members will inevitably disagree—over allocation of resources, desirability of altruism, rights and responsibilities—simply because each individual is genetically unique. When each individual does what she is designed by selection to do—maximize the rate at which her own genes are replicated—her objectives necessarily conflict with those of other family members. The only reason families are not hotbeds of extreme conflict is that their members share many genes by common descent and so have partially overlapping genetic interests. We'll discuss this matter further in Chapter 15.

Similarly, development is not just an inevitable period of immaturity, followed by maturity and senescence. Rather, it is a sequence of stages, each of which serves a function in furthering our fitness.

SUMMARY

1. Emlen defines a family as a group in which there is continued interaction between sexually mature offspring and their parents.
2. The white-fronted bee-eater is an African bird in which adult offspring delay reproduction to help their parents raise further offspring.
3. The probability of helping at the nest depends on degree of relatedness and the availability of breeding opportunities.
4. Humans show some of the same effects as bee-eater families, when adult children stay home and delay marriage during hard times.
5. Evolutionary theory predicts that conflict within families will occur simply because each member has a different genetic makeup and thus different evolutionary interests.
6. Trivers predicts parent-offspring conflict over allocation of resources because the mother views all offspring as of equal value (other things equal), whereas the child sees itself as twice as valuable as its full siblings.
7. Parent-offspring conflict does not necessarily operate consciously, and begins in the womb.
8. Sibling rivalry is a consequence of parent-offspring conflict.
9. The mother's motivation to encourage altruism in her children has an evolutionary rationale.
10. Humans practice discriminative parental solicitude when they withhold resources from sick or deformed children.
11. Vestiges of infanticide can still be seen in western society.
12. Paternal uncertainty leads to conflict between father and mother over parental investment.
13. Stepchildren are many times more likely to be abused or killed than biological children.
14. Family members' interest in which parent a child resembles stems from the problem of paternity uncertainty.
15. Food finickiness is a consequence of the fact that humans as omnivores must learn what is edible.
16. Finickiness increases at the age when children in the EEA would begin foraging for themselves.
17. Babies become anxious when separated from their mothers starting about age six months, which is about when they begin to crawl.
18. Babies show avoidance of heights, as indicated by the visual cliff, beginning about the age when they begin to crawl.
19. Humans take an unusually long time to mature, compared to other animals, possibly to give them time to learn important skills.
20. Groos suggests that child's play consists in practicing those skills the child is learning at that time.
21. Bjorklund suggests that some features of children's behavior are adaptations to childhood, rather than to later life.

22. People adjust their life course according to the existing conditions in order to accomplish important life goals, particularly reproduction.
23. Grief shown by parents over lost children depends on the age of the child in a way that closely matches the reproductive value of the child.
24. Hawkes proposes that menopause evolved to switch women's investment from producing more offspring of their own to investing in their grandchildren.
25. Men die younger than women because their potential to reproduce more rapidly biases them toward taking greater risks, both biologically and behaviorally.

12 Motivation and Emotion

When traditional psychologists talk about motivation and emotion, they are focusing on the feelings and needs that guide behavior. As evolutionists, we will also want to ask "why?" questions about those feelings and needs. What are the things that give us the most intense pleasure? A good meal, sexual intercourse, holding one's own baby or grandchild. Evolution has built us to find things that contribute to our fitness pleasurable (Dawkins, 1989). As MacDonald (1995) notes, it could hardly have been otherwise. An organism that found sex, nutritious food, and tending its offspring unpleasant would leave fewer offspring than those that enjoyed such activities.

Likewise, pain, fear, and dread are caused by those things that most directly threaten our fitness: wounding of flesh, attack by a predator, grave illness, wrath of a strong enemy. In fact, although we discussed pain in Chapter 5 under the topic of Sensation and Perception, we could just as well have included it in this chapter. Pain has a strong emotional tone and also signals actual or potential damage to our body. When we feel pain in the bottom of our foot we take off our shoe and look carefully for a small stone or other object that might be causing it. When we locate the source of the pain we remove it and prevent damage to our foot.

Motivation is generally thought of as the study of the directional and energizing aspects of behavior. Animals show periods when they are active and engaged in finding food, water, mates, and the like; at other times they rest quietly. To a casual observer the environment of the animal has not changed. What accounts for the differences in behavior when there is no difference in the animal's surroundings? Psychologists have developed the concept of motivation to explain these changes.

Animals work to satisfy motives, which often change with changes in the internal (rather than external) environment of the animal: Several hours after eating we are hungry again because we have burned up the calories we consumed, and so forth.

Emotion is commonly defined by its affective tone that is, by its pleasantness or unpleasantness. By definition there are no neutral emotions. To be sure, there are situations in which we have mixed emotions, as when you get the job you wanted but find out that an old enemy will be your boss. But emotion by definition involves affect.

EMOTION CANNOT BE SEPARATED FROM MOTIVATION

We will develop an evolutionary approach to motivation and emotion shortly. But first we need to talk about the relation between the two concepts. To a considerable extent, psychologists think about motivation and emotion separately. Textbooks and courses tend to discuss either motivation or emotion, but not the two together. One of the main points of this chapter is that the two are closely related; and some psychologists have recognized this fact. For example, Richard Lazarus (1991) notes:

> When we react with an emotion, especially a strong one, every fiber of our being is likely to be engaged—our attention and thoughts, our needs and desires, and even our bodies. The reaction tells us that an important value or goal has been engaged and is being harmed, placed at risk or advanced. (pp. 6–7.)

Emotion is our affective response to information that our goals are either being advanced or harmed. Robert Plutchik (1980) points out that emotions serve an adaptive role in dealing with survival problems posed by the environment. The sight of an enemy (stimulus) causes us to interpret the situation as dangerous (cognition), which causes fear (emotion), which in turn causes us to run (behavior). This sequence contributes to our survival and improves our chances for reproduction. Because motivation is the study of how we meet goals, it is clear that emotion and motivation are inseparable. Therefore we define *emotion* as the affective component of motivation.

You may be thinking at this point that motives and emotions can be distinguished by the fact that some motives are handled completely outside of consciousness, and involve no emotion. We agree completely that motives are often accomplished without emotion. We normally breathe without giving the slightest thought to the process. Hours or even days may go by without our being aware of breathing. (To be sure, we can consciously influence our breathing—by breathing fast or holding our breath—but only within limits: It is impossible to die by holding your breath. As soon as you pass out, your breathing reflexes take over.) But there are situations that make us acutely aware of breathing. Just get trapped under water, have an asthma attack, or choke on a piece of food, and you are certain to experience strong emotion. In other words, emotion kicks in to motivate us to solve any threat to our ability to breathe. So we are suggesting that all emotions are part of a motivational system, but motivation does not always require emotion.

That leads us to the question: When do emotions occur? We suggest that emotions are felt when it becomes important to focus attention on solving a motivational problem that isn't being handled by unconscious mechanisms. Why can't I breathe? No wonder—a piece of coral is stuck in my snorkel tube! Why am I coughing uncontrollably? Maybe I should quit smoking! Why is my nose stuffed up? Perhaps it's those flowers I just smelled! Why is my chest so congested? Maybe I have pneumonia and better get to the emergency room!

WHY WE AVOID THE TERM "INSTINCT"

For many years—going all the way back to the ancient Greek philosopher, Plato—people used the concept of instinct to explain motivation. William James (1890) says, "Instinct is usually defined as the faculty of acting in such a way as to produce certain ends, without foresight of the ends, and without previous education in the performance" (1890/1950, vol. 2, p. 383).

James's definition of "instinct" has two important parts, and serves two useful purposes. First, it makes clear that behavior is not always guided by reason, or "foresight of the ends," as he puts it. For many years, psychologists and most other people had thought of the mind as a rational entity and that we acted according to rational principles. But around the turn of the twentieth century, people began to discover the irrational side of human nature, as made popular by the writings of Sigmund Freud. Psychologists of the early 1900s invoked the concept of instinct to counteract the tendency to give reason too much emphasis in the behavior of humans and other animals.

Second, the concept of instinct permitted psychologists to talk about behavior that occurs "without previous education," as James puts it. For example, a Baltimore Oriole builds a nest, using carefully selected materials and complicated construction techniques, without ever having seen the task performed before. This kind of behavior is intriguing.

Nevertheless psychologists today generally avoid the concept of instinct for three reasons. The first reason is that calling a behavior instinctive often merely assigns a label rather than providing an explanation. Edwin Holt ridiculed this tendency as follows:

> Man is impelled to action, it is said, by his instincts. . . . If he fights, it is the "pugnacity instinct;" if he defers to another, it is the instinct of "self abasement;" if he twiddles his thumbs, it is the thumb twiddling instinct; if he does not twiddle his thumbs, it is the thumb-not-twiddling instinct. Thus everything is explained with the facility of magic—word magic." (1931, quoted by Osgood, 1953, p. 428)

Holt was right: Thinking that one has explained something by giving it a name is called the *nominal fallacy*. Naming something is only the beginning of explanation, not the end. It is necessary to understand *how* something works—under what conditions, by what mechanisms, and so forth—in order to explain it. Too often, labeling a behavior as instinctive gives people the false belief that they understand it.

The second criticism is that many behaviors once believed to be innate actually require particular kinds of experience. We already learned in Chapter 7 that cowbirds sing something close to their species-typical song without hearing it from any other cowbird. On that basis, we might conclude that the song is innate. But young males refine their songs by dropping the parts females ignore and keeping the parts they respond to. So experience is necessary in developing a song that functions effectively in courtship. Evolutionarily novel environments will disrupt even the most obligate of traits. And we have already discussed the idea that it is improper to divide the world into traits that depend on experience and traits that don't. Thus a more modern approach is to consider how a trait responds to particular features of the environment and why, not whether it is instinctive (that is, innate) or learned (Chapter 4).

The third criticism of the instinct concept was that there was no way of deciding how many instincts people had. William McDougall said there were thirteen (Hergenhahn, 1996), but others have listed over twenty-five hundred! (Weiner, 1972). Who's right; is there any way to decide? If an instinct is a type of adaptation that evolved to solve a certain problem in the EEA, then there will be as many instincts as there were problems in the EEA that instincts could solve. This number will be expected to be large, but not indefinitely so. The actual number of instincts will be discovered as scientists study them in detail—just as any mechanism is understood using the scientific method.

So we see that the concept of instinct was rejected by psychologists for three main reasons. Two of them had some validity, but the third is less worrisome when we take an evolutionary perspective. Some evolutionary psychologists use the term instinct today, being careful to avoid the nominal fallacy. But we are not going to use the term instinct because it carries too much baggage; it takes more time to clear up the misunderstandings than it is worth. Instead we will follow our standard approach of looking for evolved mechanisms—adaptations—to help us to understand the motivation of behavior.

THE EVOLUTIONARY APPROACH TO MOTIVATION

We consider motives and emotions to be adaptations that evolved to organize and stimulate behavior to solve problems that existed in the EEA. Hunger and thirst are obviously among the most important of these problems, and they have been extensively studied by psychologists. They have learned a great deal about the behavioral and physiological mechanisms that maintain proper levels of glucose, water, and other nutrients in our blood. We will not discuss these findings because we have chosen to consider some others that illustrate the contributions of evolutionary thinking more explicitly. In particular, we will emphasize the role of motivation and emotion in a social context, because social life posed many problems that faced our ancestors in the EEA and still face us today.

All Motives and Emotions are Equally Biological

Following the Standard Social Science Model, psychologists have tended to divide motives and emotions into two categories, which they variously call "basic" versus "derived," or "biological" versus "social." One of the main reasons for this distinction has been a desire to keep the list of basic motives to a small number. If there were only a few biological motives, such as hunger, thirst, and sex, then perhaps the others could be explained as built on these biological ones by learning. Thus people tried to explain motivation for work on the basis that work provides money, which can be traded for food, drink, and sexual partners, however indirectly.

This approach failed. In one of the most famous experiments in all of psychology, Harry Harlow (Harlow & Zimmerman, 1958) raised infant rhesus monkeys apart from their mothers. It is important to realize that infant monkeys spend most of their time clinging to their mothers, nursing frequently. They quickly form a strong bond to the mother and run to her for protection and comfort. Harlow wanted to find out whether they became attached to the mother because she provided food, following the principles of standard learning theory as predicted by the SSSM, or whether attachment was based on contact comfort. In place of real mothers, he made two types of surrogate mothers out of wire mesh (hardware cloth) that the baby monkeys could cling to. The first type was made of bare wire with a bottle inside; the nipple stuck through the wire and provided milk. The second surrogate mother was covered with terry cloth, but had no bottle (see Figure 12–1).

Learning theory predicts that the infant monkeys should form an attachment to the wire mother that provides the milk. Instead the monkeys became strongly attached to the terry-cloth mother. They spent all their time clinging to it, not the

Figure 12–1. *Monkeys raised on surrogate mothers.* Monkeys preferred the cloth surrogate mother over the wire model, even though they received food from the wire one.

wire one. When hungry they would stretch across from the cloth mother to nurse from the wire model. When frightened by a toy bear, they ran and clung to the terry-cloth mother. As a result of Harlow's work we know that attachment is based on contact comfort, which is just as important to infant monkeys as food.

Clearly there are many motives like attachment, curiosity, jealousy, and achievement that are not so obviously "biological." However these motives should also be seen as solutions to problems that existed in the ancestral environment. Attachment keeps the infant close to the mother and away from predators and hostile conspecifics. Curiosity solves the problem of what to do with a novel feature of the environment. Does this strange, new thing present a threat or an opportunity? Should I flee from it, or use it to my benefit? Ancestral humans that displayed a certain level of curiosity presumably were more successful than those that didn't because they gained valuable new opportunities.

> **Trail Marker:** All motives are mechanisms that evolved to solve problems that existed in the EEA, and thus are all equally biological.

Thus we see that evolutionary thinking can unify the approach to understanding motivation. Instead of dividing motives into "biological" and "social"—those motives that are caused by "innate" and "learned" mechanisms, respectively—we need to consider the entire range of problems that motives evolved to solve.

Motives Differ in Their Importance

Saying that all motives are equally biological simply means that they are equally the product of evolution; it does not mean that all motives are equally important. There is a hierarchy of motives. Without a certain level of blood glucose the animal dies, and so it is not surprising that a starving person doesn't care much about music or philosophy, or even about sex. When a person is well fed and out of imminent danger from predation and disease, other motives can be satisfied. In fact, we just saw that Harlow's monkeys would leave the cloth mother to nurse from the wire mother, showing that hunger overrode attachment.

Motives Are Not Merely "Socially Constructed"

Proponents of the SSSM often point to differences in customs around the world to argue that "social motives are socially constructed" (e.g., Barrett, 1995, p. 25). By "socially constructed" they mean that there is no biological basis for the motive, and that it is solely the result of social learning. Let us consider why this idea is wrong.

The Case of Disgust. Disgust is a good example of a universal motive/emotion that shows considerable variation across people. We say disgust is universal because people around the world both recognize the disgust face and spontaneously

Figure 12–2. *Example of disgust.* What disgusts a human may be highly attractive to another organism, depending on its evolved nature. For example, many kinds of scavenging insects would be attracted to spoiled food.

make it in response to appropriate stimuli (Ekman, 1980). See the disgust face shown in Figure 12–2. Nevertheless there is considerable variety in just what people find disgusting. The idea of eating worms and grubs will be disgusting to most readers of this book, but people in some hunter-gatherer cultures find them quite tasty (and they are very nutritious). Closer to home, Jews who keep Kosher have been known to vomit upon discovering that they have inadvertently eaten pork. One of the authors enjoys eating tripe (cow's stomach), which disgusts the rest of his family.

From an evolutionary point of view, disgust can be understood as an evolved mechanism to prevent substances that would cause pollution and disease from entering the body (Rozin & Fallon, 1987). We find feces disgusting *because* they convey disease. People who liked them didn't become anyone's ancestors. To a fly, however, a pile of dung is exactly the right place to lay eggs. It is just as attractive to the fly as a juicy steak is to us. It is all in the evolved mechanism.

So we see two aspects of disgust: It is a universal emotion, but the target of our disgust is facultatively dependent on our experience. Why should the system be designed this way? In any given locale, there is a tremendous variety of things that might either be food or be poisonous or disease bearing. In many instances, we must learn from older individuals (who have more experience) which of the multitude of potentially edible things are food, and which are not. Consider the risks of trying to learn the difference by eating a little bit of everything! Thus, children scan the environment for what other people eat and what they willingly come in contact with, and imitate them. They monitor what things people are disgusted by, and become disgusted by them too, as an efficient way of avoiding polluting substances. But this does not make disgust socially constructed. The disgust

Figure 12–3. *New Guinean showing emotion.* People with little or no contact with outsiders make the same facial expressions to emotional situations as westerners.

mechanism is present in all normal individuals in all cultures and is designed to be sensitive to the disgust reactions of our fellows so we don't have to pay the costs of trial-and-error learning.

THE QUESTION OF BASIC EMOTIONS

For many years, influenced by the SSSM, most researchers believed that biology provided some small number of innate emotions, and the rest were provided by culture and experience. J. B. Watson, the father of behaviorism, thought that babies were born with only three emotions, fear, rage, and love, and that all others were derived from these by learning. Many researchers still hold to some version of this belief (e.g., Ortony & Turner, 1990; White, 1993; Wierzbicka, 1992).

But an increasing number of researchers now see emotion in an evolutionary context. In the early 1970s, Paul Ekman and his colleagues began a groundbreaking line of research that has made the SSSM view of emotions increasingly untenable. In a nutshell, they found evidence across cultures that people everywhere express and interpret certain emotions in the same way (e.g., Ekman, 1980, 1989). In a typical study, Ekman and Friesen (1971) traveled to New Guinea and studied the emotions of people who had very limited contact with Western culture; they spoke no English and had seen no television, movies, or even photographs. First the researchers told a person a very brief story, such as the following: "Your friend has come and you are happy;" or "You see a dead pig that has been lying there a long time" (Ekman, 1980, p. 132). For each story they showed three pictures of faces that Westerners interpret as illustrating various emotions. They asked the participants to choose the picture that matched the story. The New Guineans were highly consistent in choosing the appropriate picture for the emotions of happiness, sadness, anger, disgust, surprise, and fear. Other studies have replicated these results in a number of literate cultures.

Later Ekman and Friesen videotaped other New Guineans while they asked them to show how their faces would look if they were the person in the story (see Figure 12–3). American college students correctly matched the unedited videotapes to the emotions for anger, disgust, happiness, and sadness. They tended to confuse the fear and surprise poses.

Further evidence that emotions are evolved mechanisms comes from an experiment that tested whether making the facial expressions for particular emotions would cause the emotion. Ekman and his colleagues (Levenson et al., 1990) instructed subjects to make a face using those muscles that are moved in a particular emotion. For example:

a. Pull your eyebrows down and together.

b. Raise your upper eyelid.

c. Push your lower lip up and press your lips together. (Levenson et al., 1990, p. 365)

Subjects were coached to help them make the face, but were not told that it was the face characteristic of an emotion, anger in this case. When they had succeeded in make the right face, they were asked what emotions they were feeling right then. They had a strong tendency to name the emotion that went with the face, even though the emotion hadn't been named and even in the condition in which they could not see their face in a mirror. The investigators also took physiological measures: heart rate, skin conductance, skin temperature, and body movement. These measures showed distinctive patterns for many, but not all, of the emotions.

How Many Emotions Are There?

You will recognize immediately that this question echoes the earlier debate about the number of instincts we mentioned earlier. You will recall that we said that the number of motives, to use the modern term, will be determined by discovering how many evolved mechanisms there are that solved a certain kind of recurring problem in the EEA. Part of this process is discovering commonalities among the mechanisms. The same applies to emotions, which we consider to constitute the affective component of motives.

Ekman has proposed a list of nine criteria that should be met in order to consider an emotion to be basic. They are:

1. distinct facial expression

2. presence in other primates

3. distinct physiology

4. distinct causes

5. facial expression is not separable from physiological response
6. quick onset
7. brief duration
8. automatic appraisal (that is, any cognitive evaluation of the situation that causes the emotion takes place without awareness)
9. unbidden occurrence

The reason he proposes the list is to keep the number of emotions from growing indefinitely. We will comment on a few of the criteria. Ekman includes quick onset and brief duration in order to distinguish emotions from moods, which last much longer than emotions. The automatic appraisal and unbidden occurrence distinguish emotions from other sorts of cognition that may not be emotional. A person who suddenly becomes choked with emotion while delivering a speech is usually surprised by the display, and tries to control it. If you haven't experienced this embarrassing situation, be sure that someday you will. Perhaps you will start weeping at the wedding of someone you barely know.

Certain of Ekman's criteria for basic emotions are problematic, however. First is the requirement for a distinct facial expression for each basic emotion. We discussed the emotion of sexual jealousy in Chapter 10. This emotion, which is not on Ekman's list of basic emotions, does not have a distinct facial expression, but is a well established and understood emotion. The same can be said for envy, greed, and lust. From an evolutionary point of view, what's the purpose of facial expressions? Distinct facial expressions are essential if communicating the emotion to others may help to solve the problem that caused the emotion. Obviously, there could be situations where it is better to keep the problem private; hence there is no general reason to expect every emotion to have a distinct, recognizable facial expression.

Presence of the emotion in other primates is also a problematic criterion. It is highly likely that we will share many emotions with our close relatives, including sexual jealousy. But we should not be a bit surprised if different species have different emotions simply because we have a different evolutionary history from other primates, and therefore differ in some of our adaptations. It is rather unlikely that animals of any other species experience existential dread by considering their own death.

Distinct physiology is a "measurement issue." Emotions must be sufficiently distinct to the person who experiences them to motivate the right kind of solutions. That does not mean that they will be distinct to scientists using the relatively crude measurement techniques currently available.

The problems notwithstanding, Ekman believes that there are at least five basic emotions that meet all nine criteria for basic emotions: anger, disgust, fear, happiness, and sadness. He tentatively suggests that there might be eight more, but they have not been shown to have all nine characteristics: awe, contempt, embarrassment, excitement, guilt, interest, shame, and surprise (1989).

We accept all the items in Ekman's list of five basic emotions, but we believe that there are certainly more. If by "basic" we mean that an emotion is not simply a social construction, but it is an evolved mechanism to motivate particular types of adaptive behavior, then all emotions are basic, and Ekman's criteria miss the point. The evolutionist focuses on function: Was this emotion designed to motivate solutions to a particular class of real-world problems?

ANGER IS EASIER TO DETECT THAN HAPPINESS

We said earlier in the chapter that even though all emotions are biological, they are not all equally important. Certain emotional expressions by other people may have more immediate significance for our fitness than other emotions. A happy expression on another person's face is often a good sign for us, but may not require us to do anything in particular. An angry expression, on the other hand, can mean big trouble right now. Christine and Ranald Hansen (1988) studied people's ability to pick happy or angry faces out of a crowd. The subjects were shown an array of faces. Embedded within the array was one face that had a different expression: One happy face in an angry array, or one angry face in a happy group. Subjects were much quicker and more accurate at picking out the angry face in a crowd of happy faces than they were at picking a happy face out of an angry crowd. (Other conditions examined the effects of neutral faces, either as targets or as crowds.)

The angry faces, but not the happy ones, showed a phenomenon called "pop out." Some shapes immediately pop out of an array containing other shapes, but others do not: A single *O* pops out of a field of *X*'s, but a single *R* does not pop out of an array of *P*'s and *Q*'s. Pop-out permits us to find a single *O* as fast in a large array of *X*'s as in a small one. The subjects were just as fast in picking out the angry face from a group of eight happy faces as they were from a group of three happy faces. Hansen and Hansen's work gives further evidence that the ability to detect emotions represents adaptations that solved problems in predicting other people's behavior, and that the problems differ from one context to another.

WHY WE CAN'T BE HAPPY ALL THE TIME

People through the ages have searched for the secret of happiness, mostly without success. One of the most consistent and frustrating observations about happiness is that it is fleeting. We have all seen pictures of lottery winners celebrating their sudden wealth. But research shows the sobering fact that lottery winners are no happier than other people once the initial euphoria wears off (Diener et al., 1999, and references therein).

Maybe lottery winners are unusual in some way. Would a doubling of income make the average person happier? Well, between the late 1950s and the early 1990s income in the United States more than doubled, even after inflation is taken into account. Yet the proportion of Americans that described themselves as very happy didn't budge. The converse is also true: People who suffer terrible accidents that leave them quadriplegic or paraplegic eventually adjust to their loss, and within a year or two feel just as happy as they were before the accident (Myers and Diener, 1995). Why are happiness and sadness fleeting?

Recall that evolution does not have our happiness as a goal. In order for happiness to evolve it must serve our fitness. Would a person who was happy all the time leave more offspring than one who was sometimes happy and sometimes sad? We need to respond appropriately to the situation: to be happy when our fitness has increased and be sad when it has decreased. The phenomenon of sensory adaptation that we encountered in Chapter 5 provides us with just such a mechanism. In particular, the outcome of sensory adaptation known as range shifting provides us an insight into happiness.

Think of the happiness/sadness continuum as a kind of meter of our fitness prospects. When we get an increment to our fitness we are briefly happy, but we adapt to it quickly; when we face a decrease in our fitness we are briefly sad. If we stayed happy long after each increment in fitness, our happiness couldn't keep going higher to each one. Our "happiness meter" would eventually "peg out" and fail to register any more increases. The same argument applies to unhappiness. We need a mechanism that recalibrates our happiness so that we can continue to respond appropriately to each new situation, each new opportunity or threat. The range-shifting property of sensory adaptation actually serves our fitness by allowing us to be briefly very happy and very unhappy to relatively minor events. (A gift of a leg of wildebeest makes a small contribution to our lifetime fitness, and we would be briefly happy for it. But adaptation brings us back to neutral so that we can respond appropriately to the next gift of wildebeest leg. One leg of wildebeest every week would have enormous cumulative value). Emotional adaptation keeps us responding appropriately to the environment on a constant basis.

We should not leave the impression that differences in circumstances make no long-term differences in happiness. People in rich countries are happier than people in desperately poor ones. Although adaptation happens in all the senses, there are limits to our ability to adapt to hunger, cold, and pain, and the like. It is possible to be miserable much of the time if our circumstances are bad enough. Sensory mechanisms do respond to overall level of stimulation: Although we adapt to heat, there are limits above which we are always hot; although we adapt to light, we can tell day from night, and so forth. But we must not lose sight of the fact that our sense of vision is not a light meter; it is not designed to provide an objective measure of the amount of light. If it did we would not be as sensitive to *changes* in light. Likewise the emotion of happiness is not designed to objectively measure our absolute fitness prospect, but to respond to immediate changes in it.

THE "SOCIAL" EMOTIONS

Why do we leave a tip for a waiter we will never see again, and feel guilty if we don't? One of us recalls trying to determine whether the tip was included in the bill at a restaurant in Bangkok, Thailand. The language barrier and cultural differences made communication difficult, but as far as he could tell, no tip was expected. Everyone bowed and smiled (following Thai custom) as he left the restaurant, but he had a nagging feeling that he had not done the right thing.

Precisely because humans are social organisms, our reproductive success depends to a great extent on our social skills and relationships. Randolph Nesse (1990) notes that natural selection should have crafted specialized emotional states to help us negotiate the social landscape. One of the fundamental problems facing a social species is cooperation. We have already seen in Chapter 8 how our cognitive skills are shaped by the necessity of detecting cheaters. Here we look for evidence of special emotions supporting cooperation and cheater detection.

In Chapter 4 we described the Prisoner's Dilemma, a game that has been used in many different fields to study how individuals interact when their interests are partly in common, but also partly different. There we saw that the strategy of being conditionally cooperative can be stable providing you expect to play a series of rounds.

The question remains, however: What about that waiter you don't expect to see again? Why do you cooperate the first time? Why not act as if life is a series of one-trial games, with different partners, and cheat the first time? Robert Frank (1988) calls this the commitment problem. We frequently must commit ourselves to cooperate with another person without sufficient rational basis for believing that they will carry out their end of the bargain. The best example may be marriage. A woman promises to be faithful to a man even though she has no guarantee he won't divorce her after a decade. A man commits to supporting a woman's children even though he has no guarantee they will all be his. Following Robert Trivers (1971), Frank proposes that certain emotions evolved to solve the commitment problem.

In the first place, the emotions motivate the faithfulness. A couple in love are blind to the rest of the world and each imagines that their partner is the most desirable possible. At the same time, the emotion of jealousy motivates us to deal with any signs of unfaithfulness. Second, the emotions serve as signs of the commitment. The displays of affection are costly to each partner. It is a standard source of humor that men have difficulty declaring their love. Yet a man must make a credible display of love to win the woman. An engaged or married woman wears a ring that declares to the world that she is unavailable to other potential mates. (Commonly, but not as universally, the man wears a wedding ring, but only rarely an engagement ring. There are plausible evolutionary reasons for the asymmetry, as we have discussed in Chapter 10.) And gifts to the loved one are by definition costly.

Because these signs of commitment are costly to make, they are difficult to fake. Traits such as the huge tail of a peacock, the deep voice of a male toad, and lavish displays of love by humans are called *honest signals;* they provide reliable evidence of mate quality. In this case, the quality of interest is faithfulness. The honest signals of emotional commitment help convince the partner, as well as the rest of the community, of sincerity. People comment that "Michael must really be smitten by Jennifer; he looks ridiculous following her around acting like a sick puppy."

Of course, marriage is only one example of a cooperative relationship. As social creatures we form many other kinds of cooperative relationships, with friends,

Table 12–1.   Social emotions related to the various outcomes of the Prisoner's dilemma.

SELF	OTHER	
	Cooperate	Cheat
Cooperate	Friendliness (Love)/ Friendliness (Love)	Anger/Guilt
Cheat	Guilt/Anger	Hatred/Hatred

coworkers, and the like. All of these cooperative relationships can be analysed as Prisoner's Dilemma situations. Here we are focusing on the emotions that have evolved to help us navigate such situations. Thus Table 12–1 shows some of the social emotions in relation to the cells of the Prisoner's Dilemma matrix (cf. Nesse, 1990).

We have already discussed the emotion of love, which is in parenthesis next to the less intense term, friendliness. Friendliness or love is the emotion felt between two cooperators. Because they are both cooperating, they feel the same emotions. But when one cooperates and the other cheats, they feel different emotions, not surprisingly. The cooperator is angry at the cheater who, in turn, feels guilty. When both players have cheated on each other, they feel mutual hatred.

The role of anger toward the cheater is worth considering in more detail. Trivers (1971) called this *moralistic aggression*. By punishing his or her partner the one who is cheated shows just how important the relationship is, and how much he or she is willing to risk to put it right. You may have seen people display "righteous indignation" toward others who don't meet their moral standards. Common wisdom holds that a good fight can be a sign of a healthy relationship. We are more likely to display righteous indignation to people with whom we are in a cooperative relationship. Recent research (Rutherford et al., 1997) shows that people are more willing to punish other members of a group for wrongdoing after they get to know them better. There is no point showing moralistic aggression against someone with whom you have no lasting relationship.

So we see that introducing emotions into the Prisoners Dilemma motivates cooperation when cheating might appear to be the rational choice in the short term. Some time ago the movie *Love Story* made popular the saying "Love means never having to say you're sorry." But most people who have been in real relationships, as opposed to fictional ones, have learned how false the saying is. The guilt experienced after having cheated motivates a lover to apologize and try to make amends.

The emotions also serve to establish our reputation (Frank, 1988). Conspicuous displays of emotion are seen by others, sometimes by many others, and are the topic of gossip—Did you see how Freda yelled at Joe for picking her up late? This function of emotion may explain spite, which is when we incur a cost to inflict a cost on another person. A person may blast music he hates over his own stereo in order to irritate his upstairs neighbor.

The expression "dog in the manger" describes a person who goes out of the way to prevent another from enjoying something of no value to himself. The

Figure 12–4. *Gadsden Flag.* This revolutionary war flag shows an example of the use of a credible threat.

expression comes from the fact that a dog actually will lie down in the cow's feed, preventing the cow from eating, even though the dog can't eat grain, and must go to some effort to keep the cow away. By definition spiteful people pay a cost in order to inflict a cost on others.

But why pay costs? If they actually gained nothing by their action, they shouldn't do it. People who make a credible display of fierceness may convince other people that it is not sensible to cross them. You may have had a neighbor whom everyone treated with kid gloves. Your mother may have said, "Don't go near crazy, old Mr. MacGregor's yard. Remember the time he aimed his shotgun at Billy for setting one foot on his lawn?" An action that is extreme, even irrational, can give a person a reputation that will make it easier for him to get his way in the future. It is a standard theme in fiction for a goon to use excessive violence on occasion to motivate others to cooperate with him in the future. And despots often use terror as a means of gaining the compliance of their subjects (Betzig, 1986).

Do not assume that spite is always used by people we don't admire. You may recall the flag flown by Americans during the Revolutionary period. It showed a coiled rattlesnake and the words "Don't tread on me." (See Figure 12–4.) The flag, known as the Gadsden flag, was designed to help the revolutionaries convince the British that the colonists meant business.

SHAME AND PRIDE

Next we consider two emotions, shame and pride, that are often called "self-conscious emotions" or "secondary emotions." They are often discussed separately from the "basic emotions" because they do not have stereotyped facial expressions or distinct physiology (Campos, 1995). You will recall, however, that we consider all emotions to be basic to the extent that they represent mechanisms designed by selection to solve recurring problems for humans in the EEA. You will also recall that we said that stereotyped facial expressions and distinct physiology should not be considered crucial to considering an emotion to be "basic." We consider two "self-conscious" emotions here because we believe that they do form a natural grouping, but for a different reason than usually supposed.

Humans are highly social animals, even for primates. In the EEA a lone human usually soon became a dead human. Even today, a true hermit is an extremely rare individual, and typically relies on periodic contact with others. A person's status in the community is a very important matter, and has implications for the ability to compete for all kinds of critical resources. Shakespeare captured the idea of reputation as a resource as follows:

> Who steals my purse steals trash . . .
> But he that filches from me my good name
> . . . makes me poor indeed.
>   (*Othello*, III.iii. 160–165)

Shame is defined in the Oxford English Dictionary as, "1. The painful emotion arising from the consciousness of something dishonouring, ridiculous, or undecorous in one's own conduct or circumstances. . . . 3. Disgrace, ignominy, loss of esteem or reputation." We should be careful not to rely too much on dictionary definitions of scientific concepts, because they reflect common usage. For example, the everyday definition of *work* is quite distinct from the one used in physics. But the common use of psychological terms can be a good starting point in understanding them. The dictionary definition clearly suggests that shame is related to status in the community.

Shame is closely related to guilt. In fact many authors debate whether they are in fact the same emotion. Barrett (1995), however, notes that shame and guilt differ in important ways. The emotion of shame leads one to withdraw from contact with other people, and typically involves hiding the face and averting the gaze. By contrast, guilt causes us to approach the person we have wronged in order to make amends for our action. Shame leads to a global evaluation of ourselves as bad. Guilt focuses our attention on a particular bad thing that we have done. As we discussed above in connection with the Prisoner's Dilemma, guilt involves damage to our reputation as a good cooperator. Shame, on the other hand, involves our place in the hierarchy. Contrary to popular myth, status was in all likelihood important in the EEA, and all societies have hierarchies, even those with much more even distribution of wealth than ours.

We often experience shame and guilt together for the simple reason that something we have done wrong (guilt) leads to our losing status in the community (shame). But it is significant that we are often ashamed of something that we have not done, or have no control over. We may be ashamed of growing up with a regional accent, or that our brother is a ne'er do well. The notion that shame befalls a family illustrates shame can be felt when we ourselves have done nothing to deserve it.

Looked at in evolutionary perspective, shame becomes the opposite of pride. Pride often comes from our accomplishments, of course; but, as with shame, we can be proud of things we have no control over, such as our parentage, our glossy hair, or high cheekbones. Pride is the positive emotion related to our status in the community, just as shame is the negative.

We cannot leave the topic of shame and pride without addressing the concept of *self-esteem,* a topic that is discussed in every social psychology text. Psychologists define self-esteem as our overall self-evaluation of ourselves as reasonable, decent, moral, intelligent people (Myers, 1993). There is a huge literature that holds that people are motivated to maintain their self-esteem. Much of this literature gives little indication that self-esteem has any source outside of ourselves—it is *our own* evaluation of our worth. It is called *self-*esteem, after all.

Furthermore, a major goal of many researchers who study self-esteem seems to be to show how *inaccurate* our self-esteem can be as a measure of other people's evaluation of us. Study after study shows that our self-esteem is often greater than any objective evidence would justify. Mark Leary and his coworkers (e.g., Leary & Downs, 1995; Leary, Schreindorfer, & Haupt, 1995) are exceptions to this generalization, however. They consider self-esteem to be a "sociometer," or kind of gauge of our standing with important social groups. Rather than being motivated to enhance our self-esteem, per se, as most researchers hold, Leary and his coworkers believe that "human beings appear to possess a fundamental motive to avoid exclusion from important social groups" (Leary & Downs, 1995, p. 128). Barkow (1980, 1991) holds a similar position for explicitly evolutionary reasons. He considers that self-esteem evolved from our need to evaluate ourselves as excelling at skills that lead to status in hierarchies. We agree, but believe that self-esteem would be better defined as our impression of what others think of us. The focus should be on our ability to assess our status in a hierarchy in order to compete for resources, particularly mating opportunities. A clumsier but more descriptive expression would be "our self-evaluation of our status in the hierarchy."

Is Testosterone a Status Meter?

Throughout this book we have focused on the ultimate explanations, or the answers to "why" questions, because those answers illustrate the evolutionary approach most clearly. We should not, however, imply that the proximate, or "how" questions are uninteresting or unimportant. The question of how self esteem is mediated physiologically is particularly interesting. It is well established that levels of the hormone testosterone (T) are associated with dominant and aggressive behavior in men (Mazur & Booth, 1998). For example, prisoners with higher levels of T show more dominant and antisocial behaviors. These are behaviors that would lead to increased status in a prison situation.

Most interesting is that T not only causes men to act in a dominant manner, but that changes in status affect levels of T. So elevated T is both a stimulus for dominant behavior that can increases status, and also a response to an increase in status. In other words, the cause-effect relationship goes both ways. In one clever study, T was measured before and after a chess tournament. Winners showed a rise in T after the tournament, and losers showed a decrease. So it appears that T causes dominant behavior that leads to an increase in status, and an increase in status increases T. But the result is not an ever increasing spiral of T and status. Losing a contest results in loss of status and lower T. The evolutionary significance is that we have a mechanism whereby success encourages initiative, but failure leads to withdrawal from situations that are unlikely to pay off.

CONFLICT, VIOLENCE, AND HOMICIDE

Evolution designs adaptations that increase the fitness of organisms that have them. Threats to fitness come from many sources—nonliving and living—such as extremes of heat and cold, poisonous plants and predators; but also from conspecifics in the form of enemies, rivals, and the like. Even family members have different fitness interests to some degree, as we have discussed in Chapter 11. Wives and husbands share an interest in their common children, but they still may differ about the relative importance of existing versus future offspring, for example. So it is to be expected that individuals, even in families, will have conflicts because their interests sometimes diverge.

Conflict is sometimes considered undesirable by definition. Part of the reason is that we use the term as synonymous with fighting or war. As students of behavior, however, we should consider conflict to be any situation where two individuals have incompatible interests. Take a couple that is trying to decide where to go out to eat. She wants to eat Chinese and he wants Italian. This is a conflict. Most times they settle the conflict amicably by some means such as considering how long it has been since they ate Chinese versus Italian, or who got to pick last. We were discussing nonviolent conflict resolution earlier in this chapter, when we considered the social emotions.

Some conflicts, however, are settled violently. As we discussed in Chapter 4, violence works as a means of getting some contested resource by increasing the cost of that resource to another individual. We suppose that couples rarely settle conflicts over where to eat out by resorting to violence. But men fight over potential mates, neighbors fight over boundaries, and children fight over toys. In this section we will consider some evolutionary insights into violence as an adaptation for conflict resolution.

Homicide

Why are we choosing homicide as an example of violent conflict resolution? Unfortunately, homicide is real: Violent conflicts are sometimes lethal. Martin Daly and Margo Wilson (1988) chose homicide as an "outcropping" of violent phenomena in their landmark book, *Homicide*, because incidents of it are particularly well-documented in police records. Homicide records are almost certainly less biased than self reports of violent activity would be. In addition, it is often possible to test hypotheses most easily by considering the extreme values on a dimension, as we discussed when we examined birth-order effects in Chapter 11. Much of what we say in this section is based on Daly and Wilson's work.

Note carefully that we are *not* claiming that homicide is an adaptation. It may or may not be an adaptation. Given its prevalence among contemporary hunter-gatherers (who, despite much lower population densities, have homicide rates like those of "murder capitals" like Chicago, Detroit, and Miami), homicide was probably common in the EEA. Nevertheless, we are interested in violence as the adaptation. Sometimes the psychological mechanisms that underlie violence lead to homicide, and sometimes they only lead to a bluff or a scuffle. We are treating homicide as one outcropping of violence that can be examined from an evolutionary point of view.

Most Homicides Involve Men Killing Men

You are probably not surprised to read that most homicides are committed by men. Daly and Wilson (1988) found that men were responsible for 86 percent of homicides that did not involve relatives. (The proportion is not much affected by considering all homicides.) Similarly, they found that men were responsible for 96 percent of all homicides that were committed as part of a robbery or theft. "There is no known human society in which the level of lethal violence among women even begins to approach that among men" (Daly & Wilson, 1988, p. 146). But you may be surprised to learn that the victims of homicide are also overwhelmingly male. Daly and Wilson estimate that in North America men kill other men almost forty times as often as women kill other women! Data from around the world show a similar pattern.

When Do Men Kill Each Other?

You might think that most killings happen in the course of armed robberies. In fact, data from Philadelphia show that is only the fifth most common category, after domestic quarrels, jealousy, and altercations over money. The most common category, is what criminologists call "altercation of relatively trivial origin; insult, curse, jostling, etc." A typical scenario is an argument that starts with words, continues and escalates into homicide. This category accounts for more than a third of all homicides, twice as many as domestic quarrels, and five times as many as robberies.

It is tempting to conclude from the triviality of the events surrounding these homicides that something has gone wrong in our society, or that people are acting in some new, and maladaptive way. But the evidence is clear from many societies, and throughout history, that this pattern of male violence is typical, not aberrant, however disturbing it may be. Daly and Wilson make a compelling case that what men really fight over is not whether Mohammed Ali could have beaten Joe Louis, but status and honor.

Recall our discussion of sexual selection in Chapters 2 and 10. Men and women face different selection pressures. Because of their higher potential reproductive rates, men find mates scarce and worth competing for. For every man who has two wives, one man goes without a wife, assuming an equal sex ratio. As a result men compete for women. Women in turn are choosy about whom they mate with.

One of the things women look for is a dominant male (Chapter 10). And violence is one way to assert dominance. Around the world men show behavior that is called "machismo" in Spanish. Men will pick literally any basis for an argument—somebody's driving, haircut, or hometown. The content doesn't matter because the real contest is over dominance. Tempers sometimes flare, escalation is not unusual and, if a gun is handy the outcome is all too often lethal.

The explanation offered by proponents of the SSSM for sex differences in violence, or in any behavior for that matter, is culture. It is frequently claimed that "in our culture" boys are trained to be assertive and girls passive. The main problem with this explanation is that it begs the question—it assumes without proof that there are other cultures where the reverse is true. The fact is, as we just saw, there is not a single known culture in the world where women are remotely as violent as men. Let's grant that boys are encouraged to be more aggressive "in our culture." Does this difference in training actually account for the observed difference in behavior? Although it well may make some difference, no evidence is provided by proponents of the SSSM that it can begin to account for the huge differences in the violent behavior of men and women. Nor can it explain the universality of the sex difference.

As you saw in Chapter 10, there are two human natures, male and female. Men seem to be designed to be quicker to resort to violence. This analysis is not a justification—remember the naturalistic fallacy. As usual, we study aspects of psychology not to rationalize our behavior but to understand it. Discussions about the role of society in violent behavior might productively focus on socialization methods that help boys learn to control and channel their competitive tendencies.

SUMMARY

1. Motivation is the study of the directional and energizing aspects of behavior.
2. Emotion is defined by its affective tone. Emotions are either positive or negative; never neutral.
3. Emotion is the affective component of motivation.
4. The instinct concept was rejected by psychologists for reasons that are not entirely valid today.
5. Motives and emotions are adaptations that evolved to solve problems that existed in the EEA.
6. All motives and emotions are equally biological, although not equally important.
7. Although motives are influenced by learning, that does not make them "socially constructed."
8. Disgust is a facultative trait; as omnivores humans must learn what is food and what is not.
9. Ekman has found evidence for at least five basic emotions: anger, disgust, fear, happiness, and sadness, but there are probably many more.
10. It is easier to detect an angry face than a happy one in a crowd.

11. The phenomenon of sensory adaptation explains why we can't be happy all the time.
12. The social emotions evolved to motivate social behaviors, such as can be found in the Prisoner's Dilemma.
13. The emotion of spite can establish a person's reputation as someone who must be feared, helping a person to get one's way in the future.
14. The emotions of shame and pride motivate behavior that maintains our status in a community.
15. Self-esteem is our estimate of our status in a community.
16. The hormone testosterone influences dominant and aggressive behavior in men. Winning a contest increases testosterone, and losing lowers it.
17. Homicide provides a clear example of conflict that can be analyzed for evolutionary implications.
18. Men are far more violent than women, and kill other men much more than they kill women.
19. Men often kill men in conflicts over status.

13 Health

An enormous change in human health has taken place in developed countries in the last one hundred years. Before 1900, about 25 percent of people died before age twenty-five and only 50 percent lived past age fifty. Today only 3 percent die before age twenty-five and only 10 percent die before age fifty (Committee on the Use of Animals in Research, 1991). This change can be attributed to modern medicine and public health practices. There has also been a major change in the causes of death. As recently as 1900 almost half of all deaths were caused by infectious diseases such as tuberculosis, pneumonia, and diarrhea. Today the leading cause of death is cardiovascular disease, such as heart attack and stroke, which are primarily diseases of old age (U.S. Department of Commerce, 1995 Statistical Abstract of the United States).

A startling result of the advance of modern medicine is that, more and more, the causes of death are the result of human behavior. Consider:

- The leading causes of death of young men (ages fifteen to forty-four) are accident, homicide, and suicide (U.S. Bureau of the Census, 1999).
- Lung cancer, previously rare, has become one of the most common forms of cancer as a result of cigarette smoking.
- Obesity has increased markedly in recent years, with 25 percent of U.S. adults now considered obese (Wickelgren, 1998).
- The typical American diet is a major cause of both cardiovascular disease and obesity.

The purpose of this chapter is to consider how evolutionary psychology can contribute to understanding and promoting human health. We will suggest that many of our health problems come from differences between our present lifestyle and that in the EEA, an idea called the *mismatch hypothesis*. The stone-age way of life to which we are adapted is very different from the modern, western environment.

Much of what we say in this chapter applies particularly to the North American lifestyle, which is different from that of other industrialized countries, not to mention the developing countries. We need to keep in mind that in some parts of the world infection is still the leading cause of death.

> **Trail Marker:** The mismatch hypothesis says that many problems of health are the result of a mismatch between our evolved characteristics and our present environment.

NUTRITION AND EXERCISE

Of all the differences between the stone-age and the turn of the twenty-first century, the biggest may be in our nutrition. Hunter-gatherers were, and the few remaining still are, lean and physically fit. They were taller on the average than agricultural peoples have been until the present time and were capable of remarkable feats of athleticism.

In contrast, 40 percent of American women and 25 percent of men are trying to lose weight at any given time—and another 27 percent of women and 18 percent of men are trying not to gain weight (Serdula et al., 1994). In spite of our dieting, we are getting fatter by the year—6 percent more Americans were overweight in 1993 (the most recent data available) than just seven years before (Galuska et al., 1996). We need only look at ads for diet programs, listen to people discuss their weight, or look at people walk by in the mall to realize that maintaining a healthy weight is a major problem for people in some industrial societies. Books on diet and weight loss take up about twenty-five feet of shelf space in the Carnegie Library of Pittsburgh. At the same time, mounting evidence demonstrates that diets do not work. Study after study shows that about 95 percent of people who go on a diet either do not lose weight, or gain back all they lost and more. We discuss the reasons why this happens in the next section.

Adult Human Body Weight Is Remarkably Stable

The lack of success that so many people have in their efforts to lose weight demonstrates that adult human body weight is actually remarkably stable. It takes only ten extra calories a day to gain a pound a year. This is equivalent to an extra one-tenth of a pat of butter, or one-eighth of a slice of bread—without butter—per day. And our weight remains remarkably constant over time in spite of the fact that the amount we eat varies greatly from day to day, often as much as 50 percent above or below our average. So there must be a mechanism that keeps weight constant. In fact, this mechanism explains why it is so hard to lose weight.

Why Diets Usually Don't Work. Our weight is regulated by a feedback system that has a set point. Rats and humans who have been starved below their set point eat more once food is freely available until they regain the set point; those who have been force fed eat less until they drop to the set point. This system operates without our having to think about it. We eat when we are hungry and stop when we are full. Although we have great difficulty losing (or gaining) weight, it is a good thing we don't need to regulate our weight consciously. Then we could either forget to eat and waste away or eat until we are obese.

People who do try to lose weight by going on a diet often find that their weight drops at first, but does not continue to go down. When we go on a diet our body responds by lowering the resting metabolic rate; the result is that we burn fewer calories than we did before. Our body resists the weight loss. We tend to reach a plateau even though we are eating substantially less than we did before— besides which we are hungry all the time. And when we do go off the diet, our weight may go higher than it was before, owing to the reduced metabolic rate. This is an evolutionary adaptation that permitted our ancestors to survive periods of famine by reducing their caloric needs. But it no longer functions to the benefit of most people in industrial societies where there are no periodic shortages of food.

Body fat itself is another adaptation to fluctuating and uncertain supplies of food. Because food could not be stockpiled in the EEA, we make use of the evolved mechanism of storing resources right on our bodies (in the form of fat) against the possibility of future famine. The fact that women have more body fat than men (27 percent compared to 16 percent) reflects the demands of pregnancy and lactation. The typical woman carries about enough fat to support a successful pregnancy (Frisch, 1990).

Exercise Helps in Weight Regulation

Although diets don't work very well in reducing weight, studies show that regular exercise can help, with or without dieting (Hill & Peters, 1998). Many years ago, Jean Mayer and his associates studied the food intake and body weight of men who worked at jobs requiring various amounts of physical work. They found that the workers matched their food intake to their level of activity over a wide range, resulting in regulation of weight (Mayer, 1967). They also found the same relationship in rats that were forced to exercise. Later studies confirmed these results in humans and made methodological improvements over the early human study (Schulz & Schoeller, 1994). Below a certain level of exercise, however, both the men and the rats ate more than needed to match their activity and gained weight. The upper part of Figure 13–1 shows the relationship between amount of exercise and weight. The straight-line portion of the curve shows the range of activity level over which we adjust for the increased calories burned with an increase in food intake. At some point the regulation breaks down, as shown by the upturn in the curve. People who are sedentary actually eat more than people who are moderately active. People whose exercise level is below the threshold for regulation weigh

of such a distribution would represent exaggerated or reduced levels of normal behavior and be non-optimal, by definition. Clinical depression could represent such a case.

Before we proceed with an evolutionary analysis of behavior disorders, we need to stress that some disorders may reflect more than one cause. We need to realize that a disorder may have more than one contributing factor. A person who smokes, eats a lot of saturated fats, never exercises, and has a family history of heart disease has an increased risk of heart attack. We wouldn't try to decide which one was actually responsible if that person should suffer a heart attack. Instead we would say that he had many contributory risk factors, or many possible causes. We will see below that several different causes may contribute to some disorders, such as depression.

A SURVEY OF MENTAL DISORDERS

The disorders we discuss next reflect several different causes listed above.

Post-Traumatic Stress Disorder

The Vietnam War made us familiar with the concept of post-traumatic stress disorder (PTSD). About 15 percent of U.S. Vietnam veterans suffered from social withdrawal, emotional numbing, difficulty sleeping, and flashbacks. DSM-IV recognizes PTSD as a reaction to "events so powerful that they threaten life or well being, severely tax or overwhelm coping capabilities, and challenge the assumptions that people make about the world and the way it works" (Baum et al., 1996, p. 92). It is instructive to note that the term PTSD is but the latest used to describe this disorder. During World War I the same kind of symptoms were described by the term "shell shock," because many doctors believed that it was a response to the physical concussion caused by exploding artillery. Before that, from the beginning of the Industrial Revolution, the term "railway spine" was used to describe a condition displayed by workers who had survived terrible railroad accidents. That term came from the belief that the trauma was caused by twisting or concussion of the spine. Eventually scientists became convinced that PTSD, whatever it is called, is a mental health problem, not primarily a physiological one. (We must be careful to note that we are *not* saying that it is "all in the head." Stress has real biological consequences, but mechanical damage to the nervous system is not one of them.)

The significant thing about PTSD from our perspective is that it would be expected to be primarily a disease of modern life. Events like tornadoes, cyclones and volcanoes generally produce PTSD in less than 10 percent of those who experience them. By contrast, airplane crashes, flooding caused by a broken dam, and automobile accidents cause PTSD in about 20 to 50 percent of survivors (Baum et al., 1996). You will note that the first category contains natural disasters and the second human-engineered ones (see Figure 14–1). It appears that modern society is

Figure 14–1. *Disaster scene.* Modern societies experience disasters on a scale unlikely in the EEA.

capable of organizing disasters on a scale of horror not known to our ancestors. Stone-age warfare is bad enough, but it cannot match the devastation of modern weaponry.

Thus we see that PTSD may be looked at as a susceptibility to stress that overwhelms our normal defense against threats. The frequency with which it occurs today reflects a mismatch between our evolved defenses and the modern environment.

Depression

Depression has been called the common cold of psychological disorders because so many people experience it at some time in their lives. It is characterized by low-energy level, feelings of worthlessness, sadness, inability to concentrate and to plan for the future. The distinction between clinical depression and normal sadness is based on the length and severity of the symptoms. Everyone gets the blues now and then, but not everyone becomes clinically depressed.

There are several alternative evolutionary ideas about depression. Randy Nesse (1991) has suggested that depression is nature's way of telling us that we are barking up the wrong tree. It keeps us from spending energy on activities that are unlikely to contribute to our fitness or taking senseless risk. If we have lost a contest with a rival over some resource, depression may keep us from spending more energy in a futile contest and risking even greater loss (Sloman & Price, 1987). Sloman and Price suggest that it is not mere coincidence that the loser in a contest lowers his head and avoids eye contact, behaviors typical of depression.

An evolutionary perspective suggests that people who were sad and mildly depressed when action was unlikely to succeed may have outreproduced those who didn't experience these feelings. To be effective in this way, depression would have to be properly calibrated. It should be triggered by setbacks of appropriate magnitude; it's appropriate to be depressed if your child dies or your spouse divorces you, but not if you get a fifteen-dollar parking ticket. If we imagine that each of us has a polygenically influenced "depression threshold," then it follows that many people are near the optimum, experiencing depression appropriately, when a "time-out" would be helpful. But it also follows that there will be some people whose threshold is too high and who fail to become sad and depressed even when all the signs indicate they are on the wrong track. And likewise, this view also suggests that there will be people whose threshold is too low and who experience deep and prolonged depression for very little reason. The latter would describe clinical depression. To our knowledge, systematic evidence for the former has not been sought.

Some of the hallmarks of depression seem appropriate to its postulated function. For example, people who are depressed have a lower opinion of themselves and of their prospects for success. Surprisingly, their self-assessment becomes more accurate than that of nondepressed people (Taylor, 1989)! As we discussed in Chapter 12, most people have a higher opinion of themselves than they deserve. We suggested that this inflated self-image helps us remain optimistic and effective in the never-ending competition for resources. But there are times when it is best to cut our losses. Depression strips off the rose-colored glasses through which we normally view the world. This helps us to realize that it is probably unrealistic to try to date the most attractive person we know, or compete for the highest position in our company.

An evolutionary approach suggests some additional insights into long-standing puzzles of depression. Depression is so much more common in the winter time that this form of it has been given the special name of Seasonal Affective Disorder (SAD). Perhaps SAD kept our ancestors from wasting precious energy reserves on activities that were less likely to bear fruit in the winter when food is scarce and moving about is especially metabolically expensive (Pomerleau, 1997).

The sex difference in rates of depression—women are twice as likely as men to experience depression—may also have evolutionary roots. Cynthia Pomerleau (1997) suggests that because women are physically weaker than men, they have had more to lose by entering a contest in which they could be injured. On this line of thinking she suggests that, if depression is an adaptation that removes us from a situation where we have more to lose than gain, depression may be more easily triggered in women. A variety of other ideas can also be offered. Perhaps women experience more depression because their options and scope for action are limited by the fact that men so often make the rules. Alternatively, the modern role of women may be even more out of tune with their evolved psychology than is that of men. For example, women who work outside the home often worry that they are neglecting their parental role; and women who don't work outside the home may suffer social isolation compared to women in hunter-gatherer societies who engage in more communal task-sharing. These suggestions are speculative at this point. Nevertheless they point the way for possibly productive research. For example, some (but not all) of these hypotheses predict that women's interactions with men are more likely to trigger depression than are their interactions with women.

Why is depression so common, and increasing? The mismatch between the EEA and contemporary life is vast, particularly with regard to the opportunities for frequent small successes, such as a productive foraging trip or hunt, and the opportunity to share such success with friends and relatives, and be praised for it. We did not evolve to live in such large societies where, by definition, a smaller proportion of people are visible at the top of the pecking order. And large groups contain a lower proportion of kin and allies who can be counted on to help us in times of need. We did not evolve to go to school for twelve years or more before we were ready to do productive work. We did not evolve to work at a single repetitive job forty hours a week for forty years. In the form of movie and athletic stars, mass media create beautiful and highly competent pseudo-neighbors and lead us to compare ourselves to impossible ideals. Anyone who got their ideas of what life was like in contemporary America from television would suppose that the average person is much more attractive and wealthy than is actually the case. They would suppose that life is not only a beach, it is one that swarms with multitudes of rich, beautiful people, all on permanent vacation.

O'Guinn and Shrum (1997) asked people how much television they watched and also to estimate how many Americans own convertibles, cellular phones, hot tubs, drink wine with dinner, travel abroad, and the like. The more television they watched the higher their estimates of the frequency of these signs of affluence. In Chapter 16, we consider how implicit comparisons with people we see in movies or magazines can influence our evaluations of our mates.

A different and intriguing idea about the evolutionary function of depression has recently been offered by Edward Hagen (1999). Hagen has focused principally on postpartum depression, a form of depression that affects a significant proportion of new mothers. His novel suggestion is that depression serves as a negotiation tool to extract more investment from others. This is a plausible proposal given the reproductive threshold signaled by the birth of an infant. Rearing a child to adulthood is a huge win on one's evolutionary scorecard, but doing so is fabulously expensive, and one may need to negotiate higher levels of cooperation to succeed.

> I argue that PPD [postpartum depression] may be a strategy to negotiate greater investment from father and kin, or to reduce the mother's costs by functioning somewhat like a labor strike. In a labor strike, workers withhold their own labor in order to force management to increase their wages or benefits, or reduce their workload. Similarly, mothers with PPD may be withholding their investment in the new and existing offspring, or, in cases of very severe depression, putting at risk their ability to invest in future offspring by not taking care of themselves. This may force the father and kin to increase their investment. (Hagen, 1999, pp. 346–347).

Hagen suggests this "renegotiation" strategy may also be a factor in other, nonpostpartum cases of depression.

Suicide. Depression not only causes a great deal of suffering, it sometimes leads to suicide. Suicide is the eighth-leading cause of death in the United States, accounting for 1.4 percent of all deaths (Clark & Fawcett, 1992). Suicide rates increase with age, being about 50 percent higher in elderly than young people. The serious impact of suicide can be glimpsed from the suffering that leads a person to take his or her own life and the anguish it causes the surviving family.

On the model of depression presented above, most suicides probably occur in people who have too low a depression threshold, and thus find themselves depressed much of the time. But some suicides may have an adaptive basis. At first glance, suicide would seem to contradict the principles of EP because taking one's own life puts a final end to one's reproductive prospects. But if we remember the theory of kin selection, we have the beginning of an evolutionary understanding of suicide. Recall that we can increase the frequency of our genes by furthering the reproductive efforts of our close relatives, especially our siblings and our children. Is it possible that our death can further the success of our genes? Heroic acts that save our close relatives at the expense of our life further our genes, but that is not considered suicide.

Consider the possibility that death could increase a person's genetic representation in future generations if the resources spent to keep him alive would be better spent on close relatives. As we age our reproductive value declines markedly. We can respond to that decline by shifting our efforts from producing children of our own to helping our relatives produce children. (Recall our discussion of the grandmother hypothesis in Chapter 11.) At some point, however, an elderly person becomes a net drain on resources, rather than a producer of resources—another mouth to feed. Reflecting this fact is the common desire of the elderly "not to become a burden to my children." If, as Sloman and Price (1987) suggest, depression is a reaction to loss of resources needed for reproduction, then it is not surprising that depression is a risk factor for suicide. From an evolutionary point of view, we would predict that the rate of suicide should go up as a person's capacity to promote his or her genetic interests declines: This matches the demographic fact that suicide rates increase with age.

Denys de Catanzaro (1995) tested this hypothesis by examining factors that correlate with suicidal ideation (thoughts). He studied men and women of different age groups from the general population who answered a mail survey. In addition he studied several other groups, including residents of senior citizens' housing, mental patients, people institutionalized for antisocial behavior, and male and female homosexuals.

de Catanzaro found that a large number of factors predicted suicidal ideation. We will summarize some of the more important. Perceived burdensomeness to family was a large factor for both sexes and all ages, as the hypothesis predicted. In addition, lack of success in sex was a strong predictor for young males; loneliness, poor health, and financial problems were important for older males. Loneliness was a big factor for all females; health and finances became important with older females. The greater importance of sex in predicting suicidal ideation for males is understandable from their greater variability in mating success. Men are more at risk of dying without children than women are. At the very least, de Catanzaro's results provide for the idea that some suicides are due to a sense of overburdening kin.

Why young people should consider suicide when they are unsuccessful in sex seems paradoxical. True, lack of success in sex is a negative indicator of fitness prospects, but wouldn't theory predict that one should just keep trying? Remember, although suicide may have evolved as a means of furthering the success of our genes under particular circumstances, it does not mean that it operates adaptively in all cases. If people differ in their depression thresholds (as we suggested above), then it's plausible that they differ in how likely they are to become depressed enough to contemplate suicide. Thus some people, including young people, sometimes take a temporary setback as meaning that life is hopeless.

Suicide rates may be exaggerated by a number of novel factors of modern society. The ready availability of guns, drugs, and cars would be expected to increase suicide rate by making it easy to accomplish (de Catanzaro, 1995). Finally, and most importantly, note that even if some suicides have been favored by kin selection, that has no bearing on the hotly debated issue of whether suicide is moral—remember the naturalistic fallacy!

Anxiety Disorders

As we mentioned above, it is adaptive to have a healthy fear about certain situations: about heights, unfamiliar surroundings, venomous creatures, and whether our children our safe. Too little concern about these things and we fall off cliffs, become lost, end up with rattlesnakes in our beds, and death or other mishap befalls our progeny. Some people, however, develop excessive anxiety about certain things: *acrophobia* is fear of heights; *agoraphobia* is fear of being away from home, *obsessive-compulsive disorder* is fear that we have not done some task just right, and so forth.

Interestingly, the things we develop phobias about tend to be things that were genuine dangers in the EEA. As many authors have noted, we easily develop fear of spiders, snakes, fierce creatures, heights, and blood. We do not so easily develop fear of electrical outlets, tobacco smoke, or driving without seat belts—all of which are far greater hazards than spiders. One who reads the experimental

Figure 14–2. *Two fear stimuli.* Which one looks more frightening? We are more afraid of dangerous objects and situations that our ancestors faced in the EEA.

research on phobia might get the impression that snakebite is the leading cause of death in the United States. Of course snake phobia works so well as a model for research on phobia because it taps a fear that was adaptive in the EEA.

Psychologists generally use the term fear to refer to the emotional response to a dangerous situation. The term anxiety is used to refer to a more vague feeling of threat or danger, sometimes when the object of fear is not present, but the two terms are often used interchangeably. Thus we have the related disorder of *generalized anxiety*, which is a sort of free-floating anxiety that is not focused on a specific object or situation.

We suggest two evolutionary reasons for the development of anxiety disorders. First is the mismatch between our current environment and the EEA. As we discussed above, there are kinds and levels of stressors in our society that we were not designed to deal with. Strangers are a major source of stress, as we have discussed. But industrialization brought many dangerous devices and substances that we need to be concerned about. Instead of being able to avoid dangerous things more or less automatically, we must invest conscious effort into avoiding the dangers associated with cars and electricity, for example. This increased vigilance may itself lead to anxiety disorders. And modern communication makes us aware of disasters and epidemics all over the globe, making us think the world is more dangerous than it really is.

Anxiety disorders may also be influenced by genetic reshuffling. If the tendency to be anxious is a polygenic trait, inevitably some individuals will display either a higher or lower than optimal level of the trait. Those at the high extreme would be susceptible to anxiety disorders, in the sense that their anxiety would be triggered too easily. Although we don't usually think of it, this logic would suggest that there are some people who are too low in anxiety (Nesse & Williams, 1994). The person who quits a job in a huff without a ready alternative may have too little anxiety.

Sociopathy

Sociopaths are individuals who share a number of traits: On the positive side, they are superficially charming and sociable; but they are also egocentric, impulsive, and lacking in the emotions of shame, guilt, and remorse. Also known as psychopaths, sociopaths realize they are more cold-hearted and selfish than other people, but this fact does not bother them. Although they make up only about three to four percent of the male population (there are fewer female sociopaths), sociopaths make up a high percentage (approximately 20 percent) of the prison inmates in the United States. Their crimes typically involve deceiving and manipulating other people: fraud, bigamy, and embezzlement (Mealey, 1995).

Sociopathy has a large genetic component. Sociopathy runs in families, and adopted-away children of criminals have a higher than normal likelihood of becoming sociopaths. In addition, sociopaths differ in their physiology. They show much less emotional arousal than normals do to the same stimuli. Consequently they tend to seek out situations that maintain high arousal. They are high on a personality measure known as sensation seeking.

Linda Mealy (1995) has proposed that sociopathy may be the result of frequency-dependent selection, which we discussed in Chapter 3. There we described the alternative mating strategies of certain male flies, who can either hunt their own nuptual gift or pretend to be a female in order to snatch one away from another male. Mealy suggests that sociopaths are the snatchers of the human world. As long as most people play the cooperative strategy there will be a niche for a small number of sociopaths to cheat, taking advantage of others' trust. As we discussed in Chapter 12, the social emotions motivate us to cooperate in situations like the Prisoner's Dilemma. Our tendency to give strangers the benefit of the doubt leaves us open to people who treat social encounters as a one-shot Prisoners Dilemma game, where the best strategy is to cheat.

A person who lacks the emotions of shame, guilt, and remorse can lie and cheat with a straight face, placing him at a competitive advantage to those with normal emotions. As we said in Chapter 6, self-deception can be an aid in deceiving of others. People constantly use a stranger's emotional behavior to judge their trustworthiness. ("I didn't trust him; he had shifty eyes." "Never mind your ID; you have an honest face.") What better means of self-deception than not to feel emotions?

Recently Andrew Colman and Clare Wilson (1997) suggested that the game of Chicken provides a better model of the dynamics of interacting with a sociopath than does the Prisoner's Dilemma. Chicken (also known as Hawk-Dove) is modeled in the same general manner as PD, but with payoffs sufficiently different to change its character. An excellent example is given by the game played by the characters in the famous 1955 movie *Rebel Without a Cause*, starring James Dean. In its typical version two drivers speed toward each other in the same lane. The driver who swerves first is the "chicken"; he loses the contest and the other wins. If both swerve the contest is a draw. Of course, the worst outcome for both happens when neither swerves and they crash. Colman and Wilson's mathematical analysis of the Chicken game predicts a number of features of sociopathy that PD cannot explain. It remains to be seen which analysis more closely matches the behavior of actual sociopaths.

Evolutionary Insights Into Dealing with Sociopaths. Normal people don't commit crimes because the very thought of criminal activity causes negative emotions in them. The mere knowledge that the behavior is wrong is sufficient deterrent to crime in normal people, without the threat of punishment. ("What will people think; I'll never be able to show my face in this town again.") This knowledge by itself does not deter the sociopath, however, because he doesn't have the same emotional reaction. Mealy suggests that it may be possible to deter a sociopath by convincing him of two things: first, that the action will reduce his standing in the community, and second, it is likely to lead to punishment. These two ideas may serve as a cognitive substitute, or prosthesis, for his deficient emotion; they make use of his intact cognitive ability to do a cost-benefit analysis of the contemplated action.

Another suggestion for dealing with sociopaths is to find socially acceptable outlets for their unusual tendencies. As we mentioned above, sociopaths do not completely lack emotions; they have higher thresholds for emotion. Sociopaths require greater risks than normals to produce the same level of thrill. They like bungee jumping, driving too fast, and sky diving. Mealy suggests that sociopaths might be less likely to get into trouble if they could be steered into jobs that provided enough thrills: stunt man, race car driver, or repo man. We say "man" because sociopaths are predominantly males.

As with many evolutionary hypotheses we have discussed in this book, Mealy's ideas are quite new. It will take time to evaluate them and test the predictions she makes. The journal in which she published her article is unusual in that it publishes many comments and reactions from other scientists alongside the main articles. Mealy's article stimulated a large number of comments. Interested readers may turn to the comments on her article for further discussion.

Autism

Autism is a serious disorder that affects about one person in one thousand, and is between two and four times more common in males than females, depending on the exact criteria used to define it (Bryson, 1997). Autistic individuals are markedly impaired in social interaction, particularly involving eye contact and emotional expression. Second, they show delayed or deficient language development, and often use stereotypical and repetitive language. Third, they show repetitive patterns of behavior, such as flapping of hands, and preoccupation with objects. (American Psychiatric Association, 1994). The social deficit is central to the diagnosis of autism; the other deficits may be less severe. Symptoms develop by age 3; hence it is sometimes called infantile autism. Autistic individuals are usually mentally retarded, although some autistic individuals have normal, or even high, intelligence, as we will see shortly.

Other people are an important part of every person's environment, and it is of great advantage to understand how they work. Simon Baron-Cohen (e.g., 1995) suggests that what autistic individuals lack is the ability to read other people's minds—not in the ESP sense, but in the ordinary sense of understanding other's motives, intentions, and feelings, and being able to predict how they will act. Baron-Cohen proposes that there is a module, or set of modules, that have evolved by which ordinary people solve the problems posed by our highly social existence. People who lack the ability to read minds suffer from "mindblindness." One insightful person with autism said that "Other people seem to have a special sense by which they can read other people's thoughts" (Frith et al., 1991, p. 436).

Precisely because most people can read minds effortlessly, the existence of a mind-reading module has gone undetected until now. Normal people interpret the behavior of others in terms of their intentions—their thoughts, beliefs, and desires. We readily understand that if someone opens the fridge it's because they're hungry; or if they ask if you've seen their car keys they're planning to go somewhere.

People have such a deeply programmed tendency to read intentions into actions that they even project intentions onto inanimate objects. We sometimes say that a computer with an automatic spell checker doesn't want us to misspell a word, or that the thermostat tries to keep the house warm. Many years ago, Heider and Simmel (1944, cited by Baron-Cohen, 1995) showed that people who watched a display in which two geometric shapes moved around had a strong tendency to interpret the action in terms like wanting, hesitating, trying, and so forth. Similarly, children often attribute intentions to stuffed animals, clouds, and other inanimate objects.

A clever way to test whether people attribute beliefs to others is to find out if they understand a situation in which someone would hold a belief that is false. This can be studied experimentally. Children watch a doll named Sally place her marble in a basket and then go away (Baron-Cohen et al., 1985). Another doll named Anne then takes the marble out of the basket and puts it into a box. The experimenter asks the child where Sally will look for her marble when she comes back. Normal four-year olds and eleven-year old children with Down's Syndrome had little problem with this test: They recognized that Sally could not have known that Anne had moved the marble. Autistic children (age twelve), however, usually said that Sally would look for the marble where Anne had placed it, indicating that they didn't understand the difference between physical reality and someone else's belief about reality.

Although most autistic individuals are mentally retarded, there is considerable variability. Some autistic people are highly intelligent, even getting advanced degrees and having successful careers. Physician Oliver Sacks describes his investigation of Temple Grandin, who has a Ph.D. and is a university professor, and is autistic. She has great difficulty understanding complex emotions and social situations. Grandin was interviewed by Sacks. "Much of the time," she said, "I feel like an anthropologist on Mars" (Sacks, 1995, p. 259). Grandin knew as a child that she was different:

> Something was going on between the other kids, something swift, subtle, constantly changing . . . a swiftness of understanding so remarkable that sometimes she wondered if they were all telepathic. She is now aware of the existence of these social signals . . . but she . . . cannot perceive them.

Grandin copes by keeping her life simple and studying how people react in given situations.

> [She] found the language of science and technology [to be] a huge relief. It was much clearer, much more explicit, with far less depending on unstated assumptions. (Sacks, 1995, p. 272)

The case of Temple Grandin reinforces Baron-Cohen's view of autism as mind blindness. It also suggests ways of coping with autism, even if we do not know a way to cure it.

We have treated autism so far as a single deficit—as the lack of a mind-reading module. But evidence exists that the mind-reading module is made up of submodules. Moreover, we saw above that autism involves other deficits, and that there are several varieties of autism. For these reasons, Baron-Cohen's theory of autism is not likely to be the complete explanation of autism. The mind-reading approach doesn't explain all features of autism, such as reduced verbal competence. In addition, there are other theories of autism that also propose defective information-processing modules (Rapin, 1997). Nevertheless the theory has generated considerable research that appears to shed useful light on the disorder.

TWO DISORDERS THAT MAY BE SIDE EFFECTS OF GENES WITH FITNESS BENEFITS

Throughout this chapter we have taken each disorder and considered what the causes may be from an evolutionary point of view. Many disorders seem to have more than one likely contributing cause. We deviate from that organization now to consider two disorders that may have a single cause: They may be side effects of genes with fitness benefits.

Remember genes spread if, on average, they enhance fitness. Consider the case of creativity. A gene that enhanced creativity could spread even if it sometimes caused a mental disorder, as long as the benefits of creativity exceeded the costs of the disorder. You shouldn't imagine that creativity would have been of no use to our ancestors. A more creative Stone-Age person might think of a better way to fashion an arrow, find an energy-saving foraging route, or be better at eliciting cooperation from others or outsmarting competitors. Any of these innovations could have had positive effects on fitness. But the very genes that promote creativity may also, perhaps when they occur in certain genetic combinations, have disruptive effects.

For many years popular psychology has held that creativity is often linked with madness. Vincent van Gogh, Edgar Allen Poe, Gustav Mahler, Walt Whitman, and Virginia Woolf are only a few of the mad geniuses that come to mind (Jamison, 1995). But folk psychology is not always wrong, and this is one area where

Figure 14–3. *Vincent van Gogh.* An example of a highly creative person who suffered from psychological problems. This is a self-portrait.

scientific research backs up folk psychology. A substantial literature shows a link between mental disorder and creativity. One study by Nancy Andreasen found that 80 percent of the faculty of the prestigious Iowa Writers' Workshop had suffered either depression or manic depression, compared to 30 percent of a control group (Andreason, 1987). In another study, Arnold Ludwig (1992) considered over 1,000 people whose biographies were reviewed in the *New York Times Book Review.* He found that individuals in the creative arts (e.g., architects, artists, musicians, composers, actors/directors, writers, and poets) had more psychopathology than those in other professions (e.g., athletes, business persons, scientists, military officers, and public officials). Those in creative professions had between two and three times more alcohol problems, drug use, depression, mania, and suicide.

The connection between creativity and psychopathology is not necessarily simple. It is possible, for example, that certain professions tolerate deviance more than others so people with behavior disorders gravitate to them. A person who likes to sleep until noon, wear unironed shirts and doesn't get haircuts wouldn't get very far in banking or the military. Or some professions may be bad for mental health. But examining the behavior patterns of people with mental disorders suggests a causal connection, as we discuss next.

Bipolar Disorder

Also known as manic-depression, bipolar disorder is characterized by severe mood swings. At one time the person may act depressed, but at other times experience euphoria, high-energy levels, boundless enthusiasm, and little need for sleep. A person in the manic phase of bipolar disorder may impulsively break ground for a building project without engaging in the usual planning, or go out and buy new cars for every member of the family. In the depressive phase, bipolars show typical characteristics of depression, often severe. Like all seriously depressed individuals, they are at risk of suicide. Bipolar disorder has a strong genetic component as evidenced by the fact that close relatives of bipolar individuals have an increased risk of the disorder. It is a serious illness that causes much suffering. However, it appears that the condition does promote creativity, although not all bipolar individuals are unusually creative.

Studies of people in the manic phase show that their speech contains three times more rhyming, alliteration, and idiosyncratic words than normals (Jamison, 1995). They are also able to do word-association tasks much faster. These are all characteristics of creativity. Those bipolars who are also creative are most productive during the manic phase. The composer Robert Schumann wrote four times as many musical compositions during two separate years during which he was manic than at other times. He wrote nearly 40 percent of all his compositions in just two manic years out of a twenty-four-year career (Jamison, 1995). If, in the EEA, creativity provided sufficient fitness benefits, it may have been favored despite the fact that it also inflicted some costs in terms of impaired performance during the depressive phases.

Schizophrenia

Schizophrenia is a debilitating disorder that affects about 1 percent of the population. It is characterized by a disintegration of the self. Sufferers hear voices, and experience inappropriate emotions and incoherent thoughts. Contrary to common belief, it has nothing to do with "split personality," which is properly known as multiple personality, and is quite rare. Schizophrenia occurs at about the same rate in all societies, Western and non-Western, industrialized and pastoral, etc. (American Psychiatric Association, 1994). Therefore it is not a disease of civilization, nor is it likely to be an arbitrary social invention. Virtually all scientists agree that it reflects a problem in brain function, and strong evidence from family studies (Gottesman, 1991) suggests that it is inherited.

An evolutionary perspective leads one to ask how such a disorder could arise and be maintained in the population. Because schizophrenia is so debilitating, sufferers have lower reproductive success than the rest of the population. Therefore a gene for schizophrenia cannot be conveying a reproductive advantage in those who have the disorder. At the same time the prevalence of 1 percent of the population is probably too high for the disorder to be maintained in the population by mutation of one or more genes for schizophrenia.

One possibility is that the gene for schizophrenia conveys some advantage on individuals who carry it but do not have the disorder. One way this could work is by hetrozygote superiority (see Chapter 3). In such cases, individuals who have a single copy of the relevant allele have higher fitness than individuals who have two or none. Another possibility is that the gene for schizophrenia is dominant but is only expressed in a minority of cases, for environmental reasons, or because of interactions with other genes. This mechanism is called *incomplete penetrance.*

What could be the advantage of carrying a gene for schizophrenia? Karlsson (1984, 1985, 1988) studied a population of schizophrenics and their relatives in Iceland. He found that first-degree relatives (parents, full siblings, and children) of schizophrenics were about twice as likely to be members of creative professions (professors, poets, authors, as well as honors graduates and members of Who's Who), but not lawyers, engineers or physicians, than the general population. He proposes that individuals with the schizophrenia gene but not the disorder gain an advantage in creativity.

Karlsson believes that schizophrenia is caused by a single dominant gene with incomplete penetrance. The genetics of schizophrenia is not well understood, however. Current evidence suggests that schizophrenia is the result of more than one gene, possibly many (Comings, 1997; Gottesman & McGue, 1991). It appears that Karlsson's hypothesis of a single gene with incomplete penetrance is not likely to be supported. Nevertheless we believe that the idea that one or more genes for schizophrenia convey an advantage on nonsymptomatic carriers helps to understand how the disorder may be maintained in the population.

The idea that nonsymptomatic carriers of a schizophrenia gene or genes benefit is similar to our proposal for bipolar disorder. The difference is that bipolar individuals may themselves reap a reproductive benefit, not just their relatives who presumably carry the same or some of the same genes that cause the disorder.

CAN MALFUNCTION OF A "MIND-READING MODULE" HELP UNDERSTAND SCHIZOPHRENIA?

Christopher Frith and Uta Frith (1991, C. Frith, 1994) suggest that the concept of a mind-reading module may help to understand not only autism, but also schizophrenia. The symptoms of schizophrenia are grouped into positive and negative symptoms. Positive symptoms are things a schizophrenic person has that normal people do not have: hallucinations, disorganized thoughts, paranoid delusions, and so forth. Negative symptoms describe areas where schizophrenics lack normal function: poverty of speech, blunted affect, loss of volition, and social withdrawal (Comer, 1999). Frith and Frith note that the negative symptoms of schizophrenia parallel those of autism, and suggest that both disorders reflect a problem with the mind-reading module.

We must be clear that they are not saying that autism and schizophrenia are the same disorder. Autistics and schizophrenics share only the negative symptoms, not the positive ones. Autism develops in infancy, whereas schizophrenia develops later, generally in early adulthood. Frith and Frith suggest that, unlike autistics, schizophrenics had a relatively normal mind-reading module in their youth. So, even when this module begins to malfunction, schizophrenics know that people have their own thoughts and feelings, but are unable to interpret them correctly. According to this view, their difficulty in reading minds, including their own, causes problems in social interaction and communication. They interpret their own thoughts as those of others, and so have hallucinations. They are not able to understand other people's actions and so become paranoid. Or they may simply not make any interpretations. Thus they have both positive symptoms and negative symptoms. Autistic individuals, on the other hand, grew up without the mind-reading module, and so do not attempt to make such interpretations. Thus they show only negative symptoms.

Frith and Frith's proposal is intriguing but has not yet generated much research. A number of findings, however, are consistent with the hypothesis. When schizophrenics are asked to comment on pictures of people displaying various emotions they described only physical characteristics instead of mental states, including affect (Pilowsky and Bassett, 1980). This supports the hypothesis that they do not understand the interior mental state of other people.

Another experiment tested the hypothesis that schizophrenics have difficulty telling whether an action is their own (Frith and Done, 1989). Schizophrenics and normals played a video game that required subjects to shoot a target. The circumstances of the game required them to shoot different directions according to a demanding set of rules. Thus all subjects made many errors. Normal subjects generally corrected their errors when they occurred; those schizophrenics who experienced alien control of their actions, however, seldom did. We believe that the hypothesis that schizophrenics have a malfunctioning mind-reading module has considerable promise in guiding future research on schizophrenia.

SUMMARY

1. The Diagnostic and Statistical Manual of Mental Disorders (DSM-IV) adopts a nontheoretical approach to classification.
2. Evolutionary considerations suggest behavior disorders will be explicable in one of six different ways. They may be:
   a. defenses
   b. side effects of genes with fitness benefits
   c. the consequence of frequency-dependent selection
   d. the result of a mismatch between contemporary environments and the EEA
   e. the consequence of a defective mental module
   f. the extremes of the distribution of a polygenic trait
3. Some mental disorders may have more than one cause.
4. Post-traumatic stress disorder (PTSD) is more likely to result from man-made, rather than natural, disasters.
5. Depression may be nature's way of telling us we are barking up the wrong tree.
6. As expected for polygenic traits, susceptibility to depression shows considerable variation.
7. Suicide might increase inclusive fitness when resources spent keeping a person alive could better be spent on relatives.
8. The kinds of common anxiety disorders relate to situations that were dangerous in the EEA.
9. Sociopathy may be the result of frequency-dependent selection for people who cheat on social contracts.
10. Autism is proposed to result from the lack of ability to understand other people's motives and intentions.
11. Bipolar disorder and schizophrenia may reflect side effects of genes with fitness benefits.
12. Some bipolar individuals are more creative and productive in the manic phase.
13. First-degree relatives of schizophrenics are more likely than average to be in creative professions.
14. Schizophrenics may have a malfunctioning mind-reading module, which causes difficulty in interpreting the intentions of self and others.

15 Social Behavior

In contemporary society we often interact with strangers: the check-out clerk in the grocery store, the bus driver, the customer or client you serve once, the people you nod to on the sidewalk. Although these interactions are frequent, they are brief and relatively unimportant to us in the sense that they make no lasting difference in our lives. Think of the social situations in your own life that involve strangers. How much do they matter to you? In contrast, most of our significant interactions—the ones that affect our well being—are with friends and relatives. In general, the more important the interaction is to us, the more likely it is to involve our friends or relatives. Yet social psychology, as it is conventionally studied, focuses to a large degree on interactions among strangers. This is a bizarre state of affairs. Why focus so much attention on such trivial matters?

In this chapter, we will stress the importance of thinking about social behavior from an evolutionary viewpoint. What kinds of selection pressures favor living in groups? How are the social groups of other animals organized? What are the societies of contemporary human foragers like? Why are friends and relatives so important to us?

WHY BE SOCIAL?

Sociality refers to the tendency for an animal to associate with other members of its species. Most people, including most traditional psychologists, take sociality for granted. It's a fact of life as ubiquitous and therefore as easy to overlook as the air we breathe. But like air, its withdrawal is panic-inducing. Solitary confinement is one of the worst kinds of punishment. Why are humans so intensely social? Why do we crave the company of our fellows?

The most valuable source of insight into this question comes from the comparative study of other species. Surprising as it might be to a committedly social animal like a human, many other species are characterized by solitary habits. Like gills and eyes and other adaptations, sociality has a particular distribution across the animal kingdom. Animals are social if, given their ecology, it pays them to be social. And conversely, if the costs of sociality outweigh the benefits then they will evolve solitary habits. Here it is important to remember that selection is not very efficient at crafting adaptations at the level of the group (see Box 4–2). So ordinarily, the evolution of social or solitary life ways depends on the balance of costs and benefits *to individuals,* not to the group as a whole.

Costs and Benefits of Sociality

One of the principal costs of sociality is increased competition. Animals that avoid their fellows never have valuable resources, such as a nutritious food item, snatched away by a companion. In addition, groups tend to be more conspicuous to predators than solitary animals. Obviously, attracting the attention of predators is not a good way to increase your reproductive success. On the other hand, each of these issues has a positive side too. Groups are often better at finding resources and at defending them than are solitary animals. And similarly, the members of a group may be less vulnerable to predators because there are many sets of eyes and ears to provide an early warning, and because the collective action of group members can be effective in repelling at least some kinds of predators.

> **Trail Marker:** Selection favors social habits if the benefits of associating with others outweigh the costs.

How do these costs and benefits weigh out? Obviously, for solitary species the costs must predominate, whereas for social ones the benefits must. As is the case for all adaptations, what works best depends on the circumstances. Some species may have many predators; others may have few. Some may have predators that can be repelled if enough individuals join together. But, no thank you, I don't want to try scaring off a pride of hungry lions whether I have companions or not. One key factor affecting the number of potential predators is size: small-bodied species have more predators than large-bodied ones. Consider the case of the only Asian great ape, the orangutan (*Pongo pygmaeus*). Virtually all monkeys and apes are social but orangs are solitary. First note that orangs are quite large, females and males weighing approximately 37 and 69 kilogram (81 and 152 pounds), respectively. In addition, orangs spend almost all of their lives high in the crowns of large rain forest trees. The combination of large size and arboreal habits makes them all but invulnerable to predators. These facts largely eliminate any anti-predator benefit they might gain from being social.

Trail Marker: Given their circumstances, some animals—such as orangutans—don't benefit by being social.

The effects of sociality on competition for resources can also vary from one circumstance to another. For some species, sharing food may be especially costly, but others may suffer little when they feed as a group. Sometimes food may be easy to find, but in other circumstances it might help to forage with associates who share knowledge about where the best current feeding sites are. *Patch size* is a key determinant of whether sociality helps or hurts feeding efficiency. Patch size refers to how food is distributed. It is not an absolute concept but one that must be measured relative to the nutritional needs of the consumer. Is a grasshopper a large patch of food or a small one? For a monkey it's a small patch, and hence one the monkey would rather not share. If two monkeys are foraging together and both see a grasshopper, only one of them is going to get it. The other monkey lost a resource it could have had if it had been foraging alone. On the other hand, to a tiny mite living under the wings of a grasshopper, the grasshopper is a large patch, and it loses very little if other mites join it. Let's return to the scale of the monkey's world—the tropical forest—and contemplate a fruiting tree as a resource patch.

Trail Marker: Sociality would be costly for animals whose food comes in small, scattered patches.

Temperate and tropical forests are very different. Temperate forest tend to have just a few tree species. These temperate trees often grow in pure or nearly pure stands, rather than mixed together with other species. And finally, temperate trees tend to all flower and fruit on the same cycle, keyed to the strongly seasonal patterns of spring, summer and autumn. In contrast, in tropical forests there are many hundreds of tree species, and their fruiting cycles are less coordinated. Moreover these species do not generally grow in pure stands but mix together in a complex tapestry. For a monkey, living in this tropical forest, what kind of patch is a single fruiting tree?

The tree presumably has many more fruits on it than a single monkey can eat before they rot. For this reason, the monkey may suffer only slight competition if other monkeys feed in the same tree. But because there are so many different species of trees, each with its unique fruiting cycle, fruiting trees may be few and far between—and hence difficult to find. This is an example of the kind of resource distribution that favors sociality: large patches scattered unpredictably over the habitat. Their distribution makes associates helpful in locating them, and their size reduces the cost of sharing them once found.

> **Trail Marker:** Animals whose food comes in large shareable
> patches often benefit by being social.

Of course there are other factors that can select for or against social tendencies. Some predators such as lions, hyenas, and wolves hunt socially because they can capture more or larger prey when they collaborate. Sometimes animals are social because they are attracted to a common resource but the resource is not food. For example, some open-country baboons congregate each night at sleeping cliffs where they are relatively safe from predators. Animals may group because it helps them deal with physical forces in the environment. Examples would include animals huddling together against the cold, or birds flying in formation to reduce aerodynamic drag. On the other hand, contagious diseases can select against sociality. The essential point is that, where it occurs, sociality is an evolved adaptation adjusted to the threats and opportunities posed by the animal's environment.

Selection Pressures Favoring Human Sociality

Some questions may have to wait for the invention of a time machine to be answered confidently. The selection pressures that led to the evolution of sociality in humans are shrouded in the past, and subject to considerable debate. Nevertheless, it's reasonable to explore some of the possibilities. Probably the oldest and most frequently discussed idea is that our ancestors inhabited more open, less forested country than do the other great apes—chimpanzees, gorillas, and orangutans. (These habitat reconstructions are based on analysis of the plant and animal remains associated with fossils of probable human ancestors such as *Australopithecus.*) Thus our ancestors, unlike the majority of primates, would have spent considerable time on the ground, a fact that would certainly have increased their exposure to predators. In line with this idea, all modern species of primate that live in open country are social.

In addition, unlike forests, open habitats typically contain herds of grazing animals. These herds represent a major potential food resource. Thus, a dietary shift towards more dependence on meat may have been one of the ecological factors that first separated our ancestors from the rest of the apes. Those who argue for this scenario point out that cooperating social hunters would have been more successful than solitary ones. This argument is only partially supported by comparative evidence: most modern savanna-dwelling carnivores are social, but some—for example, the cheetah—are solitary. Moreover, not all anthropologists agree that our ancestors were especially carnivorous.

Our closest living relatives, the African great apes, are social. Is that because all "advanced" primates are social? No; this idea is both theoretically and factually flawed. First, the theory: "Advanced" is a meaningless concept to the modern evolutionist. As we saw in Chapter 1, organisms are not really arranged in a ladder of complexity and sophistication. Traits are not slowly accumulated and then automatically retained in all descendant creatures. Instead traits are added, subtracted, modified, reinvented and reconfigured, depending on the suite of selection pressures shaping each species. Second, the facts: Remember that our Asian relative, the orangutan, is solitary. Each kind of organism is well adapted to its environment; it is not merely a collage of traits forming a neat bridge among its close relatives.

Nevertheless, with some caution (because the selection pressures might not be the same ones that operated on our ancestors) we might ask, why are the African apes—chimpanzees and gorillas—social? This turns out to be an interesting problem. Neither chimps nor gorillas are subject to much predation, so predator defense is an unlikely reason. What about the benefits of help in finding scattered but rich food patches?

Gorillas primarily eat leaf material. Thus, as forest-living animals they confront an essentially continuous rather than patchy food resource; they do not need associates to help them find food since leaves are so abundant. On the other hand, based on the low rates of aggression seen during foraging, feeding competition seems to be slight. In other words, for foraging gorillas, there seems to be little cost of associating with others but little benefit as well (Stewart and Harcourt, 1987).

Chimps eat fruits and leaves with the former predominating. For a large animal like a chimp (chimps are much larger than monkeys), a fruiting tree is not a very big patch. This is thought to produce significant feeding competition and to favor the chimps' peculiar type of sociality (Wrangham, 1986). Chimps live in "communities" within which all the resident animals know each other. But the whole community does not forage as a unit. In fact, the foraging parties are small, just a few animals, and party size seems to vary with the size of the patch being exploited at the moment (Wrangham, 1977).

Gorillas never hunt, but male chimps occasionally do, concentrating their efforts on other primates (e.g., monkeys) and small antelope. Male chimps do hunt cooperatively so this activity might constitute a selection pressure favoring their sociality. However, they derive well under one percent of their diet in this way, amounting to about 10 grams (one-third of an ounce) of meat per chimp per day (Hladik, 1977).

In summary then, none of the standard reasons for sociality seem to apply forcefully to either of the African apes. Currently, the predominant view is that both chimps and gorillas are social as a defense against the threats posed by other members of their own species (Wrangham, 1986). In particular, female gorillas are at risk of having their infants killed by males who did not father those infants (see the discussion of child abuse and infanticide in Chapter 12). This leads females to cluster around powerful males capable of providing protection, and explains why gorilla groups invariably include more adult females than adult males—females have more to gain by sociality than males do. In chimps, the hostilities are between communities. Here males invade neighboring communities and kill the offspring of unfamiliar females, that is, females with whom they have not mated. In addition, when they have a sufficient numerical advantage, males sometimes also kill adult males in neighboring communities (Goodall et al., 1979; Nishida et al., 1985). These kinds of risks apparently favor sociality even though associating with other chimps decreases foraging efficiency.

> **Trail marker:** The African apes are social primarily as a defense against their fellows.

Returning to the case of our ancestors, we can see there is a wide range of possible selection pressures for sociality. First, as inhabitants of open country, our ancestors were probably more at risk of predation than are the forest-dwelling apes. Second, our hominid ancestors may have eaten more animal prey than modern apes and thus gotten benefits by hunting these prey in groups. Third, regardless of the importance of meat eating, the other foods of hominids might have occurred in scattered but rich patches that were difficult to locate but readily shareable once found. Finally, hostilities among neighbors may have favored those hominids who preferred to travel in the relative safety of companions. None of these ideas are mutually exclusive: it's even possible that all of these pressures acted simultaneously.

SOCIAL LIFE IN THE EEA

Whatever pressures were at work, we can be certain that our ancestors' social lives differed from our own in a number of respects. Anthropologists often turn to contemporary foragers, that is, hunting-and-gathering peoples, as a source of insight about life in the EEA. Although the hunter-gatherers studied by anthropologists are fully modern people, they do resemble our ancestors in one key respect: They must forage for their food—both game and plants—and so face essentially the same ecological constraints as our ancestors did. Their lack of cultivated crops and domesticated animals places very low limits on the sizes of their communities. Thus contemporary foragers live in small semi-nomadic bands that range in size from 10 to 30 people. Membership in these bands is fluid, with individuals and families free to shift from one band to another if opportunities seem better elsewhere. The collection of local bands adds up to a small community of a just few hundred people, all of whom typically know each other. After the age of puberty in a foraging society you'll probably never meet a stranger, except for the rare inquisitive anthropologist! Not only are these small communities where everyone knows everyone else, but the network of kinship is dense. A large proportion of a person's acquaintances would be genetically related to her.

> In all societies the means by which interpersonal dealings are patterned are statuses of various kinds . . . but in hunting-gathering societies these statuses are nearly exclusively familistic—that is, they are kinship statuses. Hunting-gathering societies are all alike in that their social organization is formed in terms of kinship . . ." (Service, 1979: 34).

Thus, the essential features of social life among contemporary foragers, and presumably among our ancestors as well, were small populations, composed of individuals who all knew each other and who were united by bonds of closer and more distant kinship. Biological kinship and familiarity are critically important from an evolutionary perspective because they form the two possible bases for altruism: kin selection and reciprocity (see Chapter 4). The roles of kinship and familiarity in human society will be discussed in turn, and then we will discuss a factor that overlays them both, social status.

THE ROLE OF KINSHIP IN HUMAN SOCIAL BEHAVIOR

> The social behavior of a species evolves in such a way that in each distinct behavior-evoking situation the individual will seem to value his neighbors' fitness against his own according to the coefficients of relationship appropriate to that situation" (Hamilton, 1964b, p. 19).

With these words the originator of kin selection theory suggests the pervasive influence of genetic relatedness on social interactions. Genes can spread by helping their immediate bearer reproduce, through increasing her fitness. But they can also spread by inducing altruism aimed at other bearers of the same genes (see Chapter 4). Hamilton's kin selection theory has been tested in literally hundreds of different species, and the vast bulk of the data supports it. Kin selection is as close to a "fact" as we get in science. On that basis it would seem appropriate to examine the effects of genetic relatedness on human social behavior. But, strangely, social psychology has all but ignored the implications of Hamilton's work. The influences of parents and siblings are often mentioned in the context of developmental psychology. But based on the existing literature, one might form the impression that humans hatch out of test tubes and have no kin connections with any other individuals. This is a remarkable oversight, not only because of the success of kin selection theory in explaining so many features of animal society, but also because kinship is obviously and fundamentally important in shaping people's interactions, not just among foragers, but in all kinds of societies.

> **Trail Marker:** Traditional human societies are organized around kinship.

Kinship and Association

For example, group membership itself often follows along lines of kinship. The Yanomamo are horticulturalists who hunt wild animals and also farm small plots they clear from the South American rainforest. Because they farm, their villages are typically larger than the bands of foragers, ranging in size from about forty up to two hundred people. Even in these settlements relatedness is high. The thirteen Yanomamo villages studied by Chagnon (1979) averaged 102 residents. Within these settlements the average person was genetically related to 79 percent (nearly four out of five) of his or her fellow villagers. And each of those relatives shared, on average, almost 12 percent of their genes—in other words, they were as related as first cousins are.

These baseline facts are informative in themselves, but the underlying dynamics are even more intriguing. As a village grows the average relatedness among residents decreases. Tensions and fights increase in parallel. Eventually these become so disruptive that the village fissions into two. This fissioning always occurs along lines of relatedness, close relatives remaining together, with the result that relatedness is higher in each of the two new villages than it was in the larger prefissioning settlement. The same patterns seem to hold for a wide range of voluntary associations. For example, Hurd (1983) observed the acrimonious fissioning of an Amish church congregation in Pennsylvania. Genetic relatedness was higher within each of the two new churches than it was in the old one.

Kinship and Cooperation

Kinship shapes not only whom we choose as neighbors and associates but how we behave toward them. Kin are more likely to help each other than are non-kin. Data from three other groups of horticulturalists, K'ekchi' Maya, Ye'kwana, and Binumarien, indicate that people are more likely to aid their kin in clearing land, planting, and harvesting (Berte, 1988; Hames, 1987; Hawkes, 1983), and that this help makes an important difference in terms of food production. For example, among the K'ekchi' those who aided another head-of-household in planting were likely to be genetically related to the person they aided. Men who shared more genes with other members of the labor pool were able to recruit significantly more individuals to help them. And those who recruited more helpers were able to keep more acres in production (Berte, 1988). Likewise, Hames (1987) found that among the Ye'kwana in southern Venezuela, people give more aid to households where they have close relatives. Many other kinds of benefits are also aimed selectively at relatives. For example, food seems to be systematically shared with kin in both foraging and food-producing societies (Betzig and Turke, 1986; Betzig, 1988; Kaplan and Hill, 1985).

In modern industrialized societies, we often live far from our kin and we interact a great deal with nonrelatives. But even in these contexts kin seem to be a highly reliable source of aid. Susan Essock-Vitale and Michael McGuire (1985) used in-depth interviews to study the help given and received by a random sample of three hundred Los Angeles women. In this sample, genetically close relatives were more likely to help than more distant ones, and, the greater the amount of help, the more likely it was to come from kin.

> **Trail Marker:** In both traditional and industrialized societies, people systematically help their kin.

Remember Hamilton's Rule (Chapter 4): Altruism is favored whenever rb > c. This not only suggests that altruism should be more likely between close relatives. It makes two additional predictions about the circumstances that favor altruism: when the recipient can translate the aid into a large fitness benefit, and when the altruist can give aid with minimal effects on her own fitness. Thus in this Los Angeles sample, more help was given to individuals with high reproductive potential, for example young adults, where it presumably would yield a higher fitness benefit. And more help was given by women who were childless, for example, to their nieces and nephews. This too fits the theory since people without children are not inflicting costs on their own offspring when they channel resources to other relatives.

Adoption represents a very large commitment of help. There can be a variety of reasons for adoption (see Box 10–2), but given the potential costs in time, money and other resources, it would be surprising if adoptions did not show a strong kin bias. Joan Silk (1980) has studied adoption practices in Oceania, where adoption is common. There, at least, the evidence is very clear. In Silk's data set there were 146 adoptions for which the relationship between the adopter and adoptee could not be determined; these provide no relevant evidence and are thus ignored in Table 15–1. Of the remaining 1613 adoptions, 1517 (94 percent) were by relatives. And these adoptions are concentrated among the closest relatives, for example, where r = 0.25. The only exception concerns full siblings; of course people are ordinarily not in a position to adopt their brother or sister because they are too close in age.

Kinship and Aggression

The theory of kin selection not only predicts increased altruism toward genetic relatives, it also predicts decreased selfishness among kin. Homicide is the most extreme and selfish form of conflict resolution. Martin Daly and Margo Wilson (1988) were the first psychologists to realize that our tactics of conflict resolution should have been shaped by selection. In a groundbreaking book they tested a wide range of evolutionary predictions about the situational factors that make

Table 15–1.   Distribution of Adoption by Closeness of Genetic Relationship in 11 Societies in Oceania.*

r	EXAMPLE	FREQUENCY (n)	FREQUENCY (%)	CUMULATIVE FREQUENCY (%)
0.50	brother	4	0.2	0.2
0.25	niece	1041	64.5	64.8
0.125	cousin	140	8.7	73.5
0.0625	second cousin	161	10.0	83.4
0.0313	third cousin	29	1.8	85.2
<.0313		18	1.1	86.4
relatives		124	7.7	94.0
nonrelatives		96	6.0	100.0

*Data from Silk (1980). "Relatives" refers to an adoption by kin where the precise genealogical relationship was not specified. "Nonrelatives" includes all the cases where the adopter and adoptee were known to be unrelated.

homicide more or less likely. For our present purposes the question is, does genetic kinship reduce lethal violence?

One complication in answering this question is that killing requires access. For any homicide, there was some pool of potential victims available to the killer. The pool includes both blood relatives and non-relatives. If relatives compose 5 percent of the victim pool we would expect 5 percent of the real-world victims to be relatives *unless being a relative affects the chance of being killed.* Unfortunately, it's virtually impossible to define the actual victim pool for most real homicides. Daly and Wilson's (1988) clever solution was to examine domestic homicides, where one member of a household killed another. Their data base included all solved homicides in Detroit for the year 1972, when there were ninety eight domestic homicides. Using 1970 census data for Detroit, Daly and Wilson were able to determine the average household composition. The question then becomes, were relatives the victims of domestic homicide less often than we would expect on the basis of their prevalence in Detroit households? You might think that households consist exclusively of relatives, but this is not so. For example, spouses are not blood relatives; thus kin selection is not expected to influence the level of violence among spouses.

Daly and Wilson found that in 1970 (the nearest census year available) the average Detroit resident, age fourteen years or older, lived with 3.0 other persons. Age fourteen was used as a cut-off because fewer than 1 percent of the homicides in Detroit were committed by people under fourteen, but 12 percent were committed by older teenagers. Table 15–2 shows the composition of the average household. For example, the average potential homicide offender lived with 0.6 spouses. Of course no one has 0.6 of a spouse; this means that 60 percent of Detroiters over fourteen lived with a spouse. How many domestic homicides would have been spousal homicides if homicide was randomly distributed within households? This number is easy to calculate, given the mean number of coresidents (3.0) and the total number of domestic homicides (98). Spouses constituted $(0.6/3.0) = 20$ percent of the coresidents of the

Table 15–2. An analysis of homicide risk to kin and non-kin (based on Daly and Wilson, 1988, Table 2.1).

	NUMBER OF COHABITANTS	PERCENT OF COHABITANTS	EXPECTED HOMICIDES	ACTUAL HOMICIDES	RELATIVE RISK
	A	B = (A/3.0)	C = (B×98)	D	E = (D/C)
NON-KIN					
spouses	0.60	20	19.60	65.00	3.32
other non-kin	0.10	3	3.27	11.00	3.37
Total non-kin	0.70	23	22.87	76.00	3.32
KIN					
"offspring"	0.90	30	29.40	8.00	0.27
"parents"	0.40	13	13.07	9.00	0.69
"other kin"	1.00	33	32.67	5.00	0.15
Total "kin"	2.30	77	75.13	22.00	0.29
Grand Total	3.00	100	98.00	98.00	

average Detroiter. Thus, on a chance basis, 20 percent of the 98 domestic homicide victims, or 19.6 victims would have been spouses. In fact, 65 of the 98 domestic homicide victims were spouses. Now we can compute the relative risk to spouses. This is simply the number of actual homicides divided by the number of homicides expected on the basis of chance. For spouses the relative risk is $(65/19.6) = 3.32$, meaning that spouses were killed more than three times as often as we would expect, based on how many spouses there are in the average household.

If we perform similar calculations for each category of coresident a clear pattern emerges. Each type of nonrelative is killed more often than expected by chance. And each type of blood relative is killed less often than expected by chance. Finally, we can compare the relative risks to kin and non-kin. Grouping together all non-kin we see that they have a relative risk of 3.32; again, they are killed more than three times as often as expected. Doing the same calculation for kin yields a relative risk of 0.29; kin are killed less than one third as often as expected. Dividing $(3.32/0.29) = 11.35$; in other words, coresident non-kin are at eleven times greater risk of domestic homicide than coresident kin. Daly and Wilson (1988) point out even this eleven-fold difference still underestimates the differential risk to kin and non-kin. This is because some of the supposed kin in Table 15–2 are not actually genetically related, hence our use of quotation marks.

> Now, as it happens, the eight victims who were "offspring" of their killers include two 5-year-old children killed by stepfathers, as well as two infants whose beating deaths were charged solely against their mothers even though a stepfather was present . . . The effect of these cases is to exaggerate the risk to "offspring" of the killer. Similarly, both the "parent" and "other relative" categories include homicide victims who were not in fact blood kin of their killer, but were instead relatives by marriage . . . (Daly and Wilson, 1988:23).

In other words, people seem to be *much* less inclined to use extreme violence against individuals with whom they share genes. In contrast, being linked by a social category, such as stepchild or brother-in-law or even spouse, may do little to reduce violent conflict.

Trail Marker: Biological kinship seems to inhibit lethal violence.

These findings are dramatic but they are by no means limited in time or space; Detroit does not seem to be in any way special. Based on historical accounts spanning the ninth to the thirteenth centuries, Vikings in Scotland and Iceland were much more likely to murder nonrelatives than relatives, and their willingness to murder relatives increased with the potential fitness gain. Moreover they were more likely to avenge the murder of a relative, and they were more likely to form aggressive or vengeful alliances with kin than with non-kin (Dunbar et al., 1995). Similar data from the Norse Earldoms, Icelandic families and the English royalty were reviewed by Steven and Ronald Johnson. They concluded:

All three sets of data show that close biological kin were more likely to support one another and less likely to be in conflict with one another and, when conflict did occur, were less prone to kill one another than were more distant biological relatives. (Johnson and Johnson, 1991, p. 218).

More fine-grained analyses of conflict are also informative. In 1971, anthropological filmmaker Tim Asch's cameras happened to be rolling when conflict erupted in one of the Yanomamo villages where Napoleon Chagnon was conducting research. The conflict escalated from mere insults to blows with clubs, machetes, and axes, with serious injuries being inflicted. Each side attracted a dozen or more fighters as individuals joined in to support one or another of the combatants. Chagnon and his student Paul Bugos (1979) wondered whether kinship would explain people's willingness to either attack or support each other. Drawing on his extensive genealogical records of the Yanomamo, he computed the coefficients of relationship among the two groups of combatants. He found that each group of fighters was much more closely related among themselves than they were to members of the opposing group. In addition, both groups were more closely related among themselves than they were to bystanders who did not join the fight and support them.

Kinship's Effect on Attitudes and Inclinations

All of the data presented so far are anthropological rather than psychological. They focus on what people in both traditional and modern societies do. But social psychologists often try to assess the underlying attitudes and inclinations that shape social behavior. As mentioned above, very few social psychologists have taken an interest in kinship, but Eugene Burnstein and his colleagues have explicitly tried to test a range of predictions from kin selection theory (Burnstein et al., 1994). These authors asked Japanese and American undergraduates to imagine themselves in a series of hypothetical situations. In each situation there are several individuals who need help but there is only time to help one of them. The students were simply asked to say which individual they would help. Some of the scenarios portrayed dire circumstances where those who did not receive help would perish, and some were as commonplace as running an errand for someone. Those needing help were portrayed as belonging to various categories of relatives or acquaintances.

Many of the results of this study conform closely to the predictions of kin selection theory. For example, comparing across kin and non-kin categories, the tendency to help strongly paralleled the coefficient of relatedness: the students said they would be more likely to help relatives than non-relatives and they would be progressively more likely to help closer relatives. The same pattern was observed for both everyday favors and life-and-death emergencies, but the curve was steeper for emergencies (Figure 15–1). This suggests two conclusions, both of which are coincident with the theory of kin selection: 1) kinship is a dominant factor in helping decisions, and 2) kinship exerts a stronger influence in the most critical situations, i.e., where the fitness consequences are large.

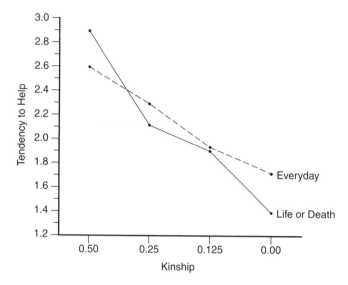

Figure 15–1. *Tendency to help nearer and more distant kin under everyday versus life-and-death conditions.* ("Some Neo-Darwinism Decision Rules for Altruism: Weighing Cues for Inclusive Fitness as a Function of the Biological Importance of the Decision" by E. Burnstein, C. Crandall, and S. Kitayama in *Journal of Personality and Social Psychology,* (1994), 67. Copyright © 1994 by American Psychological Association. Reprinted by permission of American Psychological Association, Washington, DC.)

Trail Marker: People are more inclined to help kin than non-kin and more inclined to do so when the benefit is large.

In some of the scenarios, participants were asked to imagine that they lived in a country where disease and famine were widespread, where infant mortality was high and average life-spans were short. For these scenarios the people in need were portrayed as being equally related but of different ages. For example, one might be asked to choose between helping a ten-year-old nephew (r = .25) and a 75-year-old grandfather (r = .25). In these cases, presented in Figure 15–2, students reported being less willing to help both older and younger individuals. This pattern of helping roughly parallels what evolutionists call the *reproductive value curve.* The reproductive value curve represents the age-specific expectation of future offspring. Of course reproductive value is low in older people because they are unlikely to successfully reproduce. But, it is also low in very young individuals because they may not survive to reproductive age. Reproductive value reaches a peak at sexual maturity. The distribution of helping in Figure 15–2, closely matches the likelihood that the helped individual will go on to reproduce, assuming the kind of high infant mortality that would have prevailed in the EEA. In responding to scenarios that did not stress famine, disease and high infant mortality, students showed no tendency to withhold help from very young relatives.

Parallel results were obtained by Lewis Petrinovich and his associates (Petrinovich et al., 1993). They studied what they call "moral intuitions" by posing a series of hypothetical dilemmas. Subjects were asked to imagine particular life-and-death situations where they could save one or more lives, but to do so they would have to cause one or more deaths. For example, a trolley's brakes have failed, and

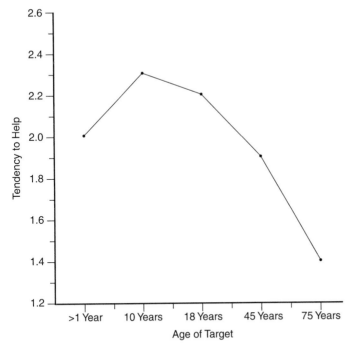

Figure 15–2. *Tendency to help different classes of relatives as a function of age and mortality regime.* ("Some Neo-Darwinism Decision Rules for Altruism: Weighing Cues for Inclusive Fitness as a Function of the Biological Importance of the Decision" by E. Burnstein, C. Crandall, and S. Kitayama in *Journal of Personality and Social Psychology,* (1994), 67. Copyright © 1994 by American Psychological Association. Reprinted by permission of American Psychological Association, Washington, DC.)

it is careening out of control down the track. There is a branch in the track as well as a switch that can cause the trolley to go either to the right or left. There are five innocent strangers on the left branch who will be killed if you take no action. Your brother is on the right branch, and he will be killed if you throw the switch to save the strangers. Their study evaluated a number of factors in addition to kinship such as political philosophy, elite social status, endangered species status, and so on. For the present discussion the key point is that closeness of biological kinship was an important determinant of whom people chose to save.

In a very recent experiment, O'Neill and Petrinovich (in preparation) tried to calibrate the relative value people place on kin versus strangers. Again in the context of the brakeless-trolley problem, their subjects were faced with saving either a kinsperson (on some trials this was a brother, on others it was a cousin) or some number of strangers (varying over trials from one to fifteen). No fewer than 70 percent of their subjects chose to save the brother, even when fifteen strangers had to be sacrificed to do so. And at least 60 percent chose to save the cousin despite the required sacrifice of up to fifteen strangers. Clearly we value our kin very highly.

Kinship and Stress

The benefits of close and regular contact with kin have other less obvious but far-reaching effects. Mark Flinn and Barry England (1995) have examined levels of the hormone *cortisol* in children growing up in a rural village on the Caribbean

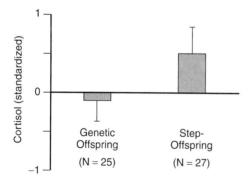

Figure 15–3. *Children who live with a stepparent have higher cortisol levels.* (From "Childhood Stress and Family Environment" by M. Flinn and B. England in *Current Anthropology,* (1995), 36. Copyright © 1995 by The University of Chicago Press. Reprinted by permission of the University of Chicago Press.)

island of Dominica. As background you should know that various kinds of psychological stress elevate cortisol. Cortisol in turn helps the body deal with those stresses. But increased cortisol levels also have harmful effects, including suppression of the immune system (the body's primary defense against infection of all kinds), inhibited growth, cognitive impairment and psychological maladjustment.

> **Trail Marker:** Living with non-kin has measurable physiological and health consequences.

Flinn and England were interested in the effects of children's domestic situation on their cortisol levels, and what they found was quite dramatic. Children who lived with a stepparent had significantly elevated cortisol levels compared to children living with their genetic parents (Figure 15–3). And the expected negative consequences follow: Children with elevated cortisol levels have higher rates of illness (Figure 15–4).

All these studies suggest that we are designed to interact with kin. We interact with kin differently than we do with non-kin, being more altruistic with the former and more selfish with the latter. Interacting with non-kin is a source of strife and

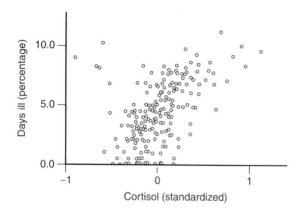

Figure 15–4. *Children who have higher cortisol levels have higher rates of illness.* (From "Childhood Stress and Family Environment" by M. Flinn and B. England in *Current Anthropology,* (1995), 36. Copyright © 1995 by The University of Chicago Press. Reprinted by permission of the University of Chicago Press.)

stress. Put another way, a variety of lines of evidence suggest that our helping algorithms are designed to be facultatively dependent on r, b, and c, in the way that Hamilton's rule predicts.

THE ROLE OF RECIPROCITY IN HUMAN SOCIAL BEHAVIOR

As you learned in Chapter 4, reciprocity is an alternative pathway to adaptive altruism. Based on the model of reciprocal altruism, organisms are expected to behave altruistically towards other altruists and to withhold altruism from cheaters. We also saw the success of the reciprocal "tit-for-tat" strategy in the iterated prisoner's dilemma game. Do these theoretical approaches accord well with the findings of social psychology?

Here's an experiment (Yinon and Dovrat, 1987) that explores several of the key variables in Trivers's theory: cost, benefit, and the requestor's potential to offer valuable help in return. The research design involves a "wrong-number technique" and a direct request for help. The experimenter dials a telephone number similar to his own but with one or more digits changed randomly. When someone answers he says that he has dialed incorrectly, that he has no more money to make another call, and that he must get a message to his wife. He tells a brief (fictitious) story about himself and the present crisis and then asks the person he has dialed to call his wife and relay the critical message.

In this experiment cost, benefit and reciprocity potential were varied systematically. For example, the cost was varied by keeping the wife's phone line busy for either thirty or sixty minutes. Benefit and reciprocity potential were varied by alterations of the story. For example, some versions depicted the situation as more urgent. Reciprocity potential was varied in terms of the fictitious profession or job the experimenter claimed in the story.

All three theoretically important variables had the predicted impact on the percentage of people who helped (Table 15–3). Other things equal, help is more likely to be given when the cost is low, the need is more urgent and the requestor has a high potential to reciprocate. Holding reciprocity potential and urgency constant, low-cost help is more likely to be given (83 > 73; 73 > 43; etc.). Holding cost

Table 15–3.   Percentage of people who gave help in response to a direct request (data from Yinon and Dovrat 1987, Table 1).

	RECIPROCITY POTENTIAL			
	HIGH		LOW	
	URGENCY			
Cost	High	Low	High	Low
High	73	43	37	20
Low	83	73	60	33

and reciprocity potential constant, high-urgency help is more likely to be given ($73 > 43$; $37 > 20$; etc.). And holding cost and urgency constant, help is more likely to be given when the requestor has a high-potential to reciprocate ($73 > 37$; $43 > 20$; etc.). These findings closely parallel the conditions outlined in Trivers's model.

> **Trail Marker:** Help is more likely to be granted when the cost is small, the benefit is large, and the requestor has the capacity to reciprocate.

Trivers's model not only makes predictions about the conditions that affect our willingness to help but also about our willingness to ask for help. Greenberg and Shapiro (1971) staged an experiment in which a pair of subjects could earn money by reaching, and more money by exceeding, a quota on two tasks. However, in each pair of subjects the second "subject" was actually a confederate of the experimenter. Two "practice" sessions, one for each task, preceded the opportunity to earn money. The results of the first practice session were staged so that it appeared that the subject would not be able to make the quota while the confederate would have an easy time doing so. The second practice session was arranged differently. All the subjects were given to believe that they would easily make the quota on this task. But for half the subjects it was made to appear that the confederate would also make quota, and for the other half it appeared that he would not. Finally, it was made clear that subjects could ask each other for help.

Thus Greenberg and Shapiro's subjects all thought, when they had an opportunity to earn money, they would need help to make quota on the first task. But half of the subjects thought that their "partner" (the confederate) would need help on the second task, and half thought that their "partner" would do fine without help. How do you think these expectations about their partner's need affected the subjects tendency to ask for help?

Of the subjects who thought their partner would need help with the second task, 71 percent asked for help themselves on the first. But of those who thought their partner would not need help, only 37 percent asked for help. Not only was an expectation about the partner's need important in determining who asked for help, but it also affected how much help subjects were willing to accept after asking. For example, several subjects asked their partner to stop helping after the quota was reached, even though more money could have been earned by exceeding the quota. Those who anticipated no opportunity to reciprocate were three times more likely to ask their partner to stop helping. Greenberg and Shapiro's (1971) interpretation of their results is that people feel that asking for help creates a responsibility to help in return, to reciprocate. Those who felt in a poor position to reciprocate were reluctant to ask for help themselves.

> **Trail Marker:** People are reluctant to ask for help when they feel unable to reciprocate.

COGNITIVE IMPLICATIONS OF SELECTION FOR RECIPROCITY

In his initial paper on reciprocity, Robert Trivers (1971) argued that friendship and the wide range of emotional systems that support it are the result of selection for reciprocal altruism in humans. He suggests that the emotions of liking and disliking evolved to motivate adaptive altruism and to facilitate the formation of partnerships only with reciprocators (see Chapter 12). Since positive emotions such as liking are open to exploitation, we should be designed to feel morally indignant when our altruism is not reciprocated. He notes that we feel gratitude in response to the magnitude of the altruism we have received and that this gratitude serves to regulate our reciprocity. Indeed we feel guilty when we fail to reciprocate. All of these characteristics generally match what we would expect in a creature designed to seek the benefits of reciprocity. But many questions remain about the motivational systems underlying altruism.

Enhanced Memory for Cheaters

In Chapter 8 you saw that people are not very good at solving certain kinds of logical problems, unless the problem involves cheater detection. This result is compatible with the idea that reciprocal altruism was important over the course of human evolution and it was thus essential for people to recognize instances of cheating. And in Chapter 2 you learned that there are very specialized mechanisms for recognizing faces. Together, these two abilities, recognizing cheating and recognizing unique individuals could provide a basis for discrimination against cheaters. Is there any evidence that these abilities are linked?

In a clever experiment Linda Mealey and her colleagues (1996) provided evidence that they are. They told their subjects they were studying attractiveness and whether judgements of attractiveness were consistent. Using this deception they asked the same people to look at a series of facial photographs on two different occasions. On the first occasion, thirty-six photographs were shown and each photograph was paired with a fictitious story that was either neutral, positive, or negative with respect to the depicted person's character. The negative stories portrayed the person as a cheater, for example, someone who had embezzled money from a church. One week later the same subjects were shown seventy-two photos, half of which were new. In addition to rating attractiveness again, the subjects were asked which photographs they remembered from the previous week.

> **Trail Marker:** Being labeled as a cheater makes a person more memorable.

As Mealey predicted, the character stories had a significant effect on recall. Overall, subjects remembered more faces that had been paired with "cheater" labels than faces that had been paired with neutral or positive labels (Mealey et al.,

1996). It's doubtful that researchers operating within the framework of SSSM psychology ever would have thought to look for a relationship between ease of recall and social reputation. As you saw in Chapter 8, Tversky and Kahneman have suggested that some memories are more "available" than others, but have not given a general theory that predicts which memories are more available. In essence Mealy and her associates have demonstrated that reputation affects availability. This is the sort of novel prediction that can emerge from evolutionary considerations.

Can People Recognize Non-Reciprocators before the Fact?

Reciprocal altruism pays. Once established, reciprocal relationships let individuals swap small costs for large benefits. But there is an initial hurdle. Individuals have to pay the cost of their initial altruism in order to find out whether a new acquaintance is a reciprocator or a cheater. Wouldn't it be better if we could tell in advance? Robert Frank and his associates (Frank et al., 1993) found that their subjects could recognize cheaters in advance. They asked Cornell undergraduates to play a single round of the Prisoner's Dilemma game. They used a payoff matrix of real dollars, rather than jail sentences (Table 15–4).

The innovative part of Frank's experiment is that the experimenters let the students interact with their partner for half an hour before the single round was played. There were no restrictions on what they could discuss. For example, they could discuss the game, their strategies, or even make promises to cooperate. Following this half-hour meeting the students were taken to separate rooms. There, each was asked to record his or her move (cooperate or cheat) and, more importantly, each was asked to predict what his or her opponent would do. The students performed significantly better than chance at anticipating whether their opponent was going to cooperate and whether he or she was going to defect (Figure 15–5). In the real world, this sort of ability would allow people to minimize the amount of altruism they waste on individuals who are never going to reciprocate.

> **Trail Marker:** People have some ability to recognize whether a new acquaintance will be a cooperator or not.

Table 15–4.   Payoff Matrix for Frank's Prisoners Dilemma Game

| | | OTHER PLAYER | |
		COOPERATES	CHEATS
YOU	COOPERATE	$2 for other player $2 for you	$3 for other player $0 for you
	CHEAT	$0 for other player $3 for you	$1 for other player $1 for you

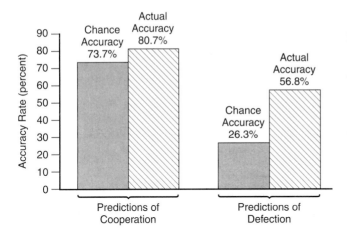

Figure 15–5. *Strangers performed significantly better than chance at predicting when their prisoners' dilemma partner would cooperate and when he would cheat.* Chance accuracy is based on the percentage of subjects who actually did cooperate or cheat. For example, because 73.7% cooperated, a prediction that one's partner would cooperate would be accurate 73.7% of the time simply by chance. (Fig. 1, "The Evaluation of One-Shot Cooperation: An Experiment" by R. H. Frank, T. Gilovitch, and D. Regan in *Ethology and Sociobiology,* (1993), 14. Copyright © Elsevier Science, Inc. Reprinted by permission of Elsevier Science, Inc.)

People Are Surprisingly Altruistic . . . If Anybody's Watching

One of the interesting results of Frank's experiment is that most—almost 75 percent—of the participants chose to cooperate rather than defect. This is a peculiar result. Remember, cooperating is a very good strategy in *iterated* Prisoners' Dilemma. But these students were not playing iterated Prisoners' Dilemma; they were playing just a single round, with a stranger. And cheating is the best strategy if the game is played only once. Look at the payoff matrix again (Table 15–3). If your partner cooperates, you should cheat because $3 > $2. If your partner cheats, you should cheat because $1 > $0. The players understood this because the payoff matrix was fully explained and because most were students in classes where the Prisoner's Dilemma was discussed. But most still choose to cooperate; why?

> **Trail Marker:** In noniterated games, most people are nicer than game theory would predict.

The first point you need to appreciate is that the results of Frank et al. (1993) are surprising for the reason just stated, but they are in no way unusual. In general, people are much nicer in non-iterated games that they "should" be, based on game theory analysis.

Consider another class of simple games called "ultimatum" games. Ultimatum games have two players, one of whom is designated as the proposer. For example, in the ultimatum game called "Divide Ten Dollars" the proposer suggests a division of the cash. If the other player accepts, each get the specified amount. If he rejects the offer, both he and the proposer get nothing. Suppose you were the proposer, how much would you offer? Game theory says the best strategy is to offer the minimal unit of currency, one dollar in this example, keeping the other nine. After all, the other player should prefer one dollar to nothing and so should

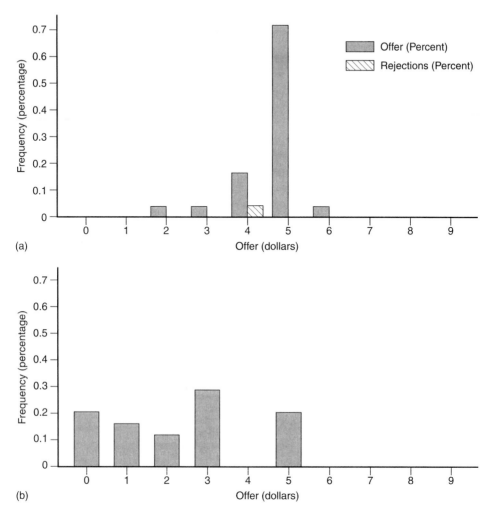

Figure 15–6. *Cash splits offered by proposers in Divide Ten Dollars.* Panel a shows results under ultimatum rules. Panel b shows results under dictator rules. N=24 in each experiment. (Data from "Fairness in Simple Bargaining Experiments" by R. Forsythe, J. Horowitz, N. Savin, and M. Sefton in *Games and Economic Behavior,* (1994), 6 and "Preferences, Property Rights and Anonymity in Bargaining Games" by E. Hoffman, K. McCabe, K. Shachat and V. Smith in *Games and Economic Behavior,* (1994), 7. Copyright © 1994 by Academic Press. Reprinted by permission of Academic Press.)

accept the proposal. But we'd bet that wasn't your answer because it's not what people typically do in Divide Ten Dollars. People typically propose a five-and-five split (Figure 15–6a). Why are people so nice?

You can probably suggest several hypotheses. Perhaps proposers feel that if they offer too little their offer will be rejected and they will end up with nothing. There's a simple way to estimate the impact of this concern on people's proposals: eliminate the possibility of rejection. This game is no longer an ultimatum game, but a "dictator" game. The proposer names a division of the cash and that's how it's divided, the other person has no say. Changing to dictator rules reduces people's niceness (Figure 15–6b); but only 20 percent of subjects match the game theoretic optimum, which in this case is to offer zero and keep the whole ten dollars. More than 20 percent of subjects still divide the cash five-and-five.

> **Trail Marker**: Cooperation decreases when one's reputation is not at stake.

Another idea about why people are relatively nice, even in dictator games, is that others are watching. After all, if humans have been subject to selection for reciprocal altruism, we should be designed to guard our reputations. Being known as a cheater would greatly restrict the amount of altruism one could expect to receive. There's also a way to isolate this "reputation" influence: perform the experiment "double-blind." Hoffman et al. (1994) performed Divide-Ten-Dollars dictator experiments double-blind, that is, insuring that neither the experimenter nor the other subjects could know what any individual proposer did. This was accomplished by having several proposers in one room and their partners in another room, and by giving the proposers envelopes in which they could privately seal a mix of dollars and blank slips of paper totaling to ten. Since the proposers and their partners never met, and since all envelopes turned into the experimenter were of equal thickness, the proposers reputations were safe, regardless of whether they were nice or not. When the envelopes were opened in the second room, the distribution of offers was decidedly less generous (Figure 15–7) than in cases where the offer is public knowledge (as in Figure 15–6).

Anonymity consistently reduces niceness (Hoffman et al., 1996). But it is also clear that, even in double-blind circumstances, many people still fail to keep all the benefits for themselves. In thinking about these results the authors conclude that it is difficult for most people to act completely selfishly because people are designed to operate in a world of repeated interactions. In the real world, the shadow of the future hangs over all our choices, and our reputations (as cheaters or as cooperators) greatly affect how others will treat us.

In summary, a variety of aspects of human social behavior are well explained if we assume a past history of selection for reciprocity. People seem to spontaneously evaluate cost, benefit and reciprocity potential. They seem disinclined to ask for help when they feel unable to reciprocate. Their memory of cheaters is especially good. And they seem to be concerned that they not be regarded as cheaters. Even in one-trial games they act as if there is a future in which their reputation matters.

RECIPROCITY AND THE ENVIRONMENT

The central idea captured by Trivers's reciprocity and Luce and Raiffa's prisoners' dilemma is very general and it has wide ranging implications for human behavior. For example, many environmental problems are essentially prisoners' dilemmas.

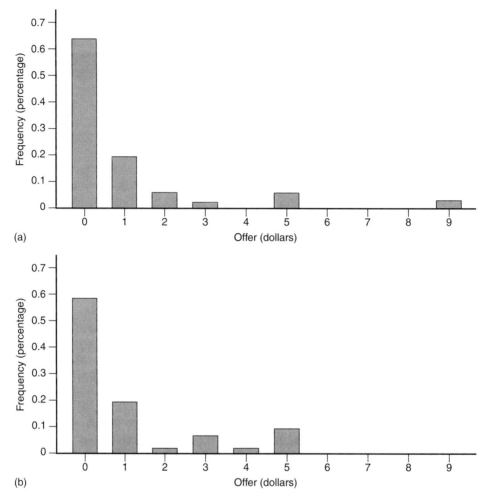

Figure 15-7.   *Cash splits offered by proposers in Divide Ten Dollars under double-blind dictator rules.* Panels a and b show two trials of the experiment, N=36 and 41.

Garret Hardin (1964) formulated the classic environmental version of the prisoners' dilemma and called it "the tragedy of the commons." The players in the commons game are herders who share a single grazing ground, the "commons." They are agreed that, to preserve the quality of the commons, a small total herd size is preferable. Keeping your personal herd small is equivalent to remaining silent in the prisoners' dilemma—it amounts to cooperating with your fellow herders. But, at any time each herder could add another animal to those he grazes on the commons. This is equivalent to confessing, because it involves cheating on your prior agreement to keep the herd small. Let's analyze the payoffs.

On the positive side, the herder who cheats and adds to the herd will receive additional revenue from the eventual sale of this animal or its products such as wool or milk. On the negative side, the addition to his herd increases the total herd on the commons and thus contributes to overgrazing, reducing the eventual value of every animal. The proceeds of the sale belong to him alone, while the decrease in value is distributed across all the animals—his and his neighbors'. Thus, the benefits *to him* outweigh the costs *to him* and he will be inclined to increase his herd. But the tragedy is that *every* rational herder is inclined to the same conclusion. When that happens, not one, but many animals are added, forage is greatly diminished, herd condition and value deeply eroded. Just as in Prisoner's Dilemma, when each person chooses her most rational alternative each ends up worse off than if she had cooperated.

> **Trail Marker:** Pollution and conservation issues can be analyzed as Prisoners' Dilemmas.

The point that Hardin was making is that the earth, the soil, water, and atmosphere are all commons. We all depend on them and use them, and when we abuse them others bear most of the cost. But, as in the tragedy of the commons, when everyone cheats and abuses them the costs mount up on all of us. Should you go to the trouble of taking your worn-out batteries to the toxic waste dump or just put them in the trash? If you take the easy route they'll certainly end up in the local landfill where they can leak toxic substances into the soil and groundwater. Disposing of them simply (cheating) is cheaper for you but disposing of them correctly (cooperating) is better for your neighbors. Should you buy an electric vehicle or a conventional gas-powered one? At least at present the electric car is more expensive and less convenient (e.g., shorter cruising range) but it produces much less pollution. In essence, buying a gas-powered vehicle is cheating, because the purchaser gets most of the benefits of lower cost and greater convenience, while the cost, in terms of further degradation of the atmosphere, is distributed over the whole planet.

Trivers (1971) showed that altruism can spread if and only if it is withheld from nonreciprocators. And Axelrod showed that tit-for-tat, which systematically withholds benefits from cheaters, is a winning strategy in iterated prisoner's dilemma situations. Their shared conclusion is that we are designed to be altruistic because cheaters have been punished over evolutionary time. But we also saw from the experiments of Hoffman et al. (1994) that when people's behavior is not obvious to others, cheating increases. Thus, environmental issues pose special problems. In many instances it's hard to tell who's cheating—who looks through your trash to see what you're failing to recycle? And what about situations where virtually everyone is already cheating, for example by driving gas-powered vehicles? Why should anyone accept the costs of being the first cooperator? This is the central problem of environmentalism: how to get people to accept initial costs in order to get eventual benefits, when others show no signs of cooperating (Olson 1965, Ostrom 1990). As policy makers are discovering, the best way is to adjust the costs and benefits. For example, if the government were to give a significant tax credit to anyone who purchases an electric vehicle, this would lower the cost of co-operating. More people would begin to do so and, as that happened, people who did not would look more and more like cheaters.

> **Trail Marker:** Government initiatives can break the deadlock in the Tragedy of the Commons and get people to start cooperating.

"Pollution credits" are another example of this kind of policy. A few years ago the U.S. government set up programs intended to get utility companies to produce electricity more cleanly. They initially gave each company a block of pollution credits equivalent to some 95 percent of the pollution they emitted in 1990. The companies were told that this percentage would decrease on a predetermined schedule. In a few years they would get credits equivalent to only 90 percent of their 1990 levels, and then 85 percent, and so on; over time they would have to clean up their act. Throughout this period, companies would only be able to emit as much pollution as they had credits to "pay" for. If they did not have enough credits they would have to buy them from other companies. Note that allowing companies to buy and sell pollution credits accomplishes two key objectives. It inflicts a cost on the cheaters who pollute more by forcing them to buy credits. And it gives a benefit to the cooperators who clean up their operations more rapidly by giving them surplus credits they can sell for cash. In short, it generates cooperation because it punishes cheaters and rewards cooperators.

THE ROLE OF STATUS AND DOMINANCE IN SOCIAL LIFE

We do not live in a world of equality: People vary in all sorts of ways that influence their fitness. Some people are stronger, smarter, or more beautiful, than others. They also control different amounts of resources. These differences are so pervasive that we should expect to find psychological adaptations for recognizing and dealing with them. Before we can go farther, however, we need to deal with a common misconception. We have emphasized throughout this book that our psychology evolved to deal with what we call the EEA—the environment of evolutionary adaptedness. It is often claimed that people in hunting-and-gathering societies, who live in a situation we believe to more closely resemble the EEA, live in non-hierarchical societies with no differences in power and status. The fact is, however, that people in hunting-and-gathering societies, like all people around the world, recognize differences in rank and status. (Recall our discussion of Donald Brown's "Universal People" in Chapter 1.) To be sure, the differences in status are often less pronounced in hunting-and-gathering cultures, where wealth is difficult to accumulate and preserve, than they are in Western societies. Nevertheless there are always some differences in status among people based on skill, knowledge, experience, intelligence, appearance, and the like.

In fact, rank is a common feature of the social life of other animals, where it serves a useful function. Individuals inevitably compete with other members of their species for scarce resources. If two individuals had to fight every time they both wanted the same food item, the same mate, or the same nesting site, they would waste valuable time and energy, as well as run the risk of injury or even death. To avoid needless fighting a great many social animals establish *pecking orders,* a term derived from observation of domestic chickens. Each pair of chickens in a flock will establish its relative rank and thereafter the higher-ranking one can peck the other with impunity. In disputes over food or other resources, all flock members defer to higher-ranking individuals. A bird in the middle of the pecking order defers to all those above it, but dominates those below it. Introduction of a new bird into a flock produces a flurry of fighting until it establishes its place in the pecking order.

In meeting others, people more or less automatically notice certain kinds of attributes and neglect others. Along with sex and age, status or dominance is among the most salient (Brewer and Lui, 1989; Hastie and Park, 1986). Even a mere still photograph of the face conveys dominance status. This signal seems not to be culture-bound because there is high cross-cultural agreement about which faces are high and low in dominance (Collins and Zebrowitz, 1995, Keating et al., 1981). In addition, facial dominance can be a reliable predictor of professional and reproductive success. For example, in 1990 Ulrich Mueller and Allan Mazur carried out a retrospective study of the 1950 graduating class of the United States Military Academy at West Point. Looking backward allowed a full assessment of these men's careers. Except for the lowest 10 percent of the class, men with higher facial dominance scores attained higher military ranks, attained them more quickly and had higher lifetime reproductive success (Mueller and Mazur, 1997).

If social dominance is so important, we might wonder, is there a social dominance module? Some evidence comes from work with preschool children (Smith, 1988). Children as young as four years are able to tell who of their playmates is the "toughest." They can rank members of their preschool class for toughness; the children's rankings agree with one another, and with dominance measured on the basis of their play interactions by an adult observer (Sluckin & Smith, 1977).

Abundant evidence suggests that humans modify their behavior in response to rank and status cues. For example, you would certainly act differently if you were meeting the governor of your state or a well-known celebrity than you do with your friends. But our responses to rank differences also penetrate to more subtle levels. For example, Susan Fiske and her colleagues (e.g., Fiske & Depret, 1996) have explored the effects of rank on the kind of information people seek about others. Subjects were recruited to work in groups. They read a brief description of the other people they expected to work with. The others were described as either more powerful or less powerful than the subject, or as merely observers. Then the subjects could look at further information about the other persons. Some of the additional information was consistent with the earlier information and some was inconsistent. The experimenters noted how much time subjects spent paying attention to the consistent versus the inconsistent information.

Subjects who were led to believe they were more powerful paid roughly equal attention to the consistent and inconsistent information. Subjects who were told they were less powerful, however, paid more attention to the inconsistent information. Fiske and her colleagues believe that these and similar experiments show that people who are less powerful seek more accurate information about others, whereas people who are more powerful seek to confirm their pre-existing notions. Fiske's work suggests that our thinking about others is sensitive to rank, and leads us to be more careful to know and understand people who are in a position to influence our lives.

SUMMARY

1. Sociality evolves when its benefits to individuals outweigh its costs.
2. Sociality can confer both antipredator and food-finding benefits.
3. The major cost of sociality is increased competition.
4. The distribution and size of food patches are important in determining whether individuals gain more from association than they lose to their associates.
5. The factors that favored human sociality are not known with certainty. Among the current suggestions are the need for better anti-predator monitoring in a terrestrial species, the possibility that our ancestors exploited patchy resources (perhaps including herds of game animals), and, on analogy with the other African apes, defense against hostile neighbors.
6. Ideas about social life in the EEA can be derived from studies of modern hunter-gatherers.
7. On this basis, humans probably evolved in small social groups where the average degree of relatedness was high and where everyone knew everyone else.
8. In line with Hamilton's theory of kin selection, all human societies are organized by kinship.
9. In traditional societies groups tend to fission when the average degree of relatedness among members drops too low.
10. In traditional and Western societies people give more aid to kin.
11. Homicide data suggest that people are relatively unlikely to kill their kin.
12. Psychological data suggest that kinship is a dominant factor in decisions about whom to help, and kinship exerts a progressively stronger influence when the fitness consequences are large.
13. Children who live with non-kin show physiological signs of stress in that they have elevated cortisol levels and higher rates of illness.
14. Altruism among non-kin depends on reciprocity, which in turn depends on discriminating against non-reciprocators (cheaters).

15. Reciprocity is another force that organizes social relationships, and various emotions such as liking, disliking, indignation, and gratitude promote the establishment and maintenance of reciprocal partnerships.
16. Memory for faces is enhanced merely by attaching the label of "cheater."
17. People are less likely to ask for help when they feel unable to reciprocate.
18. People are more likely to help when the cost is low, the benefit is large and the requestor is in a position to reciprocate with valuable aid.
19. After relatively brief periods of acquaintance, people are able to predict who will cooperate and who will cheat.
20. People are nicer than one might expect in non-iterated games; experiments suggest that the function of their niceness is to protect their reputations as cooperators.
21. Status differentials pervade human and many animal societies.
22. At least some signals of status, such as facial dominance, are reliably interpreted across cultures, and are correlated with both professional and reproductive success.
23. Children understand the notion of dominance, and can accurately assign relative dominance statuses to their peers as early as four years of age.
24. In everyday interactions, people gather more complete information about higher-status individuals.

16 ◆ Culture

Both SSSM psychologists and evolutionary psychologists agree that, the world around, humans share a common psychology. And, both agree that human behavior is variable. But SSSM psychologists and evolutionary psychologists disagree over how to reconcile these two facts. Why are there behavioral differences if humans share a common psychology? Along with most social scientists, SSSM psychologists attribute the diversity of human behavior to cultural and environmental influences. Evolutionary psychologists see these explanations as incomplete at best, and circular at the worst. Exploring the origins of the social sciences is useful in understanding this rift.

DURKHEIM'S UNFORTUNATE LEGACY

The social sciences, such as anthropology, sociology, and much but not all of psychology, have been strongly influenced by Emile Durkheim. Unfortunately, Durkheim founded the study of society on a doubtful idea. He thought that society and the social forces that shape it were separate and independent from the forces that operate in other realms; in particular, he believed that society has no basis in biology. His famous dictum was that "only social facts can explain social facts." In other words, the features of social life can only be explained in terms of other facts about society. Thus, according to Durkheim and his modern-day followers, evolutionary history is irrelevant to social behavior.

Hopefully, those who have read the first fifteen chapters of this book will realize that Durkheim's stance is peculiar. First, many nonhuman animals are intensely social. And various species of mammals, birds, and even insects show consistent differences in their social arrangements, just as they differ in other important adaptations. How have these differences come about? In Chapter 15 we identified a series of selection pressures that can favor or disfavor social tendencies. Because interactions with other members of the species can have significant effects on fitness, selection is likely to have shaped social behavior, as it shapes other aspects of the phenotype, to suit the prevailing environment. So Durkheim's claim that society is immune to biological forces, such as natural selection, seems to contradict what we know about the evolution of animal social behavior.

> **Trail Marker:** Contrary to Durkheim, animal societies seem to be strongly influenced by biological forces such as natural selection.

Another problem with Durkheim's premise that "only social facts can explain social facts" becomes obvious if we ask where the first social fact came from. It must have had its roots in the evolved tendencies of the organism; where else could it have come from?

Durkheim's Views Contradict the Unity of Science

The web of scientific explanations must form a coherent fabric. For example, there could be no finding in chemistry (e.g., "cold fusion") that contradicts the basic principles of physics. If there were, one or the other would have to be wrong and scientists would quickly get to work (as they did in the case of "cold fusion") to find out which was in error. By the rules of science, explanations must be part of the overarching fabric and are not allowed to claim exemption. Because evolution produced organisms, their traits, including their social traits, must have an evolutionary basis. Just as chemical facts must be compatible with physics, social phenomena must, ultimately, be compatible with biology. There is no separate realm of society where the principles of biology are suspended, just as there is no society where the rules of physics are suspended and people float free of gravity whenever they choose.

> **Trail Marker:** Logically, all the sciences are united, and must appeal to a consistent set of causes and principles.

"Culture" Is Not a Satisfactory Explanation for Behavioral Differences

Unfortunately, the Standard Social Science Model (SSSM) discussed in Chapter 1 and referred to throughout this book, was significantly influenced by Durkheim. Why do these people behave this way? "It's their culture" is a typical SSSM answer.

Social facts (behavior) are being explained by other social facts (culture). Does this sound like a good explanation to you? The problem is that the thinking is circular. Culture is defined as the "set of beliefs, behaviors, and life-ways that characterize a group." Thus, the explanation "They behave that way because of their culture" ends up being no explanation at all; it says they behave that way because that's the way they behave. This is not very informative. The social sciences have placed a legitimate emphasis on diversity—it's true; not everyone behaves in the same way. But the notion of culture merely describes the differences; it doesn't explain them.

> **Trail Marker:** "Culture" is a circular explanation for behavioral differences.

How about experience, the other main explanatory idea of the SSSM; can experience explain behavioral differences? Yes, but it can never give a very satisfying answer unless it is combined with an evolutionary perspective. Here's why.

Experience must act on something. Experiences don't just happen, they happen *to* individuals. Then the individual responds to the experience. But this is still just a description, not an explanation. Where does the response come from? Why does the individual respond to experience at all; why not ignore experience? The point is that we wouldn't respond to experience unless selection had endowed us with a design for responding, a design for responding *in particular ways*. We don't lighten our skin color in response to solar radiation, we darken it. We don't decrease our tendency to be violent when we see violence, we increase it. These are apparently the patterns of responsiveness that led to the highest fitness among our ancestors. Experience is an incomplete explanation unless it explains *why* the experience has the particular effect it does. And any attempt to explain why experiences have the effects they do automatically admits that the experience acts on something that has an inherent nature to respond in particular ways.

> **Trail Marker:** The effects of experience are not separate from biology; they are evolved facultative responses.

For example, we noted in Chapter 15 that memory for faces is enhanced when the face is labeled as that of a cheater. Why should this be so? Why does the label "cheater" make a face more rather than less memorable? Why doesn't the label "cheater" affect hunger or auditory sensitivity instead of facial memory. Why isn't facial memory equally responsive to other features of the local environment like temperature or sex ratio? You're right: because none of those patterns of responsiveness would be helpful. In other words, selection has designed our patterns of responsiveness to the environment. The effects of experience are not separate from biology; they are evolved facultative responses.

FACULTATIVE ADAPTATIONS AND DIVERSITY

It is important to understand what evolutionary psychology has to say about differences between individuals, about diversity. While EP often focuses on the universal aspects of human nature it certainly does not ignore diversity. For example, we agree with most SSSM psychologists that it would be important to understand why some people are more prone to violence than others. And we also agree that this kind of individual difference is largely the result of experience. But to turn this claim into an explanation we need to understand how and why particular experiences shape behavior in the specific ways that they do. EP says that humans share a common evolved psychological nature. What that nature consists of is a large set of facultative mechanisms that were crafted by selection. These mechanism were designed specifically to allow us to make appropriate behavioral adjustments in response to our experiences.

> **Trail Marker:** The effects of experience are not explanations; they need to be explained, ultimately in terms of their evolutionary basis.

Obviously, our shared psychology does not mean that we are bound to behave in identical ways. In the case of facultative traits there can be lots of diversity even if everyone has the same version of the trait. People could have precisely the same genes for melanin production (they could even be identical twins) but still differ in skin color because each is responding adaptively to her own recent exposure to ultra-violet light. Similarly, people could have the same underlying psychology but differ in their behavior because each is responding adaptively to his situation.

It's well documented that the average person becomes more violent if exposed to violence. But why? Standard attempts to answer this question merely label the finding. For example, violence breeds violence because it causes "imitation." Really? Does viewing accidental injury-producing situations, such as car crashes cause imitation? Why not? To use the notion of "imitation" as a real explanation one must be prepared to say what kinds of situations provoke it and what kinds do not. To do so one must inevitably discuss the adaptive basis, the function, of "imitation." In summary, our patterns of responsiveness must be explained, not merely labeled, if we are to have a coherent science of human behavior. We'll analyze several cultural and environmental influences in detail to illustrate how evolutionary psychologists use the notion of facultative traits to think about diversity.

> **Trail Marker:** According to a standard explanation, violence provokes "imitation." But accidentally produced injuries don't. Why not?

MATRILINEAL INHERITANCE

In most societies, men are expected to take certain responsibilities for the welfare of their wife's children. This expectation may be codified into law (e.g., child-support laws) or may be a matter of more informal customs about the husband's obligations. But there is a minority—something on the order of 10 percent—of well-described societies where men have little responsibility for their wife's children. It might seem that men are serious shirkers in these cases but there's more to the story. In this minority of societies, men do have many of the normal responsibilities for the welfare of children, but it's their sister's children who count on them, not their wife's. This is precisely the sort of situation that SSSM scientists "explain" in terms of cultural differences: That's just the way they do it in their culture.

> **Trail Marker:** In matrilineal societies, men invest their resources in their sisters' children, not their wife's children.

We hope you are more curious than that. *Why* do they do it that way? And here's another interesting question. If 10 percent of societies charge men with the care of their sister's children, how many societies charge women with the care of their brother's children? None. In how many societies are men expected to take primary responsibility for their brother's children, or women to take primary responsibility for their sister's children? None, and none again. Isn't that a bit odd? If "it's just their culture," why are some logical possibilities never found? It seems that human behavior, at least parental investment behavior, is not infinitely variable. Can you think what might cause this pattern of cultural differences?

Adults should evolve the tendency to expend resources on the young to whom they are most genetically similar. As usual, this is not a moral "should," but simply a statement of what we expect natural selection to favor. Genes for investing indiscriminately would squander resources on individuals who bear competing alleles. Genes for investing only in close relatives would tend to spread because they would often benefit copies of themselves. Can the observed patterns of parental behavior be explained by patterns of genetic relatedness? It turns out that they can.

Explaining Matrilineal Inheritance

In diploid species like *Homo sapiens*, women are always more closely related to their own children than they are to any other member of the descendant generation. A woman's child will bear 50 percent of her genes but her nieces and nephews will typically carry only 25 percent. Thus women are behaving in an evolutionarily rational way when they prefer to invest in their own children over nieces and nephews (that is, over their brothers' and sisters' children).

Perhaps you are thinking that the same argument will apply to men; but there is a key difference. Before the days of embryo transplants (for 99.99 percent of human evolution!), women were unambiguously related to the children they bore. But a man is not so certainly and automatically related to his wife's children. If the wife's child is in fact his own, then the child will carry 50 percent of his genes—just as it does hers. But it may not be his child, and thus may carry none of his genes. Obviously he should invest in the child if it is his. But how should he target his available resources when he is unrelated to his wife's child? It turns out that he is always related (by at least 12.5 percent) to his sister's children. Let's see why this is so.

> **Trail Marker:** Regardless of the degree of promiscuity, a man's sister's children always carry some of his genes.

His sister would share 50 percent of his genes on average if they were full siblings, that is, if they had the same father and the same mother. If they have only one parent in common he and his sister would share 25 percent of their genes on average. Since his sister's offspring bear 50 percent of her genes, then at worst (in the case where he and his sister are half rather than full siblings), the nieces and nephews she produces for him will bear (50 percent × 25 percent =) 12.5 percent of his genes. Now, likewise, a man is related by 50 percent to his full brothers and 25 percent to his half-brothers. But all links through males are uncertain. In other words, if a man's own paternity is in question then his brother may be in the same situation.

Note how neatly these genetic considerations match the observed patterns of parental behavior. Women are always more closely related to their own children than they are to either their sister's or their brother's children. And likewise, men are more related to their wife's children as long as they fathered those children. When they are unlikely to be the father of their wife's children, the nieces and nephews produced by their sisters, not by their brothers, are the most closely related children in the population.

Testing the Explanation

This is a tidy explanation but it should, and can, go further. We argued that behavioral diversity is not merely the product of arbitrary cultural differences. Instead, behavior should reflect facultative adaptation to key features of the environment. In the case of paternal investment, the key feature of the environment is "paternity probability," the likelihood that a man fathered his wife's children. The point is not that men sometimes invest in their sister's children. The EP approach suggests that investing in sister's children is a facultative response to low paternity probability. Thus men should invest in sister's children not in a random 10 percent of societies, but in precisely those societies where paternity probability is lowest.

> **Trail Marker:** Matrilineal inheritance is strongly associated with low paternity probability.

Several researchers have attempted to test this hypothesis and all found support for it. John Hartung's (1985) analysis is probably the most careful. He drew on a database containing information about various aspects of behavior in a large number of societies. First, based on data about frequency of and severity of punishment for extramarital sex, societies were categorized in terms of the prevailing level of paternity probability. Secondly, men's investment tendencies were measured in terms of inheritance rules. To frame a clear test of the hypothesis Hartung limited his analysis to two kinds of societies: "patrilineal" societies, where men pass all their property to wife's sons, and "matrilineal" societies, where men pass all their property to sister's sons. The prediction is then clear. Matrilineal inheritance should be restricted to societies where the probability of paternity is low.

That is exactly what Hartung found (Figure 16–1). Men put their investment where their genes are most likely to be! Not only does paternity probability explain why, despite the considerable diversity of cultures, some investment patterns simply do not exist, it also predicts *which* cultures will exhibit the matrilineal pattern. The EP approach suggests that matrilineal investment is not "just the culture" in certain societies. Instead, its distribution suggests it is an adaptive response to a particular circumstance: low paternity probability.

Was Durkheim Right?

Before proceeding to other examples it is important to explore the EP and the SSSM perspectives a little further. What would Durkheim say about matrilineal inheritance? Remember his dictum, "Only social facts can explain social facts." We have suggested that matrilineal inheritance is a response to low paternity probability, but what causes paternity probability to be low? Obviously it's people's sexual behavior, for example, relatively lax standards about marital fidelity. Were Durkheim alive to argue his case, he might say, "Ah, you see I am right: Promiscuity (one social fact) has explained matrilineal inheritance (another social fact)." This is true, as far as it goes. But how do we explain the connection between sexual practices and inheritance practices? Why should these two aspects of behavior be linked? Why does low paternity probability lead men to invest in sister's children as opposed to some other outcome, such as women investing in their brother's children, or people refusing to eat animals whose names start with vowels? The only answer that has ever been offered is a biological one: People are designed to invest in the most genetically similar children. Durkheim was right to claim that one social factor could influence other social factors, but he was wrong to claim that these influences were not based in biology.

Reconciling EP and SSSM Perspectives

There is a simple way to reconcile the EP and SSSM perspectives. The social environment is exceedingly important to human beings. Just as humans have facultative responses to aspects of the nonliving environment such as climate, we have many important facultative responses to our social environment. This is why one social fact can affect another. The contribution of EP is to *make sense* of those influences. And that is precisely what the EP explanation of matrilineal inheritance does.

Matrilineal inheritance may seem exotic to the average North American college student. Most of us have had little or no contact with cultures where matrilineal

<table>
<tr><td></td><td></td><td colspan="2" align="center">Paternity Probability</td></tr>
<tr><td></td><td></td><td align="center">Moderate or Lower</td><td align="center">High or Very High</td></tr>
<tr>
<td rowspan="2">Matrilineal</td>
<td>
Ashanti   Ponapeans
Aua   Timucua
Bemba   Trobriand
Bijogo
Chokwe
Coniagui
Dobuans
Haida
Khasi
Kingo
Liumbe
Mota
Ndoro
Nyaneka
Ponapeans
</td>
<td>
Digo
Cuanche
Kunama
</td>
</tr>
<tr>
<td align="right">N=17</td>
<td>N=3</td>
</tr>
<tr>
<td rowspan="2">Patrilineal</td>
<td>
N=5

Cagaba
Lolo
Masai
Trukese
Wogeo
</td>
<td>
N=45

Abor   Irish   Mossi
Ambara   Kachin   Jukun
Aymara   Kadara   Nuer
Aztec   Kei   Ojibwa
Basakomo   Kikuyu   Omaha
Batak   Kissi   Penobscot
Beraber   Koryak   Santal
Bhil   Lakher   Shantung
Chenchu   Lepcha   Shawiya
Coorg   Lozi   Sumbanese
Dard   Mapuche   Tanimbares
Fur   Margi   Tarasco
Ganda   Mbugwe   Telugu
Ili-Mandir   Miao   Tibetans
Ngoni   Monguor   Tswana
</td>
</tr>
</table>

Inheritance Practice

Figure 16–1.   *Matrilineal inheritance is much more likely to be the norm where paternity probability is lower.* In strict patrilineal inheritance property flows from father to son, to son's son. Is it obvious why this kind of inheritance is mainly found in societies with high paternity probability? (Based on Hartung, 1985, Table 1).

inheritance is the norm. But we don't have to look to exotic cultures to see clear examples of how our social environment triggers facultative effects on behavior.

MEDIA EFFECTS ON ATTRACTIVENESS JUDGMENTS

There is a great deal of research on how men and women evaluate each other's attractiveness. Some of the findings are reviewed in Chapter 11. But here we are concerned with the effects of culture, and whether these effects are arbitrary or functional. Douglas Kenrick and his associates have shown that attractiveness evaluations are indeed responsive to the social environment. For example, Kenrick and Gutierres (1980) showed men either facial photographs of attractive women or photographs of abstract art and then asked the men to rate the attractiveness and dating desirability of an average-looking woman. Those men shown photos of attractive women rated the average woman as both less attractive and less desirable as a dating partner than did men who were shown artwork. Such findings are called *contrast effects* because it is believed that the contrast between especially attractive stimuli and average ones causes the average ones to be more harshly judged.

Similar contrast effects were found when both male and female subjects were shown whole-body photographs instead of portraits (Kenrick et al., 1989). Subjects were shown one of three kinds of stimuli: playboy centerfolds (presumably preselected by the editors for high attractiveness), nude photos of average women, or abstract art. Then they were asked to judge the sexual attractiveness of an average woman. Those subjects shown centerfolds systematically evaluated the average

Figure 16–2. *Visual media overloaded with highly attractive people can skew people's perception of the mate pool.*

woman as less attractive than did those shown either art or average-looking nudes, and this was equally true regardless of whether women or men did the judging.

> **Trail Marker:** Contrast effects suggest that our attractiveness judgements are relative, not absolute.

In the experiments just described, the subjects are rating the attractiveness of a stranger's photograph. And it seems that strangers are indeed judged to be less attractive when they are contrasted with highly attractive stimuli. But one might ask what relevance this has for real-world relationships. Kenrick thought it was important to find out. Thus in another experiment he recruited married subjects (or those who had a similar co-resident relationship with an opposite-sex partner). In this experiment, men and women were both shown photographs of opposite-sexed nudes, taken either from *Playboy* or *Playgirl;* abstract art again provided control stimuli. In this study the subjects were then asked a series of questions about their spouse (or partner) to gauge how attractive they found their partner and how much love they felt for their partner. Do you think their feelings for their partner were similar, regardless of whether they had seen centerfolds or art? It turns out that those subjects who viewed centerfolds judged their real-world partner as less attractive and expressed less love for their partner than those who viewed art, although the differences were only statistically significant among the male subjects (Figure 16–3). Remembering what you learned about men's and women's mating preferences in Chapter 10 you might speculate that viewing erotica reduced men's commitment more because men place more emphasis than women on physical attractiveness when choosing a mate. Kenrick decided to test this hypothesis as well.

Women and men value many of the same traits in a mate, but there are a few very reliable differences. Men value physical attractiveness in a partner more than

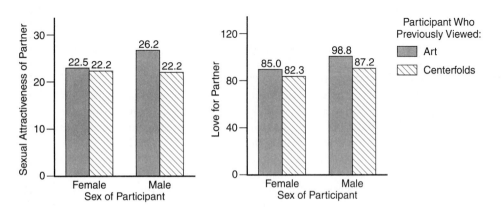

Figure 16–3. *Seeing attractive nudes of the opposite sex leads to a devaluation of ones partner.* The effect is much stronger among men. (Data from Kenrick et al., 1989, Table 2.)

women do, and women value earning power and social status in a partner more than men do (see Chapter 10). Kenrick et al. (1994) showed groups of male and female subjects photographs of attractive members of the opposite sex or photos of members of the opposite sex who were described as socially dominant. Then the subjects were asked about their commitment to their current partner. Again, seeing attractive photos led men to devalue their current partners more than it did women. But this study also yielded an interesting new contrast effect. Women who saw photos of socially dominant men devalued their partners more than did men who saw photos of socially dominant women. In other words, the contrast effects paralleled the existing mate choice criteria. When women saw what they prefer in a mate, their commitment to their current partner diminished. When men saw what they prefer, their commitment likewise fell.

> **Trail Marker:** For women and men, contrast effects parallel their mate choice criteria.

Explaining Contrast Effects

Now, let's try to think about this set of findings in terms of facultative responses to the social environment. In Chapter 10 we suggested that attractiveness is in the eye of the beholder. Men and women have evolved to prefer certain traits such as physical attractiveness or social dominance because mating with individuals who had those traits led to high reproductive success. Like most important adaptations the ability to perceive these desirable traits should be more or less universal. In very different ways Doug Jones and David Buss have demonstrated this universality. There are reliable sex differences in mating preferences (Buss, 1989a). And people of different ethnic groups agree on who is attractive and who isn't (Jones, 1996). But that agreement creates a problem: the more people agree on who's attractive, the more they end up competing for the same small set of mates. A large body of research indicates that people solve this problem by ranking themselves in the hierarchy of attractiveness and seeking a mate who's near their level, essentially driving the best bargain they can in the mate market (Elder, 1969; Murstein, 1986).

This makes sense. People who were too selective, trying to get a more desirable mate than their own desirability justified, would often fail to form any mateship at all. And people who were too unselective, accepting a less attractive mate than they could get, would have lower fitness than they might (again, on the assumption that we have evolved to see as attractive those traits that predict high fertility—see Chapter 10). So selection would refine the ability to make the necessary comparisons. And those comparisons must be based on estimates of the range of attractiveness among potential mates. In the EEA that range would be manifest in the set of opposite-sex individuals that one saw. The results of Kenrick and his associates suggest that seeing a biased set of highly attractive individuals in the popular media skews our estimates of the mate pool. If we are constantly exposed to a biased sample of physically attractive or socially dominant individuals, we form a false expectation of our chances of finding such a partner, and may be inappropriately dissatisfied with the partners we can attract.

> **Trail Marker:** Television and films are probably causing our mate-evaluation modules to malfunction.

Note that, like any adaptation, evolved facultative responses can misfire in novel environments. Matrilineal inheritance seems like an effective response to low paternity probability. But rejecting your spouse because of all the beautiful people on television and in the movies is probably maladaptive. This illustrates an important point. The EP approach does not suggest that all of human behavior is currently adaptive. It simply suggests that much of human behavior is designed—but designed to solve particular problems in the EEA. Presumably our ancestors evolved to sample the array of potential mates from visual input, that is from the potential mates they saw. This adaptation can be derailed by magazines, TV and movies that present a skewed sample of very attractive people. It would be interesting to try to estimate how much the rise of visual media has contributed to our soaring divorce rates.

In summary, EP helps us understand why people behave differently. As in the case of patrilineal versus matrilineal inheritance, each may respond adaptively to his own situation. But by specifying the kinds of problems we needed to solve in the EEA, EP also helps us understand why our evolved inclinations sometimes produce unfortunate results in the modern world.

HOW MUCH OF HUMAN BEHAVIOR CAN EVOLUTIONARY PSYCHOLOGY EXPLAIN?

We have discussed two relatively narrow examples, matrilineal inheritance and media effects of attractiveness judgments. Both have plausible evolutionary explanations. But just how much of contemporary human behavior can be explained in evolutionary terms? The honest answer is that we don't yet know. Some kinds of behavior probably have (or at least had in the EEA) strong effects on fitness. For example, investing heavily in offspring who carry a competitor's genes will often reduce one's fitness. Seriously overestimating (or underestimating) one's mating prospects probably also does not help in getting one's genes into the next generation. Evolutionary psychology may be well positioned to explain emotions, motivations, cognitions, and behaviors that have large fitness consequences. Some authors concede this point while arguing that the reverse is also true: Some psychological traits have little to do with fitness and are thus beyond the reach of evolutionary psychology.

> **Trail Marker:** Traits that have no fitness consequences are immune to selection.

There must be some truth to this critique. It's simply logical and evolutionary biologists acknowledge it: Traits that have no effect on fitness are invisible to selection. The same would be true for any kind of fitness-neutral trait, including psychological ones. On the other hand just because a trait is not strongly linked to fitness now, doesn't mean it never had any affect on fitness. Let's take an example that has seemed especially challenging: music (Pinker, 1997; Sperber, 1996). Why do humans enjoy making and hearing music? Why would these abilities ever have evolved?

As an exercise, recognizing that this is a speculative venture, let's take up the challenge of trying to explain the evolution of what we might call the musical sense. There is a reason, besides the sheer challenge, to make the effort. Music is a universal: People in every described culture have a musical repertoire and musical instruments, recognize better and worse performance, and so on. Why?

> **Trail Marker:** Because music is a cultural universal it probably has a basis in human nature.

Explaining Music

Both Steven Pinker (1997) and Dan Sperber (1996) favor the idea that music exploits or feeds preexisting mental modules. The human mind was designed, as we have argued throughout this book, as a collection of information-processing modules. Each module was specialized by evolution to accept certain kinds of information as input and produce certain kinds of output: the face-recognition module, the cheater-detection module, the emotion-recognition module, the phoneme-recognition module and so on. Beyond this, Pinker and Sperber don't precisely agree on which modules music exploits, and here we'll offer yet another suggestion.

In the EEA when humans were hunters and gatherers it seems likely that they often used their hearing to locate and predict the behavior of potential prey or potential predators. Since this is a speculative exercise we will feel free to use an anecdote. One of us (S.G.) is engaged in studying a small Sierra Madrean bird, the bridled titmouse, in its natural habitat. The research depends on finding the nests of these birds, which are very inconspicuous. By far the most useful method for finding nests has been to learn the precise vocalizations—the rhythm and sequence of pitches, the "melody"—that titmice "sing" when near their nests. Of course, it's essential to distinguish this not only from the vocalizations that they give at other times but also from the vocalizations of many other bird species. This is a useful skill for an animal behaviorist, which no amount of practice could summon if selection had not previously crafted one or more modules that accept and process this kind of rhythmic, melodic input. The suggestion here is that selection built these modules because hunter-gatherers' lives depended on the ability to distinguish among a huge array of environmental sounds, many of which signaled significant risks or opportunities.

In general, selection builds motivation into adaptive behavior. People enjoy sex, a full belly, happy progeny, reliable friends, besting our competitors; the list is long. If distinguishing environmental sounds was important to fitness, selection should have built us to enjoy attending to and parsing them. To complete the argument, once the ability to make and to enjoy making these kinds of auditory distinctions evolved, then and only then, was a sort of proto-musical ability available for cultural elaboration. Then people could begin to create and enjoy new rhythms and melodies, not because they had a designed music module, but because they had one that was tuned in the right way to appreciate music.

Sperber's (1996) explanation is similar, but he feels that it was selection for recognition of speech that created the modules subsequently exploited by music—and he, too, notes that his idea is speculative. Perhaps the two explanations are not entirely distinct: Speech-recognition modules may have been shaped by overhauling evolutionarily older modules for recognition of animal sounds. There have probably been several stages in this process. For example, at a certain point in the elaboration of the musical sense, sexual selection probably began to operate in that better performers were more attractive to the opposite sex.

> **Trail Marker:** It may be possible to test ideas about the evolutionary basis of music by studying how the brain processes music.

We may never know the precise evolutionary history of the mental modules that now process music. But, it's always a useful exercise to look for ways to test the hypotheses we advance. Here's a possible way of testing our two hypotheses about the origin of the musical sense. As you already know, many cognitive tasks are parceled out to particular parts of the brain. At the highest level, the parceling out of several important tasks follows a right-left division. For example, in most people the left side of the brain is responsible for processing language (Kimura, 1967; Studdert-Kennedy and Shankweiler, 1970) and the right side handles environmental sounds (Curry, 1967). Would you think of asking what side of the brain processes music? For most people it's the right (Zatore, 1984; Gates and Bradshaw, 1977). Perhaps you can think of better ways of testing whether the musical sense evolved out of speech modules or environmental-sound modules.

Even if neither of the ideas mentioned above turns out to be correct, there is an important message of the preceding paragraphs. If all humans have music, then even though music itself may not augment fitness, the modules that underlie our musical sense once did something important for our ancestors. In this sense, then, evolutionary psychology is relevant to just about everything humans do. We inevitably come to a deeper understanding of our behavior when we ask about the selective forces that have shaped it.

IS EVOLUTIONARY PSYCHOLOGY PESSIMISTIC?

Some people worry that the evolutionary approach to human behavior is too pessimistic. Their thinking typically goes like this. Evolved traits must have a genetic basis. Genetic traits are fixed and inflexible. If human behavior is evolved, and hence rooted in our genes, there is little hope of changing it for the better. Of course this argument is wrong. And it is our sincere hope that anyone who has followed us to the last chapter will be able to say why: Genetic traits are not necessarily fixed and inflexible. Facultative traits are highly responsive to the environment. The conclusion from EP is the same as the conclusion from traditional psychology: If you don't like the behavior, change the environment. Of course the difference between EP and SSSM psychology is that EP can draw on adaptationist thinking to deduce the nature and direction of environmental influences. For example, why would a man ever care for his sister's children instead of his own? Would paternity probability be relevant? Would high or low paternity probability lead to matrilineal inheritance? EP offers clear answers to all these questions. In contrast, traditional psychology typically uses a hit-or-miss approach to discovering environmental effects, because it has no general theory about what behavior is designed to accomplish.

> **Trail Marker:** EP and SSSM psychology are both "environmentalist" theories of behavior.

An Example of Meliorative Evolutionary Psychology: Reducing Social Disparity

Traditional psychology has discovered, by its standard empirical approach, that people's happiness is a comparative matter. People are happy when they perceive their own situation as improving and when they perceive themselves as better off than their fellows. Of course this makes evolutionary sense. How much fitness is enough? Is three offspring enough? That depends on how many offspring your neighbors (i.e., your evolutionary competitors) have. If they all have one or two, three is great. If they have four or five, three is a failure. Fitness is relative; it is comparative by its very nature. True, individuals seldom compete for fitness directly. But humans and other animals have been designed to compete for access to the resources and opportunities that are ordinarily correlated with fitness.

An important conclusion from evolutionary psychology is that people are expected to compete more intensely, taking bigger risks, when they perceive themselves to be losing badly. Let's review the relevant theory and consider its implications.

Simulating the Effects of Social Inequality

In their 1988 book on homicide, Martin Daly and Margo Wilson used computer simulation to study the evolution of competitive strategies. They imagined three kinds of competitors: a) those willing to take high risks to increase their chance of winning, b) those willing to accept only moderate risk, and c) those who avoided risky competitive strategies. Call them "High," "Medium," and "Low" for the amount of risk each will accept. In their simulations competition takes the form of contests between two individuals. In each contest there is one winner; the other individual may simply lose, or he may die. Individuals who accept higher risk are more likely to win a competitive encounter but they are also more likely to die in one; that's essentially what risky means. Of course your outcome—winning, losing, or dying—depends not only on your own strategy but on your opponent's strategy as well. For example, a High is more likely to win and less likely to die when it competes against a Medium than when it comes up against another High. Daly and Wilson proposed the payoff matrix shown in Table 16–1 to reflect this simple idea. The precise values are not critical, just so the relationships are in the right direction.

Here's how their simulation works. Start with a population of sixty potential competitors, twenty each of the High, Medium, and Low risk types, and assign each a starting score of zero. Select pairs at random to compete and determine the outcome based on the odds in Table 16–1. Add 1 to the winner's score, subtract 1 from the loser's and remove any dead individuals from the population. After a predetermined point is reached—a certain number of contests or a certain number of deaths—allow the survivors to reproduce. (There was no "mutation" in these simulations: Survivors invariably produced offspring of their own risk type.) The resulting offspring then constitute a new "generation" of competitors and again are paired randomly in a series of contests. Risk types that survived and won more contests became more common in successive generations, just as they might in natural populations. Eventually, after many generations, there was only one risk type left. Which type do you think it was?

Interestingly there is no single answer. Whether High, Medium or Low risk strategies are more successful in the long run depends on the stakes, that is, on the precise consequences of winning and losing. For example, winners might have just slightly higher fitness than losers, or alternatively they might have much higher

Table 16–1.   Chance of winning, losing, or dying for players of the strategy on the left when they compete against the strategies arrayed along the top.

	HIGH			MED.			LOW		
	WIN	LOSE	DIE	WIN	LOSE	DIE	WIN	LOSE	DIE
HIGH	.50	.10	.40	.60	.10	.30	.70	.10	.20
MED.	.40	.30	.30	.50	.40	.10	.60	.35	.05
LOW	.30	.50	.20	.40	.55	.05	.50	.50	.00

fitness. It's fairly simple to build these alternatives into the simulation. Remember, pools of competitors engage in a series of contests, with each win adding and each loss subtracting 1 point from their score. When it comes time to produce the next generation their scores translate into offspring. Daly and Wilson simulated the stakes by using a set of four different rules for translating scores into reproductive success. To simulate low stakes competition they used a very egalitarian rule (1). To simulate higher stakes competition they progressively increased the payoff from winning (rules 2–4):

1. All survivors have an equal number of offspring regardless of whether their score is positive or negative, high, or low.
2. Only survivors with a positive score reproduce, but all of these have equal reproductive success.
3. Only survivors with a positive score reproduce, and they do so in proportion to their score.
4. Only survivors with a positive score reproduce and they do so in proportion to the square of their score.

These rules are shown graphically in Figure 16–4.

Daly and Wilson found that on the relatively level playing fields of rules 1 and 2, the Low-risk strategy almost always won the simulations. The landscape changed however when competitive success translated into real differences in fitness. Under rule 3, the Medium-risk strategy won a narrow majority of the simulations and the

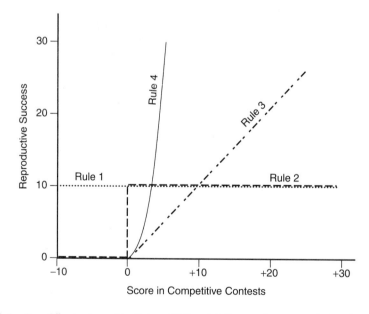

Figure 16–4. *Four different rules used by Daly and Wilson (1988) to translate contest wins into fitness.* Note that rule 1 is very egalitarian (the curve is flat) but that rules 2–4 become progressively non-egalitarian (the curves become progressively steeper).

High-risk strategy won the remainder. The sharp fitness differences produced by rule 4 favored the High-risk strategy; it won 80 percent of the simulations with the Medium risk strategy winning the rest.

> **Trail Marker:** Risky competition is favored when there are big fitness differences between losers and winners.

There is a clear conclusion from these simulations. When who wins and who loses has little effect on reproduction it's not worth taking risks to win. On the other hand, the more winning leads to reproductive success and losing leads to relative reproductive failure, the more it pays to take risks, even mortal risks, to win. It's not that High risk individuals don't die under rule 4; many do, but those who survive tend to have many more offspring than do Medium- or Low-risk individuals.

Why does this finding matter? For a very simple reason: strongly class-structured societies unwittingly implement something like rule 4 by increasing the disparity between winners and losers. For example, urban underclass men have significantly depressed chances of going to college, securing a well-paying job and marrying, and significantly elevated chances of being incarcerated or dying young. The sharp differences in opportunity and prospect between classes make the competitive stakes high, and thus foster just the kind of risky, violent competitive tactics that most destabilize society.

Measuring the Effects of Social Inequality

Wilson and Daly (1997) clearly demonstrated these effects in a recent study comparing seventy-seven Chicago neighborhoods. For each neighborhood they estimated the disparity between winners and losers and the intensity of risky competition. They used homicide rates as an indicator of risky competition because their previous work (Daly and Wilson, 1988, 1990) revealed that "a large majority of [homicide] cases involve competition for status or resources among unrelated men" (Wilson and Daly, 1997: 1271). They took two measures of the disparity between winners and losers: 1) income inequality among the households in the neighborhood, and 2) average life expectancy in the neighborhood *excluding the effects of homicide.*

> **Trail Marker:** Excluding the effects of homicide, male life expectancy still varies by as much as 23 years among Chicago neighborhoods.

You might be surprised to know that, even with the effects of homicide removed, average male life expectancy differed among neighborhoods by as much as twenty-three years! (As you might guess, life expectancies were longest in the neighborhoods with higher household incomes and less income inequality.) That's a big difference between winners and losers, and it is expected to favor risky strategies by those on track for otherwise short lives. As predicted, Wilson and Daly found that life expectancy (with the effects of homicide removed) was an excellent predictor of homicide rates. In neighborhoods where men were likely to die early of other causes, they were more likely to engage in homicidal violence. If we ask "what explains the differences in homicide rates among these seventy-seven Chicago neighborhoods?" then the answer is that more than three-quarters of the variation is explained by homicide-independent life expectancy (Figure 16–5). Income inequality, their second measure of the disparity between winners and losers, is also highly correlated with homicide rates: Neighborhoods where households differed greatly in income had the highest homicide rates.

Wilson and Daly (1997) specifically argue that the risky competition reflected in high homicide rates is an evolved facultative response. Individuals on track for failure, who anticipate short lives and minimal access to reproductively useful resources, should be motivated to employ drastic measures to try to change their life course. This is not a pretty tale, and it has a particularly nasty twist. There is a feedback loop that tends to make matters worse and worse. As people resort to more extreme competitive techniques, life expectancies go down, thereby fostering ever more risky strategies.

But remember, this is an example of how evolutionary psychology can improve our lives. The key finding is that it is inequality itself—inequality in income, in access to education, health care and opportunity in general—that fosters the kind of risky behaviors that threaten our safety and stress the fabric of society. Many social theorists have given moral or philosophical arguments against inequal-

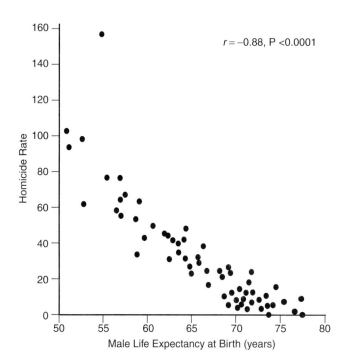

Figure 16–5. *Across 77 Chicago neighborhoods, homicide rates are very strongly correlated with homicide-independent mortality rates.* (Fig. 1 from "Life Expectancy, Economic Inequality, Homicide, and Reproductive Timing in Chicago Neighborhoods" by M. Wilson and M. Daly in *British Medical Journal,* (1997), 314. Copyright © 1997 by British Medical Journal. Reprinted by permission of BMJ Publishing Group.)

ity. These arguments may be valid in their respective spheres. Here we simply suggest that human beings have an evolved response to inequality and the high-stakes competitive landscape it creates. If we don't like that response, the solution is straightforward. If we want to reduce the violent tactics it fosters, we must reduce the level of inequality.

The question of what sorts of behavior we want to discourage and what sorts we want to encourage is ultimately a political one. But once we have collectively agreed on these objectives, evolutionary psychology can be quite helpful. The evolutionary perspective is especially good at identifying likely facultative responses. Thus it can be a powerful tool in narrowing the search for the appropriate environmental levers, levers that will naturally shift behavior in the desired direction.

SUMMARY

1. Although humans probably differ little in important aspects of their psychology, they differ markedly in their behavior: SSSM psychology and EP reconcile these two observations differently.
2. SSSM psychology suggests that behavioral differences result from the arbitrary influences of experience or culture.
3. EP suggests that behavioral differences are largely the result of designed facultative mechanisms.
4. In both views, environments play a large role in influencing behavior, but in the EP view those environmental influences are designed, where in the SSSM view they are mysterious, unexplained and arbitrary.
5. Matrilineal inheritance is an example of cultural diversity that can be explained as a facultative response (to high levels of promiscuity).
6. In a highly social species like our own, many facultative traits will depend on aspects of the social environment.
7. Facultative traits can misfire in novel environments.
8. Contrast effects lead people to devalue their mates when there seems to be an abundance of more attractive partners.
9. Visual media can apparently skew people's perception of the mate pool.
10. While traits like reading and musical ability may not have been shaped by natural selection, they depend on modules designed for related tasks like using and understanding spoken language, or distinguishing environmental sounds.
11. Selection favors risky competitive tactics when the winners of social competition fare much better than the losers.
12. Social inequality thus fosters risky competition.

Glossary

Adaptation   A trait that was preserved by natural selection because, by meeting some environmental challenge, it promoted reproduction.

ADHD   Attention Deficit Hyperactivity Disorder, characterized by easy distractibility, disruptiveness, and inability to follow instructions.

Alleles   Variant forms of a single gene; alternatives at a particular locus.

Altruistic trait   A trait that decreases the fitness of the individual manifesting the trait but increases the fitness of one or more of her neighbors.

Ambient vision   The visual system we use to move around the world. (*Compare to* Focal vision.)

Androgens   A family of hormones that are generally more abundant in males than in females.

Anxiety disorder   Excessive anxiety about particular situations or things, such as heights (acrophobia), being away from home (agoraphobia), and fear of not doing something just right (obsessive-compulsive disorder).

Artificial selection   The use of selective breeding to modify the traits of plants and animals. Analogous to natural selection except that humans intentionally choose for particular traits.

Asymmetry   A sign of developmental perturbations such as those caused by parasites and pathogens.

Attachment (of infants)   Response to a caregiver with smiling, laughing, and snuggling, accompanied after age six months by distress when caregiver leaves or stranger approaches.

Australopithecus   A genus of hominids including several species, that lived between 4 million and 1 million years ago.

Autism   Disorder characterized by severe impairment of social function and emotional expression. Autistic individuals are often, but not always, mentally retarded.

Automatic processing   Fast, effortless mental activity, characteristic of well-learned tasks. (*Compare to* Controlled processing.)

Base rate   The natural frequency of an event.

Base-rate neglect   A cognitive error that occurs when differences in the frequencies of two events are ignored; supposedly caused by certain heuristics.

Basic emotion   According to Ekman, one of a set of emotions meeting criteria such as universality, being shared with other primates, etc.; according to this book, all emotions are basic.

Behavior genetics   Branch of psychology that assesses the genetic contribution to differences in behavior between individuals.

Binding problem   The question of how the brain integrates disparate information about an object into a unified percept.

Binocular   Involving two eyes.

Biparental investment   Both sexes of parent contribute significant amounts of parental investment; the norm in human populations.

Bipolar disorder   Disorder characterized by severe mood swings, also known as manic-depression.

Categorization   The mental operation of grouping things, places and situations on the basis of similarity.

Cheater   An individual who accepts benefits (or altruism) and does not reciprocate.

Chromosome   A long string of genes.

Classical conditioning   Process by which the triggering effects of one stimulus are transferred to another, supposedly by repeated pairing of the two. Recent work shows that simple pairing is neither necessary nor sufficient for learning to occur.

Coefficient of relatedness r; the probability that two individuals share a gene by common descent. *See also* Kin selection, Hamilton's rule.

Coevolution   When two or more species influence each other's evolution.

Cognition   The mental operations of thinking.

Cognitive impenetrability   The property of many mental activities that are not available to consciousness, and are not affected by conscious attention.

Cognitive unconscious   The large portion of mental activity that is not available to consciousness.

Confabulation   Filling in the gaps in memory or knowledge by fabrication.

Continuous trait   A trait with a large number of alternative phenotypes that are often normally distributed. For example, height in humans exhibits a wide range of values with no significant gaps in the distribution. Typically shaped by genes at several loci. *See also* Polygenic trait; *contrast with* Discrete trait.

Contrast effects   Occur when the judgement of a stimulus depends on the difference between it and a previous stimulus.

Controlled processing   Slow, effortful mental activity, done while learning a task. (*Compare to* Automatic processing.)

Cooperative trait   A trait that increases the fitness of the individual manifesting the trait and increases the fitness of one or more of her neighbors.

Cortisol   A hormone produced in response to stress.

Crib death   *See* SIDS.

Critical period   Temporal window during which certain facultative adaptations are much more responsive to environmental input.

Critical-period learning   Learning which is much more effective during one part of the life span. Language learning in humans is a good example.

Degree of relatedness   Alternative term for coefficient of relatedness.

Deoxyribonucleic acid (DNA)   The chemical basis of heredity. Genes are long strands of DNA.

Differential reproduction   Refers to the fact that some individuals produce more offspring than others. The engine of natural selection.

Diploid   The condition of having two sets of chromosomes. Normal body cells are diploid.

Discrete trait   A trait with a small number of clearly separate phenotypes. For example, pea plants either have the climbing habit and are thus tall, or have the bush habit and are thus short; there are no pea plants of intermediate height. Typically shaped by genes at a single locus. *Contrast with* Continuous trait.

Discriminative parental solicitude   Investment in offspring that is conditional on parental resources, and offspring's relatedness, need, and health, etc.

Domain specific   Designed to accept a particular kind of input and produce a particular kind of output. Not functional outside it's intended domain.

Dominance hierarchy   A linear ranking of individuals in terms of their priority of access to resources.

Dominance   *See* Status.

Dominant gene   A gene that is expressed in the phenotype regardless of whether it is homozygous or heterozygous.

Durkheim, Emile   French social philosopher who believed that social phenomena could not have biological explanations.

EEA   *See* Environment of Evolutionary Adaptedness.

Electromagnetic spectrum   Range of energies that includes visible light, radio waves, ultraviolet, etc.

Emotion   The affective component of motivation.

Environment of evolutionary adaptedness (EEA)   The past environment in which current adaptations were designed by natural selection.

Evolutionary scale (or ladder)   Mistaken notion according to which organisms can be ranked as "higher" or "lower" than others. (*Compare to* Great Chain of Being.)

Extraversion   One of the "Big Five" personality traits, characterized by bold, forceful, active, and talkative behavior; on a continuum, the other end of which is called Introversion.

Facultative trait   Trait that responds to normal environmental variation. *Contrast with* Obligate trait.

Family   According to Emlen, a group consisting of parents and at least one sexually mature offspring.

Fit   Well adapted to the prevailing environment. Likely to leave more progeny than less well adapted individuals.

Fitness   The measure of how fit an individual is; the number of offspring produced by an individual.

Fluctuating asymmetry   *See* Asymmetry.

Focal vision   The visual system we use to see objects and read. (*Compare to* Ambient vision.)

Fractal geometry   Branch of mathematics useful in describing natural forms.

Fraternal twins   Twins developed from separate fertilized eggs, and thus no more genetically similar than ordinary siblings; may be same or different sex.

Frequency-dependent selection   Occurs if natural selection favors an allele when it is rare but disfavors it when it becomes more common.

Full siblings   Individuals with both parents in common, may be of either sex, related 50% on the average. (*Compare to* Half siblings.)

g   General intelligence; the factor underlying other mental abilities, what people generally mean when they describe someone as intelligent in the everyday sense.

Gambler's fallacy   The notion that events are dependent, for example, that a "head" is more likely after a series of "tails." Generally not a fallacy in the real world outside the casino.

Game theory   A branch of mathematics that models conflict situations.

Generation time   The length of time from birth to reproduction. Organisms with longer generation times tend to evolve more slowly than organisms with shorter generation times.

Genes   Particulate units of inheritance that are passed from parents to offspring.

Genetic fallacy   The mistaken idea that genes are destiny, that genetic traits cannot be changed.

Genotype   The genetic code carried by a particular individual. (*Contrast with* Phenotype.)

Grandmother hypothesis   According to Hawkes, women after a certain age can further their fitness more by investing in existing kin than by producing more offspring of their own. (*See* Menopause.)

Great Chain of Being   Mistaken notion according to which humans stand between animals and angels on a continuum from low to high.

Group selection   The spread of a trait via the differential success of alternative groups; usually an insignificant evolutionary force.

Half siblings   Individuals with one parent in common, but not both, may be of either sex, related 25% on the average. (*Compare to* Full siblings.)

Hamilton's rule   *rb>c*; the condition necessary for the spread of an altruistic gene via kin selection.

Haploid   The condition of having one set of chromosomes. Sex cells (eggs and sperm) are haploid.

Heredity   The transmission of traits from parents to offspring. Genes provide the basis for a very reliable system of heredity.

Heterozygote superiority   Results when individuals who have a heterozygous genotype are more fit than individuals who have a homozygous genotype.

Heterozygous genotype   Results when mother and father contribute different alleles for the locus in question. (*Contrast with* Homozygous genotype.)

Heuristic   A mental rule-of-thumb.

Hippocampus   A region of the brain that is important in processing spatial information and in short-term memory.

Hominids   Creatures first recognizable in the fossil record about 5 million years ago; believed to be on the human rather than the ape branch of the evolutionary tree.

Homology   Refers to the fact the evolution recycles traits when it constructs new adaptations. Thus different animals exhibit many of the same structural elements even though these elements have been modified for different functions.

Homozygous genotype   Results when mother and father contribute identical alleles for the locus in question. *Contrast with* Heterozygous genotype.

Honest signal   Costly, reliable, and hard-to-fake evidence of mate quality, such as a peacock's tail.

Hybrid cross   A mating between parents of two different types.

Hybrid   Offspring of a hybrid cross.

Identical twins   Twins developed from a single fertilized egg, and thus sharing all genes, always of same sex. (*Compare to* Fraternal twins.)

Idiot savant   (the plural is idiots savants) A person, usually retarded, with a highly uneven distribution of abilities.

Implicit learning   Learning that takes place without conscious attention, usually of skills.

Incomplete penetrance   The situation in which a gene is expressed in only a minority of cases because of environmental reasons, or interaction with other genes.

Inequality   An uneven distribution of resources and opportunities.

Innate (or instinctive)   Supposedly independent of the effects of experience. In reality no traits are fully independent of experience.

Instinct   *See* Innate.

Introversion   The opposite end of a continuum with Extraversion.

Kin   Relatives by common descent (blood relatives).

Kin selection   Mode of selection in which genes spread because of their fitness effects on other bodies likely to be carrying the identical gene; developed by W. D. Hamilton to explain the evolution of altruistic behavior.

Learning   The modification of behavior by experience.

Linear perspective.   One of the cues to depth perception, based on convergence of straight lines.

Locus   (the plural is loci) Place on a chromosome where genes affecting a particular trait occur.

Manic-depression   *See* Bipolar disorder.

Matrilineal inheritance   Pattern of inheritance in which a man's property and goods go not to his wife's sons but to his sister's sons.

Melanin   Dark pigment in skin; filters ultraviolet radiation.

Menopause   Natural cessation of ovulation and menses in women, usually around 45–50 years of age.

Mental organ   Brain module designed by natural selection to accomplish a particular mental function.

Meta-analysis   Statistical technique that permits the comparison of many different studies as if they were one, large study.

Mismatch hypothesis   The idea that many health problems result from the fact that we are adapted to an environment different from our current one.

Modular   Consisting of a set of specialized separate elements, each performing a distinct role or job.

Monocular   Involving one eye.

Monogamy   A mating system in which males and females each have only a single reproductive partner.

Moralistic aggression   According to Trivers, punishment of a cheater by the partner, accompanied by anger.

Motion agnosia   The inability to perceive movement.

Motivation   The directing and energizing aspects of behavior.

Multiple intelligences   According to Gardner, there are a number of types of intelligence, including some not taken into account in the usual intelligence tests.

Mutation   A mistake in gene copying; the ultimate source of all new alleles.

Natural selection   Mechanism of evolution proposed by Darwin. Nature—that is, the environment—judges existing alternatives in each generation; those alternatives that best promote survival and reproduction are most likely to be passed on to succeeding generations.

Naturalistic fallacy   Confusion of "is" with "ought."

Neophobia   Avoidance of novelty, particularly of food.

Neuroticism   One of the "Big Five" personality traits, characterized by worrying, nervous, and emotional behavior; opposite is emotional stability.

Nominal fallacy   The error of supposing that something is explained when it is given a name.

Norm of reaction   A graph that plots how a particular facultative trait changes in response to environmental change.

Obligate trait   A trait that resists environmental interference. *Contrast with* Facultative trait.

Overgeneralization   The extension of a learned rule to situations where it does not apply. Children overgeneralize rules of grammar; that is why they might say "we goed to the store."

Paleolithic   Old Stone Age, from about 2,500,000 years ago until about 40,000 years ago, roughly coextensive with the Pleistocene geologic period, comprising the major period of human history, and used herein as a synonym for the environment of evolutionary adaptedness.

Parental investment   Anything a parent does for a particular offspring that both increases that offspring's reproductive prospects and decreases the parent's reproductive prospects.

Patch size An ecological concept that scales the size of a typical food patch to the nutritional needs of the species in question. Patch size is large when it is sufficient to feed several individuals; it is small when it will feed only one.

Paternity uncertainty *See* Paternity certainty.

Paternity certainty Level of certainty of a biological relationship between a man and putative offspring, expressed as a fraction between 0 and 1.0.

Paternity The biological relationship of father to offspring.

Pecking order *See* Dominance hierarchy.

Phenotype The expression of a particular genotype; the result of interaction between the genotype and the environment.

Pheromone Chemical excreted by one organism that affects the behavior of another, e.g., sex pheromone.

Phonemes Distinctive vocal sounds used to mark differences in meaning; "l" and "r" are phonemes in English because "rake" and "lake" have different meanings.

Pleistocene Geologic period roughly coextensive with Paleolithic period.

Polyandry A mating system in which women may have more than one reproductive partner.

Polygenic trait Trait affected by genes at several loci. *See also* Locus.

Polygyny A mating system in which men may have more than one reproductive partner.

Post-Traumatic Stress Disorder Syndrome of emotional reactions to extremely stressful events, previously known as "shell shock."

Practice effect Refers to the fact that frequently encountered information is more accessible to memory.

Primary mental abilities According to Thurstone there are seven separate and independent factors that make up intelligence.

Prisoners' dilemma One of a suite of game theory conflicts; used to study the dynamics of reciprocity.

Promiscuity A mating system in which both sexes may have more than one reproductive partner.

Prosopagnosia The inability to recognize faces; usually results from a specific kind of head trauma or lesion.

Protein A gene product; genes specify the formulas for proteins.

Proximate questions (explanations) "How" questions (explanations) focus on mechanisms of behavior. (*Compare to* Ultimate questions.)

Psychopathy *See* Sociopathy.

PTSD Post-Traumatic Stress Disorder.

Range shifting One of the effects of sensory adaptation, whereby the sense organ adjusts its sensitivity to the ambient level of stimulation.

Recessive gene A gene that is expressed in the phenotype only when it is homozygous.

Reciprocity System in which altruism is extended only to other altruists; requires discrimination against cheaters. A model developed by R. L. Trivers.

Reproductive value   The age-specific probability of future reproduction. Reproductive value peaks shortly after sexual maturity and declines from there; the decline is steeper for women than for men.

Reproductive strategy   A coherent set of evolved tactics, not necessarily conscious, designed to maximize the number of surviving progeny.

Retention effect   Refers to the fact that recently encountered information is more accessible to memory.

Ribonucleic acid (RNA)   Chemical that transmits the gene's protein formula to the ribosome.

Ribosome   Structure that interprets the genetic message and assembles proteins.

Saccadic eye movement   Ballistic eye movement made in ordinary viewing of a scene.

Scale of nature   *See* Great Chain of Being.

Schizophrenia   Disorder characterized by incoherent thoughts, inappropriate emotions, and hearing of voices; nothing to do with "split personality."

Secondary emotion   So-called, because it is assumed by many to be different in origin from a "basic emotion."

Self similarity   In fractal geometry, the property that an object shows the same structure at different levels of magnification.

Self esteem   Our own estimate of our worth, a measure of our self-perceived status in a group.

Self-serving bias   Tendency to see ourselves as above average.

Selfish trait   A trait that increases the fitness of the individual manifesting the trait but decreases the fitness of one or more of her neighbors.

Sensory adaptation   A number of phenomena related to the steady presentation of a sensory stimulus.

Separation anxiety   *See* Attachment.

Sexual selection   Component of natural selection favoring traits that increase mating success. Often leads to the evolution of differences between the sexes.

Shared environment   When comparing two individuals, the contribution of their common experiences to their degree of similarity on a trait. (*Compare to* Unshared environment.)

Sibling rivalry   Conflict between siblings, predictable from their less-than-complete relatedness.

Siblings (also **Sibs**)   Individuals with at least one parent in common, may be of either sex. (*Compare to* Half siblings, Full siblings.)

SIDS   *See* Sudden Infant Death Syndrome.

Social clock   Ideal ages by which certain life goals should be accomplished; according to SSSM thinking, the social clock is primarily a product of social forces outside the individual.

Social Darwinism   The fallacious idea, originated by Herbert Spencer, that social inequality is justified by evolutionary theory.

Social   The tendency to seek the company of other members of one's species.

Socially constructed   Used in SSSM tradition to mean "not having a biological basis," and thus solely the result of social learning.

Sociopathy   Disorder characterized by egocentricity, impulsiveness, and lack of shame and guilt, also known as psychopathy.

Solitary   The tendency to avoid other members of one's species.

Spacing effect   Refers to the fact that items are remembered longer if they were encountered at widely separated times in the past.

Specialized   Designed for a single narrow function. Both human tools and evolutionary adaptations are specialized, simply because specialized designs are more effective. (*See also* Modular, Domain specific.)

Spiteful trait   A trait that decreases the fitness of the individual manifesting the trait and decreases the fitness of one or more of her neighbors.

SSSM   Standard Social Science Model.

Standard Social Science Model   Set of ideas common in psychology, according to which causes of behavior can be divided between nature and nurture.

Star compass   The learned celestial reference system used by some birds to orient their migratory movements.

Status   Rank; high status individuals have priority of access to resources.

Stepparent   Parent, not by blood, but by virtue of marriage or similar relationship to natural parent of the offspring in question.

Structural powerlessness hypothesis   The idea that women prefer wealthy and powerful mates because women are traditionally denied direct access to wealth and power.

Sudden Infant Death Syndrome   The sudden death while sleeping of an apparently healthy infant.

Susceptibility   Maladaptive change in the phenotype; often results from exposure to an evolutionarily novel environment.

Symmetry   Thought to be a sign of a high-quality genotype, one that is well buffered against parasites and pathogens.

Teratogen   An agent (such as a chemical or a virus) that causes developmental anomalies.

Testosterone   Principal male hormone, responsible for masculinization, but present also in lower concentrations in females; an androgten.

The Common Sense   Aristotle's answer to the binding problem, *not* the same as our everyday use of the term "common sense"

Tit-for-tat   A particularly successful strategy in the prisoners' dilemma game.

Trait   A measurable characteristic of an individual, may be discrete or continuous.

Typicality   A covert notion that structures category membership; some members of a category are regarded as more typical than others.

Ultimate questions (explanations)   "Why" questions (explanations) focus on the function a system was designed to serve. (*Compare to* Proximate questions.)

Universal People   Brown's description of behavior that is common to all human cultures.

Unshared environment   When comparing two individuals, the contribution of their different experiences to their degree of similarity on a trait. (*Compare to* Shared environment.)

Variation   Differences between individuals. Grist for the mill of natural selection.

Veridical Truthful, or not illusory.

Vestibular system Major organ for balance, closely associated with inner ear.

Visual capture See Visual dominance.

Visual dominance The phenomenon that visual information usually controls behavior when another sense provides conflicting information, equivalent to visual capture.

Visual cliff Apparatus in which an animal is placed on a horizontal surface, half opaque, and half transparent, to test its depth perception.

Vocalizations Sounds made with the vocal organs.

Voice onset time The time interval between the onset of the sound representing the consonant and the vibration of the vocal folds in making a speech unit, such as "duh."

Waist-hip ratio The size measurement of the waist at the narrowest part divided by the size measurement of the hips at the widest part; an honest reflection of hormonal status.

References

Aiken, L. R. (1996). *Assessment of intellectual functioning* (2nd ed.). New York: Plenum Press.

Allport, G. W., & Odbert, H. S. (1936). Trait-names: A psycho-lexical study. *Psychological Monographs, 47*(1, Whole No. 211).

American Psychiatric Association. (1994). *Diagnostic and statistical manual of mental disorders* (4th ed.). Washington, DC: Author.

Anderson, J. R., & Schooler, L. J. (1991). Reflections of the environment in memory. *Psychological Science, 2,* 396–408.

Anderson, K. G., Kaplan, H., & Lancaster, J. (1999, June). Paternity confidence and fitness outcomes: Abortion, divorce and paternal investment. Paper presented at the annual meeting of the Human Behavior and Evolution Society, Salt Lake City, UT.

Anderson, N., Park, M., Johnston, V., & Giddon, D. (1999, June). Anthropometric measures contributing to judgments of female facial attractiveness by four ethnic groups. Paper presented at the annual meeting of the Human Behavior and Evolution Society, Salt Lake City, UT.

Andreason, N. C. (1987). Creativity and mental illness: Prevalence rates in writers and their first-degree relatives. *American Journal of Psychiatry, 144,* 1288–1292.

Archer, J. (1997). Why do people love their pets? *Evolution and Human Behavior, 18,* 237–260.

Axelrod, R. (1984). *The evolution of cooperation.* New York: Basic Books.

Bailey, J. M., Gaulin, S., Agyei, Y., & Gladue, B. (1994). Effects of gender and sexual orientation on evolutionarily relevant aspects of human mating psychology. *Journal of Personality and Social Psychology, 66,* 1081–1093.

Baillargeon, R. (1994). How do infants learn about the physical world? *Current Directions in Psychological Science, 3,* 133–140.

Balling, J. D., & Falk, J. H. (1982). Development for visual preferences and natural environment. *Environment and Behavior, 14,* 5–28.

Bar-Hillel, M. (1980). The base-rate fallacy in probability judgments. *Acta Psychologica, 44,* 211–233.

Bargh, J. A., & Chartrand, T. L. (1999). The unbearable automaticity of being. *American Psychologist, 54,* 462–479.

Barkow, J. H. (1980). Prestige and self-esteem: A biosocial interpretation. In D. R. Omark, F. F. Strayer, & D. G. Freedman (Eds.), *Dominance relations: An ethological view of human conflict and social interaction.* NY: Garland STPM Press.

Barkow, J. H. (1991). Darwin, sex, and status. *Behavioral and Brain Sciences, 14,* 320–334.

Baron-Cohen, S. (1995). *Mindblindness.* Cambridge, MA: MIT Press.

Baron-Cohen, S., Leslie, A. M., & Frith, U. (1985). Does the autistic child have a "theory of mind"? *Cognition, 21,* 37–46.

Barrett, K. C. (1995). A functionalist approach to shame and guilt. In J. P. Tangney & K. W. Fischer (Eds.), *Self-conscious emotions: The psychology of shame, guilt, embarrassment, and pride* (pp. 25–63). New York: Guilford Press.

Bartlett, J. (1992). *Familiar quotations: A collection of passages, phrases, and proverbs traced to their sources in ancient and modern literature* (16th ed.). Boston: Little, Brown.

Baum, A., Gatchell, R. J., & Krantz, D. S. (1996). *An introduction to health psychology,* (3rd ed.). New York: McGraw-Hill.

Baxter, D. W., & Olszewski, J. (1960). Congenital universal insensitivity to pain. *Brain, 83,* 381–393.

Beecher, M., Beecher, I., & Lumpkin, S. (1981). Parent-offspring recognition in bank swallows (*Riparia riparia*): I. Natural History. *Animal Behavior, 29,* 86–94.

Beecher, M., Medvin, M., Stoddard, P., & Loesche, P. (1986). Acoustic adaptations for parent-offspring recognition in swallows. *Experimental Biology, 45,* 179–193.

Belsky, J. (1997). Attachment, mating and parenting: An evolutionary perspective. *Human Nature, 8,* 361–381.

Benton, A. (1980). The neuropsychology of face recognition. *American Psychologist, 35,* 176–186.

Berkowitz, L. (1984). Some effects of thoughts on anti- and prosocial influences of media events. *Psychological Bulletin, 95,* 410–427.

Berreby, D. (1997, January 26). Are apes naughty by nature? *New York Times Magazine,* 38–39.

Berscheid, E., and Walster, E. (1974). Physical attractiveness. In L. Berkowitz (Ed.), *Advances in experimental social psychology* (pp. 157–215). New York: Academic.

Berte, N. (1988). K'ekchi' horticultural labor exchange: Productive and reproductive implications. In L. Betzig, M. Borgerhoff Mulder, & P. Turke (Eds.), *Human reproductive behavior: A Darwinian perspective* (pp. 83–96). Cambridge, England: Cambridge University Press.

Betzig, L. L. (1986). *Despotism and differential reproduction: A Darwinian view of history.* New York: Aldine.

Betzig, L. L. (1988). Redistribution: Equity or exploitation. In L. Betzig, M. Borgerhoff Mulder, & P. Turke (Eds.), *Human reproductive behavior: A Darwinian perspective,* (pp. 49–63). Cambridge, England: Cambridge University Press.

Betzig, L., & Turke, P. (1986). Food sharing on Ifaluk. *Current Anthropology, 27,* 397–400.

Betzig, L. (1989). Causes of conjugal dissolution: A cross-cultural study. *Current Anthropology, 30,* 654–676.

Bjorkland, D. F. (1997). The role of immaturity in human development. *Psychological Bulletin, 122,* 153–169.

Bonham, G. (1977). Who adopts: The relationship of adoption and sociodemographic characteristics of women. *Journal of Marriage and the Family, 39,* 295–306.

Boster, J. (1988). Natural sources of internal category structure: Typicality, familiarity and similarity of birds. *Memory and Cognition, 16,* 258–270.

Boster, J., & D'Andrade, R. (1989). Natural and human sources of cross-cultural agreement in ornithological classification. *American Anthropologist, 91,* 132–142.

Bovill, C. (1996). *Fractal geometry in architecture and design.* Boston: Birkhauser.

Bowlby, J. (1982). *Attachment* (2nd ed.). London: Hogarth Press and the Institute of Psycho-Analysis.

Bradley, R. H., & Caldwell, B. M. (1984). The relation of infants' home environments to achievement test performance in first grade: A follow-up study. *Child Development, 55,* 803–809.

Breland, K., & Breland, M. (1961). The misbehavior of organisms. *American Psychologist, 16,* 681–684.

Bretherton, E. (1992). The origins of attachment theory: John Bowlby and Mary Ainsworth. *Developmental Psychology, 28,* 759–775.

Brewer, M., & Lui, L. (1989). The primacy of age and sex in the structure of person categories. *Social Cognition, 3,* 262–274.

Brower, L. P. (1984). Chemical defenses in butterflies. In R. I. Vane-Wright & P. R. Ackery (Eds.), *The biology of butterflies. Symposium of the Royal Entomological Society of London, Number 11.* London: Academic Press. 109–134.

Brown, D. E. (1991). *Human universals.* New York: McGraw-Hill.

Bryson, S. E. (1997). Epidemiology of autism: Overview and issues outstanding. In D. J. Cohen & F. R. Volkmar (Eds.), *Handbook of autism and pervasive developmental disorders,* 2nd ed. (pp. 41–46). New York: Wiley.

Burnstein, E., Crandall, C., & Kitayama, S. (1994). Some neo-Darwinian decision rules for altruism: Weighing cues for inclusive fitness as a function of the biological importance of the decision. *Journal of Personality and Social Psychology, 67,* 773–789.

Burton, L. M. (1990). Teenage childbearing as an alternative life-course strategy in multi-generation black families. *Human Nature, 1,* 123–143.

Buss, D. (1989a). Sex differences in human mate preferences: Evolutionary hypotheses tested in 37 cultures. *Behavioral and Brain Sciences, 12,* 1–49.

Buss, D. (1989b). Toward an evolutionary psychology of human mating. *Behavioral and Brain Sciences, 12,* 39–49.

Buss, D. (1990). Evolutionary social psychology: Prospects and pitfalls. *Motivation and Emotion, 14,* 265–286.

Buss, D. (1991). Evolutionary personality theory. *Annual Review of Psychology, 42,* 459–491.

Buss, D. (1994). *The evolution of desire.* New York: Basic Books.

Buss, D. (1997). Evolutionary foundations of personality. In R. Hogan & J. A. Johnson (Eds.), *Handbook of personality psychology* (pp. 317–344). San Diego, CA: Academic Press.

Buss, D., & Barnes, M. (1986). Preferences in human mate selection. *Journal of Personality and Social Psychology, 50,* 559–570.

Buss, D., & Dedden, L. (1990). Derogation of competitors. *Journal of Social and Personal Relationships, 7,* 395–422.

Buss, D., & Schmitt, D. (1993). Sexual strategies theory: An evolutionary perspective on human mating. *Psychological Review, 100,* 204–232.

Buss, D., Larsen, R., Westen, D., & Semmelroth, J. (1992). Sex differences in jealousy: Evolution, physiology and psychology. *Psychological Science, 3,* 251–255.

Campbell, A. (1995). A few good men: Evolutionary psychology and female adolescent aggression. *Ethology and Sociobiology, 16,* 99–123.

Campos, R. (1995). Foreword. In J. P. Tangney & K. W. Fischer (Eds.), *Self-conscious emotions: The psychology of shame, guilt, embarrassment, and pride* (pp. ix–xi). New York: Guilford Press.

Carmody, D. P., Kundel, H. L., & Toto, L. C. (1984). Comparison scans while reading chest images: Taught, but not practiced. *Investigative Radiology, 19,* 462–466.

Carroll, J. B. (1997). Pychometrics, intelligence, and public perception. *Intelligence, 24,* 25–52.

Carskadon, M. A. (Ed.). (1993). *Encyclopedia of sleep and dreaming.* New York: Macmillan.

Cashdan, E. (1993). Attracting mates: Effects of paternal investment on mate attraction strategies. *Ethology and Sociobiology, 14,* 1–24.

Cashdan, E. (1994). A sensitive period for learning about food. *Human Nature, 5,* 279–291.

Cashdan, E. (1996). Women's mating strategies. *Evolutionary Anthropology, 5,* 134–143.

Casscells, W., Schoenberger, A., & Grayboys, T. (1978). Interpretation by physicians of clinical laboratory results. *New England Journal of Medicine, 299,* 999–1000.

Catchpole, C., & Slater, P. (1995). *Bird song.* Cambridge: Cambridge University Press.

Centerwall, B. S. (1989). Exposure to television as a risk factor for violence. *American Journal of Epidemiology, 129,* 643–652.

Chagnon, N. (1979). Mate competition, favoring close kin, and village fissioning among the Yanomamo indians. In N. Chagnon & W. Irons (Eds.), *Evolutionary biology and human social behavior: An anthropological perspective* (pp. 86–132). North Scituate, MA: Duxbury.

Chagnon, N., & Bugos, P. (1979). Kin selection and conflict: An analysis of a Yanomamo ax fight. In N. Chagnon & W. Irons (Eds.), *Evolutionary biology and human social behavior: An anthropological perspective* (pp. 213–238). North Scituate, MA: Duxbury.

Chamie, J., & Nsuly, S. (1981). Sex differences in remarriage and spouse selection. *Demography, 18,* 335–348.

Chorney, M. J., Chorney, K., Seese, N., Owen, M. J., Daniels, J., McGuffin, P., Thompson, L. A., Detternam, D. K., Benbow, C., Lubinski, D., Eley, T., & Plomin, R. (1998). A quantitative trait locus associated with cognitive ability in children. *Psychological Science, 9,* 159–166.

Clark, D. C., & Fawcett, J. (1992). Review of empirical risk factors for evaluation of the suicidal patient. In B. Bongar (Ed.), *Suicide: Guidelines for assessment, management, and treatment* (pp. 16–48). New York: Oxford.

Clark, R., & Hatfield, E. (1989). Gender differences in receptivity to sexual offers. *Journal of Psychology and Human Sexuality, 2,* 39–55.

Cleveland, H. H. (1997, June). Environmental and genetic contributions to behavior problems of children of single parents: Support for a biological theory of self-selection into family structures. Paper presented at meeting of Human Behavior and Evolution Society, Tucson, AZ.

Clutton-Brock, T. H., & Vincent, A. J. C. (1991). Sexual selection and the potential reproductive rates of males and females. *Nature, 351,* 58–60.

Cohen, S. (1996). Psychological stress, immunity, and upper respiratory infections. *Current Directions in Psychological Science, 5,* 86–89.

Cole, S., Hainesworth, F. R., Kamil, A., Mercier, T., & Wolf, L. (1982). Spatial learning as an adaptation in hummingbirds. *Science, 217,* 655–657.

Collins, M., & Zebrowitz, L. (1995). The contributions of appearance to occupational outcomes in civilian and military settings. *Journal of Applied Social Psychology, 25,* 29–163.

Colman, A. M., & Wilson, J. C. (1997). Antisocial personality disorder: An evolutionary game theory analysis. *Legal and Criminological Psychology, 2,* 23–34.

Comer, R. J. (1999). *Fundamentals of Abnormal Psychology* (2nd ed). New York: Worth.

Comings, D. E. (1997). Polygenic inheritance of psychiatric disorders. In K. Blum & E. P. Noble (Eds.), *Handbook of psychiatric genetics* (pp. 235–260). Boca Raton: CRC Press.

Committee on the Use of Animals in Research. (1991). *Science, medicine, and animals.* Washington, DC: National Academy Press.

Cosmides, L., & Tooby, J. (1992). Cognitive adaptations for social exchange. In J. Barkow, L. Cosmides, & J. Tooby (Eds.), *The Adapted Mind* (pp. 163–228). New York: Oxford.

Cosmides, L., & Tooby, J. (1996). Are humans good intuitive statisticians after all?: Rethinking some conclusions from the literature on judgment under uncertainty. *Cognition, 58,* 1–73.

Crawford, C. B., Salter, B. E., & Jang, K. L. (1989). Human grief: Is its intensity related to the reproductive value of the deceased? *Ethology and Sociobiology, 10,* 297–307.

Cronbach, L. J. (1984). *Essentials of psychological testing* (4th ed.). New York: Harper & Row.

Cummins, D. D. (1998). Social norms and other minds. In D. D. Cummins & C. Allen (Eds.), *The evolution of mind* (pp. 30–50). New York: Oxford.

Cummins, D. D. (1999, June). Early emergence of cheater detection in human development. Paper presented at the annual meeting of the Human Behavior and Evolution Society, Salt Lake City, UT.

Curry, F. (1967). A comparison of left-handed and right-handed subjects on verbal and nonverbal dichotic listening tasks. *Cortex, 3,* 343–352.

Daly, M., & Wilson, M. (1982). Whom are newborn babies said to resemble? *Ethology and Sociobiology, 3,* 69–78.

Daly, M., & Wilson, M. (1988). *Homicide.* New York: Aldine de Gruyter.

Daly, M., & Wilson, M. (1990). Killing the competition. *Human Nature, 1,* 81–107.

Darwin, C. (1859). *On the origin of species.* London: John Murray.

Davis, J. N., & Daly, M. (1997). Evolutionary theory and the human family. *Quarterly Review of Biology, 72,* 407–435.

Dawkins, R. (1982). *The extended phenotype.* San Francisco: Freeman.

Dawkins, R. (1986). *The blind watchmaker.* New York: W.W. Norton.

Dawkins, R. (1989). *The selfish gene* (new ed.). Oxford: Oxford University Press.

Dawkins, R. (1996). *Climbing mount improbable.* New York: W.W. Norton.

Dawkins, R. (Undated). Science, Delusion and the Appetite for Wonder: The Richard Dimbleby Lecture. Retrieved from the World Wide Web, 20 December 1999. http://www.world-of-dawkins.com/quotes.htm

de Catanzaro, D. (1995). Reproductive status, family interactions, and suicidal ideation: Surveys of the general public and high-risk groups. *Ethology and Sociobiology, 16,* 385–394.

Dennett, D. C. (1995). *Darwin's dangerous idea: Evolution and the meanings of life.* New York: Simon and Schuster.

Dennis, W., & Dennis, M. G. (1940). The effect of cradling practices upon the onset of walking in Hopi children. *Journal of Genetic Psychology, 56,* 77–86.

Diener, E., Suh, E. M, Lucas, R. E., & Smith, H. (1999). Subjective well being: Three decades of progress. *Psychological Bulletin, 125,* 276–302.

Draper, P., & Belsky, J. (1990). Personality development in evolutionary perspective. *Journal of Personality, 58,* 141–161.

Draper, P., & Harpending, H. (1982). Father absence and reproductive strategy: An evolutionary perspective. *Journal of Anthropological Research, 38,* 255–273.

Duke-Elder, S. (1958). *The eye in evolution.* London: Kimpton.

Dunbar, R., Clark, A., & Hurst, N. (1995). Conflict and cooperation among the Vikings: Contingent behavioral decisions. *Ethology and Sociobiology, 16,* 233–246.

Eaton, S. B., Eaton, S. B. III, & Konner, M. J. (1997). Paleolithic nutrition revisited: A twelve-year retrospective on its nature and implications. *European Journal of Clinical Nutrition, 51,* 207–216.

Eaton, S. B., Shostak, M., & Konner, M. (1987). *The paleolithic prescription.* New York: Harper & Row.

Eddy, D. M. (1982). Probabilistic reasoning in clinical medicine: Problems and opportunities. In D. Kahneman, P. Slovik, & A. Tversky (Eds.), *Judgement under Uncertainty: Heuristics and Biases* (pp. 249–267). Cambridge, England: Cambridge University Press.

Eimas, P., Siqueland, E., Jusczyk, P., & Vigorito, J. (1971). Speech perception in infants. *Science, 171,* 303–306.

Einon, D. (1998). How many children can one man have? *Evolution and Human Behavior, 19,* 413–426.

Ekman, P. (1980). *The face of man: Expressions of universal emotions in a New Guinea Village.* New York: Garland STPM Press.

Ekman, P. (1989). The argument and evidence about universals in facial expressions of emotion. In H. Wagner & A. Manstead (Eds.), *Handbook of Social Psychophysiology* (pp. 143–164). Chichester: Wiley.

Ekman, P., & Friesen, W. V. (1971). Constants across cultures in the face and emotion. *Journal of Personality and Social Psychology, 17,* 124–129.

Elder, G. (1969). Appearance and education in marriage mobility. *American Sociological Review, 34,* 519–533.

Eliot, R. S., & Buell, J. C. (1981). Environmental and behavioral influences in the major cardiovascular disorders. In S. M. Weiss, J. A. Herd, & B. H. Fox (Eds.), *Perspectives on behavioral medicine* (pp. 25–39). New York: Academic Press.

Ellis, B., & Symons, D. (1990). Sex differences in sexual fantasy: An evolutionary psychological approach. *Journal of Sex Research, 27,* 27–55.

Emlen, S. (1969a). The development of migratory orientation in young indigo buntings. *Living Bird, 8,* 113–126.

Emlen, S. (1969b). Bird migration: Influence of physiological state upon celestial orientation. *Science, 165,* 716–718.

Emlen, S. (1975). Migration: orientation and navigation. In D. Farner & J. King, Eds., *Avian Biology.* Academic Press, New York.

Emlen, S. (1994). Benefits, constraints and the evolution of the family. *Trends in Ecology and Evolution, 9,* 282–285.

Emlen, S., & Wrege, P. (1988). The role of kinship in helping decisions among white-fronted bee-eaters. *Behavioral Ecology and Sociobiology, 23,* 305–315.

Emlen, S., Wrege, P. H., & Demong, N. J. (1995). Making decisions in the family: An evolutionary perspective. *American Scientist, 83,* 148–157.

Endler, J. (1986). *Natural selection in the wild.* Princeton, NJ: Princeton University Press.

Essock-Vitale, S., & McGuire, M. (1985). Women's lives viewed from an evolutionary perspective. I. Sexual histories, reproductive success, and demographic characteristics of a random sample of American women. *Ethology and Sociobiology, 6,* 137–154.

Essock-Vitale, S., & McGuire, M. (1985). Women's lives viewed in evolutionary perspective: II. Patterns of helping. *Ethology and Sociobiology, 6,* 155–173.

Euler, H., & Weitzel, B. (1996). Discriminative grandparental solicitude as a reproductive strategy. *Human Nature, 7,* 39–59.

Farthing, G. W. (1992). *The psychology of consciousness.* Englewood Cliffs, NJ: Prentice Hall.

Fiske, S. T., & Depret, E. (1996). Control, interdependence and power: Understanding cognition in its social context. In W. Stroebe & M. Hewstone (Eds.), *European review of social psychology, Vol. 7* (pp. 31–61). New York: Wiley.

Fite, K. V. (1973). Anatomical and behavioral correlates of visual acuity in the great horned owl. *Vision Research, 13,* 219–230.

Flinn, M., & England, B. (1995). Childhood stress and family environment. *Current Anthropology, 36*, 854–866.

Fodor, J. A. (1983). *The modularity of mind.* Cambridge, MA: MIT Press.

Follette, W. C., & Houts, A. C. (1996). Models of scientific progress and the role of theory in taxonomy development: A case study of the DSM. *Journal of Consulting and Clinical Psychology, 64*, 1120–1132.

Forsythe, R., Horowitz, J., Savin, N., & Sefton, M. (1994). Fairness in simple bargaining experiments. *Games and Economic Behavior, 6*, 347–369.

Frank, R. H. (1988). *Passions within reason: The strategic role of the emotions.* New York: W. W. Norton & Company.

Frank, R. H., Gilovitch, T., & Regan, D. (1993). The evolution of one-shot cooperation: An experiment. *Ethology and Sociobiology, 14*, 247–256.

Freeman, D. (1983). *Margaret Mead and Samoa: The making and unmaking of an anthropological myth.* Cambridge, MA: Harvard University Press.

Freeman, D. (1996). *Margaret Mead and the heretic: The making and unmaking of an anthropological myth.* Ringwood, Victoria and New York: Penguin.

Fridlund, A., Ekman, P., & Oster, J. (1987). Facial expressions of emotion. In A. Seligman & S. Feldstein (Eds.), *Nonverbal Behavior and Communication.* Hillsdale, NJ: Erlbaum.

Friedman, E. (1995). The role of pets in enhancing human well-being: Physiological effects. In I. Robinson (Ed.), *The Waltham book of human-animal interaction: benefits and responsibilities of pet ownership* (pp. 33–53). New York: Pergamon.

Frisch, R. (Ed.). (1990). *Progress in reproductive biology and medicine: Vol. 14, Adipose tissue and reproduction.* Basel: Karger.

Frith, C. (1994). Theory of mind in schizophrenia. In A. S. David & J. C. Cutting (Eds.), *The neuropsychology of schizophrenia* (pp. 147–161). Hove, UK: Erlbaum.

Frith, C., & Done, D. J. (1989). Experiences of alien control in schizophrenia reflect a disorder in the central monitoring system. *Psychological Medicine, 19*, 359–363.

Frith, C. D., & Frith, U. (1991). Elective affinities in schizophrenia and childhood autism. In P. E. Bebbington (Ed.), *Social psychology: Theory, method, and practice.* London: Transaction.

Frith, U., Morton, J., & Leslie, A. M. (1991). The cognitive basis of a biological disorder: Autism. *Trends in Neurosciences, 14*, 433–438.

Fullard, J. H. (1984). Acoustic relationships between tympanate moths and the Hawaiian hoary bat (*Lasiurus cinereus semotus*). *Journal of Comparative Physiology A, 155*, 795–801.

Gaddes, W. H., & Edgell, D. (1994). *Learning disabilities and brain function: A neuropsychological approach* (3rd ed.). New York: Springer-Verlag.

Gallistel, C.R. (1990). *The organization of learning.* Cambridge, MA: MIT Press.

Gallistel, C.R. (1995).The replacement of general-purpose theories with adaptive specializations. In M. Gazzaniga (Ed.), *The Cognitive Neurosciences* (pp. 1255–1267). Cambridge, MA: MIT Press.

Gallup, G. G., Jr. (1977). Self-recognition in primates: A comparative approach to the bidirectional properties of consciousness. *American Psychologist, 32*, 329–338.

Gallup, G. G., Jr. (1991). Toward a comparative psychology of self-awareness: Species limitations and cognitive consequences. In G. R. Goethals & J. Strauss (Eds.), *The self: An interdisciplinary approach* (pp. 121–135). New York: Springer-Verlag.

Galuska, D. A., Serdula, M., Pamuk, E., Siegel, P. Z., & Byers, T. (1996). Trends in overweight among US adults from 1987 to 1993: A multistate telephone survey. *Amercian Journal of Public Health, 86*, 1729–1735.

Gamboa, G., Grudzien, T., Espelie, K., & Bura, E. (1996). Kin recognition pheromones in social wasps: Combining chemical and behavioral evidence. *Animal Behavior, 51*, 625–629.

Gangestad, S., Thornhill, R., & Yeo, R. (1994). Facial attractiveness, developmental stability, and fluctuating asymmetry. *Ethology and Sociobiology, 15,* 73–85.

Garcia, J., & Ervin, F. (1968). Gustatory-visceral and telereceptor-cutaneous conditioning: Adaptation in internal and external milieus. *Communications in Behavioral Biology, Part A, 1,* 389–415.

Gardner, H. (1983). *Frames of mind: The theory of multiple intelligences.* New York: Basic Books.

Gardner, H. (1993). *Multiple intelligences: The theory applied.* New York: Basic Books.

Gates, A., & Bradshaw, J. (1977). The role of the cerebral hemispheres in music. *Brain and Language, 4,* 403–431.

Gaulin, S. (1995). Does evolutionary theory predict sex differences in the brain? In M. Gazzaniga, (Ed.), *The Cognitive Neurosciences* (pp. 1211–1224). Cambridge, MA: MIT Press.

Gaulin, S., & FitzGerald, R. (1986). Sex differences in spatial ability: An evolutionary hypothesis and test. *American Naturalist, 127,* 74–88.

Gaulin, S., & FitzGerald, R. (1989). Sexual selection for spatial learning ability. *Animal Behavior, 37,* 322–331.

Gaulin, S., McBurney, D., & Brakeman-Wartell, S. (1997). Matrilateral biases in the investment of aunts and uncles: A consequence and measure of paternity uncertainty. *Human Nature, 8,* 139–151.

Gazzaniga, M. S. (1998, January). The split brain revisited. *Scientific American, 279,* 51–55.

Gazzaniga, M. S., & LeDoux, J. E. (1978). *The integrated mind.* New York: Plenum.

Geary, D. C. (1995). Reflections of evolution and culture in children's cognition. *American Psychologist, 50,* 24–37.

Gerbner, G., Gross, L., Morgan, M., & Signorielli, N. (1986). Living with television: The dynamics of the cultivation process. In J. Bryant & D. Zillman (Eds.), *Perspectives on Media Effects* (pp. 17–41). Hillsdale, NJ: Lawrence Erlbaum,

Gibbons, A. (1997). Why life after menopause? *Science, 276,* 536.

Gibson, E. J., & Walk, R. D. (1960, April). The "visual cliff." *Scientific American, 202,* 64–71.

Gigerenzer, G. (1996). On narrow norms and vague heuristics: A reply to Kahneman and Tversky (1996). *Psychological Review, 103,* 592–596.

Gigerenzer, G., & Hoffrage, U. (1995). How to improve Bayesian reasoning without instruction. *Psychological Review, 102,* 684–704.

Gigerenzer, G., & Hug, K. (1992). Domain specific reasoning: Social contracts, cheating, and perspective change. *Cognition, 43,* 127–171.

Gleitman, L. R., & Rozin, P. (1973). Teaching reading by use of a syllabary. *Reading Research Quarterly, 8,* 447–483.

Gleitman, L. R., & Rozin, P. (1977). Structure and acquisition of reading. I. Relations between orthographies and the structure of language. In A. S. Reber & D. Scarborough (Eds.), *Toward a psychology of reading* (pp. 1–53). Potomac, Maryland: Erlbaum.

Goldstein, E. B. (1996). *Sensation & perception* (4th ed.). Pacific Grove, CA: Brooks/Cole.

Goldstein, E. B. (1999). *Sensation & perception* (5th Ed.). Pacific Grove, CA: Brooks/Cole.

Goodall, J., Bandora, A., Bergmann, E., Busse, C., Matama, H., Mpongo, E., Pierce, A., & Riss, D. (1979). Inter-community interactions in the chimpanzee population of Gombe National Park. In D. Hamburg & E. McCown (Eds.), *The Great Apes.* Menlo Park, CA: Benjamin Cummings.

Gopnik, M. (1990). Feature blindness: A case study. *Language Acquisition, 1,* 139–164.

Gordon, P. (1986). Level-ordering in lexical development. *Cognition, 21,* 73–93.

Gottesman, I. I. (1991). *Schizophrenia genesis: The origin of madness.* New York: Freeman.

Gottesman, I. I., & McGue, M. (1991). Mixed and mixed-up models for the transmission of schizophrenia. In W. M. Grove & D. Cicchetti (Eds.), *Thinking clearly about psychology,*

Vol 2: Personality and psychopathology (pp. 295–312). Minneapolis: University of Minnesota Press.

Grammar, K. (1997). The war of odours: The importance of pheromones for human reproduction. *Gynaekologisch-Geburtshilfliche Rundshau, 37,* 150–153.

Grammar, K., & Thornhill, R. (1994). Human (Homo sapiens) facial attractiveness and sexual selection: The role of symmetry and averageness. *Journal of Comparative Psychology, 108,* 233–242.

Grant, P. (1986). *Ecology and evolution of Darwin's finches.* Princeton, NJ: Princeton University Press.

Great Chain of Being. (1994). In *The new encyclopaedia britannica* (15th ed., Vol. 5, pp. 442–443). Chicago: Encyclopaedia Britannica.

Greenberg, M., & Shapiro, S. (1971). Indebtedness: An adverse aspect of asking for and receiving help. *Sociometry, 34,* 290–301.

Greenless, I., & McGrew. W. C. (1994). Sex and age differences in preferences and tactics of mate attraction: Analysis of published advertisements. *Ethology and Sociobiology, 15,* 59–72.

Greenwald, A. G. (1988). Self-knowledge and self-deception. In J. S. Lockard & D. L. Paulhus (Eds.), *Self-deception: An adaptive mechanism?* (pp 113–131). Englewood Cliffs, NJ: Prentice-Hall.

Groos, K. (1901). *The play of man.* New York: Appleton.

Gur, R. C., & Sackeim, H. A. (1979). Self-deception: A concept in search of a phenomenon. *Personality and Social Psychology Bulletin, 37,* 147–169.

Hagen, E. (1999). The functions of postpartum depression. *Evolution and Human behavior. 20,* 325–359.

Haig, D. (1993). Genetic conflicts in human pregnancy. *Quarterly Review of Biology, 68,* 495–532.

Haith, M. M., Benson, J. B. (1998). Infant cognition. In D. Kuhn & R. S. Siegler (Eds.), *Handbook of child psychology* (5th ed.), *Vol 2, Cognition, perception and language* (pp. 199–254). New York: Wiley,

Hames, R. (1987). Garden labor exchange among the Ye'kwana. *Ethology and Sociobiology, 8,* 259–284.

Hamilton, W. (1964a). The genetical evolution of social behaviour. I. *Journal of Theoretical Biology, 7,* 1–16.

Hamilton, W. (1964b). The genetical evolution of social behaviour. II. *Journal of Theoretical Biology, 7,* 17–52.

Hamilton, W., & Zuk, M. (1982). Heritable true fitness and bright birds: A role for parasites? *Science, 218,* 384–387.

Hansen, C. H., & Hansen, R. D. (1988). Finding the face in the crowd: An anger superiority effect. *Journal of Personality and Social Psychology, 54,* 917–924.

Hardin, G. (1968). The tragedy of the commons. *Science, 162,* 1243–1248.

Harlow, H. F., & Zimmermann, R. R. (1958). The development of affectional responses in infant monkeys. *Proceedings of the American Philosophical Society, 102,* 501–509.

Harm, W. (1980). *Biological effects of ultraviolet radiation.* Cambridge: Cambridge University Press.

Hartman, E. L., (1973). *The functions of sleep.* New Haven: Yale University Press.

Hartung, J. (1985). Matrilineal inheritance: New theory and analysis. *Behavioral and Brain Sciences, 8,* 661–670.

Hasher, L., & Zacks, R. (1984). Automatic processing of fundamental information: The case of frequency of occurrence. *American Psychologist, 39,* 1372–1388.

Hastie, R., & Park, B. (1986). The relation between memory and judgment depends on whether the judgment task is memory based or on-line. *Psychological Review, 93,* 258–268.

Hausfater, G., & Hrdy, S. B. (Eds.). (1984). *Infanticide: Comparative and evolutionary perspectives.* New York: Aldine.

Hawkes, K. (1983). Kin selection and culture. *American Ethnologist, 10,* 346–363.

Hawkes, K., O'Connell, J. F., & Blurton-Jones, N. G. (1997). Hadza women's time allocation, offspring provisioning, and the evolution of long postmenopausal life spans. *Current Anthropology, 38,* 551–577.

Hawkes, K., O'Connell, J. F., Blurton-Jones, N. G., Alvarez, H., & Charnov, E. L. (1998). Grandmothering, menopause, and the evolution of human life histories. *Proceedings of the National Academy of Sciences of the United States of America, 95,* 1336–1339.

Healy, S. (1992). Optimal memory: Toward an evolutionary ecology of animal cognition. *Trends in Ecology and Evolution, 7,* 399–400.

Heerwagen, J. H., & Orians, G. H. (1993). Humans, habitats, and aesthetics. In S. R. Kellert & E. O. Wilson (Eds.), *The biophilia hypothesis* (pp. 138–172). Washington, DC: Island Press.

Hefferline, R. F., Keenan, B., & Harford, R. A. (1959). Escape and avoidance learning in human subjects without their observation of the response. *Science, 130,* 1338–1339.

Hergenhahn, B. R. (1996). *An introduction to the history of psychology* (3rd Ed.). Pacific Grove, CA: Brooks/Cole.

Hill, J. O., & Peters, J. C. (1998). Environmental contributions to the obesity epidemic. *Science, 280,* 1371–1374.

Hill, R. (1945). Campus values in mate selection. *Journal of Home Economics, 37,* 554–558.

Hinde, R. A. (1970). *Animal behavior: A synthesis of ethology and comparative psychology* (2nd ed.). New York: McGraw-Hill.

Hladik, C. (1977). Chimpanzees of Gabon and chimpanzees of Gombe: Some comparative data on diet. In T. H. Clutton-Brock (Ed.), *Primate ecology: Studies of feeding and ranging behaviour in lemurs, monkeys, and apes* (pp. 481–501). London: Academic.

Hoffman, E., McCabe, K., Shachat, K., & Smith, V. (1994). Preferences, property rights and anonymity in bargaining games. *Games and Economic Behavior, 7,* 346–380.

Hoffman, E., McCabe, K., & Smith, V. (1996). Social distance and other-regarding behavior in dictator games. *American Economic Review, 86,* 653–660.

Howell, N. (1979). *Demography of the Dobe !Kung.* New York: Academic.

Hudson, J., & Henze, L. (1969). Campus values in mate selection: A replication. *Journal of Marriage and the Family, 31,* 772–775.

Hume, D., & Montgomerie, R. (1999, June). Facial attractiveness and symmetry in humans. Paper presented at the annual meeting of the Human Behavior and Evolution Society, Salt Lake City, UT.

Hurd, J. (1983). Kin relatedness and church fissioning among the "Nebraska" Amish of Pennsylvania. *Social Biology, 30,* 59–66.

Jacobs, L., Gaulin, S., Sherry, D., & Hoffman, G. (1990). Evolution of spatial cognition: Sex specific patterns of spatial behavior predict hippocampal size. *Proceedings of the National Academy of Sciences, U.S.A., 87,* 6349–6352.

James, W. (1890/1950). *The principles of psychology.* New York: Henry Holt & Co/New York: Dover Publications.

Jamison, K. R. (1995, February). Manic-depressive illness and creativity. *Scientific American, 272,* 62–67.

Jensen, A. R. (1998). *The g factor.* Westport, CT: Praeger.

Johnson, M., & Morton, J. (1991). *Biology and cognitive development: The case of face recognition.* Oxford: Blackwell.

Johnson, S., & Johnson, R. (1991). Support and conflict of kinsmen in Norse earldoms, Icelandic families, and the English royalty. *Ethology and Sociobiology, 12,* 211–220.

Jones, D. (1996). An evolutionary perspective on physical attractiveness. *Evolutionary Anthropology, 5*, 97–110.

Kagan, J., Kearsley, R. B., & Zelazo, P. R. (1978). *Infancy: Its place in human development.* Cambridge, MA: Harvard University Press.

Kahneman, D., Slovik, P., & Tversky, A. (1982). *Judgement under uncertainty: Heuristics and biases.* Cambridge, England: Cambridge University Press.

Kahneman, D., & Tversky, A. (1972). Subjective probability: A judgment of representativeness. *Cognitive Psychology, 3*, 430–454.

Kahneman, D., & Tversky, A. (1973). On the psychology of prediction. *Psychological Review, 80*, 237–251.

Kail, R. V. (1998). *Children and their development.* Upper Saddle River, NJ: Prentice Hall.

Kaplan, H., & Hill, K. (1985). Food sharing among Ache foragers: Tests of explanatory hypotheses. *Current Anthropology, 26*, 233–245.

Karlsson, J. L. (1978). *Inheritance of creative intelligence.* Chicago: Nelson-Hall.

Karlsson, J. L. (1984). Creative intelligence in relatives of mental patients. *Hereditas, 100*, 83–86.

Karlsson, J. L. (1985). Genetics of schizophrenia. *Integrative Psychiatry, 3*, 52–56.

Karlsson, J. L. (1988). Partly dominant transmission of schizophrenia. *British Journal of Psychiatry, 152*, 324–329.

Karlsson, J. L. (1991). *Genetics of human mentality.* New York: Praeger.

Keating, C., Mazur, A., & Segall, M. (1981). Culture and the perception of social dominance from facial expression. *Journal of Personality and Social Psychology, 40*, 615–626.

Kendler, K. S. (1988). The genetics of schizophrenia and related disorders: A review. In D. L. Dunner, E. S. D. Gershon, & J. E. Barrett (Eds.), *Relatives at risk of mental disorder* (pp. 247–266). New York: Raven Press.

Kenrick, D., Groth, G., Trost, M., & Sadalla, E. (1993). Integrating evolutionary and social exchange perspectives on relationships: Effects of gender, self-appraisal and involvement level on mate selection criteria. *Journal of Personality and Social Psychology, 64*, 951–969.

Kenrick, D., & Gutierres, S. (1980). Contrast effects and judgments of physical attractiveness: When beauty become a social problem. *Journal of Personality and Social Psychology, 39*, 131–140.

Kenrick, D., Gutierres, S., & Goldberg, L. (1989). Influence of popular erotica on judgments of strangers and mates. *Journal of Experimental Social Psychology, 25*, 159–167.

Kenrick, D., & Keefe, R. (1992). Age preferences in mates reflect sex differences in reproductive strategies. *Behavioral and Brain Sciences, 15*, 75–133.

Kenrick, D., Neuberg, S., Zierk, K., & Krones, J. (1994). Evolution and social cognition: Contrast effects as a function of sex, dominance and physical attractiveness. *Personality and Social Psychology Bulletin, 20*, 210–217.

Kenrick, D., Sadalla, E., & Keefe, R. (1998). Evolutionary cognitive psychology: The missing heart of modern cognitive science. In C. Crawford & D. Krebs (Eds.), *Handbook of Evolutionary Psychology* (pp. 485–514). Mahwah, NJ: Lawrence Erlbaum.

Kihlstrom, J. F. (1987). The cognitive unconscious. *Science, 237*, 1445–1451.

Kimura, D. (1967). Functional asymmetry of the brain in dichotic listening. *Cortex, 3*, 163–178.

Kimura, D., & Hampson, E. (1993). Neural and hormonal mechanisms mediating sex differences in cognition. In P. Vernon (Ed.), *Biological Approaches to the Study of Intelligence* (pp. 375–397). New Jersey: Ablex.

King, A. P., & West, M. J. (1983). Epigenesis of cowbird song—a joint endeavor of males and females. *Nature, 195*, 704–706.

Kingsolver, J. G., & Koehl, M. A. R. (1985). Aerodynamics, thermoregulation, and the evolution of insect wings: Differential scaling and evolutionary change. *Evolution, 39*, 488–504.

Kintsch, W. (1970). *Learning, memory and conceptual processes.* New York: Wiley.

Kirk, H. (1981). *Adoptive kinship: A modern institution in need of reform.* Toronto: Butterworths.

Kleiman, D. (1977). Monogamy in mammals. *Quarterly Review of Biology, 52*, 39–69.

Kreithen, M. L., & Quine, D. B. (1979). Infrasound detection by the homing piegon. A behavioral audiogram. *Journal of Comparative Physiology, 129*, 1–4.

Lalumiere, M. L., Quinsey, V. L., & Craig, W. M. (1996). Why children from the same family are so different from one another: A Darwinian note. *Human Nature, 7*, 281–290.

Langer, W. L. (1974). Infanticide: A historical survey. *History of Childhood Quarterly, 1*, 353–365.

Lazarus, R. S. (1991). *Emotion and adaptation.* NY: Oxford University Press.

Leary, M. R., & Downs, D. L. (1995). Interpersonal functions of the self-esteem motive: The self-esteem system as a sociometer. In M. H. Kernis (Ed.), *Efficacy, agency, and self-esteem* (pp. 123–144). New York: Plenum.

Leary, M. R., Schreindorfer, L. S., & Haupt, A. L. (1995). The role of low self-esteem in emotional and behavioral problems: Why is low self-esteem dysfunctional? *Journal of Social and Clinical Psychology, 14*, 297–314.

Leibowitz, H. W., Post, R. B., Brandt, T., & Dichgans, J. (1982). Implications of recent developments in dynamic spatial orientation and visual resolution for vehicle guidance. In A. Wertheim, W. Wagenaar, & H. W. Leibowitz (Eds.), *Tutorials in motion perception* (pp. 231–260). New York: Plenum Press.

Levine, J. M., & McBurney, D. H. (1986). The role of olfaction in social perception and behavior. In C. P. Herman, M. P. Zanna, & E. T. Higgins (Eds.), *Physical appearance, stigma, and social behavior: The Ontario Symposium* (Vol. 3, pp. 179–217). Hillsdale, NJ: Lawrence Erlbaum Associates.

Lewis, C. A. (1996). *Green nature/human nature: The meaning of plants in our lives.* Urbana, Ill.: University of Illinois Press.

Levenson, R. W., Ekman, P., & Friesen, W. V. (1990). Voluntary facial action generates emotion-specific autonomic nervous system activity. *Psychophysiology, 27*, 363–384.

Liberman, A. M., & Mattingly, I. G. (1989). A specialization for speech perception. *Science, 243*, 489–494.

Lightcap, J. L., Kurland, J. A., & Burgess, R. L. (1982). Child abuse: A test of some predictions from evolutionary theory. *Ethology and Sociobiology, 3*, 61–67.

Loesche, P., Stoddard, P., Higgins, B., & Beecher, M. (1991). Signature versus perceptual adaptations for individual vocal recognition in swallows. *Behaviour, 118*, 15–25.

Logan, C. A. (1999). The altered rationale for the choice of a standard animal in experimental psychology: Henry H. Donaldson, Adolf Meyer, and "the" albino rat. *History of Psychology, 2*, 3–24.

Loh, C. Y., & Elliott, J. M. (1998). Cooperation and competition as a function of zygosity in 7- to 9-year-old twins. *Evolution and Human Behavior, 19*, 397–411.

Loomis, J. M., Da Silva, J. A., Fujita, N., & Fukusima, S. S. (1992). Visual space perception and visually directed action. *Journal of Experimental Psychology: Human Perception and Performance, 18*, 906–921.

Lore, W. (1993). Epidemiology of cardiovascular diseases in Africa with special reference to Kenya: An overview. *East African Medical Journal, 70*, 357–361.

Lowe, C., & Goodman-Lowe, G. (1996). Suntanning in hammerhead sharks. *Nature, 383*, 677.

Luce, D. R., & Raiffa, H. (1957). *Games and decisions: Introduction and critical survey.* New York: Wiley.

Ludwig, A. M. (1995). *The price of greatness: Resolving the creativity and madness controversy.* New York: The Guilford Press.

Mackey, W. (1980). A sociobiological perspective on divorce patterns of men in the United States. *Journal of Anthropological Research, 20,* 419–430.

MacWhinney, B., and Snow, C. (1990). The child language data exchange system: An update. *Journal of Child Language, 17,* 457–472.

MacDonald, K. (1995). Evolution, the five-factor model, and levels of personality. *Journal of Personality, 63,* 525–567.

Marler, P. (1970). A comparative approach to vocal learning: song development in white-crowned sparrows. *Journal of Comparative and Physiological Psychology, 71,* (Suppl.), 1–25.

Marks, L. E. (1974). *Sensory processes: The new psychophysics.* New York: Academic Press.

Marsh, P., & Patton, R. (1986). Gender, social class and conceptual schemas of aggression. In A. Campbell & J. Gibbs (Eds.), *Violent transactions: The limits of personality* (pp. 59–85). New York: Basil Blackwell.

Martin, N. G., & Bailey, J. M. (1999, June). Origins of sociosexuality: A twin study. Paper presented at meeting of Human Behavior and Evolution Society, Salt Lake City, Utah.

Mayer, J. (1967). General characteristics of food intake. In C. F. Hode (Ed.), *Handbook of physiology, Section 6: Alimentary canal, Vol 1. Control of food and water intake* (pp. 3–9). Washington, D.C.: American Physiological Society.

Mayer, K. U., & Tuma, N. B. (1990). Life course research and event history analysis: An overview. In K. U. Mayer & N. B. Tuma, (Eds.), *Event history analysis in life course research* (pp. 3–20). Madison, WI: University of Wisconsin Press.

Maynard Smith, J. (1976). Group selection. *Quarterly Review of Biology, 51,* 277–283.

Mazur, A., & Booth, A. (1998). Testosterone and dominance in men. *Behavioral and Brain Sciences, 21,* 353–397.

McBurney, D. H., Balaban, C. D., Christopher, D. E., & Harvey, C. (1997). Adaptation to capsaicin within and across days. *Physiology and Behavior, 61,* 181–190.

McClintock, M. K. (1971). Menstrual synchrony and suppression. *Nature, 229,* 244–245.

McCrae, R. R., & Costa, P. T. (1990). *Personality in adulthood.* New York: Guilford Press.

McFarlan, D., McWhirter, N., McCarty, M., & Young, M. (1992). *Guinness book of records.* New York: Bantam.

McFarlane, A. (1986). *Marriage and love in England.* Oxford: Blackwell.

McGinnis, J. M., & Foege, W. H. (1993). Actual causes of death in the United States. *Journal of the American Medical Association, 270,* 2207–2212.

McGinnis, R. (1958). Campus values in mate selection. *Social Forces, 35,* 368–373.

McKenna, J. J. (1993). Co-Sleeping. In M. A. Carskadon (Ed.), *Encyclopedia of sleep and dreaming* (pp. 143–148). New York, NY: Macmillan Publishing Company.

McKenna, J. J., & Mosko, S. (1990). Evolution and the sudden infant death syndrome (SIDS): III. Infant arousal and parent-infant co-sleeping. *Human Nature, 1,* 291–330.

McKenna, J., Mosko, S., Richard, C., Drummond, S., et al. (1994). Experimental studies of infant-parent co-sleeping: Mutual physiology and behavioral influences and their relevance to SIDS (sudden infant death syndrome). *Early Human Development, 38,* 187–201.

Mead, M. (1928/1973). *Coming of age in Samoa.* New York: Morrow.

Mealey, L. (1995). The sociobiology of sociopathy: An integrated evolutionary model. *Behavioral and Brain Sciences, 18,* 523–599.

Mealey, L., Daood, C., & Krage, M. (1996). Enhanced memory for faces of cheaters. *Ethology and Sociobiology, 17,* 119–128.

Medvin, M., & Beecher, M. (1986). Parent-offspring recognition in the barn swallow (*Hirundo rustica*). *Animal Behavior, 34,* 1627–1639.

Mehler, J., Jusczyk, P., Lambertz, G., Halsted, N., Bertoncini, J., & Amiel-Tison, C. (1988). A precursor to language acquisition in young infants. *Cognition, 29,* 143–178.

Mendel, G. (1865/1965). *Experiments in Plant Hybridization* (reprint in English translation). Cambridge: Harvard University Press.

Mennella, J. A., & Beauchamp, G. K. (1993). Beer, breast feeding, and folklore. *Developmental Psychobiology, 26,* 459–466.

Mennella, J. A., & Beauchamp, G. K. (1996). The human infant's response to vanilla flavors in mother's milk and formula. *Infant Behavior and Development, 19,* 13–19.

Minsky, M. (1986). *The society of mind.* New York: Simon and Schuster.

Monty, R. A. (Ed.). (1976). *Eye movements and psychological processes.* Hillsdale, NJ: Erlbaum.

Moore, E. O. (1981–1982). A prison environment's effect on health care service demands. *Journal of Environmental Systems, 11,* 17–34.

Morgan, M. (1983). Symbolic victimization and real world fear. *Human Communication Research, 9,* 146–157.

Mueller, U., & Mazur, A. (1997). Facial dominance in *Homo sapiens* as honest signaling of male quality. *Behavioral Ecology, 8,* 569–579.

Murdock, G. (1967). *Ethnographic atlas.* Pittsburgh: University of Pittsburgh Press.

Murstein, B. (1986). *Paths to marriage.* Newbury Park, CA: Sage.

Myers, D. (1993). *Social psychology* (4th ed.). New York: McGraw-Hill.

Myers, D. (1996). *Social psychology* (5th ed.). New York: McGraw-Hill.

Myers, D. G. (1998). *Psychology* (5th Ed.). New York: Worth Publishers.

Myers, D., & Diener, E. (1995). Who is happy? *Psychological Science, 6,* 10–19.

Nesse, R. M. (1990). Evolutionary explanations of emotions. *Human Nature, 1,* 261–289.

Nesse, R. M. (1991, June). What good is feeling bad? The evolutionary benefits of psychic pain. *The Sciences, 31,* 30–37.

Nesse, R. M., & Berridge, K. C. (1997). Psychoactive drug use in evolutionary perspective. *Science, 278,* 63–66.

Nesse, R. M., & Williams, G. C. (1994). *Why we get sick: The new science of Darwinian medicine.* New York: Times Books.

Neugarten, B., Moore, J. W., & Lowe, J. C. (1965). Age norms, age constraints, and adult socialization. *American Journal of Sociology, 70,* 710–717.

Nishida, T., Hiraiwa-Hasegawa, M., Hasegawa, T., & Takahata, Y. (1985). Group extinction and female transfer in wild chimpanzees. *Zeitschrift fur Tierpsychologie, 67,* 284–301.

O'Guinn, T. C., & Shrum, L. J. (1997). The role of television in the construction of consumer reality. *Journal of Consumer Research, 23,* 278–294.

Olson, M. (1965). *The logic of collective action: Public goods and the theory of groups.* Cambridge: Harvard University Press.

O'Neill, P., & Petrinovich, L. (in prep.) The effects of kinship on decision making.

Orans, M. 1996. *Not even wrong: Margaret Mead, Derek Freeman, and the Samoans.* Novato, CA: Chandler and Sharp.

Orians, G. H., & Heerwagen, J. H. (1992). Evolved responses to landscapes. In J. H. Barkow, L. Cosmides, & J. Tooby (Eds.), *The adapted mind: Evolutionary psychology and the generation of culture* (pp. 555–579). New York: Oxford.

Ortony, A., & Turner, T. J., (1990). What's basic about basic emotions? *Psychological Review, 97,* 315–331.

Osgood, C. E. (1953). *Method and theory in experimental psychology.* New York: Oxford University Press.

Ostrom, E. (1990). *Governing the commons: The evolution of institutions for collective action.* Cambridge: Cambridge University Press.

Panskepp, J. (1998). Attention deficit hyperactivity disorders, psychostimulants and intolerance of childhood playfulness: A tragedy in the making? *Current Directions in Psychological Science, 7,* 91–98.

Papka, M., Ivry, R. B., & Woodruff-Pak, D. S. (1997). Eyeblink classical conditioning and awareness revisited. *Psychological Science, 8,* 404–408.

Payne-Gaposchkin, C., & Haramundanis, K. (1970). *Introduction to astronomy* (2nd ed.). Englewood Cliffs, NJ: Prentice-Hall.

Pearson, K. (1924). *The life, letters, and labours of Francis Galton, Vol 2.* Cambridge: Cambridge University Press.

Peitgen, H.-O. & Saupe, D. (Eds). (1988). *The science of fractal images.* New York: Springer Verlag.

Petrinovich, L., & Bolles, R. (1954). Deprivation states and behavioral attributes. *Journal of Comparative and Physiological Psychology, 47,* 450–453.

Petrinovich, L., O'Neill, P., & Jorgensen, M. (1993). An empirical study of moral intuitions: Toward an evolutionary ethics. *Journal of Personality and Social Psychology, 64,* 467–478.

Phillips, D. P. (1974). The influence of suggestion on suicide: Substantive and theoretical implications of the Wether effect. *American Sociological Review, 39,* 340–354.

Pilowsky, I., & Bassett, D. (1980). Schizophrenia and the response to facial emotions. *Comprehensive Psychiatry, 21,* 236–244.

Pinker, S. (1994). *The language instinct.* New York: Morrow.

Pinker, S. (1997). *How the mind works.* New York: W. W. Norton.

Pitcher, T. J. (Ed.). (1993). *Behavior of teleost fishes* (2nd ed.). London: Chapman-Hall.

Plomin, R. (1987). *Development, genetics, and psychology.* Hillsdale, NJ: Erlbaum.

Plomin, R., DeFries, J. C., McClearn, G. E., & Rutter, M. (1997). *Behavioral genetics* (3rd ed.). New York: W. H. Freeman and Company.

Plutchik, R. (1980). A general psychoevolutionary theory of emotion. In R. Plutchik & H. Kellerman (Eds.), *Emotion: Theory, research, and experience: Vol. 1, Theories of emotion* (pp. 3–24). New York: Academic Press.

Pomerleau, C. S. (1997). Co-factors for smoking and evolutionary psychobiology. *Addiction, 92,* 397–408.

Popper, A. N., & Fay, R. R. (Eds.). (1995). *Hearing by bats.* New York: Springer-Verlag.

Povinelli, D. J., & Cant, J. G. H. (1995). Arboreal clambering and the evolution of self-conception. *The Quarterly Review of Biology, 70,* 393–421.

Proffit, D. R., & Kaiser, M. K. (1995). Perceiving events. In W. Epstein, & S. J. Rogers (Eds.), *Perception of space and motion. Handbook of perception and cognition* (2nd Ed.). (pp. 227–261). San Diego, CA: Academic Press.

Rapin, I. (1997). Classification and causal issues in autism. In D. J. Cohen & F. R. Volkmar (Eds.), *Handbook of autism and pervasive developmental disorders,* 2nd ed. (pp. 847–867). New York: John Wiley & Sons.

Real, L. (1991). Animal choice behavior and the evolution of cognitive architecture. *Science, 253,* 980–986.

Reber, A. S. (1992). An evolutionary context for the cognitive unconscious. *Philosophical Psychology, 5,* 33–51.

Ree, M. J., & Earles, J. (1992). Intelligence is the best predictor of job performance. *Current Directions in Psychological Science, 1,* 86–89.

Regalski, J. M., & Gaulin, S. (1993). Whom are Mexican infants said to resemble? Monitoring and fostering paternal confidence in the Yucatan. *Ethology and Sociobiology, 14,* 97–113.

Rescorla, R. (1988). Pavlovian conditioning: It's not what you think it is. *American Psychologist, 43,* 151–160.

Resnick, S., Berenbaum, S., Gottesman, I., & Bouchard, T. (1986). Early hormonal influences on cognitive functioning in congenital adrenal hyperplasia. *Developmental Psychology, 22,* 191–198.

Ridley, M. (1993). *Evolution.* Boston: Blackwell Scientific.

Ridley, M. (1996). *Evolution* (2nd ed). Cambridge, MA: Blackwell Science.

Rips, L. J. (1975). Inductive judgments about natural categories. *Journal of Verbal Learning and Verbal Behavior, 14,* 665–681.

Rips, L. J., Shoben, E. J., & Smith, E. E. (1973). Semantic distance and the verification of semantic relations. *Journal of Verbal Learning and Verbal Behavior, 12,* 1–20.

Robinson, I. (Ed.) (1995). *The Waltham book of human-animal interaction: Benefits and responsibilities of pet ownership.* New York: Pergamon.

Roeder, K. D. (1965, April). Moths and ultrasound. *Scientific American, 212,* 94–102.

Rosch, E. (1973). On the internal structure of perceptual and semantic categories. In T. Moore (Ed.), *Cognitive Development and the Acquisition of Language* (pp. 111–144). New York: Academic.

Rosch, E. (1975). Cognitive representations of semantic categories. *Journal of Experimental Psychology: General, 104,* 192–233.

Rosch, E., & Mervis, C. (1975). Family resemblances: Studies in the internal structure of categories. *Cognitive Psychology, 7,* 573–605.

Rose, L. (1986). *The massacre of the innocents: Infanticide in Britain 1800–1939.* London: Routledge & Kegan Paul.

Rozin, P. (1990). Getting to like the burn of chili pepper: Biological, psychological and cultural perspectives. In B. Green, R. Mason, & M. Kare (Eds.), *Chemical senses, Vol 2: Irritation* (pp. 231–269). New York: Marcel Dekker.

Rozin, P. (1996). Sociocultural influences on human food selection. In E. D. Capaldi (Ed.), *Why we eat what we eat: The psychology of eating.* Washington, DC: American Psychological Association.

Rozin, P., & Fallon, A. E. (1987). A perspective on disgust. *Psychological Review, 94,* 23–41.

Rozin, P., & Gleitman, L. R. (1977). The structure and acquisition of reading. II. The reading process and the acquisition of the alphabetic principle. In A. S. Reber & D. Scarborough (Eds.), *Toward a Psychology of Reading* (pp. 55–141). Potomac, Maryland: Erlbaum.

Rubin, K. H., Fein, G. G., & Vandenberg, B. (1983). Play. In P. H. Mussen (Ed.), *Handbook of child psychology.* (Vol. 4). (pp. 693–774). New York: Wiley.

Rutherford, M.D., Kurtzban, R., Tooby, J., & Cosmides, L. (1997, June). Cooperation and Punishment in Groups: Economic tradeoffs. Paper presented at the meeting of the Human Behavior and Evolution Society, Tucson, AZ.

Sacks, O. (1995). *An anthropologist on Mars.* New York: Alfred A Knopf.

Sanders, C. M. (1980). A comparison of adult bereavement in the death of a spouse, child and parent. *Omega, 10,* 303–322.

Scheper-Hughes, N. (1992). *Death without weeping: The violence of everyday life in Brazil.* Berkeley: University of California Press.

Schneider, W., & Shiffrin, R. M. (1977). Controlled and automatic human information processing: I. Detection, search and attention. *Psychological Review, 84,* 1–66.

Schulz, L. O., & Schoeller, D. A. (1994). A compilation of daily energy expenditures and body weights in healthy adults. *American Journal of Clinical Nutrition, 60,* 676–681.

Segal, N. (1988). Cooperation, competition, and altruism in human twinships: A sociobiological approach. In K. B. MacDonald (Ed.), *Sociobiological perspectives on human development* (pp. 168–206). New York: Springer-Verlag.

Segal, N., & MacDonald, K. (1998). Behavioral genetics and evolutionary psychology: Unified perspective on personality research. *Human Biology, 70,* 159–184.

Sekuler, R., & Blake, R. (1994). *Perception* (3rd Ed.). New York: McGraw-Hill.

Seligman, M. E. P. (1971). Phobias and preparedness. *Behavior Therapy, 2,* 307–320.

Serdula, M. K., Williamson, D. F., Anda, R. F., Levy, A., Heaton, A., & Byers, T. (1994). Weight control practice in adults: Results of a multistate telephone survey. *American Journal of Public Health, 84,* 1821–1824.

Sergent, J., Ohta, S., & MacDonald, B. (1992). Functional neuroanatomy of face and object processing. *Brain, 115,* 15–36.

Service, E. (1979). *The hunters* (2nd ed.). Englewood Cliffs, NJ: Prentice-Hall.

Settersten, R. A., & Mayer, K. U. (1997). The measurement of age, age structuring, and the life course. *Annual Review of Sociology, 23,* 233–261.

Shanks, D. (1996). Learning and memory. In D. Green (Ed.), *Cognitive science: An introduction* (pp. 276–309). Oxford: Blackwell.

Shapley, R., & Enroth-Cugell, C. (1984). Visual adaptation and retinal gain controls. In N. N. Osborne & G. J. Chader (Eds.), *Progress in retinal research* (3rd ed.) (pp. 263–346). Oxford: Pergamon Press.

Sharkey, J. (1997, September 28). You're not bad, you're sick. It's in the book. *The New York Times,* Section 4, pp. 1, 5.

Sherry, D., Forbes, M., Khurgel, M., & Ivy, G. (1993). Greater hippocampal size in females of the brood parasitic brown-headed cowbird. *Proceedings of the National Academy of Sciences U.S.A., 90,* 7839–7843.

Sherry, D., Jacobs, L., & Gaulin, S. (1992). Spatial memory and adaptive specialization of the hippocampus. *Trends in Neuroscience, 15,* 298–303.

Sherry, D., & Vaccarino, A. (1989). Hippocampus and memory for food caches in black-capped chickadees. *Behavioral Neuroscience, 103,* 308–318.

Sherman, P. (1981). Kinship and demography in Belding's ground squirrel nepotism. *Behavioral Ecology and Sociobiology, 8,* 251–259.

Shiffrin, R. M., & Schneider, W. (1977). Controlled and automatic human information processing: II. Perceptual learning, automatic attending, and a general theory. *Psychological Review, 84,* 127–190.

Silk, J. (1980). Adoption and kinship in Oceania. *American Anthropologist, 82,* 799–820.

Silk, J. (1990). Human adoption in evolutionary perspective. *Human Nature, 1,* 25–52.

Singh, D. (1993). Body shape and women's attractiveness: The critical role of waist-to-hip ratio. *Human Nature, 4,* 297–321.

Singh, D., & Luis, S. (1995). Ethnic and gender consensus for the effect of waist-to-hip ratio on judgement of women's attractiveness. *Human Nature, 6,* 51–65.

Skinner, B. F. (1956). A case history in scientific method. *American Psychologist, 11,* 221–233.

Skoyles, J. R. (1999). Brain size and expertise. *Psycoloquy,* 99.10.002 (http://www.cogsci.soton.ac.uk/cgi/psyc/newpsy99.10.002).

Sloman, L., & Price, J. S. (1987). Losing behavior (yielding subroutine) and human depression: Proximate and selective mechanisms. *Ethology and Sociobiology, 8,* 99–109.

Sluckin, A. M., & Smith, P. K. (1977). Two approaches to the concept of dominance in preschool children. *Child Development, 48,* 917–923.

Smith, P. K. (1988). The cognitive demands of children's social interaction with peers. In R. W. Byrne & A. Whiten (Eds.), *Machiavellian intelligence* (pp. 94–110). Oxford: Oxford University Press.

Sober, E., & Wilson, D. S. (1998). *Do unto others: The evolution and psychology of unselfish behavior.* Cambridge, MA: Harvard University Press.

Sorlie, P. D., Backlund, E., & Keller, J. B. (1995). US mortality by economic, demographic, and social characteristics: The National Longitudinal Mortality Study. *American Journal of Public Health, 85,* 949–956.

Spelke, E. (1994). Initial knowledge: Six suggestions. *Cognition, 50,* 431–445.

Sperber, D. (1996). *Explaining culture: A naturalistic approach.* Oxford: Blackwell.

Sprecher, S., Sullivan, Q., & Hatfield, E. (1994). Mate selection preferences: Gender differences examined in a national sample. *Journal of Personality and Social Psychology, 66,* 1074–1080.

Stern, K., & McClintock, M. K. (1998). Regulation of ovulation by human pheromones. *Nature, 392,* 177–179.

Sternberg, R. J. (1998). *The theory of successful intelligence.* Unpublished manuscript.

Sternberg, R. J. (2 December 1998). Psychology Colloquium, Carnegie Mellon University.

Stewart, K., & Harcourt, A. (1987). Gorillas: Variation in female relationships. In B. Smuts, D. Cheney, R. Seyfarth, R. Wrangham, & T. Struhsaker (Eds.), *Primate Societies* (pp. 155–164). Chicago: University of Chicago Press.

Stimmel, B. (1996). *Drug abuse and social policy in America.* Binghamton, NY: Haworth Press.

Stoddard, P., & Beecher, M. (1983). Parental recognition of offspring in the cliff swallow. *Auk, 100,* 795–799.

Strassmann, B. I., & Clarke, A. L. (1998). Ecological constraints on marriage in rural Ireland. *Evolution and Human Behavior, 19,* 33–56.

Strauss, M. S., & Curtis, L. (1984). The development of quantitative knowledge in infancy. In: C. Sophian (Ed.), *The origins of cognitive skill* (pp. 131–155). Hillsdale, NJ: Erlbaum.

Studdert-Kennedy, M., & Shankweiler, D. (1970). Hemispheric specialization for speech perception. *Journal of the Acoustical Society of America, 48,* 579–594.

Sulloway, F. J. (1996). *Born to rebel: Birth order, family dynamics, and creative lives.* New York: Pantheon Books.

Sundquist, J., & Johansson, S. E. (1997). Self-reported poor health and low educational level predictors for mortality: A population based follow up study of 39,156 people in Sweden. *Journal of Epidemiology and Community Health, 51,* 35–40.

Symons, D. (1979). *The Evolution of Human Sexuality.* New York: Oxford University Press.

Symons, D. (1995). Beauty is in the adaptations of the beholder: The evolutionary psychology of human female sexual attractiveness. In P. R. Abramson et al. (Eds.), *Sexual nature, sexual culture* (pp. 80–119). Chicago: University of Chicago.

Taylor, S. E. (1989). *Positive illusions: Creative self-deception and the healthy mind.* New York: Basic Books.

Thornhill, R. (1979). Adaptive female-mimicking behavior in a scorpionfly. *Science 295,* 412–414.

Thornhill, R. (1998). Darwinian aesthetics. In C. Crawford & D. L. Krebs (Eds.), *Handbook of evolutionary psychology: Ideas, issues, and applications* (pp. 543–572). Mahwah, NJ: Lawrence Erlbaum Associates.

Thornhill, R., & Gangestad, S. (1994). Human fluctuating asymmetry and sexual behavior. *Psychological Science, 5,* 297–302.

Thornhill, R., & Gangestad, S. (1999a). The scent of symmetry: A human sex pheromone that signals fitness? *Evolution and Human Behavior, 20,* 175–201.

Thornhill, R., & Gangestad, S. (1999b, June). The scent of men's symmetry may honestly advertise fitness. Paper presented at the annual meeting of the Human Behavior and Evolution Society, Salt Lake City, UT.

Tiger, L. (1992). *The pursuit of pleasure.* Boston: Little, Brown and Company.

Tiger, L. (1997, May 29). Prudish military denies human nature. The Ottawa Citizen, final edition, p. A15.

Tinbergen, N. (1958). *Curious naturalists.* New York: Basic Books.

Tooby, J. (1982). Pathogens, polymorphism and the evolution of sex. *Journal of Theoretical Biology, 97,* 557–576.

Tooby, J., & Cosmides, L. (1990). On the universality of human nature and the uniqueness of the individual: The role of genetics and adaptation. *Journal of Personality, 58,* 17–67.

Tooby, J., & Cosmides, L. (1992). The psychological foundations of culture. In J. H., Barkow, L. Cosmides, & J. Tooby (Eds.), *The adapted mind: Evolutionary psychology and the generation of culture* (pp. 19–136). New York: Oxford.

Tooby J., & DeVore, I. (1987). The reconstruction of hominid behavioral evolution through strategic modeling. In W. Kinzey, (Ed.), *Primate models for the origin of human behavior* (pp. 183–237). New York: SUNY Press.

Townsend, J. (1989). Mate selection criteria: A pilot study. *Ethology and Sociobiology, 10,* 241–253.

Trivers, R. L. (1971). The evolution of reciprocal altruism. *Quarterly Review of Biology, 46,* 35–57.

Trivers, R. L. (1972). Parental investment and sexual selection. In B. Campbell (Ed.), *Sexual selection and the descent of man* (pp. 136–179). Chicago: Aldine.

Trivers, R. L. (1974). Parent-offspring conflict. *American Zoologist, 14,* 249–264.

Tutin, C., & McGinnis, P. (1981). Chimpanzee reproduction in the wild. In C. Graham (Ed.), *Reproductive biology of the great apes* (pp. 239–264). New York: Academic.

Tversky, A., & Kahneman, D. (1974). Judgment under uncertainty: Heuristics and biases. *Science, 185,* 1124–1131.

Tversky, A., & Kahneman, D. (1983). Extensional versus intuitive reasoning: The conjunction fallacy in probability judgment. *Psychological Review, 90,* 293–315.

Uchino, B. N., Cacioppo, J. T., & Kielcolt-Glaser, J. K. (1996). The relationship between social support and physiological responses: A review with emphasis on underlying mechanisms and implications for health. *Psychological Bulletin, 119,* 488–531.

Ulrich, R. S. (1984). View through a window may influence recovery from surgery. *Science, 224,* 420–421.

Ulrich, R. S. (1993). Biophilia, biophobia, and natural landscapes. In S. R. Kellert & E. O. Wilson (Eds.), *The biophilia hypothesis* (pp. 73–137). Washington, DC: Island Press.

U. S. Bureau of the Census (1998). *Statistical abstract of the United States: 1998* (118th ed.). Washington, DC: U.S. Government Printing Office.

U. S. Bureau of the Census. (1999). *Statistical Abstract of the United States.* (Retrieved 20 December 1999 from the World Wide Web: *http://www.census.gov/prod/www/ statistical-abstract-us.html*

U.S. Department of Health and Human Services. (1996). State- and sex-specific prevalence of selected characteristics—Behavioral risk factor surveillance system, 1992–1993. *Morbidity and Mortality Weekly Report, 45(SS-6),* (whole no. SS-6).

Wakefield, J. C. (1992). The concept of mental disorder: On the boundary between biological facts and social values. *American Psychologist, 47,* 373–388.

Wehner, R., & Flatt, I. (1972). The visual orientation of desert ants *Cataglyphis bicolor* by means of terrestrial cues. In R. Wehner (Ed.), *Information Processing in the Visual System of Arthropods* (pp. 295–302). New York: Springer.

Wehner, R., & Srinivasan, M. (1981). Searching behavior of desert ants, genus *Cataglyphis* (Formicidae, Hymenoptera). *Journal of Comparative Physiology A, 142,* 315–338.

Wehr, T. A., Moul, D. E., Barbato, G., Giesen, H. A., Seidel, J. A., Barker, C., & Bender, C. (1993). Conservation of photoperiod-responsive mechanisms in humans. *American Journal of Physiology, 265,* R846–R857.

Weiner, B. (1972). *Theories of motivation: From mechanism to cognition.* Chicago, IL: Markham.

Weiner, J. (1994). *The beak of the finch.* New York: Vintage.

Weller, A. (1998). Communication through body odor. *Nature, 392,* 126–127.

Weller, A, & Weller, L. (1997). Menstrual synchrony under optimal conditions: Bedouin families. *Journal of Comparative Psychology, 112,* 143–151.

West, M. J., & King, A. P. (1988). Female visual displays affect the development of male song in the cowbird. *Nature, 334,* 244–246.

White, G. M. (1993). Emotions inside out: The anthropology of affect. In M. Lewis & J. M. Haviland (Eds.), *Handbook of emotions,* 29–40. New York: Guilford Press.

Wickelgren, I. (1998). Obesity: How big a problem? *Science, 280,* 1364–1367.

Wiederman, M. (1993). Evolved gender differences in mate preferences: Evidence from personal advertisements. *Ethology and Sociobiology, 14,* 331–352.

Wiederman, M., & Allgeier, E. (1992). Gender differences in mate selection criteria: Sociobiological or socioeconomic explanation? *Ethology and Sociobiology, 13,* 115–124.

Wierzbicka, A. (1992). Talking about emotions: Semantics, culture, and cognition. *Cognition and Emotion, 6,* 285–319.

Williams, G. (1966). *Adaptation and natural selection.* Princeton, NJ: Princeton University Press.

Williams, T. M. (1986). *The impact of television: A natural experiment in three communities.* Orlando, FL: Academic Press.

Wilson, M., & Daly, M. (1997). Life expectancy, economic inequality, homicide and reproductive timing in Chicago neighborhoods. *British Medical Journal, 314,* 1271–1274.

Wolfe, A. (1996, 23 December). Up from scientism. *The New Republic,* 29–35.

Woodruff, G., & Premack, D. (1979). Intentional communication in the chimpanzee: The development of deception. *Cognition, 7,* 333–362.

Wrangham, R. (1977). Feeding behaviour of chimpanzees in Gombe National Park, Tanzania. In T. Clutton-Brock (Ed.), *Primate ecology: Studies of feeding and ranging behaviour in lemurs, monkeys, and apes* (pp. 504–538). London: Academic.

Wrangham, R. (1986). Ecology and social relationships in two species of chimpanzee. In D. Rubenstein & R. Wrangham (Eds.), *Ecological aspects of social evolution* (pp. 352–378). Princeton, NJ: Princeton University Press.

Wrangham, R. (1987). The evolution of social structure. In B. Smuts, D. Cheney, R. Seyfarth, R. Wrangham & T. Struhsaker (Eds.), *Primate Societies* (pp. 282–296). Chicago: University of Chicago Press.

Wright, R. (1995). The evolution of despair. *Time, 146(9),* 50–57.

Wynne-Edwards, V. C. (1962). *Animal dispersion in relation to social behavior.* Edinburgh: Oliver and Boyd.

Yinon, Y., & Dovrat, M. (1987). The reciprocity-arousing potential of the requestors occupation, it's status and the cost and urgency of the request as determinants of helping behavior. *Journal of Applied Social Psychology, 17,* 429–435.

Zatore, R. (1984). Musical perception and cerebral function: A critical review. *Music Perception, 2,* 196–221.

Zillmann D. (1989). Aggression and sex: Independent and joint operations. In H. Wagner & A. Manstead (Eds.), *Handbook of Social Psychophysiology: Emotion and Social Behavior* (pp. 229–259). Chichester: John Wiley.

Trail Markers

Chapter 1:

Evolution does not mean progress, only change.

Absence of a behavior at birth is not proof that it results from experience.

It is a mistake to divide the causes of behavior between nature and nurture.

The brain can't be a general purpose computer; computers need task-specific software.

Proximate answers explain how a mechanism works; ultimate answers explain why the mechanism exists, in terms of the function it serves.

The naturalistic fallacy confuses "is" with "ought." Something is not morally acceptable simply because it is "natural."

Social Darwinism is a prominent example of the naturalistic fallacy. It also mistakenly holds that evolution means progress.

Chapter 2:

Natural selection refers to the fact that those who are better suited to the current environment tend to produce more offspring.

Natural selection produces designs for reproduction called adaptations.

Adaptations are complex, integrated and show design for a clear function that contributes to reproduction

Natural selection cannot design behavior directly. It designs psychological organs that produce adaptive behavior.

Selection works by choosing among existing alternatives, not by inventing entirely new ones.

Evolution is cumulative with new adaptations being layered on older ones.

Adaptations were designed to solve past environmental problems and may not perfectly match present challenges.

Sexual selection favors traits that provide benefits only in the mating context.

Unlike natural selection, sexual selection typically leads to the evolution of sex differences.

Sex differences in reproductive rates affect the availability of mates for males and females.

Sex differences in reproductive rate cause sexual selection by making mates scarce for just one sex.

Chapter 3:

For polygenic traits, the population will always include considerable scatter around the optimum value.

The genetic fallacy is the mistaken idea that genetic traits cannot be changed.

Chapter 4:

Darwin's original theory does not predict altruism.

Advantages for the group are generally not sufficient to spread a trait.

Kin selection favors altruism that is selectively aimed at relatives.

Kin selected altruism facultatively depends on the relationship among r, b, and c.

Evolution builds simple rules of thumb to guide behavior.

Animals can estimate r, b, and c by simple rules of thumb.

Reciprocal altruism can spread if altruism is withheld from cheaters.

Iterated Prisoner's Dilemma provides an opportunity to punish cheaters.

Organisms should be designed to bestow favors on those who reciprocate, and to withhold favors from those who don't.

When asking about the causes of a trait, it's a mistake to separate nature and nurture.

Instead or asking "Is it nature or nurture?" ask "Why does the environment have this particular effect?"

Violence is one tactic animals use to get disputed resources.

Violence may facultatively depend on the frequency of violence in the population.

Norms of reaction provide the key to understanding the influence of environment on behavior.

Adaptations often fail in novel environments.

Many of our adaptations are geared more to life in the EEA than to life in the present.

Chapter 5:

Evolution does not have our happiness as a goal, only our reproductive success.

Coevolution leads to evolutionary arms races, resulting in a spiral of adaptation and counter-adaptation.

Chapter 6:

Scientists are able to study consciousness even though they don't have a complete definition of it.

Voluntary behavior does not always operate by way of conscious sensations.

Learning can take place outside of consciousness.

Scientists use the term unconscious in a way that has nothing to do with Freudian notions.

Organs that evolve for one purpose are often later adapted for an entirely different purpose.

The unity of the self is an accomplishment, not a necessity.

Deception is a predictable outcome of natural selection.

Chapter 7:

Learning occurs when behavior is modified by experience.

All behavior depends on some kind of experience.

Instinctive (or innate) behaviors are relatively obligate; but even they can be perturbed by novel environments.

Learning mechanisms are facultative adaptations.

Like all adaptations, learning mechanisms are designed to solve particular real-world problems; hence learning mechanisms are specialized.

Migratory birds learn a star compass suited to the earth's tilt during their lifetimes.

Critical-period learning is specialized to happen once, usually early in life, and then be resistant to revision.

Desert ants constantly learn where they are by vector summing.

Human infants learn which sounds signal a difference in meaning.

Overgeneralization shows that children do not merely imitate; they deduce the rules of grammar.

Selection favors individual recognition where the young of many parents mix.

Temporal contiguity alone does not produce learning.

Temporal contiguity is not even necessary for learning.

The ease of learning a task depends on how well it matches a real-world situation.

Chapter 8:

Many natural categories seem to be organized by typicality.

Typicality-based categories reflect the nested hierarchy of relatedness among living things.

"Typical" species are those with many close relatives.

It remains to be seen whether all categories are organized by typicality.

An efficient memory would forget the less useful items.

To see what an ideal memory would have to do, Anderson and Schooler studied the pattern of events in the world.

The practice, retention, and spacing effects seem to match the pattern of real-world events.

Our evolved tendencies toward reciprocity help us solve certain logical problems, but not others.

According to Kahneman and Tversky, "availability" and "representativeness" may bias our judgments.

No one has yet described how the availability and representativeness heuristics work.

Probability is an evolutionarily novel concept.

People are much better intuitive statisticians when they are given frequency data in place of probability data.

In the real world, the gambler's fallacy is seldom a fallacy!

Sex differences in verbal and spatial ability are well documented.

Sex differences in ranging behavior lead to the evolution of sex differences in spatial ability.

Chapter 9:

Evolutionary psychology mainly focuses on adaptations that are common to all people, not on differences.

The concepts of intelligence and personality reflect our evaluation of others as potential resources.

Because modern intelligence tests were developed to predict success in school, an evolutionarily novel setting, we should not be surprised if they neglect many abilities that are obviously intelligent.

An intelligence test designed for hunter-gatherers would probably test different skills than ones designed to predict school success.

The things we go to school to learn make use of modules that evolved for other purposes.

Children are not intrinsically motivated to practice math and reading skills because these tasks are not the natural products of adaptations.

Chapter 10:

A woman's reproduction is limited by her physiological investment capacity.

A man's reproduction is limited by his access to fertile women.

Monogamy is evolutionarily novel in humans.

Even in monogamous societies, infidelity, divorce, and remarriage allow effective polygyny.

Because of a tendency toward weak polygyny, women are expected to be somewhat choosier, men somewhat more competitive.

On average, women are choosier about their sex partners, but men are not wholly indiscriminate.

Biparental investment is most likely to evolve in species with helpless young.

Both sexes invest economically in offspring; only women invest physiologically.

"Beauty is in the adaptations of the beholder." (Symons 1995).

Youth, health, vigor and symmetry are key components of attractiveness.

Women prefer partners with good economic potential.

Structural powerlessness does not explain women's preference for economically promising partners.

Men prefer physically attractive partners.

Men prefer youthful partners.

Men prefer partners with a low waist-hip ratio.

Women playing a mixed reproductive strategy would accept genes and investment from different men.

Men playing a mixed reproductive strategy would invest heavily in one partner but still attempt to attract additional mates.

Women are especially selective about the physical attractiveness of their one-night-stand partners.

Both women and men are expected to guard against the mixed reproductive strategies of their partner.

Patterns of sexual jealousy reflect the different risks that men and women face.

Both men and women adjust their mating strategies to their expectations about the availability of male investment.

Chapter 11:

Abilities develop when they are needed.

Chapter 12:

All motives are mechanisms that evolved to solve problems that existed in the EEA, and thus are all equally biological.

Chapter 13:

The mismatch hypothesis says that many problems of health are the result of a mismatch between our evolved characteristics and our present environment.

Chapter 15:

Selection favors social habits if the benefits of associating with others outweigh the costs.

Given their circumstances, some animals—such as orangutans—don't benefit by being social.

Sociality would be costly for animals whose food comes in small, scattered patches.

Animals whose food comes in large shareable patches often benefit by being social.

The African apes are social primarily as a defense against their fellows.

Traditional human societies are organized around kinship.

In both traditional and industrialized societies, people systematically help their kin.

Biological kinship seems to inhibit lethal violence.

People are more inclined to help kin than non-kin and more inclined to do so when the benefit is large.

Living with non-kin has measurable physiological and health consequences.

Help is more likely to be granted when the cost is small, the benefit is large, and the requestor has the capacity to reciprocate.

People are reluctant to ask for help when they feel unable to reciprocate.

Being labeled as a cheater makes a person more memorable.

People have some ability to recognize whether a new acquaintance will be a cooperator or not.

In noniterated games, most people are nicer than game theory would predict.

Cooperation decreases when one's reputation is not at stake.

Pollution and conservation issues can be analyzed as Prisoners' Dilemmas.

Government initiatives can break the deadlock in the Tragedy of the Commons and get people to start cooperating.

Chapter 16:

Contrary to Durkheim, animal societies seem to be strongly influenced by biological forces such as natural selection.

Logically, all the sciences are united, and must appeal to a consistent set of causes and principles.

"Culture" is a circular explanation for behavioral differences.

The effects of experience are not separate from biology; they are evolved facultative responses.

The effects of experience are not explanations; they need to be explained, ultimately in terms of their evolutionary basis.

According to a standard explanation, violence provokes "imitation." But accidentally produced injuries don't. Why not?

In matrilineal societies, men invest their resources in their sisters' children, not their wife's children.

Regardless of the degree of promiscuity, a man's sister's children always carry some of his genes.

Matrilineal inheritance is strongly associated with low paternity probability.

Contrast effects suggest that our attractiveness judgements are relative, not absolute.

For women and men, contrast effects parallel their mate choice criteria.

Television and films are probably causing our mate-evaluation modules to malfunction.

Traits that have no fitness consequences are immune to selection.

Because music is a cultural universal it probably has a basis in human nature.

It may be possible to test ideas about the evolutionary basis of music by studying how the brain processes music.

EP and SSSM psychology are both "environmentalist" theories of behavior.

Risky competition is favored when there are big fitness differences between losers and winners.

Excluding the effects of homicide, male life expectancy still varies by as much as 23 years among Chicago neighborhoods.

Index